JUST WAR THINKERS

This volume offers a set of concise and accessible introductions to the seminal figures in the historical development of the just war tradition.

In what, if any, circumstances are political communities justified in going to war? And what limits should apply to the conduct of any such war? The just war tradition is a body of thought that helps us think through these very questions. Its core ideas have been subject to fierce debate for more than 2,000 years. Yet they continue to play a prominent role in how political and military leaders address the challenges posed by the use of force in international society. Until now there has been no text that offers concise and accessible introductions to the key figures associated with the tradition. Stepping into this breach, *Just War Thinkers* provides a set of clear but detailed essays by leadings experts on nineteen seminal thinkers, from Cicero to Jeff McMahan. This volume challenges the reader to think about how traditions are constituted – who is included and excluded, and how that is determined – and how they serve to enable, constrain, and indeed channel subsequent thought, debate, and exchange.

This book will be of much interest to students of just war tradition and theory, ethics and war, philosophy, security studies and IR.

Daniel R. Brunstetter is Associate Professor in the Department of Political Science at the University of California, Irvine, USA.

Cian O'Driscoll is Senior Lecturer in Politics at the University of Glasgow, UK.

War, Conflict and Ethics

Series Editors: Michael L. Gross
University of Haifa
and James Pattison
University of Manchester
Founding Editor: Daniel Rothbart
George Mason University

This new book series focuses on the morality of decisions by military and political leaders to engage in violence and the normative underpinnings of military strategy and tactics in the prosecution of the war.

JUST WAR THINKERS

From Cicero to the 21st Century

*Edited by Daniel R. Brunstetter and
Cian O'Driscoll*

Routledge
Taylor & Francis Group

LONDON AND NEW YORK

First published 2018
by Routledge
2 Park Square, Milton Park, Abingdon, Oxon OX14 4RN

and by Routledge
711 Third Avenue, New York, NY 10017

Routledge is an imprint of the Taylor & Francis Group, an informa business

British Library Cataloguing-in-Publication Data
A catalogue record for this book is available from the British Library

Library of Congress Cataloging-in-Publication Data
Names: Brunstetter, Daniel R., editor. | O'Driscoll, Cian, editor.
Title: Just war thinkers : from Cicero to the 21st century / edited by Daniel R. Brunstetter and Cian O'Driscoll.
Description: Abingdon, Oxon ; New York, NY : Routledge is an imprint of the Taylor & Francis Group, an Informa Business, [2018] | Series: War, conflict and ethics | Includes bibliographical references and index.
Identifiers: LCCN 2017009808| ISBN 9781138122475 (hbk) | ISBN 9781138122482 (pbk.) | ISBN 9781315650470 (ebk)
Subjects: LCSH: Just war doctrine--History.
Classification: LCC U22 .J89 2018 | DDC 172/.42--dc23
LC record available at https://lccn.loc.gov/2017009808

ISBN: 978-1-138-12247-5 (hbk)
ISBN: 978-1-138-12248-2 (pbk)
ISBN: 978-1-315-65047-0 (ebk)

Typeset in Bembo
by Saxon Graphics Ltd, Derby

CONTENTS

NOTES ON CONTRIBUTORS

Alex J. Bellamy is Professor of Peace and Conflict Studies and Director of the Asia Pacific Centre for the Responsibility to Protect at the University of Queensland, Australia. He is also Senior Adviser at the International Peace Institute, New York and Fellow of the Academy of Social Sciences in Australia.

Chris Brown is Emeritus Professor of International Relations at the London School of Economics. He is the author of numerous articles and of *International Society, Global Polity* (2015) *Practical Judgement in International Political Theory: Selected Essays* (2010), *Sovereignty, Rights and Justice* (2002), *International Relations Theory: New Normative Approaches* (1992), editor of *Political Restructuring in Europe: Ethical Perspectives* (1994) and co-editor (with Terry Nardin and N.J. Rengger) of *International Relations in Political Thought: Texts from the Greeks to the First World War* (2002). His textbook *Understanding International Relations* (2009 4th edition) has been translated into Arabic, Turkish, Portuguese and Chinese, with a Basque edition forthcoming.

Daniel R. Brunstetter is Associate Professor in the department of political science at the University of California, Irvine. His work on the ethics of force has appeared in *Ethics & International Affairs*, the *Journal of Military Ethics, Political Studies, Review of International Studies, International Journal of Human Rights, Raisons politiques* and elsewhere. He is the author of *Tensions of Modernity: Las Casas and His Legacy in the French Enlightenment* (w/Routledge) and co-editor of *The Ethics of War Revisited: Moral Challenges in an Era of Contested and Fragmented Sovereignty.*

Stephanie Carvin is an Assistant Professor of International Relations at the Norman Paterson School of International Affairs. Her research interests are in the area of international law, security, terrorism and technology. Currently, she is teaching in the areas of critical infrastructure protection, technology and warfare and foreign policy. Stephanie holds a PhD from the London School of Economics and published her thesis as *Prisoners of America's Wars: From the Early Republic to Guantanamo* (2010). Her most recent book is *Science, Law, Liberalism and the American Way of Warfare: The Quest for Humanity in Conflict* (2015), co-authored with Michael J. Williams. In 2009 Carvin was a Visiting Scholar at George Washington University Law School and worked as a consultant to the US Department of Defense Law of War Working Group. From 2012–2015, she was an analyst with the Government of Canada focusing on national security issues.

Theodore Christov is Associate Professor of History and International Affairs at George Washington University in Washington DC, where he teaches intellectual history and political theory. He is the author of *Before Anarchy: Hobbes and His Critics in Modern International Thought* (2016), which examines how and why Hobbes and anarchy have come to be seen as synonymous. His research interests lie in international political thought, and early modern and modern political theory. In his next research project on global governance and the idea of a world state, he examines competing proposals for a global political order in the aftermath of imperial disintegration.

Rory Cox is Lecturer in Late Mediæval History at the University of St Andrews. His research combines intellectual history and military history, focusing particularly on the often discordant relationship between just war doctrine and military conduct. He is currently engaged in a broad comparative analysis of justifications for war across multiple cultures in the Mediterranean and Europe, *Justifying Warfare: From Antiquity to the End of the Middle Ages*, to be published by Princeton University Press.

G. Scott Davis received his A.B. from Bowdoin College (*summa cum laude*) and his Ph.D. from Princeton University. He works in philosophy of religion, moral theory, and the history of western thought, with an emphasis in ethics. He has written on a wide range of issues directly relevant to just war thinking and its history, and his work has been published in, among other venues, the *Journal of Religion and Violence*, the *Journal for Peace and Justice Studies*, and *Soundings: An Interdisciplinary Journal*. His monograph, *Warcraft and the Fragility of Virtue*, was published in 1992 and he has contributed to numerous edited volumes and collections since. He taught at Stanford University, Columbia University, and Princeton University before joining the University of Richmond as the Lewis T. Booker Professor of Religion and Ethics in 1994.

Luke Glanville is a fellow in the Department of International Relations at the Australian National University. He is the author of *Sovereignty and the Responsibility to Protect: A New History* (2014) as well as articles in journals including *International*

Studies Quarterly, European Journal of International Relations, and *Ethics & International Affairs*. Luke is co-editor of the quarterly journal, *Global Responsibility to Protect*.

Adam Hollowell is Visiting Lecturer in the Sanford School of Public Policy at Duke University and Director of Student Ministry at Duke Chapel. He holds a PhD in Theological Ethics from the University of Edinburgh, Scotland. He is the author of *Power and Purpose: Paul Ramsey and Contemporary Christian Political Theology* (2015).

James Turner Johnson (Ph.D., Princeton 1968) is Distinguished Professor *emeritus* of Religion at Rutgers University, where he served on the faculty from 1969 through 2015. His work centers on the Western and Islamic moral traditions on war, peace, and statecraft. Recipient of Rockefeller, Guggenheim, and National Endowment for the Humanities fellowships, he has authored eleven books, of which the most recent is *Sovereignty: Moral and Historical Perspectives*, and edited or co-edited six more, of which the most recent (with Eric Patterson) is *The Ashgate Research Companion to Military Ethics*. He was founding Co-Editor of the *Journal of Military Ethics*.

John Kelsay is Distinguished Research Professor at the Department of Religion, Florida State University. He focuses on religious ethics, particularly in relation to the Islamic and Christian traditions. His current work deals with religion and politics. Professor Kelsay serves as editor of Soundings: An Interdisciplinary Journal and as Director of the Center for Humanities and Society at Florida State University. He has published several monographs, including *Arguing the Just War in Islam* (2007) and *Islam and War: A Study in Comparative Ethics* (1993). John has also published a number of scholarly articles in leading journals, including *Ethics & International Affairs, Studies in Christian Ethics*, and the *Journal of Religious Ethics*.

Anthony F. Lang, Jr. is a Professor of International Political Theory in the School of International Relations at the University of St Andrews, where he founded the Centre for Global Constitutionalism. He has published articles and books on humanitarian intervention, the just war tradition, punishment and responsibility in international law, Middle East politics, and global constitutionalism. He is the co-editor of the forthcoming *Handbook on Global Constitutionalism* (2017) and is the author of the recently published *International Political Theory: An Introduction* (2014).

Cian O'Driscoll is a Senior Lecturer in Politics at the University of Glasgow. He completed his PhD in 2006 at the University of Wales. Prior to this he studied at the University of Limerick, Dalhousie University, and the University of Oslo. Cian's first monograph, *The Renegotiation of the Just War Tradition and the Right to War in the 21st Century* was published in 2008. He co-edited *Just War: Authority, Tradition, Practice,* which was published in 2013. Cian has also published a number of journal articles on the ethics of war, contributing to *International Studies Quarterly,*

Review of International Studies, Ethics & International Affairs, Millennium, International Relations, the *Journal of Military Ethics,* and the *European Journal of Political Theory.* Cian is currently working on a monograph entitled *Triumph and Tragedy: The Victory of Just War.* He is a member of the Royal Society of Edinburgh's Young Academy and the co-convenor of the Glasgow Global Security Network.

Brian Orend is Professor of Philosophy at the University of Waterloo in Canada. His core fields of research include: human rights; international relations; and the ethics of war and peace. He is perhaps best known for his work on post-war justice, and the book *The Morality of War* (2nd ed, 2013). Recent publications include being the editor of a new edition of Kant's *Perpetual Peace* (2015). Forthcoming books include: the updated second edition to his *Introduction to International Studies* (2018); an edited anthology on *War Ethics* (2018); plus a monograph, *War and Political Theory* (2018).

Gregory M. Reichberg is Research Professor at the Peace Research Institute Oslo (PRIO) and Adjunct Professor in the Department of Political Science at the University of Oslo. He heads the Oslo-based Research School on Peace and Conflict and is an associate editor of the *Journal of Military Ethics.* From 2009-2012 he was director of the PRIO Cyprus Centre in Nicosia, where he coordinated research and dialogue activities on the search for a political settlement to the island's division. Over the last ten years he has been engaged in religious dialogue on social/political issues, most recently in Iraq, where PRIO contributed toward drafting the Erbil Declaration. Reichberg's recently published work includes a monograph *Thomas Aquinas on War and Peace* (2017), and several co-edited volumes: *Religion, War, and Ethics: A Sourcebook of Textual Traditions* (2014); *World Religions and Norms of War* (2009); and *The Ethics of War: Classic and Contemporary Readings* (2006). He has also published a number of articles in leading journals. He was appointed to the Pontifical Academy of Social Sciences by Pope Francis in 2016.

Nicholas Rengger is Professor of Political Theory and International Relations at the University of St Andrews and a member of the *Academia Europaea.* His most recent book is T*he Anti-Pelagian Imagination in Political Theory and International Relations: Dealing in Darkness* (2017), which contains two essays on the work of Jean Elshtain. He has written extensively on the just war tradition, most especially in his *Just War and International Order: The Uncivil Condition in World Politics* (2013). He is currently working on a study of the significance of Weber's essay *Politik als Beruf* for five contemporary ethico-political dilemmas and a major study entitled *Political Philosophy and World Order.*

Heather M. Roff is a Senior Research Fellow at the University of Oxford and a Research Scientist in the Global Security Initiative at Arizona State University. She is also a national Cybersecurity Fellow and Future of War Fellow at the New

America Foundation. Her research interests include international ethics, international law, emerging military technologies, the philosophy of Immanuel Kant, and feminist theories. She has held faculty positions at the Josef Korbel School of International Studies at the University of Denver, the University of Waterloo and the United States Air Force Academy. She is author of *Global Justice, Kant and the Responsibility to Protect* (2013) and more than a dozen articles relating to international ethics and emerging military technologies, particularly autonomous weapons and cybersecurity.

Gavin Stewart is a PhD candidate in Politics at the University of Glasgow. Prior to commencing his doctoral studies, he completed an MRes in International Relations and an MA in Politics, both also at the University of Glasgow, graduating with merit in the former and first class honours in the latter. He is currently researching classical formulations of justice in warfare, with a particular focus on the theoretical and historical significance of Cicero's writings in terms of the development of the tradition.

Nahed Artoul Zehr is the executive director of Faith & Culture Center in Nashville, TN. She spent 2013–2017 as an assistant professor of religious studies at Western Kentucky University in Bowling Green. Zehr is the author of *The War against al-Qaeda: Religion, Policy, and Counter-Narratives.*

FOREWORD

War is mankind's oldest story. In the *Iliad* war is presented as a choice of the gods. Insecure, vengeful and proud, it is the gods who direct soldiers into brutal and deadly combat. As Homer tells it, the force of war is so deeply ingrained in the human experience it is beyond the capacity of mere mortals to control.

The just war tradition is a centuries-long project to assert control over human conflict. As Andrew Carnegie wrote in 1914, "It is the killing of each other that stamps man still the savage. That this practice is not soon to pass away from civilized man is unthinkable, since history proves that from age to age, by a law of his being, he has been slowly yet surely developing from the beast". For Carnegie, moral progress was possible – it was visible in the abolition of practices such as slavery and dueling and in the development of new institutions of international law and organization. Carnegie believed that human society would ultimately make an evolutionary leap to eradicate war as a legitimate human enterprise.

Two world wars and the genocides of the 20th century proved the limits of Carnegie's vision. Yet the idea that war can and should be regulated has never been more widely debated. This book appears as atrocities in Syria, Sudan, Congo and Burma continue. Great power military confrontation simmers over claims in Ukraine, Crimea, and the South China Sea. Possibilities for nuclear proliferation hover over the Middle East, South Asia, and East Asia. Drone strikes and cyber-attacks occur daily. Internet-linked terrorist networks remain a genuine threat. The frame for all of these conflicts continues to be the just war and the principles it suggests.

In his speech at Hiroshima in June 2016 President Barack Obama said, "Technological progress without an equivalent progress in human institutions can doom us. The scientific revolution that led to the splitting of the atom requires a moral revolution as well". He concluded that we should choose "a future in which Hiroshima and Nagasaki are known not as the dawn of atomic warfare but as the start of our own moral awakening".

This moral awakening, as Obama put it in his Nobel lecture in 2009, should be built on two propositions. First, "We must begin by acknowledging the hard truth: We will not eradicate violent conflict in our lifetimes. There will be times when nations – acting individually or in concert – will find the use of force not only necessary but morally justified". Second, "Where force is necessary, we have a moral and strategic interest in binding ourselves to certain rules of conduct".

The rules that Obama refers to are embedded in the principles of the just war. These rules respect sovereignty and human dignity. They invoke the principles of discrimination (between combatants and non-combatants) and proportionality. These rules are not revealed by a higher authority nor invented by elites. These rules are passed down from theologians and jurists, soldiers and statesmen. They arise out of the hard experience of war itself. They are the product of real people dealing with the horrors of the wars of their day.

This book tells the story of the just war tradition through its main protagonists. Each chapter gives insight into the life and times of the most significant just war thinkers. Through these characters we see the tradition grow, evolve, and change over time. We see the tradition as it emerges from ancient and classical roots through the early years of the state system, and eventually to the contemporary post-colonial milieu. We see individuals as well as institutions. Crucially, we see that the just war thinkers do not live in a world of theory. They live in a world where ideas and life experience develop together, where principles often conflict and hard choices must be made.

All of the contributors to this book – and all of the thinkers profiled – would agree that the just war is a dynamic concept. Each generation must renew for itself the meaning and use of the principles the tradition suggests. To that end, we are much in debt to Daniel Brunstetter and Cian O'Driscoll for assembling such an engaging group of scholars. The open and critical dialogue exhibited in these pages is evidence that the tradition is in good hands and fit for duty in these unstable and insecure times.

Joel H. Rosenthal
President, Carnegie Council for Ethics in
International Affairs, New York, NY

ACKNOWLEDGEMENTS

Cian O'Driscoll would like to thank a number of people for their assistance in producing this volume. Each and every one of the contributors to this book have been a pleasure to work with, rendering the process of compiling the manuscript a far easier and more enjoyable task than it probably ought to have been. A special word of thanks to Heather Roff whose addition to the team was rather late in the day, but who nevertheless delivered a superb chapter. Andrew Humphrys and Hannah Ferguson ensured that we met our deadlines by keeping a steady hand on the tiller at Routledge. John Emery also contributed hugely by reading and commenting on drafts of every single chapter – this is a better book for his efforts. Two doctoral candidates at the University of Glasgow, Louis Bujnoch and Gavin Stewart, offered thoughtful feedback on the purpose and composition of the volume. As ever, Andrew Hom was on hand to offer his own brand of cynical but supportive counsel, while Phil O'Brien, Ian Clark, and Toni Erskine have been a constant source of encouragement. Tom and Felix Spelman were great wrestling partners – even if they were occasionally mistaken about who their favourite uncle is. It is also necessary to thank the Economic and Social Research Council, who provided the funding for my time on this project (ES/L013363/1 – Moral Victories: Ethics, Exit Strategies, and the Ending of Wars). Last but certainly not least, I would like to thank my co-editor and friend, Dan Brunstetter, for his extraordinary contribution to this book. I had wanted to work with Dan for some time before we agreed to take on this particular initiative, and the experience is one I will treasure. I learned a great deal from working with Dan, and am hoping there will be more opportunities to do so in the future.

Daniel Brunstetter would like to thank many people who helped to make the volume possible. First and foremost, Cian O'Driscoll, a kindred spirit and fellow traveller along this journey we call life. The idea for the book emerged out of a conversation at a café in a Paris train station, with Cian's vision for the book filling the space on many napkins – in my infinite wisdom, I had no paper on which to write. Not quite the parchment of old and far from technology of today, I managed, but only just, to keep pace with the flow of his ideas by writing on what happened to be on hand. It has been a pleasure to see the volume through its journey from ancient Rome to today, and conversing about the chapters with him along the way. Of course, I have our authors to thank for the depth of their contributions, and their patience as I offered comments (upon more comments). Two doctoral candidates at UC Irvine deserve a special shout-out: John Emery – yes he deserves to be thanked twice! – helped in more ways than seemingly possible, and Hallee Caron provided timely and meticulous copyediting. My own chapter benefited greatly from conversations I had at the Bartolomé de las Casas: History, Philosophy, & Theology in the Age of European Expansion conference held at Providence College in 2016. In particular Matthew Restall, David Lantigua, David Orique and Rady Roldán-Figueroa provided erudite council. I owe a special debt to the late Daniel Castro, whose own work on Las Casas has been an inspiration. In addition to thanking the editorial team at Routledge, I also wish to extend my gratitude to the War, Conflict and Ethics series editors, Michael Gross and James Pattison, for their invaluable advice on the scope and structure of the book. Finally, I want to thank my students, many of who come from war-torn histories, for sharing their stories and inspiring me to work on this subject. Sahira's story was particularly inspiring to me. From an Iraqi refugee following the 2003 U.S. led invasion, to an undergraduate student in southern California, to her pursuits of post-graduate studies in peace and conflict at one of the world's most prestigious universities – her journey is a symbol of the ability of the human spirit not simply to endure, but to strive to make the world a better place. I dedicate this book to those she left behind, who suffer from the folly of our moral misgivings. May these pages offer some insight to the current and future generation of leaders to make better decisions …

INTRODUCTION

An intimation of possibilities

Daniel R. Brunstetter and Cian O'Driscoll

The just war tradition is a body of thought that addresses the rights and wrongs of warfare. It boasts a venerable history, with scholars in general agreement that it can be traced back to the sunset of the Roman Empire, if not further. Over this period, the tradition has coalesced around three thematic concerns. The first of these is the *jus ad bellum*. Its focus is the question: In what circumstances or under what conditions might the use of force ever be justified? The answer to this question is usually parlayed into a series of principles. Thus the resort to force may be justified in cases where the actor in question bears a just cause to initiate hostilities, possesses the requisite authority to levy warfare, is animated by a right intention, and has reasonable grounds to believe that the recourse to force is a last resort, likely to result in military success, and to yield more good than harm. The second thematic concern is the *jus in bello*. Its remit is the conduct of warfare. It asks: What are the limits to the justified use of force? Three principles are typically cited in response to this inquiry. First, the use of force must be limited by necessity. This proscribes wanton violence and cruelty. Second, the level of force employed must always be proportionate to the objective. And third, force must only be directed at legitimate targets, with all other parties spared the ravages of war so far as this is possible. This is known as the principle of discrimination or non-combatant immunity. The third thematic concern is the *jus post bellum*. It is concerned with how wars may be concluded justly. It does not generate a neat set of principles, but instead is focused on the responsibilities of belligerents in the immediate aftermath of war.

Unfortunately, there is no shortage of reasons why we should familiarize ourselves with these ideas. War is, of course, an ever-present on the international landscape. Barely a week goes by without reports streaming in of battlefield atrocities taking place in some or other trouble spot around the globe. Meanwhile, terrorist attacks continue to tear at the very fabric of societies the world over. The consequence of this is that very few lives remain untouched by warfare. Even if one escapes the front lines, the taxes we pay go toward, among other things, training soldiers, stocking armouries, and funding the military adventurism of our leaders. As Leon Trotsky reputedly said, you may not be interested in war, but it is certainly interested in you.

Acknowledging the ubiquity of warfare is one thing. Accepting that it is appropriate to speak about war in relation to justice is a different matter. Yet unless we wish to reject the use of force outright and in every instance, we invariably find ourselves treating war in precisely these terms. Writing against the backdrop of WWII, Albert Camus (cited in Zinn, 2002, p.73) encouraged his readers to make the gamble "that words were more powerful than munitions". Yet Camus was not a thoroughgoing pacifist. He was a member of the armed resistance that took the fight to the occupying Nazis. His experience suggests, then, that these are complex matters, and that there may sometimes be a link between justice and warfare. Discerning this link begins by asking a series of simple, but very important, questions: Can war ever be justified? If so, what threshold requirements must be met? How should a just war be prosecuted? What is the correct balance to strike between the dictates of military necessity and the offices of humanity? Finally, how, if at all, can war lead, in the end, to some semblance of a just peace? Once one finds oneself asking these questions, one has already engaged with the idiom and ideas of just war.

The purpose of this book

The purpose of this book is to introduce the just war tradition. Many readers will already be accustomed to reading just war terminology in the newspapers and to hearing it debated on radio and television shows. Terms such as just cause, last resort, proportionality and civilian immunity pepper the reportage of current events related to war, often defining the scope of debates about the latest international crisis – from events in the Ukraine to the struggle against the so-called Islamic State (IS) in Syria and Iraq. This language, which is closely linked to modern notions of international law and human rights, has a long and storied pedigree that perceptibly informs the way we think and talk about war today. The chapters that follow are not meant to tell the reader what he or she should think about the relationship between war and justice. Rather, they seek to expose him or her to the historical roots and contemporary significance of the terms and concepts that often arise when war is under discussion. The hope is that, by gaining a deeper knowledge of how just war ideas have developed over time the reader will be in a better position to interrogate and perhaps, with critical insights gained from this foray into the history of ideas, even refine his or her own views on the on the rights and wrongs of warfare.

If this goes some way toward explaining why we might wish to think more deeply than heretofore about "just war", it says precious little about what is meant by "tradition". Some might be baffled about why we have chosen to use such a dusty word when seemingly more amenable options, such as "theory", are available. This is a valid query and it points to the main reason that we consider this book to be a necessary and useful addition to an already busy field.

To think about just war as a tradition entails a rejection of the idea that it denotes a single, monolithic theory. The notion of just war as a tradition involves conceiving of it as a multiplicity of closely related but competing voices that, when combined, constitutes a unified field of inquiry and practical judgment. Ian Clark (2015, p.33) captures something of this when he writes:

> It is not possible to speak of a single doctrine of just war; nor can we point to the linear development of any single idea. At best, just war appears as a tradition, a set of themes and tropes that has developed across the centuries, and drawing from diverse strands of intellectual endeavor. These recurrent themes in the discussion of warfare reflect a general philosophical orientation (and hence can be loosely referred to as a continuing tradition), but they have been subject to constant revision and adaptation.

In a similar vein, James Turner Johnson (2009, p.252) likens the just war tradition to, "a stream that moves through history like a river, remaining the same yet putting down elements, and picking up others as it flows, from time to time dividing into different channels and then, perhaps, recombining". The implication of this is that a tradition should, to the degree that it is possible, be viewed in its totality, as a rolling story, the sum of its parts, rather than as an index of individuated contributions. Like the Bayeux Tapestry – a detail from which is featured on the cover of this volume – it is only possible to gain a proper understanding of the tradition by viewing it, not as a series of static and independent parts, but as a protean whole. This raises the vexed questions of how we determine where that story begins and whose voices to count as bona fide contributions to the tradition (Reichberg, Syse, and Begby, 2006, pp.x–xi).

These questions do not brook easy answers. They do, however, invite us to consider the risks associated with thinking about the ethics of war in light of the historical just war tradition. Most notably, it is all too easy to drift toward a facile conservatism that, on the one hand, discounts new thinking on the grounds that it marks a departure from the teachings of our forefathers, and on the other, fetishizes "classic", that is, old, categories as abiding truths. The problem is compounded by the fact that, with the honorable exception of Jean Bethke Elshtain, and perhaps also Christine de Pizan, the figures identified as the luminaries of the just war tradition usually happen to be dead white males (Kinsella, 2011). Consequently the vitality of the tradition – its flexibility, self-reflexivity, and indeed relevance – risks being diminished, overpowered by a propensity for closure and reification. In this way a tradition that, to borrow Jaroslav Pelikan's (1984, p.65) pleasing turn of phrase, ostensibly stands for the "living faith of the dead" flirts with a form of sclerotic traditionalism that is better described as "the dead faith of the living".

Many of these criticisms lie behind the recent "revisionist" turn in just war theory. Scholars such as Jeff McMahan have derided fidelity to the just war tradition as a case of misplaced loyalty. He has criticized the tradition as a form of received wisdom or unquestioned orthodoxy, and has dismissed its tenets as "obviously absurd" (2009, vii). For many who have followed McMahan, any devotion shown to investigating the history of the just war tradition is at best an indulgence, at worst a surrender to the mistakes and follies of the past.

The perils associated with thinking about the ethics of war in light of the just war tradition are real, but they are also avoidable. Engagement with the history of the tradition can enrich our ethical reasoning without exhausting it or taking it hostage. The work of Alex Bellamy (2007), Nigel Biggar (2013), James Turner Johnson (2014), John Kelsay (2007), Larry May (2012), Gregory Reichberg (2016), and Nick Rengger (2013), among others, attests to this. On the one hand, their writings indicate that while the principles of the just war tradition should not be mistaken for empty shells to be filled however one chooses, without any regard for their provenance and development over time, nor are they entirely determined by their past usage. It is possible to tweak or re-fashion them to meet new demands. On the other hand, they also demonstrate that some knowledge or awareness of how these principles evolved, that is, how some interpretations of just war principles have been challenged or rejected over time, can be very helpful when thinking about how they should be interpreted and applied in today's world. As Johnson puts it (1984, p.15), the just war tradition supplies "a fund of practical moral wisdom, based not in abstract speculation or theorization, but in reflection on actual problems encountered in war as these have presented themselves in different historical circumstances". The point is that cultivating a sense of the past need not enslave us to it. Rather, the hope must be that it will bestow upon us a deeper, more variegated perspective on the challenges we face today.

The challenges to be confronted

This book introduces the just war tradition by way of a set of essays on the key figures associated with it. The aim is to provide the reader with a sense of how just war thinking evolved over time, and how it might be understood as a tradition. As such it confronts four challenges. We have already alluded to some of them. The first is the not insignificant matter of where to start. This connects to a very thorny question indeed: When did the just war tradition originate? Put differently, who was the first just war thinker? A number of candidates present themselves for consideration. One might, for instance, be minded to attribute the honor to Aristotle, who appears to be the first person to commit the term "just war" to record. Alternatively, one could turn to Cicero, who devoted portions of his masterwork, On Duties, to discussing the "justice of warfare". Yet another option would be Saint Augustine, who many people have celebrated as the father of the just war tradition (Barnes, 1988, p.71; Mattox, 2006, p.1). Were one to be more cautious, one might decide that a recognizable articulation of the just war idea did not actually emerge until the 13th century writings of Saint Thomas Aquinas. Our view is that the selection of any of these options would be defensible. Where one decides to start the story is, to a large extent, simply a matter of personal preference – a reflection of the particular story one wishes to tell about the tradition. The key in all instances is that the scholar bears in mind that his or her choice of starting point is always to some greater or lesser degree tendentious and subject to challenge.

With that caveat discharged, we have opted to begin our survey with Cicero. Our rationale is that he is the first thinker to offer a systematic account of the "justice of warfare", and the template he establishes is hugely helpful for understanding the later writings of Saint Augustine and others. Cicero is cited as a source of authority by later thinkers across the centuries, including Augustine, Gratian, Las Casas, Grotius and Vattel. Even though the thought of these thinkers differs greatly, the turn to Cicero provided a common source from which to begin their arguments, namely that the very concept of a just war, and a war waged justly, exists. The fact that contemporary scholars tend to skim over Cicero's contribution to the just war tradition only adds to the appeal of beginning with him. As with all the chapters that follow, the entry on Cicero is written in clear and accessible style that is intended to cater to novices and experts alike. Our hope is that, while there should be enough detail to satisfy the experienced scholar, the undergraduate student picking this book up will find the essays it contains both stimulating and easy to follow.

The second challenge will be familiar to anyone who has ever played the parlor game of selecting their all-time dream time in whatever their favorite sport might be. Who should be included, and who should be omitted? And on what grounds should this decision be made? Ought space be made for critics of the tradition, that is, those figures that engage just war thinking by refuting it? An affirmative answer to this question would bring characters such as Erasmus into the mix. Or should chapters be reserved exclusively for the central thinkers of the just war tradition? We have attempted to be as inclusive as we possible. The result is nineteen chapters devoted to thinkers spanning the various sub-traditions and disciplines that have constituted the just war tradition from the 1st century BCE to the present day. Thus we have included chapters on classical orators, early Christian theologians, canon lawyers, scholastics, humanists, early modern jurists, enlightenment philosophers, formulators of military doctrine, and contemporary political theorists, moral philosophers, and religious ethicists. We have attempted, so far as it is possible, to strike a happy balance between mainline just war thinkers and more marginal figures whose engagement with just war thinking reveals something about the dilemmas and applicability of the inherited ideas of just war. Thus, for every Augustine or Grotius, there is a Bartolomé de las Casas (who used the Catholic just war tradition he inherited to criticize the Spanish wars of conquest) or Immanuel Kant (who listed Grotius among the tiresome comforters of war-minded statesmen and focused on *jus post bellum*). In each case, we have asked leading experts on the figure in question to write the entry. Besides directing the reader to the Table of Contents, and the chapters themselves, there is, we hope, no need to gloss the final line-up.

Covering such a broad span of thinkers invites certain problems, not least regarding coherence. Sprawling from the 1st century BCE to the present day, and sampling so many disciplines, there is a very real possibility that a volume such as this could descend into a scattershot affair. We have attempted to circumnavigate this problem by mandating that all chapters address their subject in a similar fashion and follow the same general format. Consequently, all the chapters contained in this volume are organized around the same thematic concerns. Each thinker is treated in relation to the historical context in which he or she worked, the key texts he or she produced, the principal tenets of their just war thought, their contribution to the tradition, and any legacy they might boast, with an eye towards gauging their contemporary relevance. This way of arranging matters not only makes the text more manageable to digest. It will also help the reader to discern patterns of continuity between and across various historical figures, critical breaks from the ideas of the past, and to note how ideas propagated by one thinker feed into the writings of his or her successors and shape the subsequent development of the tradition as a whole.

The third challenge pertains to how one relates the just war tradition to other cultural or religious approaches to thinking about war. What crossover is there, for instance, between just war thinking and pacifism, or just war thinking and the Islamic tradition of *jihad*? Or is it really possible to understand the just war tradition as a discrete body of thought void of any overlap with other cultural traditions? The answer to the latter question has to be in the negative. There is an abundance of evidence that just war thinking often co-mingled and even cross-fertilized with approaches drawn from other traditions. For reasons of space and focus, however, we have chosen to bypass this challenge, which others have taken up elsewhere (Johnson and Kelsay, 1990; May, 2015; Reichberg and Syse, 2014). The volume you have in front of you concentrates solely on the western tradition of just war thought. We have sacrificed breadth for depth, and focused our analysis on the tradition that is most closely connected to international law and the law of armed conflict.

The fourth and final challenge is the twin peril of anachronism and antiquarianism. Anachronism involves reading present-day ideas into the past. Antiquarianism is the opposite: it reflects an interest in the past purely for its own sake. Each is troublesome in its own way. If anachronism risks distorting the historical record by indexing it to contemporary concerns, antiquarianism goes too far the other way by ignoring those concerns altogether. The challenge, then, is to chart a course between these rocks. This behooves the scholar to find some way, without eliding their nuances, or misconstruing their arguments, of interpolating the particularities of a range of historical texts so that they are intelligible to today's reader. Accordingly, the contributors to this volume have sought to foreground historical context in their exegeses, introduce their particular subject in his or her own words where possible, and offer remarks on the contemporary relevance of that thinker's ideas. Whether or not they have been successful will be for the reader to judge.

An intimation of possibilities

Winston Churchill once quipped that the Balkans have produced more history than is good for them (MacMillan, 2010, p.89). Whatever the veracity of this statement as it applied to the Balkans, readers could be forgiven for thinking it holds true when it comes to the ethics of war. With a long and winding history that dates all the way back to antiquity, just war thinking in particular can often seem to come with more baggage than any scholar could reasonably be expected to carry. The result of this is that the historical just war tradition itself is often dismissed as a patrimony to be escaped rather than a store of learning to be claimed and engaged. This is an unfortunate oversight that this volume seeks to remedy. As the chapters that follow will hopefully show, the tradition is a resource that helps us to gain a deeper, richer, more variegated perspective on the ethical dilemmas that we confront in the context of contemporary armed conflict. To paraphrase John Tosh (2008, pp.28-29), it is not a dead weight on the present, but an intimation of possibilities.

Works cited

Barnes, Jonathan. 1982. The Just War. In Kretzmann, N., Kenny, A., and Pinborg, J. eds. *The Cambridge History of Later Medieval Philosophy: From the Rediscovery of Aristotle to the Disintegration of Scholasticism 1100-1600.* Cambridge: Cambridge University Press.

Bellamy, Alex J. 2006. *Just Wars: From Cicero to Iraq.* Cambridge: Polity.

Biggar, Nigel. 2013. *In Defence of War.* Oxford: Oxford University Press.

Clark, Ian. 2015. *Waging War: A Philosophical Introduction—2nd edition.* Oxford: Oxford University Press.

Johnson, James Turner. 1984. *Can Modern War be Just?* New Haven: Yale University Press.

Johnson, James Turner. 2009. Thinking Historically about Just War. *Journal of Military Ethics* 8(3), pp.246-259.

Johnson, James Turner. 2014. *Sovereignty: Moral and Historical Perspectives* Washington DC: Georgetown University Press.

Johnson, James Turner and Kelsay, John. eds. (1990). *Cross, Crescent, and Sword: The Justification and Limitation of War in Western and Islamic Tradition.* Westport: Greenwood Press.

Kelsay, John. 2007. *Arguing the Just War in Islam.* Harvard NJ: Harvard University Press.

Kinsella, Helen. 2011. *The Image Before the Weapon: A Critical History of the Distinction Between Combatant and Civilian.* Ithaca, NY: Cornell University Press.

MacMillan, Margaret. 2010. *The Use and Abuse of History.* London: Profile.

Mattox, John Mark. 2006. *Saint Augustine and the Theory of Just War.* New York: Continuum.

May, Larry. 2012. *After War Ends.* Cambridge: Cambridge University Press.

May, Larry. 2015. *Contingent Pacifism: Revisiting Just War Theory.* Cambridge: Cambridge University Press.

McMahan, Jeff. 2009. *Killing in War.* Oxford: Oxford University Press.

Pelikan, Jaroslav. 1984. *The Vindication of Tradition.* New Haven, CT: Yale University Press.

Reichberg, Gregory M. 2016. *Thomas Aquinas on War and Peace.* Cambridge: Cambridge University Press.

Reichberg, Gregory M., Syse, Henrik, and Begby, Endre. eds. 2006. *The Ethics of War: Classic and Contemporary Readings.* Oxford: Blackwell.

Reichberg, Gregory M. and Syse, Henrik. eds. 2014. *Religion, War, and Ethics: A Sourcebook of Textual Traditions.* Cambridge: Cambridge University Press.

Rengger, Nicholas. 2013. *Just War and International Order.* Cambridge: Cambridge University Press.

Tosh, John. 2008. *Why History Matters.* Basingstoke: Palgrave.

Zinn, Howard. 2002. *The Power of Non-Violence: Writings by Advocates for Peace.* Boston: Beacon Press.

1

MARCUS TULLIUS CICERO (106 BCE–43 BCE)

Gavin Stewart

Introduction

Marcus Tullius Cicero (106 BCE–43 BCE), statesman, orator and philosopher of the late Roman republic, was among the first thinkers to offer a systematic ethical project in which the concept of just war had a firm place. His ideas would find a marked presence in a number of important just war thinkers in history – Augustine and Grotius to name two – and provide many of the basic building blocks with which we all try to understand justice in warfare today. Cicero's broader ethical project was to bring Greek philosophy to bear on Roman practice and, in doing so, instill a sense in the Roman people of what constituted virtuous behavior. This endeavor can be described on many levels: the uniting of the moral and the political, the rational and the actual, nature and custom, philosophy and rhetoric, justice and warfare. More than merely compiling and transmitting the philosophy of his predecessors, Cicero, as one scholar notes, "deftly appropriates, transforms, and, at times transcends" their work (Atkins, 2013, p.2). The moments of transcendence can perhaps be attributed to his rare position as both statesman and philosopher. It is precisely this status that makes him such an important figure in the just war tradition. As John Adams would say of Cicero in the 18th Century, "as all the ages of the world have not produced a greater statesman and philosopher united in the same character, his authority should have great weight" (*Ibid.*, p.1).

This identity as statesman-philosopher speaks to the intimate relation between the events of Cicero's life and his theorizing. His extraordinary rise and fall in politics at such a pivotal moment in western history is deserving of our close attention, but there is space here to set out only some of the key events (Rawson, 1994). He was born into a wealthy but non-senatorial family in the town of Arpinum, 60 miles or so outside of Rome. The family's landed wealth and powerful connections ensured that he received the best education from some of the leading orators and philosophers of the day. Following a brief stint of unexceptional military service and further philosophical education, Cicero entered politics and within a few years had secured the consulship – the highest elected political office – at the minimum age of 42. This was a remarkable achievement at the time for a gentleman of his social class with very little military experience. The year of his consulship saw the conspiracy of the populist senator Catiline to seize power by force at Rome. The conspiracy was exposed, Catiline fled into exile and, after a *senatus consultum ultimum* (a senatorial decree designed to replace the office of dictatorship in times of existential threat to the commonwealth), Cicero had five of the conspirators executed without trial and was thereafter hailed as "the father of his country".

Even though he was relatively absent from the battlefield himself, the ubiquity of war, both internal and external, would exert a significant influence on Cicero's political thought. An interesting example that foreshadows some of his thought on just war is his powerful speech on the Manilian law in 67 BCE, which granted an extraordinary command to Gnaeius Pompeius Magnus (Pompey) in the Third Mithridatic war. Cicero lamented that even though Mithridates had been defeated in previous wars, he was left with enough power to rebuild and threaten again. Thus any post-war peace was only temporary. In his speech, Cicero implies that Pompey had the virtue and military wherewithal to make sure this did not happen again by prosecuting the war differently, and thus restoring Rome's reputation. This speech significantly increased Cicero's own personal standing, winning him important allies and ensuring his steady rise through the *cursus honorum* (the "career ladder" of public offices at Rome) in the process. But the winds of fortune soon changed with his enemy Clodius gaining power in 58 and declaring Cicero an exile for his brutal suppression of the Catilinarian conspirators. He would return to a glorious welcome shortly after, and despite some periods of withdrawal to write philosophy, he continued to play a leading role in Roman politics in his later life. But the tumultuous times, marked by the power struggles of military generals such as Julius Caesar, Marcus Crassus and Pompey, culminated in his proscription and execution at the hands of Mark Anthony's death squad in 43 BCE.

Contexts

It is important to set Cicero's thought on just war in the broader context of international relations in antiquity. His conception of the *ius gentium*, which is key to his international ethics, was partly conditioned by the general sense of international obligation that had already existed among a number of states across the Mediterranean for some time (Bederman, 2001). As one historian describes these international relations, certain states were part of a community that "had a very conscious sense of dealing with one another as equals and within a system that regarded each as being 'civilized' and not barbaric" (*Ibid.*, p.43). The norms regarding warfare were part of this sense of mutual understanding.

Rome's conquest of central Italy in the 4th century BCE increased her international standing, brought her into a wider sphere of geopolitics across the Mediterranean and contributed to an increase in the number of treaties she struck with others. The Mediterranean state system of the 3rd and 2nd centuries, consisting of powers such as Macedon, Syria, Egypt, Carthage, Rhodes and the Greek city-states, was grounded in a sense that all of the constituent nations, despite their divergent cultures, were civilized enough that their relations could be based on *good faith*, that is, mutual trust. To seal this trust, treaties were ritualized, taking a kind of hybrid religious-legal form where oaths would be sworn, inviting the wrath of the gods should they be broken. This also gave rise to certain formal procedures and limitations in the declaration and prosecution of war (what we now refer to as *jus ad bellum* and *jus in bello*). The initiation and conduct of hostilities between members of this state system tended to be less the result of aggression, and more from a perceived wrong that had been committed, or good faith that had been broken. War in this way performed the function of religious-legal redress or punishment. There is, of course, the question of whether talk of just war at this time was anything more than mere rhetoric to legitimize aggressive military actions. Livy's narrations of the Roman history of this period offer a window into the Roman rhetoric of just war (both in the period he narrates and in his own time). For his part, Cicero (as we will see below) sought to embed this rhetoric in a broader philosophical system with justice at its core.

Rome herself was a highly militarized community. The conquest of Italy in the 4th century BCE was formative in terms of developing this military culture, which would find further expression and development in her victories over the western Mediterranean in the 3rd century and the Greek world in the second. Central to Roman military success was the value her citizens placed upon glory. This concept signifies great fame or renown, bestowed by the people on those who perform great deeds in preserving and protecting their liberty. Consuls (the most senior political officials) had only one year in office to demonstrate their military prowess in pursuit of the people's liberty and were very adept at finding opportunities for doing so (Harris, 1979). This led to a rapidly expanding empire and the dissolution of the existing state system. As the 2nd and 1st centuries progressed, questions about justice, war and glory would become more urgent for Romans to address.

As Rome expanded, the senate found it increasingly difficult to govern such a far-flung empire. Bonds of loyalty strengthened between armies and their generals, increasing the powers of the latter to the extent that they could overwhelm the government with force should they find any senatorial decisions unfavorable. Intemperate passions for glory pitted both general against general and Rome against other nations. The 1st century was thus marked by the dissolution of senatorial solidarity, ever-changing groupings of allies, complex intrigues, and a series of both civil and foreign wars. The Roman republic eventually dissolved in 27 BCE, when Julius Caesar's nephew Octavian (Caesar Augustus) established the Principate.

Cicero lived through much of this chaotic period. In order to preserve and protect the commonwealth, he tried earnestly to restore the dignity and solidarity of the senatorial class both in his theoretical writings and in his practice. As we will see below, Cicero would try to keep glory in check by rooting it in virtuous behavior. It is important to note here that he expounds his political theory with historical examples, but he narrates history in such a way that it reconciles with his theory. Thus, Roman history often emerges in Cicero's writings as a kind of "golden age" of warfare, aligning with his own ideas about justice, so that it can be compared favorably against the injustices of his own time (Fox, 2007).

Texts and tenets

Cicero was a prolific writer. His surviving works include important speeches that were preserved in written form, letters to his friends, colleagues and family, and a number of philosophical and rhetorical treatises. On the subject of warfare, we can point to several important texts that provide the broader intellectual contours shaping his political thought. These include *De Re Publica* and *De Legibus*, two philosophical dialogues written in the 50s BCE (both of which survived in fragmented form).[1] *De Re Publica* is a conversation about the best kind of commonwealth and citizen, set in the midst of a political crisis in 129 BCE when the agrarian reforms of the recent past had begun to threaten the stability of the commonwealth. The text apparently enjoyed considerable popularity both in Cicero's own time and after. Tacitus seems to have engaged with it, and Augustine refers to it on multiple occasions in his *City of God*. For the Christians of late antiquity, the *De Re Publica* arguably represented the culmination of pagan thinking about politics. *De Legibus* is set in Cicero's own day, with the author as one of the characters discussing the best kind of laws for the best kind of commonwealth with his friend Atticus and brother Quintus. It was left incomplete and most likely unpublished in his own lifetime. Some references are made to it in late antiquity (again, Augustine is worthy of note in this respect) but it was mainly from the Middle Ages onwards that the work would exert an important influence.

Despite the difficulties the modern scholar has in interpreting these dialogues, they provide a number of insights into key elements of Cicero's just war thinking, particularly in relation to his theory of natural law. Through the voice of Laelius, one of the interlocutors in *De Re Publica*, we have a definition of natural law that has echoed loudly down the history of political thought. In Book III, he says:

> True law is right reason, consonant with nature, spread through all peoples. It is constant and eternal; it summons to duty by its orders; it deters from crime by its prohibitions … There will not be one law at Rome and another at Athens, one now and another later, but all nations at all times will be bound by this one eternal and unchangeable law, and the god will be the one common master and general (so to speak) of all people. He is the author, expounder and mover of this law ….

> (Rep. *3.33*)

Written laws, institutions and practices are seen to be imperfect expressions of, or *in accordance with*, the natural law insofar as they are shaped by its orders and prohibitions (*Leg.* 2.13). Cicero gives a more detailed account of the natural law in Book I of *De Legibus*, while in Books II and III the dialogue revolves around religious and constitutional laws for Rome. The *ius gentium* will emerge in his later works (somewhat ambiguously) as an unwritten and imperfect expression of the natural law:

> And these things are common divisions of the law, those things which are written and those which without writing are upheld by the law of nations (*ius gentium*) or the customs of our ancestors … those [laws] which are unwritten owe their force either to custom or to the agreements and, as it were, common consent of men.
>
> *(Part. Or. 37.130)*

Although there is some debate over Cicero's use of the concept, it seems that, unlike the natural law itself, the *ius gentium* is historically and socially contingent. It emerges as different nations or peoples emerge from a primordial (non-legal) condition and develop certain customs in their dealings with one another, which are in accordance with the natural law (Conklin, 2010). The laws of war would come to have their place in this schema, as customs held in common across a certain group of nations. These customs are based ultimately on right reason and it is each nation's internal development of this reason that gives rise to virtue in their actions towards one another. Thus, immediately prior to his discussion of just war in the *De Officiis*, Cicero writes: "… certain duties must be observed even towards those at whose hands you may have received unjust treatment. There is a limit to revenge and to punishment …" (I.33).

Although the better-preserved part of *De Re Publica* focuses on constitutional theory and Roman history (Books I and II), we can discern from later fragments that the best kind of commonwealth is also one that respects the laws of war in international society. There is a general duty for states to uphold what we would refer to today as certain *jus ad bellum* and *jus in bello* principles. These propositions from the *De Re Publica* on when recourse to war is warranted were not lost on later thinkers. Augustine refers to a lost passage from book III of the text, stating, "unless I am mistaken, it is argued [there] that no war is undertaken by a good state except on behalf of good faith or for safety" (Rep. 3.34a). St. Isidore (circa 560–636 CE), whose encyclopedic *Etymologies* played a major role in preserving Roman learning in the medieval west and influenced Gratian, quotes the following passage from *De Republica*: "Those wars are unjust which are undertaken without cause. For aside from vengeance or for the sake of fighting off enemies no just war can be waged … No war is considered just unless it is announced and declared and unless it involves the recovery of property" (Rep. III.35a). These passages on just war preserved by Augustine and Isidore are set in the context of a broader discussion of natural law in Book III of *De Republica* (specifically in Laelius' defense of natural law against the skeptical arguments of Philus). While we should be careful of how later thinkers interpreted Cicero and how they might have taken the passages out of context (especially Gratian [see chapter 4], who also took other authorities' words out of context – notably Augustine), this view on just war is broadly consistent with what Cicero would have to say in the *De Officiis*.

The *De Officiis* is a work on practical ethics, written in the form of a letter to Cicero's son who was studying in Athens at the time. Modeled on a work by the Stoic philosopher Panaetius (now lost), it consists of three books. The first asks: what is honorable (*honestum*)? The second asks: what is beneficial (*utile*)? And the final book is given over to examples where the honorable and beneficial appear to be in conflict. It is written as a practical guide towards "appropriate actions", or duties (*officiis*): "everything that is honourable in a life depends upon [duty's] cultivation, and everything dishonourable upon its neglect (I.4)". Cicero takes for granted the Stoic doctrine that whatever is honorable is beneficial, whatever is beneficial is honorable, and any conflict between the two is illusory. The main discussion of just war comes in Book I after a broader discussion around the nature of justice and injustice.

Cicero's deliberations on just war as set down in the *De Officiis* can be understood as written expressions of the *ius gentium*. As noted above, there are duties owed even to those who wrong us; this is as true between individuals as it is between commonwealths. Cicero begins his discussion of justice in warfare with a sonorous fusion of what we now refer to today as *jus ad bellum*, *jus in bello* and *jus post bellum*:

> There are two types of conflict; the one proceeds by debate, the other by force. Since the former is the proper concern of man, but the latter of beasts, one should only resort to the latter if one may not employ the former. Wars, then, ought to be undertaken for this purpose, that we may live in peace, without injustice; and once victory has been secured, those who were not cruel or savage in warfare should be spared.
>
> (Off. *1.34–35*)

In the context of Cicero's wider project, this passage is very rich in meaning and can lend itself to a number of different interpretations. I wish to highlight here two elements I regard as important in understanding Cicero's thoughts on war. First, that one must wage war only where discussion is impossible. This is not quite the same thing as the modern *jus ad bellum* concept of last resort, in which peaceful measures should always be tried first. Rather, it is left to the statesman to judge whether the problem is a situation of debate or a situation of war. Second, wars must only be fought for the sake of some future peace without injustice. Consideration must be shown to the defeated so that a just peace can endure, and protection ought to be given to those who lay down their arms or ask for mercy. In this respect, beneficence – acting kindly to promote fellowship – is a key aspect of justice in the *in bello* and *post bellum* context (I, 42–59). Such actions may include receiving a defeated people into Roman citizenship, as was the case with the

Tusculans and Sabines, among others. But at times, achieving a just peace (from the statesman's perspective) may require more drastic measures, including the utter desolation of one's enemy, as was the case with Carthage and Numantia (I.39). We will return to the moral challenges posed by such actions later in the discussion, but for now it is important to stress the overall purpose of the *De Officiis*: to instill *virtue* in potential statesmen, so that such terrible decisions are made only when *necessary*.

For Cicero, only such virtuous statesmen have the requisite authority to wage war in the first place. Turning to ancestral tradition to demonstrate Rome's justice in this respect, Cicero writes:

> A fair code of warfare has been drawn up, in full accordance with religious scruple, in the fetial laws of the Roman people. From this we can grasp that no war is just unless it is waged after a formal demand for restoration, or unless it has been formally announced and declared beforehand.
>
> (Off. *1.36*)

The *fetiales* were a college of priests tasked with the oversight of international affairs.[2] The procedure involved the striking of treaties and the performing of rites, which called the gods to witness the swearing of oaths. Any perceived violation of a treaty would involve more rites, the contents of which were essentially a formal demand for restoration made in the presence of relevant individuals of the foreign power. A period of time would be provided for restitution to occur, but if this time elapsed without redress, the *fetiales* would approach the Roman government, informing them that a just cause for war was present, which in turn would then decide whether or not to wage the war. If it was to be waged, the *fetiales* were tasked with issuing a formal declaration of war to the rival power, which took the form of more rites and a bloodied spear hurled into its territory. The idea behind the institution was to ensure that Rome never fought aggressive wars and upheld the good faith essential to international society. But spears could only be hurled so far; with the expansion of Rome beyond Italy it is not clear how active the fetial laws remained in Roman warfare. What *is* clear is why Cicero would argue that they *should* be a central feature of Roman practice: they would be in accordance with the natural law (*Leg.* 2.21).

Cicero continues the discussion of just war in *De Officiis* by distinguishing between two different types of wars: those fought for the sake of supremacy, which he describes as among *rivals* (those protected by the *ius gentium*), and those fought for the sake of survival, which he describes as against *enemies* (those outside the protections of the *ius gentium*) (I.41). While both should only be commenced when deliberation is impossible and for the sake of living in peace without injustice, the scope of actions appropriate to each is different. A war for supremacy – i.e. glory – "must be carried out with less bitterness" (I.41); while the implication is that a war for survival need not require such moderate behavior. Thus, while praising Roman restraint in her wars against the Tusculanes, the Sabines, and others, Cicero shows no remorse that Carthage and Numantia were razed to the ground. The

Carthaginians "were breakers of truces and Hannibal [its leader] was cruel". Cicero saw them as grievously violating the *ius gentium*, and so Carthage was not spared in battle. He also regarded the Celtiberians as cruel, so the destruction of their settlement at Numantia, after a vicious twenty-year battle, was seen as necessary for the survival of the commonwealth. Significantly, the destroyer of both cities was Scipio Aemilianus, the chief character of *De Republica*, whose virtue Cicero holds in high regard. What becomes apparent in Cicero's writings on warfare is an underlying tension between justice and necessity.

Controversies

War was, it seemed for Cicero, an inevitable part of life. It was used as a vehicle to rise in stature in society, a means to spread Rome's influence in the Mediterranean world, and a way to preserve her values and traditions from rivals and enemies. His philosophical interest in war raises important questions about the link between war and glory, necessity and anticipatory war, and whether or not the laws of war can ever apply to relations with those deemed outside the *ius gentium*.

Cicero recognized that there was a link between just war and the international standing of the Roman commonwealth. Key to understanding this link is the notion of glory. Glorious deeds require a courageous disposition. This quality is essential in the good statesman, but on its own Cicero regards it as a threat to the stability of the commonwealth and so he sought (quite radically) to rework the concept of glory for Romans by rooting it in other virtues as well, including justice. *True* glory, he argues, comes from keeping faith with others and procuring their love and admiration, rather than breaking faith and ruling unjustly with fear and intimidation (II.31–45). It is an open question as to whether Cicero theoretically succeeds in rooting glory in the other virtues.[3] In practice, the more spirited the generals in charge of Rome's glory, the greater is the risk that they will succumb to a *selfish passion* for it at the expense of justice (I.26, I.65). Caesar is held up as the prime example here that can serve as a warning to others; in his quest for preeminence, he "overturned all the laws of gods and men" both nationally and internationally (I.26). Thus Cicero warns: "men are led most of all to being overwhelmed by forgetfulness of justice when they *slip* into *desiring* positions of command or honour or glory" (I.26, emphasis added). Cicero's theory seeks to correct this, regarding the glory of Rome's empire, and wars fought for it, as being more firmly rooted in virtue as a whole. And at the same time, this glory is useful in terms of maintaining a just peace in the universal commonwealth. Nevertheless, there are indications that he is less than fully confident in his own theory, insofar as he acknowledges that glory is a very "slippery" concept, which can so easily lead to injustice (I.65).

The destruction of Corinth serves as a good example for drawing out the tensions involved here. Corinth had been a member of the Achaean League, a confederation of Greek city-states that had been allied to Rome for some fifty years. There were a number of heated debates in the League, which led to an uprising in 146 BCE against Rome and, in a marked departure from her foreign policy in the region, Rome utterly destroyed Corinth in the ensuing war, before breaking up the League itself. Cicero would have "preferred" that his forefathers had not destroyed Corinth, but recognized it was possible that they "had some specific purpose in doing so ... to prevent the location itself from being some day an incitement to war" (I.35). Corinth's strategically advantageous location is seen here to represent an existential (if distant) threat to the Roman commonwealth. Later in the *De Officiis*, however, Cicero implicitly questions the prudence of his forefathers in what he sees as Corinth's *unnecessary* and therefore *unjust* destruction: "in public affairs, wrong is very often done because of the appearance of benefit. An example is our own destruction of Corinth" (III, 46).

Greed for glory (and wealth) is arguably at the center of this controversy. Booty was a key motivation for soldiers enlisting to fight and the rich pickings of Corinth, especially with the unprofitable wars being fought in the west at the time, certainly must have been tempting.[4] Although the general who led the destruction, Lucius Mummius, showed self-restraint with his plunder by using it to bestow gifts on some Italian provinces instead of himself, he was only *seeming* to be just. His actions had the effect of garnering the love, trust and admiration of some Roman citizens and thereby increasing his own personal glory. At the same time, the senatorial decision to destroy Corinth instilled fear, intimidation and obedience across the rest of the Greek world, making for an easier, but less beneficent, management of Rome's empire. All of this seems a far cry from the beneficence and good faith Cicero counsels in wars with other commonwealths, as well as from the virtuous depiction of glory in his theory. Indeed, Cicero emphasizes that the ostensible benefits of acting unjustly are not, in fact, benefits at all. He cites several examples from Greek and Roman history, and he concludes the discussion by saying: "Let this, then, be fixed: if something is dishonourable, it is never beneficial, not even when you acquire something you think beneficial (III.49)".

It bears repeating, however, that Cicero appears to restrict such principles only to those who are members of international society (and it seems, in the end, that he saw Corinth as such a member). At times, there may be no other option but to act cruelly when the survival of the commonwealth is *truly* at stake. Matters of glory are of no concern to the ideal statesman in these situations (Rep. VI.25). When the commonwealth confronts those whose actions or dispositions place them outside of the universal fellowship of humanity, it seems that, for Cicero, the virtue holding that fellowship together – justice – does not exist. All of this begs the question: who is part of international society and based on what criteria? This is a theme with which many thinkers covered in this volume – including Gratian, Vitoria, Las Casas, Gentile, Grotius and Vattel – have grappled.

Returning to Cicero, it seems that the link between the honorable and the beneficial is erased when necessity arises (III.32; III.107). The moral and legal limitations of war can only exist among the more or less civilized: *commonwealths* who have deliberated, written their own civil laws, and recognize universal duties to others. Enemies, or what Cicero also refers to at times as barbarians or savages, such as the Celtiberians, Cimbrians, and Carthaginians (at least during the Third Punic War when Carthage was destroyed by Rome), do not appear to be protected by his just war principles. In an important sense, he believes they are not commonwealths at all, and this is why they appear to sit outside the protections of the *ius gentium*.[5]

Deciding whether or not the commonwealth's survival is threatened, which could legitimize certain aggressive acts to neutralize the threat, involves making a prior judgment, which is by no means straightforward or trivial. Getting it wrong involves committing injustice against another commonwealth, which in turn threatens the fabric that holds international society together as a whole. For Cicero, such desperate situations cannot be theorized; they cannot be brought under a set of rules or principles to be followed at all times. Rather, they are to be taken up on a case-by-case basis, and the judgments made require a great deal of prudence so that conditions of necessity are correctly recognized and dealt with appropriately. To this end, Cicero is very concerned to discover the properties of the ideal statesman and offer practical advice based on this ideal.[6] Recalling his discussion about the two types of conflict discussed above, the ideal statesman ought to be able to understand whether he is in a situation of debate or a situation of war. If persuasion is impossible, the ideal statesman will know when to employ any type of force necessary to ensure the survival of the commonwealth, and he will also know when to fight "with less bitterness", that is, to apply justice in warfare, because he is fighting other members of international society.

In the context of necessity, the ideal statesmen may need to face the prospect of anticipatory war. Cicero provides no theoretical discussion of anticipatory wars. We have already seen his doubts around Corinth, but he accepts Rome's destruction of Carthage and Numantia, both of which he sees as unequivocal instances of anticipatory war. Importantly, the statesman involved in destroying Carthage and Numantia, Scipio, is held out in the *De Re Publica* as someone very much approaching the ideal, with Cicero's treatment in the *De Officiis* of these wars demonstrating that he concurs with Scipio's judgments. This underscores what has already been said: rules for Cicero, including that of only waging war after receiving some sort of injury, are meaningless when the commonwealth's survival is at stake. Such crises require instead the impeccable foresight of the wise and prudent statesman to perceive existential threats when (or better, before) they appear on the horizon.

In summary, to capture the deep tensions that Cicero confronts, we can say that there is, in one sense, a radical separation between justice and necessity; but in another sense, they come together in the virtue (specifically, the wisdom and prudence) of the ideal statesman (*Leg.* 1.19). Justice is the supreme *social* virtue for Cicero, rooted in the natural law and forming the very basis of society, whether national or international. It requires good faith, mutual trust, which is only possible amongst those who recognize moral duties *to one another*. If, for example, a rival were seen to threaten the survival of the commonwealth, this would be taken as a sign that it recognized no such moral duties to others and could not therefore be a recipient of good faith, or justice. In this scenario, the rival is transformed into a deadly enemy who sits outside of international society, and thus outside of the protections of the *ius gentium*. Determining the veracity of this threat becomes all-important because it entails actions that would be unjust *within* international society, though they might be necessary to save the commonwealth from existential threats outside of it.

This, of course, places a great deal of responsibility on the statesman to understand what justice and necessity are in times of war, and what threat means when dealing with a deadly enemy disposed to wreak havoc in international society. How successful Cicero is in approaching these matters should be of great concern to students and scholars of the just war tradition. Connecting war to justice, glory and empire is fraught with theoretical and practical difficulties, but as John Adams recognized, Cicero as statesman-philosopher was in a uniquely well-founded position to address such matters. Whether or not his theory and advice are sound, it is clear that his treatment of these themes would form a very important foundation of just war thinking for centuries to come.

Legacy and enduring relevance

Cicero's legacy for the just war tradition is far-reaching and diverse, feeding into and significantly shaping both its Christian and secular streams of thought. The next chapter will draw out the complexities and fragmentary nature of Augustine's own just war thinking, but here it is appropriate to touch upon some of its Ciceronian flavors which would be carried forward into the Christian ethics of warfare. Augustine was very well read in Cicero and although critical of some of his arguments, he would respect and retain many others. As Johnson notes in his chapter, Augustine roots just war in wisdom and prudence in Book XIX of his *City of God*, which carries loud echoes of Cicero's ideal statesman (albeit in a Christian context). Other aspects of Cicero's writings, such as waging war only for the sake of a just peace (itself of Platonic provenance) and the duty of showing mercy to the defeated, would also be taken up by Augustine and carried over into the Middle Ages and beyond.

Cicero would continue to be a significant authority in the just war tradition as it moved into a more secular age. Grotius quotes him on many occasions in his *De Iure Belli ac Pacis*, drawing extensively on his thinking around the natural law and *ius gentium* to create some of his own foundations for a modern international law, independent of God's will. Cicero's *ius gentium* would also be a towering presence in Vattel's *Le Droit des Gens* in the 18th Century. Grotius and Vattel, as we will see later in this volume are both important figures in the just war tradition, but as with their forerunners and successors, they interpret Cicero in particular contexts and with particular purposes.

And yet his writings are of more than historical significance. Cicero speaks directly to many of the challenges we confront today when thinking about justice in warfare: who is to be protected by the laws of war? Who is a member of international society and based on what criteria? When, if at all, do concerns of justice fade into the background in warfare? How do we reconcile justice and necessity in both *jus ad bellum* and *jus in bello*? How do we reconcile *jus post bellum* with wars of the utter desolation of one's enemy? Cicero's thought blends a form of realism (the necessity of wars of survival) and just war (based on reciprocal duty), but it is important to remember that his realism is embedded in a framework of *virtue* that seeks to limit its applicability as far as possible in the name of justice. Indeed, justice and necessity come together in the wisdom and prudence of the ideal statesman. Thus, a return to Cicero's broader philosophy regarding what the ideal statesman is, and how one comes to approach that ideal, is a return to an untapped source of inspiration, one that might differ significantly, say, from the Christian-based virtue ethics of Aquinas (who was a monumental influence on the just war tradition past and present). In this vein, Cicero's own speeches and letters, which we have not had space to explore, offer great insight into his own deliberations and practical judgments concerning the politics and warfare of his own day, and perhaps across the ages as well.

Notes

1   Excerpts from these texts have been reproduced in Reichberg, Syse, and Begby (2006).
2   For an excellent discussion of the fetial laws, see (Ando, 2010).
3   There are some complex issues involved here. For a more detailed discussion of Cicero's treatment of glory, see (Long, 1995).
4   Cicero was a staunch defender of private property, as long as it was acquired with justice, see (Wood, 1988, ch.VI).
5   The extant portions of *De Re Publica* provide us with some theoretical arguments as to what Cicero regards as a commonwealth, but by and large he views the line to be drawn here as an essentially practical problem, and so his thoughts on the matter tend to emerge more in his oratory than his philosophy. A key aspect is how he develops the concept of *humanitas*, see (Gildenhard, 2011).
6   Unfortunately, the main discussion of Cicero's ideal statesman is in Book V of *De RePublica*, which has been all but lost in transmission. However, there are a number of extant passages in *De RePublica* and elsewhere in his oeuvre that allow us to reconstruct his ideal to some extent. On this subject, see for example: (Zarecki, 2014).

Works cited

Ando, Clifford. 2010. Empire and the Laws of War: A Roman Archaeology. In: Straumann, B. ed. *The Roman Foundations of the Law of Nations: Alberico Gentili and the Justice of Empire.* Oxford: Oxford University Press, pp.30–53.

Atkins, Jed W. 2013. *Cicero on Politics and the Limits of Reason.* Cambridge: Cambridge University Press.

Bederman, David J. 2001. *International Relations in Antiquity.* Cambridge: Cambridge University Press.

Cicero. 1991. *On Duties.* Griffin, M.T. and Atkins, E.M. eds. Cambridge: Cambridge University Press.

Cicero. 1999. *On the Commonwealth and On the Laws (De Re Publica)*. Zetzel, James E.G. ed. Cambridge: Cambridge University Press.

Conklin, William E. 2010. The Myth of Primordialism in Cicero's Theory of *Jus Gentium*. *Leiden Journal of International Law*. **23**(3), pp.479–506.

Fox, Matthew. 2007. *Cicero's Philosophy of History*. Oxford: Oxford University Press.

Gildenhard, Ingo. 2011. *Creative Eloquence: The Construction of Reality in Cicero's Speeches*. Oxford: Oxford University Press.

Long, A.A., 1995. Cicero's Politics in *De Officiis*. In: Laks, A. and M. Schofield. eds. *Justice and Generosity: Studies in Hellenistic Social and Political Philosophy; Proceedings of the Sixth Symposium Hellenisticum*. Cambridge: Cambridge University Press, 213–241.

Harris, William V. 1979. *War and Imperialism in Republican Rome 327–70 BC*. Gloucestershire, U.K.: Clarendon Press.

Rawson, Elizabeth. 1994. *Cicero: A Portrait*. Bloomsbury, U.K.: Bristol Classical Press.

Wood, Neal. 1988. *Cicero's Social and Political Thought*. Oakland, CA: University of California Press.

Zarecki, Jonathan. 2014. *Cicero's Ideal Statesman in Theory and Practice*. London: Bloomsbury.

2

ST. AUGUSTINE (354–430 CE)

James Turner Johnson

Introduction

Augustine is likely the most cited single authority on just war, but just war literature has approached his thought in very different ways. I have elsewhere (Johnson, 1987, pp.50–66) offered my own survey of Augustine on just war and his relationship to other early Christian thinkers. Here, though, I will focus on the approaches taken by others.

A baseline of sorts is offered by prominent historical treatments of Augustine that have focused on exploring his thought and its meaning in the context of his life and times. Of such works Peter Brown's personal and intellectual biography *Augustine of Hippo* (1967 and 2000) is in a class of its own, placing Augustine's major works in the context of his life as it developed, while his *Through the Eye of a Needle* (2012) adds important perspectives on the larger historical and religious context of Augustine's life; yet useful as these works are for the broader historical context of Augustine's thinking, they do not examine his thinking on just war. The various works of R.A. Markus (especially 1970) dealing with Augustine and late classical Christianity add further texture to the background in which Augustine lived and wrote, but it is Markus's short essay, "St. Augustine's Views on the 'Just War'" (1983) that stands out in providing a pithy, tightly focused examination of what Augustine wrote bearing on just war, locating particular passages on this subject in works on various topics written for diverse purposes, and connecting Augustine's treatment of just war to his changing view of politics at different stages in his life. In discussing the historical approach to Augustine on just war below under the heading "Contexts" I principally follow Markus's analysis, expanded by Brown's dating of the works mentioned, seeking to place what Augustine said about just war in its historical frame.

The second approach examined in this chapter is to focus on how Augustine was understood and his influence was carried forward during the Middle Ages and into the early modern period, including the use made of his thought in the systematic treatments of just war that first appeared in the high Middle Ages. I have elsewhere in various places examined the medieval development of the idea of just war (Johnson, 1975, pp.26–80; 1981, pp.121–170; 1987, pp.67–132); the present discussion adds to those treatments and extends them, focusing specifically on Augustine.

Approaching the transmission and use of Augustine's thought in this period involves acknowledging the importance of the collections of excerpts from his writings on different subjects that began to appear not long after his death, alongside passages excerpted from other Christian authorities. In these collections the excerpted passages became *canones*, canons, rules providing guidance for Christian behavior. For the entire Middle Ages and for the early modern period up till the invention of the printing press, such collections provided the major access to the thought of those authorities excerpted in them and in particular of Augustine, whose influence was magnified over time by these collections. The passages gathered and transmitted through different editions of these canonical works (most of which have been lost, but with their content carried over into new collections) present Augustine as he was known for centuries after his death, and it is particularly interesting to see the differences between Augustine's thought on war as viewed from this perspective and as viewed from the perspective of recent interpreters.

In work on just war from the last half-century Augustine's work has largely been approached as a source for ideas from which the contemporary writers draw to make arguments fundamentally their own. This is the third perspective on Augustine's thinking on just war examined in this chapter. In general terms this approach has been to focus on Augustine as a theologian whose just war thought expresses his theology of Christian love and/or his theological understanding of history. Recent writers employing this approach do not attempt to place Augustine's work on just war in its own historical context, and they do not engage his historical legacy in the medieval shaping of just war thought. Prominent examples of this recent idea-focused approach include the just war work of Paul Ramsey (1961 and 1968), Oliver O'Donovan (2003), Jean Bethke Elshtain (2003), and Nigel Biggar (2013). All these have produced important conceptions of just war, but among them only Ramsey, though working from only a limited selection from Augustine's writings, engages his thinking on both love and history closely and at some length. In the discussion below, under the heading "Controversies", I focus on Ramsey's interpretation of Augustine, an interpretation whose influence also appears in the other three writers named, though in their own particular ways.

The following pages examine Augustine on war from the perspectives of the three approaches described above: that of historians interested in Augustine's historical context and his thought within that context, the view of Augustine's thinking on war provided in the passages collected and preserved in the medieval collections of *canones*, and the approach of an influential late 20th-century just war theorist. The conclusion then briefly weighs these approaches against one another for what they reveal about Augustine on just war.

Contexts

While the pattern among recent just war thinkers who draw from Augustine's thought has been to ignore the changes in Augustine's thought during his lifetime, both Markus and Brown pay close attention to these changes. Markus comments, "whatever can be said about almost any aspect of his thought is unlikely to be true of it over the whole span of his career as a writer and a thinker" (Markus, 1983, p.2). He goes on to observe that Augustine treated the morality of warfare in three different contexts during his life.

Augustine's earliest treatment of the subject of war was in his early philosophical dialogue, *De Libero arbitrio*. This work was begun in 388 CE and finished in 391 CE, when Augustine was in Milan (Brown, 2000, p.64). The brief passage relating to war in this work, whose main purpose and content were focused on refuting Manichaean teaching, has to do with whether killing is always sinful. His answer is that sometimes killing is not a sin:

> If killing a man is indeed homicide, it sometimes can happen without sin. For neither a soldier killing an enemy, nor a judge or his minister killing a criminal, nor someone inadvertently or imprudently throwing a spear would sin, in my opinion, when they killed a man.
>
> *(De Libero arbitrio, Book 1, cited from Reichberg,*
> *Syse, and Begby, 2006, p.119)*

From Augustine's intellectual and religious perspective at this stage in his life, observes Markus, he was seeking to reject his earlier Manichaeism and account for good and evil in terms drawn from Neo-Platonism. Thus he sought to explore human freedom, the general subject of this early work, "within the over-arching order he had come to see running through the *cosmos*", an order "in principle accessible to a well-educated and well-exercised intellect" (Markus, 1983, p.3). This led him to examine three levels of law: the *lex aeternae* overarching everything, the *lex naturae* by which the natural order is governed, and human law, by which human societies are ruled. For each lower level of law to be just, he argued, it must be in accord with the one superior to it, and thus the justice of human law depends ultimately on the eternal law of God. In this frame, comments Markus, "Like the public hangman in another of [Augustine's] early dialogues [*De ordine*], war, in the appropriate circumstances, is part of a well-ordered society's means of conforming to God's universal order and is rightly sanctioned by law" (*Ibid.*).

Augustine did not return to the discussion of the morality of war until some years later in another anti-Manichaean work, his *Contra Faustum*, written in 397–98, by which time he had returned to North Africa and had become Bishop of Hippo Regius (Markus, 1983, p.5; Brown, 2000, p.178). In contrast to the rationalist method of *De Libero arbitrio*, here his focus was more on Scripture. In *Contra Faustum* XXII Augustine "vindicated the Old Testament patriarchs against [Faustus's] calumnies" (Markus, *ibid*, n.9), and he did so by "defending Moses, who waged war on God's command, avoiding the sins which would make war blameworthy: love of violence, vengeful cruelty, strife and implacable enmity, savagery, lust for power and so forth" (Markus, *ibid*. and n.10). In the full passage (*Contra Faustum* XXII.74; see Reichberg, Syse, and Begby, 2006, p.73) these sins, all of which are rooted in the *libido* (lust) of *cupiditas* (wrongly ordered love), are contrasted to death, which Augustine notes matter-of-factly comes to all as part of the order of the world, while wars aimed at punishing sin are described as "commanded by God or some other legitimate ruler and … undertaken by the good". Here, notes Markus, though Augustine is still taking aim at the Manichees, his argument has shifted from what it was in *De Libero arbitrio*: if God can command war, as the Old Testament shows he has done, it cannot be inherently immoral. Though Augustine's focus in this later stage of his life is the Old Testament, he finds enough evidence from the New Testament to refute the Manichaean argument that the New Testament God is a different one. While Markus does not mention it, this is also the period in which Augustine began to write his biblical commentaries, in which the subject of war also appears (Brown 2000, p.178 and p.282).

The shift in Augustine's manner of argument is deeply important, Markus argues (1983, pp.6–7). His youthful confidence in a rationally ordered universe, where justice can be realized through rational control, had been replaced by a chastened conviction of the pervasiveness of sin and man's inability to free himself from it by his own power, so that he must depend on God's grace and moral guidance. His earlier view had depended on a reason-based legal theory about the relationship among eternal, natural, and temporal law. Though he continued to argue for the justification of war, he now put this in the context of a different theory of law, one in which the natural order has been corrupted by sin, with temporal law itself a product of sin, so that God has had to step in to seek to reshape this and restore justice in the world. This phase of Augustine's thinking Markus associates with his optimism about the effect of the Emperor Theodosius's establishment of Christianity as the Roman state religion and use of imperial authority and power to enforce Christian orthodoxy: these times, thought Augustine, are "Christian times" when the world is itself being transformed into a Christian Empire (Markus, 1983, p.8). "[I]t can be no accident", writes Markus, "that [Augustine's] classic statement on warfare [that in *Contra Faustum* XXII.74] occurs in one of his works dominated by this way of thinking" (Markus, 1983, p.9).

In the third phase of Augustine's life, Markus argues, this optimism about the world disappeared, though his conception of just war survived to be placed in another new context. In this third and final part of Augustine's life his major work was the *City of God*, which he wrote over several years from 413 CE to 425 CE (Brown 2000, p.280 and p.380). In this work, written after the death of Theodosius had brought an end to Augustine's belief that the Roman world was being reordered towards a Christian Empire, Markus observes that his conception of political power and the purpose of war has shifted to become "a means of securing some minimal barriers against the forces of disintegration" with "institutions of political and judicial authority serv[ing] to keep conflict in check" (Markus, 1983, p.10) The purpose of just war here is to seek to hold the world together: "The quest for justice and order is doomed; but dedication to the impossible task is demanded by the very precariousness of civilized order in the world" (*Ibid.*). Markus cites two books from *City of God*, XIX and XXII, as the place where Augustine's final views on politics and war found expression. These were among the last books in this work, written in 425 CE, only five years before Augustine's death (Brown, 2000, p.380). Augustine's letters to Count Boniface date to this last period also and should be read as expressing the same perspective on the purpose of Christian responsibility to wage just war. As Augustine puts the matter to Boniface, "Some … fight for you against invisible enemies by praying; you [the soldier] toil for them against visible barbarians by fighting" (*Letter 189 to Boniface*).

As we will see later in this chapter, Ramsey too focused on *De Libero arbitrio* and *City of God* XIX for his understanding of Augustine on just war, though he, in common with other recent just war writers who employ Augustine as a source for ideas, did not take note of the very different intellectual and religious perspectives that shaped each, and Ramsey did not treat *Contra Faustum* XXII at all. Nor do the other recent just war writers mentioned above. Indeed, the full discussion of the Old Testament wars in *Contra Faustum* can pose real problems for a just war theorist, as here Augustine can seem to countenance the idea of war commanded by God – holy war. Markus's placement of this idea in the frame of Augustine's own religious and intellectual development stands as a corrective to Christians who might want to draw such a conception from this work. Rather, for Augustine's perspective in the final phase of his life, just war ultimately cannot be so grand; rather it can only express the responsibility to preserve as much order, justice, and peace as possible in a world where these values, the ultimate goods of politics, are everywhere prone to disintegration. On Markus's reading, the Augustine of *Contra Faustum* prepares the way for the Augustine of *City of God* XIX, though the change in historical context transforms Augustine's optimistic view as to the achievement of the goods of political life into a pessimistic one, where these goods appear endangered at every hand.

Legacies

In the centuries following Augustine's life very few readers had access to complete copies of works like *De Libero arbitrio*, *Contra Faustum*, and *City of God* – or indeed of any of Augustine's works. What they had instead, as noted above, was various collections of passages excerpted from his works and those of other Christian authorities, presented as "canons" or rules to guide Christian living. The term canon, originally Greek (*kanon*), was first used in the Christian context to denote the actions of ecumenical councils. But by Augustine's time in the Latin Church regional councils of bishops and even individual bishops could issue canons to guide the behavior of the faithful in their sees. It was a small step to term the collected passages canons and to understand them as having universal authority wherever they were promulgated.

The development and transmission of the canonical collections was particularly important for what Augustine wrote on war, because in fact he wrote relatively little about this subject. By contrast to the topic of sexuality, for example, on aspects of which he wrote six individual treatises besides discussions of various sorts in other works, Augustine never wrote a systematic treatment on war. His writings on this subject were fragmentary, consisting of passages of different lengths found in works of varying purpose written in different stages of his life, where the comments on war served the purpose of the longer works in which they were placed. Nor was the total volume of these scattered passages particularly large. The most comprehensive present-day collection of passages relating to war from Augustine's works is that provided in chapters 7 and 10 of Gregory Reichberg, Henrik Syse, and Endre Begby's *The Ethics of War* (2006), and even with the editors' commentary these chapters total only 40 pages. In the medieval canonical collections, though, the excerpted passages stood on their own terms and, considered together, took on a more cohesive character than they had had in their original contexts; moreover, as canons, individually and together they had a higher profile than originally. At the same time, however, they were stripped from their original historical and literary contexts, so that the medieval legacy of Augustine's words on just war was to present his thought as timeless guidelines for Christian thinking and action.

The canonical collections served an important practical purpose. In Augustine's time and on through the centuries to the invention of the printing press, books were extraordinarily expensive and, therefore, comparatively rare. Peter Brown comments that in the fourth century "[e]ach copy of the Gospels alone cost as much as a marble sarcophagus" (Brown, 2012, p.275), and the relative cost would have been similar all through the following centuries. By contrast to our own time, when books are plentiful and cheap, and whole libraries in digital format can fit on a CD-ROM or a USB memory stick or be accessed online,[1] during Augustine's time and for centuries afterwards the possession of books was limited to only the wealthiest individuals or families or, increasingly during the Middle Ages, wealthy monastic houses and bishops of wealthy sees. While today Augustine is widely known for his *Confessions* and *City of God*, these works were not available in their entirety to the general Christian population of Europe for centuries after Augustine's death – not, indeed, until after the invention of the printing press. Moreover, most people would have been unable to read them, or indeed any of Augustine's works in which the subject of just war is treated, even if these works had been available. So the collection of excerpts from Augustine and other Christian authorities responded to a real economic need: to make core elements of those authorities' thought more widely available throughout the Church.

The collections of canons, though, also served a religious purpose that guided the selection of the passages excerpted as well as their use: to provide guidance to Christians in their efforts to avoid sinful behavior. Presented in the format of rules for Christian thinking and action, what Augustine wrote on war developed a new priority, as it was immediately relevant to the lives of Christians who belonged to the medieval knightly class, all the way from individuals in the profession of arms up to the higher nobility who ruled territories and commanded armies. The passages on war also served the complementary purpose of showing why individuals of all classes should not take arms on their own authority for their own benefit. On Augustine's terms members of the knightly class could in good conscience bear and use arms on higher authority in the service of the order, justice, and peace of the political community; yet the passages from Augustine also showed that individuals should not take arms on their own authority and for their own behalf without committing mortal sin.

The medieval collections of passages from Christian authorities went hand-in-glove with the development of penance as a Christian sacrament. Through the canonical collections, either directly or at second or third hand, clergy in the confessional could determine whether an individual Christian was guilty of a sin or not and if so the gravity of the sin, and thus determine the penance to be done. This immediate spiritual purpose of the collected passages thus gave them an important role not only in the lives of the Christian faithful but also in the development of the institutional Church during the Middle Ages.

What, then, were the references to war collected as canons? They included passages on war drawn from works of considerable diversity. In each of their original contexts the passages on war served a distinct purpose: in the *Contra Faustum*, for example, what Augustine said about war was part of his overall argument against Manichaean body-soul dualism, while in the letters to Boniface Augustine's aim was to guide a nominally Christian high Roman official in the performance of his duty, including his command of a large military force. Once excerpted from their original contexts and included in a collection of canons, though, the diverse passages took on a more general force and purpose, and this raised their standing relative to those passages excerpted from works on subjects Augustine had treated at more length, as well as shaping how the passages in question were interpreted and used in the changing historical, social, and political contexts of the Middle Ages.

The canonical collections of passages from Augustine about war came to fruitful focus when the canonist Gratian, working principally from collections of passages from Christian authorities assembled by the canonists Anselm of Lucca and Ivo of Chartres (themselves working from earlier collections of canons), prepared his *Concordia discordantium canonum/Concordance of Discordant Canons*, soon referred to as the *Decretum*, completing it in or about 1148. Gratian's treatment of the subject of war in Part II, *Causa* 23 is the first comprehensive and systematic statement of the idea of just war, and it depends heavily on passages (canons) from Augustine, which far outnumber those from other authorities.

Gratian's work in the *Decretum* and that of his immediate successors (the Decretists and the Decretalists) is the subject of the next chapter in this book, but it is in order here to note the commanding role passages from Augustine occupied in this foundational work in the development of the just war idea. Today the canonists are generally ignored, while Aquinas's question "On War" (*Summa theologiae* II/II, Q. 40) is far better known as a statement of the idea of just war from this period; yet what Aquinas says there depends directly on the work of the canonists from the century and a quarter immediately before him and would have been impossible without that work. Aquinas is particularly known for the three conditions for a just war he lists in *Summa theologiae* II/II, Q. 40, Article I – princely authority, just cause, and right intention – but these conditions were not original to him: they summarized conclusions reached in the canonical developments that began with Gratian, and the passages Aquinas chose to give authority to each of the three conditions were all from Augustine, drawn from the *Decretum*. The same can be said of the question "On War" as a whole. As explored in chapter 4 of this volume, Aquinas's original contribution here was not the substance of the just war idea, which was essentially canonical, backed up by passages from Augustine, but its placement in his theological ethics, which opened the door for later developments in the just war idea.

Part II, *Causa* 23 of the *Decretum* provides an authoritative window on the medieval understanding of Augustine on war, an understanding expressed through canons, rules to guide Christian living. What we find here is passages from a broad diversity of kinds of Augustine's works – apologetic (*Contra Faustum*), philosophical (*De Libero arbitrio*), exegetical (Augustine's works on Genesis, Exodus, Numbers, the Pentateuch as a whole, the Gospel of Matthew and Christ's sermon on the Mount), sermons on various topics, some of his letters, and even *City of God*, though Book I and not Book XIX of this work. All in all, this is a far greater variety of sources than typically cited by recent just war thinkers in their references to Augustine. Yet the passages Gratian included are employed as proof-texts, separated from their purpose in their original contexts and from their historical and personal contexts in Augustine's life. They provide very useful knowledge of what Augustine said about war, to be sure, but Gratian and his successors had their own context and their own purposes in using this material from Augustine. The same can be said of the Spanish scholastics – including Vitoria and Suárez, both taken up in subsequent chapters.

Controversies

Though references to Augustine are widespread in recent work on just war, including not only those works reflecting a religious perspective, the dominant recent pattern of the use of Augustine's thinking has been one that ignores the original historical context of particular elements of that thinking as well as the medieval legacy of understanding passages on just war from Augustine's works as canons, rules of timeless validity for Christian living. This dominant recent pattern varies from author to author, but collectively the effect has been to reshape how Augustine's influence is perceived and understood as ethically meaningful. One especially important recent writer on just war, Paul Ramsey, provides an example of the larger phenomenon.

Ramsey's two books from the 1960s, *War and the Christian Conscience* (1961) and *The Just War* (1968), together began the recovery (or reinvention) of just war thinking in the latter part of the twentieth century. While Ramsey makes occasional references to Augustine in the later book, his closest and most extended engagement with Augustine's thought occurs in the earlier book, in chapter 2 ("The Just War According to St, Augustine") and chapter 3 ("The Genesis of Noncombatant Immunity"). In the former chapter Ramsey employs a theological exegesis of Augustine to develop his own distinctive conception of just war as a Christian moral theory proceeding from the requirements of Christian love. Briefly, for Augustine all human behavior proceeds from what is loved. Fallen Adam loves wrongly: his love, cupidity or *cupiditas*, leads him to seek worldly goods that cannot satisfy his ultimate need, which can be satisfied only by loving God. Ramsey (1961, p.16) quotes Augustine's language on this: "Thou hast made us toward thyself, and our hearts are restless until they rest in Thee". Love of God is impossible for fallen Adam, but the gift of grace turns his cupidity into charity, love oriented toward God. Ramsey's initial discussion of Augustine focuses here, using the latter's *On the Morals of the Catholic Church*, XV, and *The City of God*, V and XIX (Ramsey 1961, pp.16–17 and pp.1–5). Ramsey's aim to establish Augustine's theological foundation is underscored by the fact that *On the Morals of the Catholic Church* includes nothing at all on the specific matter of just war. On this subject what is particularly important in what Ramsey reads out of Augustine is the discussion of politics in *City of God* XIX, which Ramsey treats over his next several pages. He locates the Augustinian idea of *justum bellum* here, building on what Augustine says in Chapter VII:

> But, say they, the wise man will wage just wars. As if he would not rather lament the necessity of just wars, if he remembers that he is a man; for if they were not just he would not wage them, and would therefore be delivered from all wars. For it is the wrong-doing of the opposing party which compels the wise man to wage just wars, and this wrong-doing, even though it gave rise to no war, would still be a matter of grief to man because it is man's wrong-doing.
>
> *(Ramsey 1961, p.27 and n. 29)*

Now, this passage is about war as a result of sin, and Augustine here roots just war in prudence or wisdom, not in charity. But for Ramsey charity is present nonetheless. In this he follows Augustine scholar Ernest Barker's argument that for Augustine charity raises human justice to a higher plane, where it "ceases to be a system of right relations between men ... and it becomes a system of right relations between man and God" (Barker, quoted by Ramsey, p.21 n.14). Ramsey does not, though, accept Barker's conclusion, to understand Augustine's view of the state as "a coadjutor of the City of God" (Ramsey, 1961, p.22). Ramsey instead looks ahead to Chapter XXIV of Book XIX, where Augustine, after rejecting Cicero's definition of a commonwealth, offers his own, as an "assemblage" of people bound together by agreement as to what they love. In the City of Earth the object of common love is the state, but in the City of God that object is none other than God. This distinction,

Ramsey notes, keeps Augustine from elevating the idea of just war into an idea of war sanctioned by God. Staying with Book XIX, Ramsey follows Augustine into his discussion of peace as the end aimed at by war, where he notes that "[e]ven the heavenly city … while in its state of pilgrimage, avails itself of the peace of earth" (Augustine, Book XIX, Chapter XVII, quoted by Ramsey, p.29 and n.32). Just war, by aiming at peace in the earthly city, thus serves the love fulfilled only in the City of God. Yet, Ramsey observes, even though Augustine could speak positively about the peace and justice of the Roman order relative to that of Rome's enemies, he still regarded this order as shaped by sinful loves and standing under "the judgment of God". "And so", comments Ramsey, "the 'just' war which seeks peace … has its own intrinsic limits which it may overstep" (Ramsey, 1961, p.30).

Ramsey's conception of "the just war according to St. Augustine" thus rests heavily on Book XIX of *The City of God*, drawing from Augustine's discussion there of the different loves of the earthly and heavenly cities, the different forms of peace available to both, and the need for Christians during their earthly life to make best use of the peace offered by the earthly city, supporting its justice and seeking to rectify and punish wrongdoing. Though one would not know this from Ramsey's analysis, Augustine does not say much directly about war in this book, though he says a good deal about peace, and his overall discussion leads to a theory of the Christian's proper involvement in politics. In the end the shape of this larger political involvement is Ramsey's own major concern, as telegraphed by the title of his book: how far the Christian conscience allows participation in the affairs of the political order of the "city of earth", including especially war.

The love commandment in the New Testament is twofold: to love God and to love one's neighbor as oneself. The discussion on which Ramsey draws from Book XIX of *The City of God* has principally to do with the former and the difference between love towards God, which defines the Heavenly City, and the love of earthly things, which defines earthly political communities. In chapter 3 of *War and the Christian Conscience* Ramsey turns to the second part of the love commandment, love of neighbor, further developing his conception of just war as one which is both permitted (even commanded) and limited by such love. His use of Augustine shifts here as well. He begins with Augustine's *De Libero arbitrio/On the Freedom of the Will* and its treatment of *libido* (lust) as a characteristic element in fallen human love, quoting at length a passage from Augustine already cited in connection with Markus's treatment of *De Libero arbitrio* above, in which he discusses the right of self-defense against attack and the right of a soldier, acting on superior authority, to kill enemies for the protection of citizens (Ramsey, 1961, pp.35–36). But the purpose Ramsey draws from this passage is different from that found by Markus, and Ramsey notes nothing about the anti-Manichaean nature of this early work of Augustine's. Rather, for Ramsey, the focus is the matter of rightful love in the act of killing, which is not developed in the original context at all. Ramsey rather projects back onto this early passage a theology of love not developed until later in Augustine's thought, interpreting the passage according to this thinking. Killing in self-defense, as Ramsey reads Augustine's reasoning, cannot be just for a Christian, since self-defense is motivated by wrongful love. To illustrate this Ramsey quotes a passage from Augustine's mentor Ambrose: the Christian cannot return the blows of an armed robber "lest in defending his life he should stain his love toward his neighbor" (*Ibid.*, p.37). This Christian standard is higher than that set by natural justice, on which the law of self-defense was based. Thus in the passage Ramsey quotes, Augustine refuses to countenance self-defense, even in the face of an unjust attack. But by contrast, for Augustine the soldier's killing of enemies is morally possible, since the soldier is not acting out of his own self-love but is obeying superior orders: the soldier's action can thus be taken without wrong desire (*Ibid.*, p.38). Though Ramsey does not dwell further on this argument, for him it marks a significant nodal point in Augustine's reasoning about war, since early Christian morality forbade self-defense. So does Augustine, but, he reasons, the soldier acting on superior orders is in a different moral frame from the individual acting to defend himself. This is the fundamental argument from which Augustine allows Christian participation in just war.

At this point in his text Ramsey turns to other thinkers than Augustine and does not return to him, though he continues to work out of the distinction he finds in the passage quoted from *De Libero arbitrio*. In the end he reaches a position that he thoroughly elaborates only in his 1968 book: the justification for Christian participation in war is to protect one's neighbors, whom one is commanded to love; yet the enemy is also a neighbor, and so one should not do to him more than needed to prevent his attack from succeeding, and in any case the justification for fighting extends only to enemy combatants and not noncombatants, for they too are among the neighbors the Christian is commanded to love (Ramsey, 1968, chapter 6). This goes somewhat beyond what Augustine argued in *De Libero arbitrio* or, for that matter, anywhere else in his work, but Ramsey regarded it as following from Augustine's understanding of love of neighbor.

This way of thinking about the moral justification and limitation of Christian participation in war yields what Ramsey identified as two moral principles: discrimination (the principle behind noncombatant immunity) and proportionality. Though in his thinking these are connected to the obligation of love of neighbor, they have come to have a more general life, becoming widely disseminated as the defining principles of the *jus in bello* in subsequent just war thinking. Whether both principles can be traced to Augustine is not at all clear: in deriving them Ramsey, as noted, turns to other authorities and to his own reasoning. Historical just war thinking makes direct use of Augustine's argument about soldiers' actions under superior authority and uses it to define the right of just war as opposed to other forms of the use of armed force. But the historical tradition derives its *jus in bello* differently.

Conclusion

The medieval approach to Augustine on war through excerpted passages from his works made into canonical guides for Christian living reflected both economic factors (the expense and relative unavailability of complete books and libraries of books) and spiritual ones (the practical purposes of avoiding sin and performing penance). By the time the collected canons were systematically forged into a coherent conception of just war other factors had also come into play: the rediscovery of Roman law, particularly its conception of natural law and *jus gentium* and its conception of political order in terms of the goods or ends of order, justice, and peace; the beginning of the emergence of an idea of human rights; the political need to form unified commonwealths out of a culture long defined by self-interest and use of armed power. Though the particulars are different, the understanding of Augustine found in recent work on war is shaped by similar factors. The economics are still present, though different: Ramsey could rely on easily obtainable English translations of *City of God* for his discussion of Book XIX, but a medieval thinker had to depend on the collections of canons, and he had to be able to read them in Latin. While medieval thought used Augustine on love as a guide to personal sanctity, Ramsey's focus on the idea of love of neighbor reflected a different conception of the purpose of Christian living, one dominant in Protestant Christianity at the time. When Ramsey adapted Augustine to the service of a conception of just war prioritizing protection of noncombatants, it was not only because of what he found in Augustine but also because of his own conception of the relation of Christian ethics to just war. And of course, the background of Ramsey's work – which is not discussed above because it does not directly involve use of Augustine but is covered in detail in chapter 15 of this volume – was a particular political need: in this case, to deal with the threat posed by nuclear weapons. The worth of Augustine's thinking is marked here by its being able to inform such very different contexts.

At the same time, though, each of these approaches is an interpretation, and to get at what Augustine himself actually thought about war requires something more like what is provided by Markus and Brown – an effort to read Augustine in his own context and understand him there. Despite the substantial work already done by these and other historians, a good deal more remains to be done, specifically with respect to the idea of just war. Such an effort would provide new purchase on thinking critically about later interpretations of Augustine on this subject – both those of the medieval canonical tradition and those of recent theorists of just war.

Note

1   For example the collection of works by Augustine and a long list of other Church fathers at www.newadvent.org/fathers

Works cited

Augustine. Works. *New Advent*. Available from: www.newadvent.org/fathers
Biggar, Nigel. 2013. *In Defence of War*. Oxford: Oxford University Press.
Brown, Peter. 2000. *Augustine of Hippo*. Berkley, Los Angeles, and London: University of California Press. (Originally published London: Faber and Faber 1967).

Brown, Peter. 2012. *Through the Eye of a Needle*. Princeton and Oxford: Princeton University Press.

Elshtain, Jean Bethke. 2003. *Just War Against Terror*. New York: Basic Books.

Johnson, James Turner. 1975. *Ideology, Reason, and the Limitation of War*. Princeton and London: Princeton University Press.

Johnson, James Turner. 1981. *Just War Tradition and the Restraint of War*. Princeton and Guildford, Surrey.

Johnson, James Turner. 1987. *The Quest for Peace*. Princeton and Guildford, Surrey.

Markus, Robert A. 1970. *Saeculum: History and Society in Saint Augustine's Theology*. Cambridge: Cambridge University Press.

Markus, Robert A. 1983. Saint Augustine's Views on the 'Just War', in Sheils, W. J. ed., *The Church and War*. Basil Blackwell for The Ecclesiastical History Society, pp. 1–14.

O'Donovan, Oliver. 2003. *The Just War Revisited*. Cambridge, New York, et al.: Cambridge University Press.

Reichberg, Gregory, Henrik Syse and Endre Begby. 2006. *The Ethics of War: Classic and Contemporary Readings*. Oxford: Blackwell.

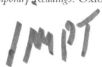

3

GRATIAN (CIRCA 12th CENTURY)

Rory Cox

Introduction

Gratian is arguably the single most influential figure in the history of the Western just war tradition. This is a bold claim, but it is based upon the fact that Gratian's law book, the *Concordia discordantium canonum* ("A concordance of discordant canons"), is *the* foundational text of the Western just war corpus.[1] More commonly known as the *Decretum Gratiani*, or simply *Decretum*, Gratian's law book created for the first time a truly systematic analysis of the relationship between war and justice. Furthermore, the *Decretum*'s influence extends far beyond the field of just war studies. As Landau (2008a, pp.53–54) observes, the "*Decretum* forms the bedrock of European legal culture. Its content and methodology shaped the core of the Western legal tradition".

Gratian's compilation of previous thought on the uses, merits and evils of war, combined with his own ethical-legal analysis, provided the basic structure and components of much of the just war thought that exists today. But Gratian did more than merely provide a set of "building blocks" (Reichberg, 2008, p.13) to be used by later theorists in constructing their ethics of war; rather, he constructed an original doctrine of his own. While Augustine is often identified as the "father" of the Western just war tradition,[2] his teaching on war only became authoritative from the 12th century as a direct result of Gratian's compilation and analysis (Johnson, 1981, p.121; 1987, p.58). Moreover, as Johnson explains on his chapter on Augustine in this volume (chapter 2), it is problematic to refer to Augustine's ideas on war as a "doctrine", for they lack the cohesiveness and consistency implied by this term. Gratian's contribution to the just war tradition cannot be limited to the role of a passive transmitter of Augustinian just war doctrine (e.g. Hubrecht, 1955, pp.166–167) because in reality no such "doctrine" existed prior to Gratian (Haggenmacher, 1983, pp.24–25). What is commonly thought of as the Augustinian formulation of the just war is in fact an intellectual hybrid – a synthesis of Augustine's *and* Gratian's interpretations of what constitutes justifiable violence. It is best to think of Gratian as a translator, producer, and disseminator of just war thought.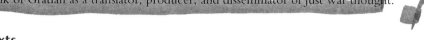

Texts

The *Decretum* is a massive collection of canon law, that is, the law of the Christian Church. The work is divided into three parts.[3] The first part contains 101 *Distinctiones* ("Distinctions") that explain the principles and methodology of canon law, analyze specific legal concepts, and explore the functions of different clerical positions. The second part is made up of thirty-six *Causae* ("Causes," or cases), each subdivided into questions that explore a range of moral, institutional, and procedural issues faced by the medieval Church, clergy, and laity. It is within Part 2, Causa 23, that one finds Gratian's main treatment of war and violence (Gratian 1879, pp.889–965).[4] The third part, referred to as *De consecratione*, consists largely of a discussion of the nature of the sacraments and contains five further *distinctiones*.

In its entirety, the *Decretum* contains thousands of authoritative "canons", consisting of excerpts from authoritative texts (*auctoritates*). Writings from Scripture, the Church Fathers, early popes, the decisions of church councils, and Roman law make up the majority of the canons, but classical Greek and Roman authors are also included.[5] These canons are accompanied by Gratian's own commentary (*dicta Gratiani*), in which he outlines problems and questions and seeks to resolve the contradictions apparent in the canons. The *causae* of Part 2, including Causa 23 on war, usually adopt the form of scholastic dialectical reasoning known in the Middle Ages as the *sic et non* ('yes and no') method. A question is posed, arguments for and against are proffered using a variety of canons, and finally a solution is reached that attempts to reconcile the aforementioned authorities. It was in his critical analysis of the canons and the construction of these original syntheses that Gratian broke genuinely new ground in canonical jurisprudence, distinguishing his *Decretum* from previous compilations of canon law by canonists such as Burchard of Worms (circa 960–1025), Anselm of Lucca (circa 1036–1086), and Ivo of Chartres (circa 1040–1115). Gratian's selection of canons in Causa 23 was not especially original, with numerous canons being lifted directly from the Ivonian *Panormia* in particular, but the rapidity with which the *Decretum* superseded these highly successful collections evinces just how original, instructive, and popular Gratian's approach was.[6] Hundreds of copies of the *Decretum* survive in medieval manuscripts, complemented by forty-five incunable editions printed prior to 1501, and more than 150 editions printed after this time.[7]

Contexts

Yet we know virtually nothing about the individual who created the *Decretum*. Over the years, many "facts" have been asserted about Gratian: that he was born at Ficulle or Chiusi in central Italy; that he was a brother of the famous theologians

Peter Lombard (circa 1096–1160) and Peter Comestor (died circa 1178);[8] that he was a Camaldolese monk; that he hailed from the monastery of Saints Felix and Nabor; that he was a teacher of canon law at the medieval law school of Bologna; that he was a bishop; that his first name was John. The reality is that most of these "facts" were ascribed to Gratian several centuries after his death and that "almost all of what we know of Gratian is hearsay" (Noonan, 1979, pp.146–147 and pp.157–158). Even the date of his death is unknown, although he probably died in the late 1140s, as canonists in the 1150s write as if he is no longer alive (Landau, 2008a, p.24).

There is a similar lack of certainty concerning the date at which the *Decretum* was composed. Up until the turn of the 20th century, it was believed that the work dated to circa 1150–1151. Since the work of Fornier (1898, pp.253–280), there has been a broad consensus that the *Decretum* was actually composed a decade earlier, circa 1140–1141.[9] Unfortunately, even this tentative chronology becomes problematic in light of evidence that the *Decretum* was significantly edited and elaborated during the first few years of its existence. Research has revealed that it is almost certain that the *Decretum* was created in two distinct phases: a much shorter First Recension and a slightly later, more discursive, Second Recension, containing much more Roman law and technical language. The differences between the two recensions are so pronounced that it is possible that they are the work of more than a single author. However, Part 2 – including Causa 23 on war – appears to be part of the older original text (Noonan, 1979, pp.163–169; Winroth, 2000, pp.3–4, pp.136–145, pp.193–195, pp.197–222).

Notwithstanding the deficiencies in our knowledge about Gratian's biography and the intricate processes that led to the creation of the *Decretum*, we may say with some confidence that a man named Gratian did indeed compose the core of what is known as the *Decretum Gratiani*, including that part which discusses just wars. We can also say that Gratian had a good grounding in theology and especially in law, and that the *Decretum* was probably completed in Bologna, the foremost center of legal study during the 12th century. Given the didactic nature of the law book itself, it seems reasonable to suppose that Gratian was a teacher of canon law at Bologna, and that the *Decretum* was designed to be used by students and teachers alike.

The *Decretum* emerged out of a European society that, from the turn of the second millennium AD, was increasingly legalistic and sensitive to the possession and protection of rights, recognizing a strong relationship between right (*ius*) and power (*potestas*) (Tierney, 1997, pp.54–58). As the greatest landholder in medieval Europe and as an institution that was itself made up of myriad competing communities and individuals, the Church and its clergy were foremost among those concerned with rights. From as early as the 4th century AD, canon law had developed into an autonomous legal system that operated alongside the numerous secular legal systems found throughout Christendom. Canon law was unique in that it was supranational, becoming "a working and often quite effective international law"; indeed, "the canons embodied a system of law often parallel to, sometimes in conflict with, and occasionally victorious over, the competing civil jurisdictions of kings and princes" (Brundage, 1995a, p.3, p.17, p.177). Canon law was also distinctive in that it was founded on the basis of written law – i.e. authoritative texts – rather than the oral or customary legal traditions that were dominant in Europe prior to the 11th century.

Around 1050 a definite shift is identifiable in the formalization of law in Western Europe. This can be accounted for by a variety of factors, but chief among these was a commercial revolution (Landau, 2008b, p.115). Population growth, urbanization, agricultural intensification, and trade expansion increased the number of disputes requiring settlement and produced a desire for enhanced legal security regarding obligations such as private contracts, communal charters, and financial credit. To make this possible, a widely recognized set of legal texts was required. The compilation of Roman laws made by the Emperor Justinian between 529 and 534 AD, commonly referred to as the *Corpus iuris civilis* ("The Body of Civil Law"), met this demand.[10] Crucially, during the late 11th century the fifty books of the *Digest* – a collection of legal writings and opinions dating principally from the 2nd and 3rd centuries AD and given force of law by Justinian in 533 – were gradually rediscovered. The *Digest* provided a methodological model for legal analysis and a key to interpreting the Justinian corpus. This spurred a new professionalization of civil jurisprudence that deeply influenced the development of canon law (Landau, 2008b, p.147). Armed with the *Digest*, the law school of Bologna became the focal point for both branches of jurisprudence: civil and ecclesiastical.

The second factor that encouraged the production of written law in this period was the jurisdictional strife associated with the Investiture Contest (circa 1070–1122).[11] This competition for jurisdiction encouraged lay and ecclesiastical lords to ground their own claims to authority in "fixed" and "authoritative" legal traditions, embodied in codified law. Pope Gregory VII (1073–1085) not only stubbornly fought for what he understood to be ecclesiastical and (specifically) papal rights; he also "revolutionized the Christian view of warfare" (Brundage, 1976, p.104). By promoting the concept that war in defense of the Church was not only free from sin but also potentially spiritually meritorious, Gregory VII opened the door to later theories of just war, holy war and crusade. Gratian's *Decretum* was forged in the crucible of this reformatory period and was perhaps its most important product, marking the beginning of classical canon law and just war doctrine proper (Tooke, 1965, p.87; Haggenmacher, 1983, p.23).

Tenets

> Certain bishops, together with the people in their charge, lapsed into heresy; with threats and tortures they began to compel neighboring Catholics into embracing this heresy. Having learned of this, the pope ordered the Catholic bishops of the surrounding regions, who had received civil jurisdiction from the emperor, to defend the Catholics from the heretics and, by any means possible, to compel them to return to the true faith. The bishops, upon receiving these commands from the pope, gathered their soldiers and began

to fight against the heretics both openly and by ambushes. Finally – after some of the heretics had been killed, some had been despoiled of their private and ecclesiastical property, and still others had been confined to jail or the workhouse – they were forced to return to the unity of the Catholic faith.

(Gratian, C.23, prologue)[12]

Thus begins Causa 23 of the *Decretum*. It is coercion against heretics within the Church and the concomitant destruction of life and property that provides the context for Gratian's analysis of war. However, while the initial context is firmly ecclesiastical, Gratian develops a wide-ranging analysis of coercion and violence in general. He poses eight key questions, which are worth quoting in full as they determine the structure of Causa 23 itself and, as a result of the *Decretum's* influence, shaped the concerns and direction of the medieval and post-medieval just war debate:

> Here it is asked first, whether it is a sin to wage war [*militare*[13]]? Second, what war is just, and in what way did the children of Israel fight just wars? Third, whether an injury to one's associates may be repelled by arms? Fourth, whether vengeance ought to be inflicted. Fifth, whether it is a sin for a judge or his minister to kill the guilty. Sixth, whether evil men are to be compelled to the good. Seventh, whether heretics should be deprived of their goods and the goods of their church, and ought he who takes possession of these goods be said to possess the property of others [i.e. possess them illicitly]? Eighth, whether it is permitted to bishops or clerics to take up arms, on the authority of the pope or by the command of the emperor?
>
> *(Gratian, C. 23, prologue)*[14]

As one can see, these questions blend both moral and legal concerns: whether war was a sin and could the evil be compelled to do good, contrasted with whether war was an act of vindictive justice, the character of war as part of a legal process initiated by a judge and executed by his ministers, and the legal ownership of property seized as a result of war.

To answer the eight questions laid out above, Gratian generally utilizes his *sic et non* method, offering first a number of canons from scripture (particularly the New Testament) that prohibit violence, notably the well-known injunction to "turn the other cheek" (Mt. 5:39) and Christ's command to Peter to "Put your sword back in its sheath" (Mt. 26:52–3). The problem, as Gratian – and many other Christians before him – saw it, was that warfare was "instituted either to repel injury or to inflict vengeance … and both things are prohibited by the law of the gospels". Christ commanded non-violence and vengeance should be reserved to God alone (Deut. 32:35; Rom. 12:19): "it appears, therefore, that to wage war is a sin" (C. 23, q. 1 d.a.c. 1).

However, Gratian was no pacifist. At the very beginning of the *Decretum* (D. 1, d.a.c. 1), Gratian stated that: "The human race is ruled by two things, namely natural law and customs". Gratian's understanding of natural law owed significantly to the Visigothic bishop, Isidore of Seville (circa 560–636 AD), whose encyclopedic *Etymologies* played a major role in preserving Roman learning in the medieval West. Gratian turned to Isidore to show that self-defense was licit because it was founded in nature: "Natural law is common to all peoples (*omnium nationum*), in so far that everywhere it is held by instinct of nature rather than by decree, such as … the repulsion of violence by force" (D. 1, c. 7).[15] Because natural law was founded on divine law (D. 1, cc. 1–6), the instincts of nature could not be unjust.[16] Alongside this justification of self-defense on the grounds of natural instinct, Gratian devoted significant effort in Causa 23 in creating a legal and moral-theological approach to warfare that drew especially on Augustine's moral theology of Christian violence.[17] The most distinctive characteristic of Augustine's justification of war was his effective separation of acts from intentions. This divorce made possible the spiritual preservation of *caritas* – charity, love, patience – while at the same time permitting physical acts of violence (C. 23, q. 1 d.p.c. 1; c. 2; Russell, 1975, p.60; Cox, 2014, pp.27–28). According to this interpretation, physical coercion could be exercised without *spiritual* violence because, just as a parent chastises a wayward child out of love, coercion was undertaken for the benefit of the sinner. Thus the battlefield deathblow could be conceived of as a *coup de grâce* in a physical and metaphysical sense.

Plato, Aristotle, and Cicero had made famous the maxim that war ought only to be waged for the sake of peace.[18] Gratian repeated this ideal through his use of Augustine: Christian soldiers must be motivated by a desire for peace and justice, so that "even in war, be a peacemaker" (C. 23, q. 1 c. 3; cf. Reichberg, Syse, and Begby, 2006, p.111). The absence of motives such as hate, avarice, personal vengeance, or the desire to dominate others was a prerequisite of this "peaceful violence" (C. 23, q. 1 c. 4; cf. Reichberg, Syse, and Begby 2006, p.112). As Syse (2007, p.37) notes, Augustine's primary presumption was against *injustice* rather than war, and Gratian followed Augustine in believing that the evil of permitting injustice and allowing the wicked to persist in their sin (thus exacerbating their spiritual damnation) was a greater evil than using force to coerce the wicked. Concluding Question 1, Gratian explicitly accepted the possibility of just wars: "to wage war is not a sin, and the precepts of patience are to be observed in the preparation of the heart, not in the ostentation of the body" (C. 23, q. 1, d.p.c. 7).

Nevertheless, this was very far from an open-ended justification of violence. There were clear limitations on who could declare and fight a just war, and for what reasons. Gratian understood war to be a form of legal process; therefore prosecuting war was the duty of lay soldiers acting under a public authority. Just as only an officially appointed minister could execute the punishment proscribed by a public judge in a court of law, so only soldiers could administer the violence of war proscribed by the public authority (C. 23, q. 1 c. 4; q. 8 c. 33).[19] War was a *public* not a private instrument. Indeed, the treatment of war in Causa 23 is distinct from earlier canonical collections in that Gratian does not treat war primarily as a problem of murder and penance. Developing a pre-existing Christian theological debate about the moral risks of using violence in self-defense, Gratian formulated a doctrine that established just war as a kind of judicial instrument to punish injuries (a theme that Las Casas, discussed in chapter 7, picks up on).[20] While preserving the subjective assessment of violence based on a person's intention, Gratian also emphasized a more objective framework for assessing the justice of war, based on the Greco-Romano criteria of sufficient public authority (*potestas/imperium*) and reasonable cause (*iniuria*). However, because *ius* (justice) and *iniuria* (injury) were broadly conceived to include both moral and material injuries – here the influence of Augustine was writ large – Gratian created a just war doctrine that incorporated the right of self-defense as well as the obligation to defend others, to punish material injuries, and to punish moral injuries against justice, the Church and the faith. Consequently, the potential application of Gratian's just war was remarkably broad.

But who or what was the public authority? Augustine stated that "the authority and choice to undertake wars belongs to princes [*principes*]" (C.23, q. 1 c. 4; cf. Reichberg, Syse, and Begby, 2006, p.112). In Augustine's era (370–430 AD), the *princeps* was the non-military title of the Roman emperor. But in the Middle Ages, this Latin term was translated as meaning "prince" or "chief" more generally, creating numerous possible claimants for the authority to declare war: German emperors, popes, kings, bishops, or barons. On this vital issue of identifying the locus of proper authority, Gratian elaborated slightly but fell short of elucidating. He cited Isidore of Seville, that: "A just war is that which is waged by an edict [*ex edicto*] in order to restore goods, or to repel enemies" (C. 23, q. 2 c. 1).[21] Synthesizing Isidore's restorative and defensive definition of just war with Augustine's emphasis on war as an instrument of punitive justice, Gratian formulated his own succinct definition: "a just war is that which is waged by an edict and through which injuries are avenged" (C. 23, q. 2 d.p.c. 2; cf. Reichberg, Syse, and Begby, 2006, p.113). Gratian's interpretation of proper authority was that it resided in any person or institution that could issue an authoritative edict. It would appear, therefore, that Gratian was happy to accept a reasonably expansive interpretation of proper authority, recognizing the authority to wage war in a large number of individual *principes*. If one had the jurisdiction to issue a public decree, then one had the authority to declare war. Importantly, this included the princes of the Church, principally the pope.

In Question 8, Gratian discussed at length how clerics and prelates could participate in war. Gratian upheld the traditional prohibition on clerics bearing arms. Clergy who polluted themselves through shedding blood – either through direct action or direct command – were barred from handling the holy sacraments (C. 23, q. 8 c. 30).

Clerics who died in battle were to receive no oblations or prayers, and any cleric caught bearing arms was condemned to lose his clerical degree and obliged to do penance (C. 23, q. 8 cc. 4–6).[22] Nevertheless, while priests "must not take up arms with their own hand it is lawful for them to exhort others to do so for the sake of defending the oppressed and to fight against the enemies of God" (C. 23, q. 8

d.p.c. 6). Heretics and infidels were perceived to be the main threats to the Church (as the prologue to C. 23 suggests), thus it was natural that the obligation and authority to defend the faithful against such threats fell especially to the pope (C. 23, q. 8 cc. 7–9; cc. 17–18; d.p.c. 18). Likewise, those bishops who had been endowed with secular jurisdictions were like the "princes of this world" and were thus obliged to participate in the just wars of secular lords, at the consent of the pope (C. 23, q. 8 d.p.c. 20; c. 22; d.p.c. 25; cc. 26–8). Those who died fighting the "enemies of the holy faith", under the exhortation of the pope, were promised "a heavenly reward" (C. 23, q. 8 c. 9), although the prohibitions against clergy shedding blood in person remained in place (C. 23, q. 8 d.p.c. 28; cc. 29–31).[23]

Controversies

It has been remarked that canonistic analysis of the just war focuses on *ius ad bellum* norms (rights of going to war) and consequently ignores more practical *ius in bello* (rights in the conduct of war) considerations.[24] While it is true that *in bello* norms are not prominent in the *Decretum*, the consideration of such norms is not entirely absent from the analysis. For example, Gratian turns to Old Testament examples (citing Augustine) to show that there was no obligation to restrict the tactics employed during a just war. Following a divine command, Joshua had used an ambush to overcome the citizens of Ai (Josh. 8:1–29), resulting in the mass slaughter of the men and women of the city, which was then razed to the ground. The conclusion is that, when a legitimate ruler "has undertaken a just war, it is of no concern to justice whether he wins by open warfare or by ambush" (C. 23, q. 2 c. 2; cf. Reichberg et al., 2006, p.113). We know that Gratian compiled the *Decretum* after the Second Lateran Council (1139), yet he chose not to include Lateran II's prohibition of using bows and crossbows in wars against Christians.[25] If a war was just (as all wars should be, otherwise they should not be waged in the first place), then they should be prosecuted by whatever tactical means necessary in order to bring them to a swift conclusion.[26] The requirement of ending just wars as swiftly as possible also applied to *when* wars could be waged. Beginning in the late 10th century, the *Pax Dei* (Peace of God) and *Treuga Dei* (Truce of God) had attempted to protect non-combatant property and persons, and to prohibit violence on holy days. Significantly, Gratian rejected limitations on the timing of warfare, citing a letter of Pope Nicholas that "if unavoidable necessity presses", then war in defense of one's person, country, or customary laws could be waged "even during the Lenten season". The rationale behind this was that to act otherwise would present an unreasonable risk to one's life and the lives of others, thereby seeming "to tempt God". Of course, the caveat was that if war was not necessary, "there is to be abstention from battles not only during Lent, but at all times" (C. 23, q. 8 c. 15; cf. Reichberg, Syse, and Begby, 2006, p.124). Gratian was more sympathetic to aims of the Peace of God, which stipulated that non-combatants such as pilgrims, monks, children, widows, and the unarmed poor should be protected from the violence of war, under pain of excommunication.[27]

Therefore, *in bello* considerations did feature in Gratian's analysis, but *in bello* restraints were de-emphasized as a result of them being understood as secondary to, and dependent on, *ad bellum* legitimation. Moreover, it seems that clerical commentators on the just war assumed that soldiers who went to war from a proper desire to restore justice and to defend the innocent would not indulge in the sort of flagrant rapine that is typically considered the hallmark of unjust wars (C. 23, q. 1 cc. 3–4). This was consonant with the basic reasoning that "good" motives generated just violence while "evil" motives generated unjust violence.

Legacies

At the beginning of this chapter I claimed that Gratian is the single most influential figure in the history of the Western just war tradition. This is largely a result of the immense popularity and influence of the *Decretum* during the medieval and early modern periods. The widespread adoption of the *Decretum* as a legal textbook and reference work ensured that Gratian's formulation of the just war established the direction, focus, and boundaries of future discussion. By the late 12th century, questions about war and violence were already accepted as part of standard scholastic interests, especially within canon law (Russell, 1975, pp.213–257; Brundage, 1995b, p.674; Landau, 2008b, p.129). Yet Gratian had left many issues unresolved or open to debate. For example, nine different (albeit overlapping) categories of war are cited in the *Decretum*: war (unspecified); carnal war; spiritual war; war on the authority of God; just war; war to pacify; judicial war; public war; and secular war (Brundage, 1995b, p.692). The lack of specific distinctions and clarifications within the *Decretum* generated a great deal of subsequent analysis and debate, and an ever-growing body of just war literature.

Despite this frequent lack of specificity, Causa 23 not only provided an important vision of what a just war was and what just wars required, it also determined the types of questions and material that were considered pertinent to the evolving just war discourse. From as early as 1148, legal scholars were commenting on the *Decretum* ("decretists") in order to clarify ambiguous issues such as what constituted a just cause and who or what possessed sufficient authority to declare war.[28] Pope Innocent IV's (1243–1254) assertion that just wars could only be declared by authorities with no superior, which narrowed the definition of *princeps*, paved the way for the dominant modern view that the authority to wage war is limited to sovereign states. Innocent IV conceded that anyone could licitly use violence in self-defense or defense of private property, although he insisted that such defense must be immediate (*incontinenti*) and proportionate to the injury (*moderamen inculpatae tutelae*), and that private defense was not "proper war" (*bellum*) in the full legal sense.[29] Around 1216 a canonist named Johannes Teutonicus (d. 1245) finished an authoritative "ordinary gloss" (*glossa ordinaria*) of the entire *Decretum*; this was updated by Bartholomew of Brescia (d. 1258) in the years between 1234 and 1241 (Weigand, 2008, p.84, pp.89–91). This commentary elaborated on many details of Gratian's analysis – Causa 23 alone generated 864 individual addenda – and frequently appears alongside the main text in late medieval manuscript copies and early printed editions of the *Decretum*. This interpretative activity stoked the furnaces of the medieval just war debate and lead to ever more sophisticated and nuanced treatments, the apotheosis of which was John of Legnano's exhaustive *Tractatus de bello, de represalis et de duello* ("Treatise on war, reprisals and duels"), written circa 1360 (Legnano, 1917).

Gratian's continuing influence can also be seen in the work of those early modern theologians and jurists who made up the so-called "School of Salamanca".[30] Francisco de Vitoria (see chapter 6), regarded as the founding father of this "school," structures his discussion in *On the Laws of War* around four problems: "1) Whether it is lawful for Christians to wage war at all; 2) On whose authority war may be declared or waged; 3) What may and ought to be the causes of the just war; 4) What Christians may lawfully do against enemies, and to what extent" (1991, p.295). One can immediately detect the similarities to the questions that frame *Decretum* Causa 23. As a neo-scholastic, Vitoria adopted the same *sic et non* mode of analysis as used by Gratian and Aquinas, and Vitoria's discussion of war is littered with citations of biblical, Patristic, and Roman law texts taken from Causa 23. This is not to say that Vitoria simply parroted Gratian – far from it. The impact of Aristotle's *Politics* and *Nicomachean Ethics* (not available in Latin until the 13th century) is evident in Vitoria's analysis of who or what possesses authority to wage war.[31] As discussed in chapter 6, he also provides a carefully considered, and at times innovative, exposition of what constitutes just causes to wage war.[32] More generally, Vitoria's development of natural law as a basis for the law of war and his detailed treatment of *ius in bello* norms clearly distinguishes him from his 12th-century predecessor.[33] Nonetheless, the principal direction and questions asked by Vitoria, as well as many of the texts and assumptions underlying his discussion, owed directly to Gratian's thought on war. Indeed, Gratian's role in defining the body of texts that served as the authoritative material for Western just war doctrine was still being played out when Hugo Grotius gathered the materials for his famous *De jure belli ac pacis* (1625) (Haggenmacher, 1983, p.31).

Enduring relevance

It should be self-evident that if one wishes to understand the nature of contemporary just war doctrine, then one must understand its underlying concepts and assumptions. However, if one lays aside the crucial role played by Gratian in the historical development of the Western just war tradition, one might ponder: Can this 800 year-old text still speak to us today about the justice of violence and the conditions under which it can be utilized?

Military intervention, and humanitarian intervention more specifically, is a fiercely contested issue in contemporary international politics. Notwithstanding potential abuse of the rhetoric by political actors, the basic ethical and legal justification for humanitarian intervention is the concept of the obligation to defend others against injustice. This area of just war thought was ancient even in Gratian's time. In the 1st century BC, Cicero (1991, pp.10–11) stated:

> Of injustice there are two types: men may inflict injury; or else when it is being inflicted upon others, they may fail to deflect it, even though they could ... the man who does not defend someone, or obstruct the injustice when he can, is at fault just as if he had abandoned his parents or his friends or his country.

This obligation to defend others against injustice was repeated by early Christian thinkers (it formed the basis of Ambrose of Milan's acceptance of limited just warfare),[34] and Gratian in Causa 23, Question 3, explored it: "Whether an injury to one's associates is to be repelled with arms?" Similar to Cicero and Ambrose, Gratian concludes that "the perverse are to be opposed, and the injury of one's fellows is to be repelled with arms ... He who does not do this, consents to the injury" (C. 23, q. 3 d.p.c. 10). This justified the use of interventional force against injustice on behalf of others; no limitation was imposed by concepts of the inviolability of sovereignty or territory that are the hallmarks of post-Westphalian international law (see chapter 12 on Vattel). In modern international relations, territorial violation is a major obstacle for any "lawful" intervention, and defense of "sovereign territory" is considered the paradigmatic just cause for war.[35] In contrast, the punishment of injustice was paramount for Gratian and for most medieval writers on the just war. Since injustice could be found at both home and abroad, one's obligation to combat injustice did not stop at one's geographic borders, which were often in flux during the Middle Ages.

Applied to a contemporary context, if one contends that the violation of human rights is intrinsically unjust – as UN (1948) *Universal Declaration of Human Rights* assumes – then humanitarian intervention could be justifiable regardless of whether the threat to human rights arises from a party exterior to the state in which the violations are taking place (e.g. as a result of aggressive foreign invasion), or from a party within the state itself (e.g. a tyrannical regime). Because the central motivation is action against injustice (wherever it may occur), such interventions have a potentially universal application. With Gratian's emphasis on violations of justice rather than violations of territorial integrity, the *Decretum* offers an approach to the use of just war and intervention that is clearly identifiable in contemporary just war discourse. Whether or not one agrees with such a classic just war revival or not (the attempts by Elshtain (chapter 17) and Johnson (chapter 18) are not without controversy), the contemporary context is such that a good deal of contemporary just war thought may be far more medieval in its basic assumptions than is openly acknowledged. To borrow a phrase from Hedley Bull (2012, pp.245–246), we may be witnessing a "new medievalism" in contemporary just war doctrine.

Regardless of whether one accepts the direct relevance of Gratian's ideas to contemporary international relations – Las Casas's take on humanitarian intervention in chapter 7 for example offers a more critical perspective not too far removed from Gratian's influence – the enormity of his contribution to the just war tradition as a whole, in terms of helping to establish the scope, content, and methodology of its enquiry, is indisputable. What this chapter has made clear, I hope, is Gratian's importance as a just war thinker. In the Western just war tradition, he is a giant upon whose shoulders others have stood.

Notes

1   The standard Latin edition of the *Decretum Gratiani* is by Emile Friedberg (Gratian 1879). All translations from the *Decretum* are my own, but I am indebted to Professor Giulio Silano, who made available to me his translation of Causa 23 and its accompanying gloss; this translation has influenced my own renderings of Gratian's text. Selected translations touching on war are also available in Reichberg, Syse, and Begby (2006, 109–24), and wherever possible I have included references to this volume. An English translation of the first twenty *Distinctiones* of *Decretum* Part 1, the so-called 'Treatise on Laws', is also available (Gratian 1993).

2   Nussbaum (1943, p.455); Hubrecht (1955, pp.163, 166–7); Russell (1975, p.16); Corey and Charles (2012, p.10). For further references to Augustine as the "father" of just war, see O'Driscoll (2015, p.1).

3   See Landau (2008a, pp.35–38) for an overview of the structure of the *Decretum*. Conventional citation of the *Decretum* provides the relevant 'Distinction' (D.) or 'Cause' (C.), the Question (q.), and the canon/canons (c./cc.). Therefore, a reference to *Decretum*, Part 2, Causa 23, Question 4, canons 2–3, would appear as: *Decretum*, C. 23, q. 4 cc. 2–3. Gratian's commentary preceding or following specific canons is referred to as *dicta ante canonum* (d.a.c.) or *dicta post canonum* (d.p.c.). I will cite relevant parts of the *Decretum* using these conventions rather than using page references to the 1879 edition.

4   Causa 33 of Part 2 is unusual in that the third question consists of a lengthy discussion of penance, and is itself divided into seven *distinctiones*. This excursion is typically treated as a semi-autonomous tract and referred to as *De Poenitentia*.

5   More than two thirds of the canons of Causa 23 consist of Patristic texts (Landau 2008a, p.29).

6   The Ivonian *Collectio tripartita* was also an important source (Hubrecht 1955, p.164, 167; Landau 2008a, p.31). Bauer and Lesaffer (2005) provide an important assessment of Ivo's treatment of just war and his influence on Gratian.

7   Landau (2008a, pp.49–50). About 160 manuscripts of the *Decretum* survive from the twelfth century alone (ibid. 48): a remarkably large number by medieval standards. Given that medieval historians usually assume a destruction rate of at least 90 per cent for medieval texts, then one can begin to appreciate the *Decretum*'s popularity.

8   Lombard (2007, vii).

9   Noonan (1979, pp.158–60). The inclusion of canons from the Second Lateran Council (1139) means that the *Decretum* cannot have been completed earlier than 1139 (Fornier 1898, pp.255–6).

10 This body of law included the *Codex Justinianus*, the *Institutes*, the *Novellae*, and finally the *Digest* (or *Pandectae*). Landau (2008b, pp.118–26) provides a concise overview of the *Corpus iuris civilis* and the early growth of Roman and canon law in Bologna and elsewhere.

11 On the Investiture Controversy, see for example Tellenbach (1948) and Robinson (1978). Tierney (1964, pp.33–95) provides a range of pertinent primary sources in translation.

12 Cf. Reichberg, Syse, and Begby (2006, p.109).

13 The Latin infinitive verb *militare* can be translated to mean 'to fight/wage war' in a general sense or 'to serve as a soldier/serve in the army' in a more personal sense. Given the broad nature of Gratian's first question, I have preferred the more universal sense of 'to wage war'.

14 Cf. Reichberg, Syse, and Begby (2006, p.109).

15 See Isidore (2006, p.117). Isidore was drawing on Roman law: 'it is permissible to repel force by force, and this right is conferred by nature. From this it appears ... that arms may be repelled by arms'. *Digest* (1985, 4:584), bk. 43, ch. 16.1, §27.

16 On the use of natural law by Gratian and the canonists, see Tierney (1997, pp.23–5, 58–69).

17 *Decretum*, C. 23, q. 1 cc. 2–6; see Reichberg et al (2006, pp.111–12) for cc. 2–4. Reid (2011, p.78) suggests that in the *Decretum* 'the right of self-defense was grounded on natural law while the right to wage war grounded on the law of nations'.

18 For the development of this maxim, see Plato (1975, pp.51, 292); Aristotle (1981, p.434; 1999, p.289); Cicero (1991, pp.14–15, 32). See also Barnes (1982, p.780).

19 Cf. Cicero (1991, p.16): 'it is not lawful for one who is not a soldier to fight with the enemy'.

20 Russell (1975, pp.62–3); Brundage (1976, p.109); Bauer and Lesaffer (2005, pp.44, 48–52); Reichberg (2008, p.14).

21 Isidore (2006, p.359). Note that Gratian's citation of Isidore includes the phrase 'ex edicto', meaning 'by/from an edict', whereas in Isidore's *Etymologiae* (bk. 18, ch. 1, §2) the original phrase is actually 'ex praedicto', meaning 'from a formal declaration' (Isidore 2010). See also Hubrecht (1955, p.169).

22 Gratian did allow that, if absolutely unavoidable (i.e. to save one's own life), those clergy who had shed blood would not remain permanently irregular and could be reinstated to the priesthood once they had fulfilled a penitential sentence: *Decretum* D. 50 c. 6 and c. 36; although compare D. 46 c. 8, which forbade ordination to those who had avenged private injuries. See also Reid (2011, pp.76–7); Duggan (2013, pp.129–30).

23 On clerical arms bearing in canon law post-Gratian, see Duggan (2013, pp.131–80).

24 Johnson (1975, pp.7–8, 36; 1981, p.123).

25 *Concilium Lateranenses II*, canon 29, Alberigo et al (1973, 203).

26 A common exception was the prohibition of breaking faith with the enemy if an oath had been sworn (e.g. *Decretum*, C. 23, q. 1 c. 3).

27 *Decretum*, C. 23, q. 3 c. 10; q. 5 c. 23; C. 24, q. 3 cc. 22–5. See also Russell (1975, pp.70–1).

28 For example, Rufinus (1902, p.405). See also Baldwin (1970, 1:206).

29 Innocent IV (1581, f. 96r, col. B); Reichberg, Syse, and Begby (2006, pp.141–2, 150–1).

30 Principally, Francisco de Vitoria (circa 1492–1546), Domingo de Soto (1494–1560), Luis de Molina (1535–1600), and Francisco Suárez (1548–1617).

31 *On the Law of War*, qu. 1, article 2 (Vitoria 1991, pp.299–302). Cf. *On the American Indians*, qu. 1, article 1; qu. 2, article 1; qu. 3, article 1 (Vitoria 1991, pp.239–40, 252–8, 278–84).

32 *On the Law of War*, qu. 1, article 3 (Vitoria 1991, pp.302–4).

33 *On the Law of War*, qu. 1, article 4; qu. 3, articles 1–9 (Vitoria 1991, pp.304–6, 314–26).

34 Ambrose (2002, 1:193, 195–7, 221, 289, 367). Cited by Gratian at *Decretum*, C.23, q. 3 c. 5, c. 7; cf. Reichberg, Syse, and Begby (2006, pp.114–5).

35 UN (1945, Article 2 (4) and Article 51); Smith (1998, pp.66, 67); Johnson (2014) provides a stimulating discussion of evolving concepts of sovereignty and their impact on justifications of force.

Works cited

Primary

Alberigo, J. et al., eds. 1973. *Conciliorum Oecumenicorum Decreta*. Bologna: Istituto per le scienze religiose.

Ambrose. 2002. *De Officiis*. Davidson, I. J. ed. trans. Oxford: Oxford University Press.

Aristotle. 1981. *The Politics*. Sinclair, T. A. trans. Revised and re-presented by Saunders. Trevor J. London: Penguin.

Aristotle. 1999. *Nicomachean Ethics*. Ostwald, Martin. trans. Upper Saddle River, NJ: Prentice Hall.

Augustine. 2010. *De libero arbitrio*. Library of Latin Texts, Online, ser. A.. Turnhout: Brepols.

Augustine. 2001. *Augustine: Political Writings*. Atkins, E. M. and Dodero R. J. eds. Cambridge: Cambridge University Press.

Cicero, Marcus Tullius. 1991. *On Duties*. Griffin, M. T. and Atkins, E. M. eds. Cambridge: Cambridge University Press.

The Digest of Justinian. 1985. Latin text edited by Theodor Mommsen with the aid of Paul Kreuger, English translation edited by Alan Watson. 4 vols. Philadelphia: University of Philadelphia Press.

Gratian. 1879. *Decretum Magistri Gratiani, Corpus Iuris Canonici, Volume 1*. Friedberg, Emil. ed. Leipzig: Bernhard Tauchnitz.

Gratian. 1993. *The Treatise on Laws (Decretum DD. 1–20)*. Augustine, Thompson. trans. *With the Ordinary Gloss*, Gordley, James. trans. and an introduction by Christensen, Katherine. Washington D.C.: The Catholic University of America Press.

Innocent IV, Pope. 1581. *In Quinque Libros Decretalium*. Turin: Nicolai Beuilaquae.

Isidore of Seville. 2006. *The Etymologies of Isidore of Seville*, Barney, Stephen A., Lewis, W. J., Beach, J. A. and Berghof, Oliver. eds/trans. Cambridge: Cambridge University Press.

Isidore of Seville. 2010. *Etymologiarum sive Originum libri XX*. Library of Latin Texts, Series A, based on the edition of Lindsay, W. M. Oxford: Oxford University Press, 1911. Turnhout: Brepols.

Legnano, Giovanni da [John of Legnano]. 1917. *Tractatus De Bello, De Represalis et De Duello*. Holland, Thomas Erskine. ed. with an English translation of the Text by Brierly, J. L. Oxford: Oxford University Press.

Lombard, Peter. 2007. *The Sentences. Book 1: The Mystery of the Trinity*. Silano, Giulio. trans. Toronto: Pontifical Institute of Mediaeval Studies.

Plato. 1975. *The Laws*. Saunders, Trevor J. trans. Harmondsworth: Penguin.

Reichberg, Gregory M., Syse, Henrik, and Begby, Endre. eds. 2006. *The Ethics of War: Classic and Contemporary Readings*. Oxford: Blackwell.

Rufinus. 1902. *Die Summa Decretorum des magister Rufinus*. Singer, H. ed. Paderborn: Ferdinand Schöningh.

Schaff, P., ed. 1994. *A Select Library of the Nicene and post-Nicene Fathers of the Christian Church, Volume 1*. 1ˢᵗ ser. (1886–90). Grand Rapids, MI: Eerdmans.

United Nations (UN). 1945. *Charter of the United Nations. Chapter I, Articles 1–2.* Available www.un.org/en/sections/un-charter/chapter-i.

United Nations. *Chapter VII, Articles 39–51.* Available: www.un.org/en/sections/un-charter/chapter-vii.

United Nations. 1948. *Universal Declaration of Human Rights.* Available: www.un.org/en/universal-declaration-human-rights/.

Vitoria, Francisco de. 1991. *Political Writings.* Pagden, Anthony and Lawrance, Jeremy. eds. Cambridge: Cambridge University Press.

Secondary

Baldwin, J. W. 1970. *Masters, Princes, and Merchants: The Social Views of Peter the Chanter and His Circle.* 2 vols. Princeton: Princeton University Press.

Barnes, Jonathan. 1982. The Just War. In Kretzmann, N. Kenny, A. and Pinborg, J. eds. *The Cambridge History of Later Medieval Philosophy: From the Rediscovery of Aristotle to the Disintegration of Scholasticism 1100–1600.* Cambridge: Cambridge University Press, pp. 771–784.

Bauer, Dominique and Randall Lesaffer. 2005. Ivo of Chartres, the Gregorian Reform and the Formation of the Just War Doctrine. *Journal of the History of International Law.* **7**(1), pp.43–54.

Brundage, James A. 1995a. *Medieval Canon Law.* New York: Longman.

Brundage, James A. 1995b. The Hierarchy of Violence in Twelfth- and Thirteenth-Century Canonists. *The International History Review* **17** (4), pp.670–692.

Brundage, James A. 1976. Holy War and the Medieval Lawyers. In Murphy, Thomas Patrick. ed. *The Holy War.* Columbus, OH: Ohio State University Press, pp. 99–140.

Bull, Hedley. 2012. *The Anarchical Society: A Study of Order in World Politics.* 4th edition. Basingstoke: Palgrave Macmillan.

Corey, David D. and J. Daryl Charles. 2012. *The Just War Tradition: An Introduction.* Wilmington, DE: ISI Books.

Cox, Rory. 2014. *John Wyclif on War and Peace.* Woodbridge: The Royal Historical Society/ The Boydell Press.

Duggan, Lawrence C. 2013. *Armsbearing and the Clergy in the History and Canon Law of Western Christianity.* Woodbridge: The Boydell Press.

Fournier, Paul. 1898. Deux controversies sur les origins du Décret de Gratien. Deuxième Partie: La Date du Décret de Gratien. *Revue d'histoire et de literature religieuse* **3**, pp.253–80.

Haggenmacher, Peter. 1983. *Grotius et la doctrine de la guerre juste.* Paris: Press Universitaires de France.

Hubrecht, Georges. 1955. La 'Juste Guerre' dans le Décret de Gratien. In Forschielli, Jos and Stickler, Alph M. eds. *Studia Gratiani, Volume 3.* Bologna: Institutum Gratianum, pp.160–77.

Johnson, James Turner. 1975. *Ideology, Reason, and the Limitation of War. Religious and Secular Concepts 1200–1740.* Princeton: Princeton University Press.

Johnson, James Turner. 1981. *Just War Tradition and the Restraint of War: A Moral and Historical Inquiry.* Princeton: Princeton University Press.

Johnson, James Turner. 2014. *Sovereignty: Moral and Historical Perspectives.* Washington, D. C.: Georgetown University Press.

Landau, Peter. 2008a. Gratian and the *Decretum Gratiani*. In Hartmann, Wilfried and Pennington, Kenneth. eds. *The History of Medieval Canon Law in the Classical Period, 1140–1234: From Gratian to the Decretals of Pope Gregory IX*, Washington, D.C.: The Catholic University of America Press, pp.22–54.

Landau, Peter. 2008b. The Development of Law. In Luscombe, David and Riley-Smith, Jonathon. eds. *The New Cambridge Medieval History, Volume 4, c. 1024–1198, Part 1*. Cambridge: Cambridge University Press, pp.113–147.

Noonan Jr., John T. 1979. Gratian Slept Here: The Changing Identity of the Father of the Systematic Study of Canon Law. *Traditio* **35**, pp.145–172.

Nussbaum, Arthur. 1943. "Just War: A Legal Concept?" *Michigan Law Review* 42 (3): 453–79.

O'Driscoll, Cian. 2015. "Rewriting the Just War Tradition: Just War in Classical Greek Political Thought and Practice." *International Studies Quarterly* 59 (1): 1–10.

Reichberg, G. 2008. *Jus ad Bellum*. In May, Larry, ed. *War: Essays in Political Philosophy*, New York: Cambridge University Press.

Reichberg, Gregory M.; Henrik Syse; & Endre Begby, eds, (2006) *The Ethics of War: Classic and Contemporary Readings*. Oxford.

Reid Jr., Charles L. 2011. "The Rights of Self-Defence and Justified Warfare in the Writings of the Twelfth- and Thirteenth-Century Canonists." In *Law as Profession and Practice in Medieval Europe: Essays in Honor of James A. Brundage*, edited by Kenneth Pennington and Melodie Harris Eichbauer, 73–91. Farnham, UK and Burlington, VT: Ashgate.

Robinson, Ian S. 1978. *Authority and Resistance in the Investiture Conflict: The Polemical Literature of the Late Eleventh Century*. Manchester and New York: Manchester University Press.

Russell, Frederick H. 1975. *The Just War in the Middle Ages*. Cambridge: Cambridge University Press.

Smith, Michael J. 1998. "Humanitarian Intervention: An Overview of the Ethical Issues." *Ethics and International Affairs* 12 (1): 63–79.

Syse, Henrik. 2007. "Augustine and Just War: Between Virtue and Duties." In *Ethics, Nationalism, and Just War: Medieval and Contemporary Perspectives*, edited by Henrik Syse and Gregory M. Reichberg, 36–50. Washington, D.C.: Catholic University of America Press.

Tellenbach, Gerd. 1948. *Church, State and Christian Society at the Time of the Investiture Contest*, translated by R. F. Bennett. Oxford: Basil Blackwell.

Tierney, Brian, ed. and trans. 1964. *The Crisis of Church and State 1050–1300*. Englewood Cliffs, NJ: Prentice Hall.

Tierney, Brian. 1977. *The Idea of Natural Rights. Studies on Natural Rights, Natural Law and Church Law 1150–1625*. Atlanta: Scholars Press.

Tooke, Joan D. 1965. *The Just War in Aquinas and Grotius*. London: S P.C.K.

Weigand, Rudolf. 2008. "The Development of the *Glossa ordinaria* to Gratian's *Decretum*." In *The History of Medieval Canon Law in the Classical Period, 1140–1234: From Gratian to the Decretals of Pope Gregory IX*, edited by Wilfried Hartmann and Kenneth Pennington, 55–97. Washington, D. C.: The Catholic University of America Press.

Winroth, Anders. 2000. *The Making of Gratian's "Decretum"*. Cambridge and New York: Cambridge University Press.

4

THOMAS AQUINAS (1224/5–1274)

Gregory M. Reichberg

Introduction

Prima facie, war was an altogether marginal issue for Thomas Aquinas (1224/5–1274). The one text where he did provide an exposition on this theme – the "Quaestio de bello" (Question on War) – occupies a scant five pages in his *Summa theologiae* (*ST*), a work still unfinished at his death but that nevertheless runs over two thousand five hundred pages long.[1] Moreover, his personal and professional calling would seem to place him at a far remove from the harsh realities of war. Prohibited by priestly vow from any direct participation in battle or military exercises of any kind, as a Dominican friar he lived his entire adult life within the quiet of religious houses of study, occupying himself with prayer, teaching and writing, chiefly on matters of speculative theology.

The fame of Aquinas's "Quaestio de bello" is attributable in large measure to its brevity. Whereas the medieval canon lawyers had offered more complex lists of the requirements that must be met if a war is to be considered just, Aquinas simplified these to only three. And by devoting a distinct chapter (termed a *question* – Latin *quaestio* – in the nomenclature of medieval scholasticism) to just war in his *ST*, he thereby put this theme on the map for succeeding generations of thinkers. Under the impetus of the celebrated commentary (completed 1517) that Thomas de Vio (better known as Cardinal Cajetan) wrote on the *ST*, from the 16th century onwards the *ST* became the leading textbook in Western theology, around which successive generations of professors organized their teaching. Cajetan's rather detailed account of the three criteria (especially the first two) in his commentary to q. 40[2] was emulated by other scholastic thinkers; thus we find Vitoria and Suárez – both covered in later chapters in this volume, as well as their peers also commenting on this same question.

Contexts

And yet, Aquinas's life[3] was not as removed as one might think from the things of war. His father and brothers were knights. He witnessed military exercises from an early age and was surely privy to numerous family conversations on the technicalities of fighting and the ongoing military-political events – particularly the growing conflict between the pope and emperor that would eventually take the life of his brother Renauld (who was captured and executed by the forces of Frederick II). Sent at the tender age of five to be educated at the Benedictine Abbey of Monte Cassino, the young Thomas was moved by his parents to the safer location of Naples after the famous monastery came under threat of armed attack as the result of political intrigues. This personal proximity to war and military life left an unmistakable imprint on St. Thomas's writings, which are filled with martial examples, apparently to a greater degree than his theological contemporaries (Synan, 1988). This family background also likely accounts for his acquaintance with the popular military manuals that were circulating in his day; hence we find Aquinas citing from the *Stratagems* by Frontinus and the *Epitoma Rei Militaris* by Vegetius – hardly standard sources for his fellow theologians.[4] In the same vein we find him highlighting issues that largely escaped the attention of these same contemporaries, the military modalities of both practical wisdom (*prudentia*), and Christian courage (*fortitudo*), most notably.

It goes without saying that St. Thomas was well aware of the political debates then ongoing in Christendom. These provided the larger historical background for his reflections on war and peace. Writing toward the end of the feudal period, thus at a time when the growing influence of cities would soon lead to the formation of nations and later (in early modernity) of states, he crafted a theory of political authority that was in tune with these developments. In this connection he recognized the legitimacy of multiple centers of temporal political autonomy and resisted the more archaic conception of Hostiensis (as the decretalist Henry of Suse was called) and other lawyers, who approved of the emperor's claim to be head over the "Holy Roman Empire" (Reichberg, Syse, and Begby, 2006, chs.15&18).[5] Favoring the competing view of Pope Innocent IV, who promoted a multi-polar Europe as counter-weight to the Emperor's claim to hegemony, Aquinas elaborated a concept of legitimate war-making authority that was structured around a multitude of independent princes (*Ibid.*, ch.13).[6] Moreover, he quietly displaced the focus from loyalty to the person of the prince to respect for the underlying subject of this competence – the political community.

The fact that Aquinas speaks of "public authority" to declare war (*ST* II–II, q. 41, a.1, ad 3), as an equivalent for the more traditional term of "princely authority", shows to what degree he had moved beyond the confines of medieval feudalism that was oriented around personal bonds of fealty to one's lord. A glimmer of the emerging "concert of nations" can be discerned in his writings. And having been influenced by Aristotle to view political communities as inherently "natural" groupings, Aquinas articulated a theory of peace that was premised on shared ties of humanity rather than of religious faith. Along these lines it is quite striking how Aquinas largely remained silent on the Crusades in his general account of just war in the "Quaestio de bello", in contrast to other authors of his period, for instance Hostiensis[7] and Humbert of Romans[8] who placed war against the "Saracen infidels" at the heart of their accounts.

In reflecting on just war Aquinas was visibly dependent on St. Augustine and Gratian. Building on their work, Aquinas was one of the first theologians of the 13th century (along with Alexander of Hales[9]) to engage on the question of just war. Traces of Augustine are visible at different stages of Aquinas's argumentation. Augustine's idea, for instance, that the peace of this world is inherently imperfect – as opposed to the peace to be experienced in the heavenly Jerusalem – is employed by Aquinas to explain why it can be right to wage war: against the "evil peace" of the wicked, the sword of war can and should be exercised by "princes" so that human beings "may find a more perfect peace than that which they had heretofore".[10] Just war has value precisely insofar as it is an instrument of peace, not any peace whatsoever, but the sort of peace that St. Augustine had earlier defined as the "tranquillity of order".[11] On this understanding, the peace of this world is inherently unstable. Human frailty is such that our sinfulness, and with it a propensity for violence, must be held in check by a public authority that can wield the sword of war against internal malefactors and external enemies. Within q. 40 "On War", and *inter alia* the subsequent q. 64, a. 7, on self-defense, Augustine is likewise cited in abundance. But in so doing, Aquinas did much more than simply collate sentences from his learned predecessor. His purpose, rather, was to anchor the idea of just war within a systematic moral philosophy that merged the Augustinian outlook on sin, redemption, and grace with Aristotelian insights on nature, virtue, and political community.

Alongside the citations from Augustine, Gratian's *Decretum* also figured in Aquinas's discussion of just war. This can be seen, for instance, in article 2 of the "Quaestio de bello", where a set of passages from causa 23 are cited in support of the view that clerics and even bishops may take part in warfare (Reichberg, Syse, and Begby, 2006, pp.178–180). While he eventually disagrees with this position (on grounds that as "representatives" of Christ they should refrain from spilling blood as he did), Aquinas wholeheartedly supports Gratian's contention that Christianity does not require pacifism; on the contrary, he follows Gratian in asserting that the Christian community should be protected by force of arms, although more explicitly than Gratian he holds that laymen, rather than clerics, have responsibility for bearing arms.

Aquinas was also well versed in the writings of his confrère Raymond of Peñafort, an influential canon lawyer who had considered how soldierly participation in war should be taken up in the confessional (*Ibid.*, ch.12). Although Aquinas showed some interest in the objective morality of military actions (for example the determination of just cause), following the lead of Raymond (and of course St. Augustine) he was more intent on displaying how right and wrong conduct in war is first and foremost a matter of moral *character*. This emphasis on character led Aquinas to place his account of just war within a broader treatment of the virtues and vices.

Texts

Numerous comments on military pursuits may be found throughout Aquinas's writings. Although just war is mentioned in his commentary on the *Sentences* of Peter Lombard (1252–1256), and is again alluded to in his short work *On Kingship* (ca. 1267),[12] this topic drew Aquinas's sustained attention only in the "Second Part" of the *ST*, which was written ca. 1270. As already noted, just war was the express topic of question 40 in *ST* II–II, q. 40. Here, in the first article, Aquinas sums up his thought on the three requirements of a just war (Reichberg, Syse, and Begby, 2006, pp.176–178). The tendency by and large has been to read this first article of "Quaestio de bello" – "whether any war can be just" – as a stand-alone piece. But this approach to the text is misleading, for two reasons.

First of all, reading the "Quaestio de bello" in detachment from its textual surroundings misconstrues the basic hermeneutics of the *ST*, as will be explained in a moment. Secondly, and by extension, the isolated reading of q. 40 has reinforced the assumption that Aquinas was intent on advancing a just war casuistry, namely the search for objective moral criteria by which to judge a wide selection of concrete cases. But read in this light, the reader is quickly disappointed, as the account in article one is so broad, and conducted at such a high level of generality, that it is of little use in reaching firm conclusions about particular situations. Reasoning from his three criteria of legitimate authority, just cause, and right intention, it is always possible to reach diametrically opposed conclusions on any specific case. Moreover, this misidentification of Aquinas's approach with casuistry had led to a neglect of what could be his most important contribution to just war theorizing – namely his outline of the moral dispositions (virtues) that ought to undergird the resort to armed force, both *ad bellum* and *in bello*. By situating his treatment within a typology of the virtues Aquinas made the theory of just war very relevant to practitioners. The highly refined imaginative modeling (so called "trolley cases") that has come to dominate much contemporary philosophical theorizing on the ethics of war (see *infra* the chapter on Jeff McMahan) remains largely inaccessible to military practitioners who must often decide under conditions of urgency – in the face of strong emotions that make cool-headed reflection difficult if not impossible. Aquinas's virtue approach has, by contrast, the advantage that it is designed specifically for such settings; thus instead of first separating reflection from practice and then facing the challenge of reuniting the former with the latter, Aquinas attempts a unified account that joins the two from the beginning.

The linkage of just war to virtue is largely invisible in "Quaestio de bello", article 1 apart from the brief mention of "right intention" toward the end of the article. Indeed, read alone, it is unclear in this article how exactly just war stands in relation to virtue. The centrality of this relation becomes apparent only when we step back and consider the hermeneutics that Aquinas put into effect within the

broader *ST*. Far from being written after the fashion of an encyclopedia, the work was designed by its author to be a synthesis of Christian wisdom. In constructing this synthesis, Aquinas gave careful thought to the placement of each individual topic (*quaestio*), with the supposition that the explanatory power of the whole would be advanced through a careful ordering of these different *quaestiones*. None of these were intended to be read independently, in isolation from the others.

The "Quaestio de bello" is anchored in a section of the *ST* known as the "Secunda-secundae pars" (literally, "the second part of the second part", or "II–II" in the standard abbreviation). The section is organized around a typology of the virtues. A great variety of individual topics are therein classified according to the two main types of virtue – theological and moral – and each category in turn is subdivided into its respective kinds: faith, hope, and charity (theological virtues) and justice, prudence, fortitude, and temperance (cardinal) virtues) (Reichberg, 2016, pt.1).

Just war is first mentioned in the opening sequence of questions on faith, where it serves as an example to illustrate how not all the truths contained in the Christian faith need be believed explicitly. In the act of faith, as in the acts of other virtues, some aspects are essential while others are incidental only. For instance, belief in God's providence is essential to faith while affirmation that Abraham had two sons is aleatory. In like manner, Aquinas explains, it is essential to courage that one willingly risk death in a just war while confronting an enemy for the sake of the common good; but that one do so with a particular sort of weapon – say a sword – is incidental to the formal object of the virtue (see *ST* II–II, q. 2, a. 5). Use of this example in a setting otherwise alien to the things of war shows how from the very beginning of his survey of the virtues in the "Secunda-secundae pars", Aquinas was already thinking about just war in its relation to courage. But the direct examination of this relationship he deferred to a much later *quaestio*, namely q. 123, a. 1 on "whether courage is specifically about the dangers of death that arise in war" (Reichberg, Syse, and Begby, pp.187–189). The article suggests that just war is at once a condition of virtuous courage (bravery at the service of an unjust cause would not qualify as true courage) and its effect (those participating in actual fighting will meet the criterion of right intention only if they react emotively in the way that a virtuous man would). A parallel treatment is accorded within q. 50, on prudence (*prudentia*). A special mode of this virtue (termed *phronesis* by Aristotle) is likewise assigned for its exercise in military settings. This *prudentia militaris* represents a moral disposition to make battlefield decisions in line with the demands of virtue. It is a virtue especially of commanders, but even rank-and-file soldiers are expected to have a share in it insofar as they too, during combat, make choices that engage their comrades in arms.[13]

Some authors have made much of the fact that, even before discussing just war in relation to the virtues of prudence and courage, Aquinas had already highlighted connections between just war and charity. While it is true that the "Quaestio de bello" is set within a section of the *ST* that is devoted to this theological virtue (a choice that Suárez would later follow in the 16th century), the context is very different than the later consideration of prudence and courage. In contrast to these two moral dispositions which assure the virtuous exercise of martial acts, in q. 40 Aquinas does not present just war as an act of charity (say to protect the innocent under attack). Nor does he say that charity should place special restrictions on the exercise of just war. Rather, his reason for placing his treatment of just war within the section on charity is negative; he wants to account for the fact that traditionally within Christianity "war" is the name of a sin. If war, like hatred and greed, is an indicator of our sinful condition, what are we to make of the idea, also traditional (since it can be found in Augustine and Ambrose) that there is such a thing as *bellum justum*? It is to sort out this seeming contradiction that Aquinas asks "whether there can be a just war" within his wider analysis of "sins against charity" (Reichberg, 2016, ch.1).

Key tenets

The substance of "Quaestio de bello", a. 1 is taken up with outlining the famous three requirements ("princely authority", "just cause" and "right intention") that must be met if any war is to be considered just. Read as a stand-alone piece it might seem that this account is overly parsimonious, as other significant requirements (proportionality and discrimination, for instance) here receive no mention. However, as can be gleaned from the summary below, Aquinas does allude to these requirements in other passages within the *ST*.

Aquinas provided two arguments in q. 40, a. 1 for the necessity of *princely authority* (also termed by him "legitimate" and "public" authority),[14] one based on the juridical principle "no higher redress" (just war becomes operative only in the absence of established judicial procedures) and the other on the need for coordinated command – namely that defense of the common good requires a chain of command with the prince at its head.

The "no higher redress" argument (*ST* II–II, q. 40, a. 1) is framed normatively around the idea of temporal jurisdiction. It builds on the premise that war-making will be ruled out as a procedure for achieving justice between two parties whenever *de jure* their dispute can be adjudicated by a superior with authority over them both. For this reason (second premise), private individuals and subordinate communities are prohibited from waging war. Hence the conclusion: solely those who have no temporal superior – namely princes – are permitted to initiate war. This was not an original argument in Thomas's day. His brief statement was meant to sum up a reasoning that had been more amply developed by his predecessors when they had sought to explain why the medieval feud (*faida*) – a practice whereby private individuals had employed violence to avenge perceived wrongs – should no longer be allowed.

The second argument for legitimate authority (*ST* II–II, q. 40, a. 1) is framed by him on the basis not of right, but of efficacy. Victory in war will be most assured when it proceeds as the effect of a unified force, "for many persons acting together can pull a load which could not be pulled by each one taking his part separately and acting individually".[15] As the collective activity of a multitude-in-arms, engagement in war depends on a chain-of-command that can be set in motion and effectively coordinated only by a unitary first agent. Mobilization for such a task cannot be done by the initiative of private persons, otherwise disorder and defeat would likely result.

That princes alone should occupy the office of supreme command, "calling the multitude to action as happens in wars", Aquinas deduces from their principal duty, which is "to care for the polity". While all upright citizens should act for the promotion of the common good, this they do mainly by carrying out their own limited tasks. By contrast, deciding on matters that impact the entire community is proper to those who have been entrusted with oversight of the common good; first and foremost this role falls to "princes", the term used in Aquinas's day to signify the holders of executive power within polities. In overseeing their respective realms, princes, in addition to the normal tasks associated with governance, must also provide effective protection against internal disturbers of the peace. Likewise princes must adopt measures to safeguard against attacks launched by external enemies. To this dual end of protection, princes are thereby accorded the power of the sword. Failure to exercise this office of protection could lead to their deposition.

By framing the public use of force in terms of protection, Aquinas launched a new concept into just-war reflection, namely that of *defensive war*. Whereas the ancient Romans had spoken of defense in terms of the action that private individuals could undertake by their own initiative (this was regulated by civil law whereas war was set within the sphere of public law), under the influence of Aquinas, subsequent scholastics (e.g., Cajetan, Vitoria, and Suárez) contrasted defensive and offensive war. Both were in principle considered legitimate – they in turn were differentiated from territorial aggression and other modes of illicit war.

Aquinas's second requirement, *just cause*, is tersely stated by him as follows: "In order for a war to be just … in second place a *causa justa* is required, so that those who are attacked deserve this attack by reason of some fault (*culpam*)".[16] Immediately following, and in support, Aquinas cites a passage whereby Augustine (*Questions in Hept., q. X, super Jos*) had written that, "A just war is wont to be described as one that avenges wrongs, when a nation or state has to be punished, for refusing to make amends for the wrongs inflicted by its subjects, or to restore what has been seized unjustly". A very different statement on just cause may be found in his earlier *ST* discussion on the Old Law (*ST* I–II, q. 105, a. 3). Making no reference to the theme of punishment, Aquinas observes that as the Old Law contained "suitable precepts" regulating "hostile relations with foreigners" it commanded that war should be justly initiated. Before launching into an armed offensive in prosecution of a legitimate grievance, justice requires that one's adversary be offered "terms of peace", namely an opportunity to make amends. Underlying this requirement is the acknowledgment that war is not an ordinary procedure for resolving disputes; rather war has the character of a last resort that should be implemented only after less violent means of dispute settlement have failed. In framing just cause in this way, Aquinas provided a very early formulation of the criterion that goes under the name of "necessity" in modern international law.[17]

Regarding the third requirement, right intention, Aquinas said very little, apart from the very general statement that those waging war should "intend the advancement of good" and the "avoidance of evil". He adds that this intention can very well be lacking even should the war effort be undertaken by a legitimate authority, and for a just cause. Such an absence will be sufficient to render the war "illicit". Referring to a famous passage ("what is rightfully to be blamed in war"[18]) from Augustine's *Contra Faustum*, Aquinas suggests that those engaged in warfare, whether as commanders or rank-and-file soldiers, should not only observe due measure in their outward actions, but in addition they should cultivate an inner emotional state that is compatible with virtue. By the same token, vices such as cruelty, avarice, unbridled anger, or hatred, should be shunned.

In other passages of the *ST* we find Aquinas alluding to some other moral conditions ("requirements" or "criteria") that today standardly receive mention in discussions of just war.[19] His treatment of just rebellion provides an early formulation of *ad bellum* proportionality: "There is no sedition in rising up against a [tyrannical government], unless indeed the tyrant's rule is opposed so inordinately that his subjects [one's fellow citizens] suffer greater harm from the consequent uprising than from the very rule of the tyrant".[20] Discrimination is not addressed by him directly, although in his general *ST* treatment of homicide he states very emphatically "it is in no way permitted to slay the innocent" (ST II–II, q. 64, a. 6). In his discussion of the judicial precepts of the Old Law he notes how the advantage of victory should be sought with moderation, by sparing women and children, and by not cutting down the fruit trees on enemy territory (ST I–II, q. 105, a. 3). This nod in favor of the emerging consensus on non-combatant immunity was not followed up by him in more detail. Aquinas was nonetheless concerned to explain how some types of action should *in se* be prohibited in war; lying and the breaking of promises he cited in particular.[21]

Regarding *in bello* proportionality, in particular the causation of side effect harm to non-combatants,[22] Aquinas is often cited in connection with the "doctrine of double effect" (DDE), a prominent and controversial point of reference for contemporary discussions of "collateral damage".[23] DDE holds that from our good actions harmful side effects can foreseeably result, and we are not obligated to refrain from these good actions to prevent the said side effects from occurring. Thus, in contemporary military ethics it is generally recognized that some missions will be justified, on grounds of DDE, in spite of a recognition that civilian casualties will ineluctably follow.

DDE accordingly teaches that agents will be absolved from the liability, which ordinarily attaches to the production of harmful side effects, only if (at a minimum) the deliberate activity which gave rise to the said side effects was itself not blameworthy. By contrast, the negative side effects that follow from the commission of a crime (or, more generally, from any morally wrongful deed) are ascribable to the agent as an aggravating condition for which he will be held accountable, and this regardless of the fact that these were wholly undesired by him and in no way contributed toward the commission of his crime or the enjoyment of its illicit gains.

The seminal formulation of DDE is usually traced to *ST* II–II, q. 64, a. 7 ("whether one individual may licitly kill another in self-defense") (Reichberg, Syse, and Begby, 2006, pp.190–191). The article is focused on self-defense as exercised by private individuals in peacetime. Aquinas has in mind the situation that can arise when, for example, someone is attacked by roadside thieves. He begins this passage with the observation that "nothing hinders a single act from having two effects", "an intended effect", on the one hand, and an effect that "lies outside of [the agent's] intention" (*praeter intentionem*), on the other. From this principle he infers that self-defensive killing by private individuals will be allowable provided that two conditions are met; first of all, the defender must have for sole aim the protection of self from harm ("saving one's own life is what is intended"), and secondly, the amount of force used must be proportionate to this aim; should one exceed this measure, the self-defense will be illicit. Aquinas concludes this passage with a brief reflection on homicidal self-defense as carried out by public officers of the law (soldiers or police). Their killing is not restricted by the sole aim of self-protection, for "even while intending to kill another in self-defense", they do this for the sake of the "public good". But even soldiers would sin should they not measure their killing to the needs of public order and justice, but do so rather to achieve some private end (say to eliminate a rival or avenge a personal wrong).

As can be seen from this summary, *ST* II–II, q. 64, a. 7 is not concerned with the problem of collateral damage in wartime. No mention is made of harm done to civilian lives and property. Indeed, Aquinas's treatment looks wholly to harm directed against assailants. This notwithstanding, it is undeniable that what since has come to be called the doctrine of "double effect" is indeed taken from the first sentence in article ("nothing hinders a single act from having two effects"). However, whether this article does in fact articulate a *doctrine* of double effect is a matter of some dispute.[24] Some commentators maintain that this is clearly the case. They read Aquinas as holding that private persons may not deliberately kill in self-defense; while their defensive actions can foreseeably result in the death of their assailants, they must not *intend* this effect.[25] In other words, the outcome in question will be blameless only when it arises as a pure side effect of an otherwise justifiable action (a blocking motion, for instance).

By contrast, others such as Matthews (1995) have maintained that Aquinas' purpose in writing this passage was rather to differentiate between purely defensive killing, on the one hand, and killing for punitive ends, on the other. On this reading, Aquinas construed self-defense as an aim that might justify the application of necessary and proportionate force against an assailant, even to the point of deliberately causing his death. Recognizing that lethal force could also be applied with a very different aim in mind, namely to punish wrongdoing, Aquinas held that that this sort of killing was prohibited to all private persons, and could only be considered justifiable when undertaken by public officers of the law. In such a case violence would then be imposed not strictly as a means of self-preservation, but rather for the public good, in order to rectify an injustice. Under this scenario, killing *qua* punishment would have the character of an end. As such, it would be *intended* in the strong sense of the term. Defensive killing, by contrast, not being aimed at as an end, was qualified as by Aquinas as "outside of the agent's intention" (*praeter intentionem*). Having the character of a pure means, such killing would in no way be sought for its own sake, and thus could permissibly be undertaken by private individuals.

In other, related passages (for instance *ST* I–II, q. 73. a. 8), Aquinas explicitly addresses the question whether agents can permissibly cause harms that are foreseen but not directly intended. Interestingly, on these occasions he seems very restrictive in his assessment. Thus, reflecting on the Gospel command to forebear from uprooting the cockle in order to spare the wheat (Matt., chap. 13), Aquinas comments that "vengeance should be delayed until the last judgment, rather than that the good be put to death together with the wicked" (*ST* II–II, q. 64, a. 2, ad 1). Elsewhere he likewise suggests that when a particular side effect is inherently bound up with a deliberate act (i.e., follows from that act in a predictable manner), the side effect should be deemed in some measure intentional. Although none of these texts deal expressly with military settings, it seems clear, at the very least, that one should be circumspect in assigning to Aquinas a permissive view of side effect harm. On the contrary, he would seem to favor a restrictive approach to targeting when civilian lives are placed in danger.

Enduring legacy

Because of his central place in the history of just war theorizing, as well as his prominence within Catholic theology, Aquinas's positions have frequently served as a flashpoint for wider controversies on war and ethics. He has stayed relevant over the centuries in large measure because of these controversies. Able to size up the crux of an issue in few words, by its very succinctness his thought has lent itself to contrasting interpretations, thereby stimulating reflection in this domain. Already mentioned above in our consideration of double effect, this can be illustrated by a few additional examples.[26]

First, there is the debate, now ongoing for more than two decades, concerning the correct starting point for moral reflection on war.

According to one line of reasoning, moral reflection about war should begin with the obligation "do no harm". From this obligation there derives, it is said, a strong presumption against the use of force, a presumption that can be overridden only in "exceptional circumstances" (Miller, 1991, p.16). On this understanding, as articulated *inter alia* by the American Catholic Bishops:

> Just war teaching … establish[es] a set of rigorous conditions which must be met if the decision to go to war is to be morally permissible. Such a decision, especially today, requires extraordinarily strong reasons for overriding the presumption *in favor of peace* and against war.
>
> *(1983, p.27)*

By contrast, other authors have argued for a more proactive conception of military force. Moral thinking about war should begin, they argue, with a reflection on the duty of civic leadership to oppose grave wrongdoing. Its starting point, in the words of James Turner Johnson, is a presumption against *injustice*.

> [T]he development of Christian just-war tradition follows a line of reasoning focused on the rightness of the resort to force to combat the evil of injustice, and that development did not construe at any point the use of force to be a moral problem in itself … What Christian just-war doctrine is about, as classically defined, is the use of the authority and force of the rightly ordered political community … to prevent, punish, and rectify injustice. There is, simply put, no presumption against war in it at all.
>
> *(Johnson, 1996, p.30)*

Significantly, each of these rival versions of just war theory appeals to Thomas Aquinas as a source for their respective views. Thus, American Catholic Bishops write that,

> in the twentieth century, papal teaching has used the logic of Augustine and Aquinas to articulate a right of self-defense for states in a decentralized international order and to state the criteria for exercising that right.
>
> *(1983, p.27)*

From the opposing perspective, James Turner Johnson writes that,

> the position of Thomas Aquinas looms as especially important [for the development of just war thinking along the lines of a presumption against injustice] … What is morally condemnable in war [for Aquinas] … is not force itself but the use of force with the wrong intention.
>
> *(Johnson, 1996, p.29)*

Thus, on the one hand, we have those who view participation in war as morally suspect, and hence as standing in need of the most stringent justification if it is to have any ethical warrant at all. Recourse to military force should be as restrictive as possible, and availed to only in the most pressing circumstances. It should not be thought of as part of the ordinary functioning of political leadership. On this understanding, pacifism and just war "share a common starting point: a moral presumption against the use of force" (Miller, 1991, p.16).[27] Opponents of this view make the case that it underestimates the weight of injustice in human affairs, hindering the ability of moral leaders to counter it effectively.

The other debate[28] concerns the interpretation of Aquinas's famous formulation (cited above) of just cause: "those who are attacked deserve this attack by reason of some fault". Nowadays the objection is frequently raised that, on this conception, war is essentially a punitive endeavor whereby the just side is entitled to bring the utmost suffering upon its unjust adversary. Those prosecuting a just war would be bound by few rules of restraint, an idea clearly as odds with the modern conception that fundamental norms of war apply to all participants in war, just and unjust alike. In this vein, Augustine Regan observes how in our modern age "we can no longer see the soldier as one going out, armed with divine authority to kill enemy soldiers, as though they were so many criminals, an idea clearly reflected in St. Thomas …" The "idea of a punitive war", he adds, "is completely unreal and outdated" (Regan, 1979, p.77). A similar criticism has been advanced more recently by Jeff McMahan, who maintains that Aquinas's conception of just cause is overly expansive insofar as it posits retribution as the chief aim of a just war. Punishment would (on Aquinas's account as read by McMahan), necessarily be pursued in a just war even when it would not prevent, deter, or rectify any other harm or wrong (McMahan, 2005).[29] Rejecting this supposition, McMahan advances a liability-based account of just cause (see chapter 19 of this volume).

Does Aquinas's formulation of just cause entail a punitive conception of war? Against this reading it has been maintained that despite Aquinas's use of the term "fault" (*culpa*) within the passage in question, his theory of just cause does not hinge specifically on the dual concepts of culpability and desert.[30] The hinge is rather the idea of injustice or injury done (*iniuria*). The underlying or primary aim of just war is to efface an injury, to re-establish a right that has been wrongly violated. The notion of a violated right is at the foreground of his analysis, while culpability plays a background or supporting role. This was how Vitoria interpreted Aquinas's formulation of just cause: where the latter had spoken of *culpa,* the former discreetly substituted *iniuria*[31] – to describe the same state of affairs. This shift in vocabulary is not accompanied by the slightest hint of criticism for Aquinas's earlier usage. The rephrasing seems intended instead to render more manifest a dimension effectively present in the master's own thinking, namely that the concept of objective wrongdoing prescinds from the ascription of personal guilt. On this understanding, someone can be *liable* for wrongdoing yet not bear *culpability* for this same misdeed.

Which of these two readings of Aquinas's *causa justa* (the one premised on liability, the other on culpability) is the more accurate? Given the terseness of his account, it is nearly impossible to say. The fact that he employs the language of culpability and desert clearly militates in favor of the penal conception.[32] That said, it remains uncertain whether Aquinas intended to ascribe so central a position to punishment. As emphasized by Vitoria, Molina and later exponents, other elements in Aquinas's thought lend themselves very plausibly to the contrasting liabilist reading.

Notes

1   Counting from the double-columned English translation by the Fathers of the English Dominican Province (Thomas Aquinas 1948).
2   See Reichberg, Syse, and Begby, 2006, chap. 22, pp.240–249, for background information on Cajetan as well as selected passages in English translation.

3   For an intellectual biography of Aquinas, see Torrell 2005.
4   See (Reichberg, 2016, pp.67–68), for a representative sampling of citations.
5   See Reichberg, Syse, and Begby 2006, chaps. 15 (160–168), and 18 (199–202).
6   See Reichberg, Syse, and Begby 2006, chap. 13, 148–155.
7   On Hostiensis, see Reichberg, Syse, and Begby, 2006, chap. 15 (160–168).
8   See the translated selections from Humbert's *Opus tripartitum* reproduced in Riley-Smith 1981, 103–117.
9   On Alexander of Hales, see Reichberg, Syse, and Begby 2006, chap. 14, 156–159.
10 *ST* II–II, q. 29, a. 2, ad 2; Reichberg, Syse, and Begby 2006, chap. 16, 173.
11 Aquinas cites this formula in *ST* II–II, q. 29, a. 2, in corp.; Reichberg, Syse, and Begby 2006, chap. 16, 173.
12 For discussion of the relevant passages from these two works, see Reichberg 2016, 76, 131–132.
13 See, in particular, article 4 of this question 50 (in Reichberg, Syse, and Begby 2006, chap. 16, 186–187), and Reichberg 2016, 67–81.
14 The relevant passage is reproduced in (Reichberg, Syse, and Begby, 2006, chap. 16, p.177); see (Reichberg, 2016, pp.116–134), for discussion of the two arguments.
15 *De regno*, bk. 1, chap. 3, in St. Thomas Aquinas, 1938, 43.
16 *ST* II–II, q. 40, a. 1; in (Reichberg, Syse, and Begby, 2006, chap. 16, p.177).
17 "Necessity is commonly interpreted as the requirement that no alternative response be possible" (Gray, 2008, p.150).
18 This quote (cited above) figures as canon 4 "What is rightfully to be blamed in war" in *Decretum,* book II, causa 23, q. 1 In (Reichberg, Syse, and Begby, 2006, chap. 10, p.112).
19 For a discussion of these criteria as they appear in contemporary treatments of just war, see Begby, Reichberg, and Syse 2012.
20 *ST* II–II, q. 42, a. 2, ad 3 (Reichberg, Syse, and Begby, 2006, chap. 16, p.186); translation slightly modified).
21 *T* II–II, q. 40, a. 3 (Reichberg, Syse, and Begby, 2006, chap. 16, 180–181).
22 The observation of proportionality in the direct infliction of harm is briefly mentioned by Aquinas in *ST* II–II, q. 64, a. 7 (Reichberg, Syse, and Begby, 2006, chap. 16, p.190), where he notes how even an act "proceeding from a good intention ... will be rendered illicit, if it be out of proportion to the [intended] end. Thus, if a man in self-defense, uses more than necessary violence, this will be illicit, because according to the jurists 'it is licit to repel force by force, provided one does not exceed the limits of blameless defense'".
23 See the essays assembled in (Woodward 2001).
24 See (Reichberg 2016, chap. 8, "Self-Defense", pp.173–201), for the specifics of this debate.
25 See *inter alia* Boyle 1978 and Finnis 1998.
26 Due to limitations of space I leave aside other noteworthy debates, for instance on the question whether or not Aquinas's doctrine supports the "moral equality of combatants" (Reichberg, 2016, pp.223–256).
27 See also (Miller 2002), who maintains that, for Aquinas, charity places special restrictions on the exercise of just war.
28 See Reichberg (2016, pp.142–172).
29 McMahan (2005).

30 See (Reichberg 2016, chap. 7, "War and Punishment", pp.142–172), for the details of this debate.

31 *De iure belli*, q. 3, a. 4, fourth point: "the sole and only just cause for waging war is when harm (*iniuria*) has been inflicted" (Reichberg, Syse, and Begby, chap. 27, p.314).

32 This conception was developed most notably by Cajetan; see (Reichberg, Syse, and Begby, 2006, chap.22, pp.240–250).

Works cited

Aquinas, Thomas. 1938 (revised edition). *On the Governance of Rulers*. Phelan, Gerald B. trans. Toronto: Pontifical Institute of Medieval Studies.

Aquinas, Thomas. 1948 (revised edition). *Summa Theologica*. Complete English Translation in Five Volumes, by the Fathers of the English Dominican Province. London: Benzinger Brothers.

Begby, Endre, Reichberg, Gregory M. and Syse, Henrik. 2012. The Ethics of War. Part II: Contemporary Authors and Issues. *Philosophy Compass* **7**(5), pp.328–347.

Boyle, Joseph. 1978. *Praeter Intentionem* in Aquinas. *The Thomist*. **42,** pp.649–665.

Finnis, John. 1998. *Aquinas: Moral, Political, and Legal Theory*. Oxford: Oxford University Press.

Gallagher, Thomas. 2002. *Assault in Norway: Sabotaging the Nazi Nuclear Program*. Guilford, CN: The Lyons Press.

Gray, Christine. 2008. *Intenational Law and the Use of Force* (3rd edition). Oxford: Oxford University Press.

Johnson, James Turner. 1996. The Broken Tradition. *The National Interest*, pp.27–36.

McMahan, Jeff. 2005. Just Cause for War. *Ethics & International Affairs*. **19**(3), pp.1–21.

Matthews, Gareth. 1995. Saint Thomas and the Principle of Double Effect. In MacDonald, Scott and Stump, Eleonore. eds. *Aquinas's Moral Theory*. Ithaca and London: Cornell University Press, pp.63–78.

Miller, Richard B. 1991. *Interpretations of Conflict: Ethics, Pacifism, and the Just-War Tradition*. Chicago: University of Chicago Press.

Miller, Richard B. 2002. Aquinas and the Presumption against Killing and War. *Journal of Religion*. **82**, pp.173–204.

National Conference of Catholic Bishops. 1983. *The Challenge of Peace: God's Promise and Our Response*. Washington, D.C.: United States Catholic Conference.

Regan, Augustine. 1979. *Thou Shalt Not Kill*. Dublin and Cork: The Mercier Press.

Reichberg, Gregory M. 2016. *Thomas Aquinas on War and Peace*. New York: Cambridge University Press.

Reichberg, Gregory M., Syse, Henrik and Begby, Endre. eds. 2006. *The Ethics of War: Classic and Contemporary Readings*. Oxford: Blackwell Publishing.

Synan, Edward A. 1988. St. Thomas Aquinas and the Profession of Arms. *Medieval Studies*. **50** pp.404–37.

Torrell, Jean Pierre. 2005 (revised edition). *Saint Thomas Aquinas*. Vol. 1: *The Person and his Work*. Royal, Robert.trans. Washington, D.C. The Catholic University of America Press.

Woodward, P.A. ed. 2001. *The Doctrine of Double Effect: Philosophers Debate a Controversial Moral Principle*. Notre Dame, Indiana: Notre Dame University Press.

5

ℳ𝓈. CHRISTINE DE PIZAN (c. 1364–c. 1430)

Cian O'Driscoll

Introduction

Christine de Pizan has variously been described as "ahead of her times", a "proto-pacifist", "France's first woman of letters", and "the quintessential outsider" (Le Saux, 2004, p.93; Willard, 1984, p.15; and Forhan, 2002, p.vi). Born in Venice in 1364, she moved with her family to Paris in 1368 when her father, Tomasso, was appointed as the royal astronomer in the court of King Charles V. Christine's father encouraged her love for books, and she enjoyed privileged access to the library of Charles V, who was well known as a patron of learning.[1] Upon turning sixteen, Christine married a young notary, Etienne du Castel. It appears to have been a happy marriage (Margolis, 2011, p.6). Etienne supported Christine's desire to educate herself, and they had three children together. Hard times were around the corner, however. On a national level, the death of Charles V ushered in a period of great difficulty for France, while, domestically, the death of Christine's father and the untimely passing of Etienne in 1389 left Christine an unsupported widow and mother of three at the age of 25. Christine's response was to turn to a life of letters, composing poetry and prose, first for consolation, but latterly as a means of supporting her family. She experienced great success in this domain, and will be forever remembered for her influence upon both French Literature and Women's Studies. As we will discover, she also had much of interest to say about the ethics of war, and made a significant contribution to the tradition of just war thinking. In particular, she played a vital role in bridging church and lay approaches to the regulation of violence.

Contexts

Christine's life and writings were indelibly marked by the times in which she lived. The Great Schism (1378–1417) and the Hundred Years War (1337–1453) ensured that the entirety of her life was played out against a particularly turbulent political backdrop. Her family's move to Paris took place not long after successive French defeats at Crecy (1346) and Poitiers (1356), and she was a first-hand witness to the civil unrest that followed these reverses. In addition to suffering one defeat after the other to the English, this was a period during which France was "racked by internal divisions, feuding and repeated civil conflicts, and the countryside was constantly terrorised by the brutal behaviour of garrisons and rampaging bands of unemployed soldiers (Taylor, 2013, p.19)". Christine (quoted in: Adams, 2014, p.1) referred to these sad developments as a "sickness that so tears through the land".

Events came to a head when Charles V died in 1380 without any plans for a secure succession in place. Until such time as his 11 year old son, Charles VI, was ready to ascend to the throne, Louis, the duke of Anjou was to rule France by regency. Alongside this, arrangements had been put in place for Philip the Bold, the duke of Burgundy, and Louis II, the duke of Bourbon, to act as guardians to Charles VI. When Charles VI finally assumed the throne in 1388 he found himself caught between the machinations of Philip the Bold and his own younger but much more capable brother, Louis of Orleans. His difficulties were compounded when in 1392 he suffered a debilitating bout of insanity. This turned out to be a recurring condition, and there followed frequent extended spells when the King was incapable of governing. An opening was thus created that both Louis of Orleans and Philip the Bold, and later his son, John the Fearless, sought to exploit. If the situation was a powder keg waiting to blow, the fuse was lit when John the Fearless commissioned the assassination of Louis of Orleans in November 1407. Violent feuding ensued, with both camps seeking the support of the English against their fellow Frenchmen. To make matters worse, in 1415 the English King, Henry V, led an invasion of France and crushed the French army at the battle of Agincourt. The resultant Treaty of Troyes effectively sidelined Charles VI and disinherited his only living son and heir to the throne, the Dauphin, Charles of Guyenne. All appeared lost. It was only the appearance of Joan of Arc and French victory at Orleans in 1429 that turned the tide back in France's favor. In the wake of that famous triumph, the terms of the Treaty of Troyes were scrapped, the Dauphin was crowned Charles VII, the French reclaimed the territories they had lost to the English, and final victory was declared for France in 1453.[2]

Christine was very close to these events. As a member of the court of Charles V, she not only mourned his death, she also directed her literary efforts to preserving his legacy so far as this was possible. To this end, she wrote a succession of works, many of which were in the "mirror for princes" format, intended to instruct the leading men of France in how to act responsibly and in the best interests of their country. And while there is some debate regarding whether Christine's sympathies lay with the Orleanist or the Burgundian cause (see: Adams 2014; Willard 1984), it is clear that she presented the chivalric license claimed by warring nobles as both the source of and the (partial) solution to the problems confronting France.

We will direct our attention to Christine's most important writings on these general themes momentarily. To set the stage for this discussion, it will, however, be helpful to first say a few words about chivalry and the regulation of violence during this period.[3] Two issues present themselves for special consideration in this regard. In the first instance there is the question of how knightly violence should be managed and constrained. Church and lay sources addressed this question in slightly different ways. Church sources, engaging with both canon law and theological precepts, were inclined to address the subject of waging violence in relation to the demands of the Christian conscience. On this account, virtues such as piety, humility, kindness, mercy, and chastity assumed a central role, and victory was conceived as the heavenly reward awaiting those who fought justly and in accordance with God's laws.[4] Lay sources, that is, proponents of the chivalric code that was held to govern relations between fighting men, placed greater emphasis on the earthly values of honor, glory, and physical prowess. This approach was not so concerned with the prizes that might await the virtuous knight in the sweet hereafter as it was with the esteem he could win in the here-and-now for the performance of valorous feats of arms.[5] Christine, as we shall see, played an important part in connecting these different approaches to one another – a key development in the evolution of the just war tradition.

Second, following from this, is the tricky matter of how the wisdom imparted by these sources could profitably be related to the particularities of warfare in Christine's day. How, for instance, might chivalric norms and the dictates of civil and canon law be extended to a period marked by the emergence of national kingdoms, new modes of fighting, and the increased importance of rank-and-file common soldiers (as opposed to gentlemen knights) on the battlefield?[6] Once again, Christine's writings furnish us with a window into both how these issues were worked out, and how they influenced the development of the just war tradition. As we turn to examine these issues in more detail, it will be important to bear in mind that Christine's engagement with them arose not from a detached scholarly interest, but from her deep involvement with the hurly-burly of French political life at the turn of the 15th century.

Texts

Christine was the author of a great many texts that spanned a great many genres. Her writing career began with poetry that addressed, among other things, the experience of bereavement and the loneliness she encountered as a widow in French society. However, she swiftly moved on to other styles of writing and topics. Nadia Margolis (2011, pp.69–126) offers a sense of the breadth of Christine's range when she divides her later work into four categories: [i] books directed to advocating the cause of women in French society (e.g., *The Book of the City of Ladies*; *Epistle to the Queen*); [ii] morality tales (e.g., *The Epistle to Othea*; *Moral Teachings to Her Son*); [iii] religious writings (e.g., *A Prayer on Our Lady*; *The Hours of Contemplation on Our Lord's Passion*); and [iv] military and political works (e.g., *Book of the Deeds and Good Practices of the Wise King Charles V*; *Book of Peace*). While all of Christine's writings hold a certain amount of intrigue, it is the latter category that is most pertinent to our interests. Within this, two works in particular stand out. They are *The Book of Deeds of Arms and of Chivalry* and *The Book of the Body Politic*. The purpose of this section is to examine them in depth with a view to teasing out the contribution they make to the development of just war thinking in the Middle Ages.

The Book of Deeds of Arms and of Chivalry

Written in 1410 at the behest of John the Fearless, the duke of Burgundy, *The Book of Deeds of Arms and of Chivalry* (henceforth *The Book of Deeds*) is a "technical treatise on the art of warfare" (Forhan, 2007, p.112). John was a deeply controversial character. It was, the reader will recall, his decision to order the murder of Louis of Orleans in 1407 that plunged France into turmoil. Although he fled Paris immediately after Louis' death, the courage he displayed in the French victory at the Battle of Othée in 1408 earned him a reprieve and ultimately a return to his nation's capital. Back in Paris, he gained the trust of the queen, Isabeau of Bavaria, and was appointed as the guardian to the then Dauphin, Louis of Guyenne. (Louis was the older brother of Charles of Guyenne, mentioned above, but he died in 1415 before he could mount the throne.) John the Fearless took it upon himself to cure Louis of Guyenne, a decadent youth given to folly and excess, of his bad habits. To this end he commissioned Christine to write a book that would educate the Dauphin in the ways of military discipline and virtue. Christine gladly accepted the charge. It was, after all, closely related to her lifelong interests in both educating the young and furnishing the leaders of France with a model of virtuous rule that they could then emulate (Willard, 1999, pp.4–5). She was also well qualified for this task, having already authored an encomium to the Dauphin's grandfather, Charles V, and written extensively on chivalry.

Christine's previous writings had equipped her with a deep knowledge of the writings of, among others, Vegetius, Valerius Maximus, Frontinus, and Honore Bouvet, and their influence pervades *The Book of Deeds*. The text is divided into four parts. Part I introduces the notion of just war alongside a discussion of the tactical and logistical matters that have a bearing on the practice of warfare. Part II pillages Roman military history and strategic thought for lessons on how to accomplish victory in war, with special reference to sieges and stratagems. Part III treats the rights of arms according to the written law of the day. And Part IV treats a variety of questions pertaining to private combat and duels, among other things. Christine's aim in treating these matters is, she writes, to serve "the welfare of noble men engaging in the profession of arms" (I.I). In other words, her intention was to produce a practically oriented discussion of the moral and legal issues pertaining to warfare that would prove helpful to those men charged with fighting France's wars. With this in mind, she composed the book "in the plainest possible language so that, with God's help, I may make clear and comprehensible to all readers the doctrine set forth by the several authors whose works I have consulted" (I.I). If this sounds like Christine was hiding her authorial light behind the bushel of her sources, this was a deliberate strategy. Perhaps mindful of her status as a woman and her lack of direct military experience, she was keen to anchor the text in the authority of her sources and also, interestingly, in the spirit of those whom she suggests speak through her. In the Prologue, for instance, she presents herself as the mouthpiece of the Roman goddess Minerva, while Parts III and IV ostensibly report a dream Christine had wherein she was instructed in the rights and wrongs of war by a wise old man who, though unnamed, bears an uncanny resemblance to Honoré Bouvet.

Although the treatment of just war in Part I opens with a reference to Cato the Censor, its real locus is medieval Christian thought. The spirit of Saint Augustine haunts the text, while elements of Christine's analysis are redolent of Giovanni da Legnano's writings on war, which were in turn influenced by Gratian as well as heavily cited by Honoré Bouvet, whose work she turned to liberally.[7] The discussion begins with a familiar question: Can war, which is often the cause of "detestable and improper" acts, ever be justified (I.II)? There is no attempt to distract from the fact that the exercise of arms precipitates extortion, rapine, arson, and all manner of grievous deeds (I.II). Rather she lays the unvarnished realities of warfare bare. Despite this, Christine professes that, "wars undertaken for a just cause are permitted by God" (I.II). This argument is supported by reference to biblical passages – the same ones cited by Augustine, Gratian, Thomas Aquinas, and John of Legnano – wherein God commanded wars to be waged. She elaborates: "Holy writ also says of God that He is the Lord and Governor of Hosts and battles, and that wars and battles waged for a just cause are but the proper execution of justice, to bestow right where it belongs" (I.II). She further notes that both divine law and civil and canon law grant people permission to use force to "repress the arrogant and evildoers" (I.II). As for the misdeeds that accompany warfare, Christine discounts them with the observation that, rather than undermining the rightness of war itself, they should be understood as an abuse of it (I.II). While this may sound rather red in tooth and claw, the effect of this discussion is not to glorify just war but to restrict it to a remedial response to evildoing.

What, then, counts as a just cause? Christine offers a well-developed answer to this question (I.IV). She comments that five causes are generally cited for going to war, but adds the proviso that only three of them have any basis in law. These lawful causes she lists as follows: [i] war may be undertaken to "maintain law and justice"; [ii] to "counteract evildoers who befoul, injure, and oppress the land and the people"; and [iii] to "recover lands, lordships, and other things stolen or usurped for an unjust cause by others who are under the jurisdiction of the prince, the country, or its subjects" (I.IV). When unpacked, these causes generate further, more specific permissions. Christine argues, for instance, that the first cause cited above creates a moral and juridical basis for princes undertaking war to "uphold and defend the Church and its patrimony against anyone who would defile it" (I.IV). All Christian princes, she adds, should regard this as their duty. The second cause cited above speaks to the obligation of lords to act on behalf of those whose wellbeing they are pledged to protect, i.e., their vassals and subjects. However, the lord is only entitled to use force if all others means of providing that protection have proven futile. The third cause cited above is arguably more interesting. It pertains to the defense of allies and draws on traditional chivalric notions of defending the weak and the vulnerable. If it pleases him, Christine writes, the prince "may justly go to the aid of any other prince, baron, or other ally and friend of his, or to help any country or land, if the need arises and if the quarrel is just. In this point are included widows, orphans, and all who are unjustly trampled under foot by another power" (I.IV). Once again she stresses that where such conditions prevail, a prince is not only entitled to go to war, he is obliged to do so.

Christine also takes great care to dismiss the two bogus causes often cited for going to war. These putative justifications, namely that war may be used to both inflict vengeance upon an adversary for an injury received and to conquer foreign lands, rest on will alone with no basis in law. Although heroes of the past, such as Alexander the Great and the Romans, went to war against other nations on these grounds, Christians must recognize that such actions would be contrary to their faith – at least when the enemy is also a Christian nation. As Christine puts it, "I do not find in divine law or in any other text, for causes such as these without any other ground, that it is acceptable to start any kind of war or battle upon any Christian land, but rather the contrary" (I.IV).[8] This is correct, she supposes, for God proscribes men from seizing that which is another's and, ultimately, reserves the right to vengeance to Himself and Himself alone. It is, however, worth noting that Christine's account of what may qualify as a just cause for war is inclusive of (even if not focused upon) crusades, a point she briefly returns to elsewhere in the book (III.III). Yet she does not go anywhere near as far down this road as, say, Bernard of Clairvaux.[9] That is to say, she does not glory in the idea of fighting for God; rather she acknowledges its basis in law, and seeks to limit it.

Christine also addresses the tricky question of proper authority (I.III). She restricted the title to declare war to kings, princes, emperors, lords, and dukes, that is to say, to those who are duly and rightfully constituted as "heads of temporal jurisdictions" (I.III). On this account, the right to war was denied to any man or person who was not sovereign in his own domain. Conversely, it is the duty of whoever is sovereign to protect and maintain the rights of those who are subject to his power (I.III). As we will see a little later, working out what this meant in practice could be devilishly difficult. Interestingly, in a move that foreshadows policies later advocated by Francisco de Vitoria and Francisco Suárez, Christine insists that, even if he is sovereign, a prince should not declare war on a whim, or simply on his own say-so. Instead, prudence dictates that he should commission advice from "a great council of wise men" before committing his nation to war (I.IV; also III.VII). The reason for her insistence on this procedural device is quite straightforward. It is Christine's awareness that the decision to go to war is a great and weighty matter that touches "the lives, the blood, and the honour and the fortunes of an infinite number of people" (I.V).

There are many other interesting points developed in *The Book of Deeds* but we do not have the space to cover them all here. Before we move on, though, it is incumbent upon us to note the logic that underlies its development of the just war idea. Christine is very clear that while war may (and in some cases must) be waged to right wrongs, it should be waged so far as possible in a manner that does not impose unjust burdens upon the innocent. In Christine's words, "For a just war may keep on to recover what is right, of which the limits may not be overstepped by any means, which is to say, by pillaging friendly lands and various other sorts of grievances that men-at-arms carry out frequently" (III.VII). Regrettably, she does not say a great deal more about what counts as wrongful conduct, but it is very clear that she has some notion of what we might call *jus in bello* restrictions that pertain to the innocent in mind. It is also the case, however, that these restrictions might fairly be overridden in a just war. Employing a style of reasoning that evokes Augustine's providential view of war, Christine argues that even though a war will necessarily involve some killing of the innocent, something that is presumptively wrong, it may nevertheless be justified if the cause is meritorious. "For it is in the very execution of justice that God suffers and permits it, to the end that wrong may be made right, even though God suffers wars to be fought sometimes against all right and reason; this is like the scourge of God and the punishment for the sins of the people" (III.VII). But, Christine cautions, men must take care that the wars in which they serve are justified, otherwise they risk damnation. "You should know that if the quarrel is unjust, he that exposes himself in it condemns his soul; and if he dies in such a state, he will go the way of perdition without great repentance through divine grace at last" (III.VII).[10]

The Book of the Body Politic

Christine wrote *The Book of the Body Politic* between 1404–07, shortly before the assassination of Louis of Orleans. Though it is dedicated to Charles V, it appears to have been written, like *The Book of Deeds*, with the upbringing of Louis of Guyenne in mind. Christine presents *The Book of the Body Politic* as a "mirror for princes" designed to steer the Dauphin away from the perils of tyranny and inculcate in him an appreciation for virtuous government. As with all books of this genre, it draws heavily on moral fables (*exempla*) culled from classical history, and wears its influences – among them, John of Salisbury, Giles of Rome, and Cicero (see chapter 1 of this volume) – on its sleeve. Where the ethics of war is concerned, it covers many of the same issues as *The Book of Deeds*, and mostly arrives at the same conclusions. What is different, and indeed interesting, about it is how it is framed.

The book is structured around the metaphor of the community as a body, with Part I detailing the conduct required of princes in a well-ordered society, Part II treating the behavior expected of knights and nobles, and Part III examining the duties of the common people. Within this, what catches the eye is the manner by which Christine articulates the role of the prince. She treats the responsibilities of the sovereign in terms that evoke both Augustine and Aquinas. The prince, she notes, is ultimately accountable to no one but God, and advises him to avoid placing any stock in "those worldly goods and honours which are so perilous and short lived" (I 7). Moreover, she urges the prince to think about the duties of his office in terms of caring for the common good: "he will live and govern by the laws of a prince of good habits and virtue, and will exercise his office to the best of his ability for the common good of his kingdom and country" (I.7). Moreover, Christine is explicit that these duties may extend to the use of force. The prince, she argues, should love and guard his country in a manner akin to how the shepherd cares for and protects his flock (I.9). To employ a metaphor that Christine herself uses, just as the shepherd tends to his animals and works to ensure that they are safe from wolves and other wild beasts, so "the good prince is mindful of the defence and care of his country and people" (I.9).

If it is the prince who is comparable to the shepherd, his knights may fairly be likened to the shepherd's dog. Their obligation is to protect the people from external threats and to check them from lawlessness (I.9). Christine develops this point by reference to the chivalric code that governed the activities of fighting men, which she in turn (following others such as Bouvet) roots in the warrior traditions of the classical world, especially Rome (I.13; I.29; II.2; II.3; II.4). As Christine interprets it, this code enjoins knights to obey six principles of conduct in their relations with both one another and the common people (II.5). First, knights should dedicate themselves to mastering their arms. This entails discipline and commitment and reflects moral seriousness (II.5–6). Second, they must display "constancy in their courage" by standing their ground in battle and refusing to flee from the enemy (II.5; II.7–8). Third, they should support one another, or, as Christine puts it, "they ought to give heart and steadiness to each other, counselling their companions to do well, and to be firm and steadfast" (II.5; II.9–12). Fourth, they should keep their word to uphold their fealty (II.5; II.13). Fifth, they ought to love and strive for honor and glory above all worldly things, including riches. While chasing earthly glory is, as Augustine warned, a source of sinfulness and to be avoided, the desire to earn honor and esteem may operate as a lever ensuring the just conduct of knights (II.5; II.14–17). As Christine puts it, the good and noble ought to "desire glory, despite the fact that Boethius argues in his third book not to quest too ardently for glory in thus world, and not at all in the spiritual life. But for those who live morally in the active life, to desire glory in a just cause is not a vice" (II.17).[11]

The sixth and final principle is especially interesting. It is that knights ought to be "wise and crafty against their enemies and in all deeds of arms" (II.5; II.18–21). To illustrate this point, Christine furnishes several examples (extracted from classical history) wherein military leaders deployed a variety of ruses and forms of stratagem to good effect. "And by these stories", she writes, "one can clearly see that subtle tricks are sometimes good and profitable (II.21)". Christine does not remark upon the tensions between this edict and the fourth principle of knightly conduct, to maintain fealty. She does, however, draw a distinction between trickery and perfidy, which would later feature prominently in the writings of, among others, Hugo Grotius (see chapter 10 of this book) and Emer de Vattel (chapter 12).[12]

Christine's engagement with chivalric ideas and themes is an interesting development in its own right. While church authorities – and we may think here of Gratian and Aquinas, as well as generations of Decretists and Decretalists – were painfully aware of the problems that knightly violence posed for the social order, they sought solutions to it in canon and civil law as well as philosophy and theology.[13] They did not take into consideration the social mores and customs that were endogenous to the knightly class, or the norms and protocols that circumscribed knightly combat.[14] Yet Christine did precisely this: her writings – especially *The Book of Deeds* and *The Book of the Body Politic* – reflect a desire to extrapolate from the chivalric code an account of the distinction between legitimate and illegitimate knightly violence. Moreover, although they derive from different sources, a level of overlap is discernible between the norms cited by Christine and the nascent *jus in bello* ideas found in Gratian (chapter 3) or Aquinas (chapter 4), as well as those that are more explicitly developed in Vitoria and onwards. Indeed, it is fascinating to note that the discussions she pursues regarding who or what should qualify for immunity from combat, and the proper treatment owed to a prisoner of war, anticipate modern approaches to the principle of discrimination.

Legacy

Posterity has not been especially kind to Christine, at least in respect of her writings on the just war tradition. In her own time and shortly afterward, this was a function of her gender. Scholars who referenced her work were, perhaps predictably, prone to disguising the fact that the author of the book they were discussing was in fact a woman (Le Saux, 2004, p.94). Later, Christine's contribution to the development of just war thought was obscured by her propensity to quote extensively from other writers, most notably Bouvet, but also Vegetius and Valerius Maximus. This tendency earned for Christine a reputation for reproducing other people's ideas rather than developing her own. As James Turner Johnson (1975, p.72) expresses it, Christine

> is not the theorist [Bouvet] is; her book, while heavily dependent on [Bouvet's], abridges his arguments again and again in the interest of presenting a more colloquial, even chatty, treatment of the subject of war. ... Pizan is what we would today call a popularizer, and for her day she was a good one.
> (p.72)

This judgment is not entirely unfair. The careful reader of, say, *The Book of Deeds* cannot fail to notice how closely it follows in the footsteps of Bouvet in particular: many discussions (e.g., III.XI) scan like a more accessible facsimile of the related passage in Bouvet's *Tree of Battles*. It is in this light that one might interpret one recent description of *The Book of Deeds* as a "tapestry of the known experts in the field" (Forhan, 2002, pp.150–51).

Yet this appraisal understates the importance of both what Pizan was doing, and its effect. On the one hand, it does not acknowledge the degree to which Christine challenged her sources. As Francoise le Saux (2004, pp.93–94) writes, Christine's writings on war offer "more than a mere compilation. The shortcomings of old authorities such as Vegetius are recognised ... Similarly, Christine does not hesitate to disagree with Bouvet". On the other hand, and arguably more importantly, the depiction of Christine as a popularizer does not account for the fact that, more than anybody before her, she sought to incorporate the relevant aspects of the chivalric code into the formal discussion of the ethics of war. This involved bridging the gap between what I earlier referred to as lay and church sources, but which might be better understood as those bodies of thought on the rights and wrong of war deriving from, respectively, the knightly class themselves (i.e., those who did the actual fighting) and canon and civil lawyers as well as religious thinkers. This would prove to be a crucial step toward the formation of what Johnson (see chapter 18 of this volume) called the "classic just war doctrine" in the period immediately following the Hundred Years War.

It also played some part in tempering chivalric zeal for war. While Christine advanced chivalric ideas in her writing, and ransacked Roman history for examples of courageous deeds performed by great warriors, she also countered the romanticization of warfare. She is sparing rather than enthusiastic in her references to "honor" and "prowess", and careful to highlight the gap between the heroes of classical antiquity and the realities of warfare in her own day. Indeed she opens *The Book of Deeds* with the candid admission that warfare is often the cause of a great many "wrongs, extortions, and grievous deeds" (I.II). Warfare, she writes, is a hard master that, like "the scourge of God", punishes the innocent and the guilty alike (III.VII). Princes should not be hasty in turning to it, but instead should regard it as a bitter medicine that must sometimes, when the worst comes to pass, reluctantly be administered. Viewed in this light, Christine's writings played at least some minor role in turning the discourse of chivalry away from militarism and toward a more modest, more realist register. One ought to keep this in mind as one thinks of the warrior's code today. Thus, a contrast could be drawn between Christine and Lieber (chapter 14) whose ideas, imbued with a love for war, had a profound influence on ethical military code of the modern era.

Christine's writings also play an important role in updating just war thinking to meet the changing political and military realities of the period. This is most obvious in respect of her treatment of the question of how feudal obligations to serve one's master in war should be configured and cashed out in an era of centralizing national kingdoms. But it is also evident in the careful way that she tackles the use of new weapons, such as cannons, and parses the issue of who should enjoy immunity from attack in times of war.[15] On a more negative note, Christine's writings dispensed with the elaborate typology of warfare that had been carefully crafted by her predecessors (e.g., Giovanni da Legnano). Instead of distinguishing between public wars, private wars, duels, and reprisals, she jumbled them all together in a manner that would soon become the norm. Recent developments in just war thinking pertaining to the changing character of warfare (see Clark, 2015, pp.1–3) suggest that this may have been a wrong turn.

Conclusion

Although Christine de Pizan may not be cited across the tradition as a source of authority like many of the authors covered in this volume, hers is an important voice. Often discounted as a popularizer, her contribution was to broker a dialogue on the subject of the rights and wrongs of warfare between bishops and lawyers on the one hand and those who took up the profession of arms on the other. This paved the way for incorporating the cares and beliefs of those who did the actual fighting into what scholars would later call the classic just war doctrine of the high Middle Ages. It also gave her a platform for speaking to and influencing the conduct of the princes of her day – those very men who were waging the Hundred Years War. All the while, and befitting her role as a widow in a country racked by civil unrest, she never lost sight of the costs of war.

Notes

1 Following the lead of Charity Cannon Willard, the foremost authority in the field, this chapter refers to the subject by her first name, "Christine", rather than her surname, "Pizan". Excerpts from these texts have been reproduced in Reichberg, Syse, and Begby (2006).

2 Readers interested in the Hundred Years War will find Jonathan Sumption's multi-volume history a lengthy but worthwhile investment (1999; 2011; 2009; and 2015). For a more manageable primer, see Kate Langdon Forhan's essay on Christine in Syse and Reichberg (2007).

3 The analysis that follows is informed by a number of sources, chiefly: (Johnson, 1975, p.64–73) and (Kaeuper, 1999; 2009). For an excellent general overview of political thought in this period: (Black, 1992).

4 Chapters 2, 3, and 4 (on Augustine, Thomas Aquinas, and Gratian) provide a more detailed analysis of both the theological and canonical streams that inform church thinking on war in the early Christian and medieval period.

5 For more on the idea and practice of chivalry, see: (Keen, 1965; 2005); (Strickland, 1996); (Huizinga, 1999); and (Stacey, 1994).

6 For historical background on these issues: (Contamine, 1986).

7 Christine's principal source appears to be Giovanni da Legnano, whose writings on war follow in the footsteps of Gratian, through whom an Augustinian inflection is transmitted. It is possible that Christine only knew John's work through the filter of Honoré Bouvet, whom she cites extensively. That Bouvet is not so well known today may be because his writings fell outside the mainline of the Christian canon and neoscholastic traditions.

8 She repeats the notion of a higher standard for Christians elsewhere (III.XVII).

9 This is neither the time nor the place to indulge in a discussion of the Crusades or Bernard of Clairvaux. For an excellent introduction to the former: (Riley-Smith, 2014) and (Rubenstein, 2011). For more on Bernard: (Leclercq, 1976).

10 This formulation calls to mind recent "revisionist" articulations of just war theory, albeit from a different moral framework. See chapter 19 for more details.

11 Christine's writings on this theme evoke Cicero's take on the importance, and tensions created by, the coupling of glory and just war (see chapter 1). Indeed, she refers at

length to the Roman triumph procession, an institution that was close to Cicero's heart.

12   Also: *The Book of Deeds* (III.XIII). For more on trickery in medieval and contemporary just war thinking see (Whetham, 2009).
13   Russell (1975) is an excellent source on this.
14   For a set of interesting reflections on the utility of "warrior codes" for the regulation of contemporary warfare see: (French, 2003); (Ignatieff, 1999); and (Kinsella, 2011, pp.24–52).
15   See *The Book of Deeds* (II.XXII; III.XVIII–XXII).

Works cited

Adams, Tracy. 2014. *Christine de Pizan and the Fight for France.* Pennsylvania: Pennsylvania State University Press.

Black, Antony. 1992. *Political Thought in Europe, 1250–1450.* Cambridge: Cambridge University Press.

Clark, Ian. 2015. *Waging War: A Philosophical Introduction – 2nd edition.* Oxford: Oxford University Press.

Contamine, Philippe. 1986. *War in the Middle Ages.* Jones, Michael. trans. Oxford: Blackwell.

Forhan. Kate Langdon. 2002. *The Political Theory of Christine de Pizan.* Aldershot: Ashgate.

Forhan, Kate Langdon. 2007. Poets and Politics: Just War in Geoffrey Chaucer and Christine de Pizan. In Syse, Henrik and Reichberg, Gregory M. eds. *Ethics, Nationalism, and Just War: Medieval and Contemporary Perspectives.* Washington DC: Catholic University of America Press, pp.99–117.

French, Shannon E. 2003. *The Code of the Warrior: Exploring Warrior Values Past and Present.* Oxford: Rowman & Littlefield.

Huizinga, Johan. 1999. *The Waning of the Middle Ages.* Hopman, F. trans. Mineola, NY: Dover.

Ignatieff, Michael. 1999. *The Warrior's Honour: Ethnic War and the Modern Conscience.* London: Penguin.

Johnson, James Turner. 1975. *Ideology, Reason, and the Limitations of War: Religious and Secular Concepts, 1200–1740.* Princeton: Princeton University Press.

Kaeuper, Richard W. 1999. *Chivalry and Violence in Medieval Europe.* Oxford: Oxford University Press.

Kaeuper, Richard W. 2009. *Holy Warrior: The Religious Ideology of Chivalry.* Philadelphia: University of Pennsylvania Press.

Kenn, Maurice. 1965. *The Laws of War in the Middle Ages.* London: Routledge and Kegan Paul.

Keen, Maurice. 2005. *Chivalry.* New Haven: Yale University Press.

Kinsella, Helen M. 2011. *The Image Before the Weapon: A Critical History of the Distinction between Combatant and Civilian.* London: Cornell University Press.

Le Saux, Francoise. 2004. War and Knighthood in Christine de Pizan's *Livre des Faits d'armes et de Chevallerie.* In Saunders, Corinne, le Saux, Francoise, and Thomas, Neil. eds. *Writing War: Medieval Literary Responses to Warfare.* Cambridge: D.S. Brewer, pp.93–105.

Leclercq, Jean. 1976. *Bernard of Clairvaux and the Cistercian Spirit.* Lavoie, Claire. trans. Kalamazoo, MI: Cistercian Publications.

Margolis, Nadia. 2011. *An Introduction to Christine de Pizan*. Gainesville, FL: University Press of Florida.

Pizan, Christine de. 1994. *The Book of the Body Politic* Forhan, Kate Langdon. trans. Cambridge: Cambridge University Press.

Pizan, Christine de. 1999. *The Book of Deeds of Arms and of Chivalry*. Willard, Sumner. trans. Philadelphia: Pennsylvania State University Press.

Riley-Smith, Jonathan. 2014. *The Crusades: A History—3rd edition*. London: Bloomsbury.

Rubenstein, Jay. 2011. *Armies of Heaven: The First Crusade and the Quest for Apocalypse*. New York: Basic Books.

Russell, Frederick R. 1975. *Just War in the Middle Ages*. Cambridge: Cambridge University Press.

Stacey, Robert C. 1994. The Age of Chivalry. In Howard, Michael, Andreopoulos, George J., and Shulman, Mark R. eds. *The Laws of War: Constraints on Warfare in the Western World*. New Haven: Yale University Press, pp.27–40.

Strickland, Matthew. 1996. *War and Chivalry: The Conduct and Perception of War in England and Normandy, 1066–1217*. Cambridge: Cambridge University Press.

Sumption, Jonathan. 1999; 2015. *The Hundred Years War: Vols. I–IV*. London: Faber and Faber.

Taylor, Craig. 2013. *Chivalry and the Ideal of Knighthood in France During the Hundred Years War*. Cambridge: Cambridge University Press.

Whetham, David. 2009. *Just War and Moral Victories: Surprise, Deception and the Normative Framework of European War in the Later Middle Ages*. Lieden: Brill.

Willard, Charity Cannon. 1984. *Christine de Pizan: Her Life and Works*. New York: Persea.

6

FRANCISCO DE VITORIA (1492–1546)

Alex J. Bellamy[1]

Introduction

Francisco de Vitoria (1492–1546) was a towering figure of traditionalism in a time of tumult and discovery. He was born in Alava and raised in the Castillian town of Burgos. He joined the Dominican Order in 1504 and in 1506 served, still in his hometown, in the Dominican Monastery of San Pablo. Soon after, Vitoria began his academic career at the College Saint-Jacques in Paris, where he studied until 1512, under the tutelage of Peter Crockaert and others. There, he was schooled not only in the scholastic work of Thomas Aquinas, but also in the new precepts of humanism and nominalism (Hamilton, 1963, pp.4–5). He earned his doctorate in theology a decade later, in 1522, whereupon he returned to Spain. His first academic posting was at the College of San Gregorio, in Valladolid, where he taught theology. In 1526, Vitoria was appointed Prima Professor of Theology at the University of Salamanca, where he offered his now famous teachings on the moral dimensions of war.[2] He taught there for twenty years until his death in 1546 (Reidy, 1959, pp.vii–viii).

Contexts

In the year of Vitoria's birth, 1492, Christopher Columbus discovered the Americas. In Europe, meanwhile, Protestant Lutheranism, humanism and realism were challenging Catholic orthodoxy. Amidst all this turmoil, and on the very eve of the birth of the modern mind, arrived unprecedented creativity and debate about the moral questions raised by war. Traditional scholastic reasoning, which for the previous four hundred years at least had defined moral thinking and of which St. Thomas Aquinas was among the greatest exponents, now came under withering attack from humanists and others who claimed that the whole approach was anachronistic (Norena, 1975, p.42; Corbett, 1975). This was the time of Desiderus Erasmus and his blistering critique of war, which claimed that it was all but impossible to maintain Christian values of peace, charity and love in the midst of war's brutal violence (Erasmus, 1907, p.46). Popular playwrights also turned their minds to the ethical problems posed by war. From the 1590s to 1610s, Shakespeare's plays canvassed the full spectrum of views from "fatalism" ("warism") to pacifism ("anti-warism").

Amidst this intellectual tumult, emerged one of the most innovative, influential – and arguably controversial – contributions to just war thinking. Schooled in the humanism of the time, Vitoria applied scholastic thought and methods to the chief moral problems of the day and, in doing so, inspired a renaissance in scholastic just war thinking (known as "Neo-Scholasticism" or "the Spanish/Salamanca School") that would have a lasting impact. Not only did Vitoria shed light on the principles of just war themselves, offering one of the first complete rendition of principles recognizable today as "just war criteria", he also broke new ground in thinking about *how* humans ought to make moral decisions and the broader legitimacy of those decisions. And although his was a self-consciously Catholic and scholastic ethics of war, Vitoria's account of the just war laid the crucial foundation stones for the tradition's later secularization. For instance, it provided an account of political life that grounded the origins of human sociability and the state within nature itself and that therefore acknowledged that different types of states with different religious practices could be legitimate or perfect polities with all the rights to dominion that this entailed (Monahan, 1994, p.155). In his own time, this account offered a radically new way of thinking about the rights of non-Europeans. With retrospect, it stands at the beginning of an emerging modern conception of sovereignty resting on the equal rights of all human societies.[3] But Vitoria's was also an account that sparked controversy. Among other things, later critics complained that Vitoria offered only an apology for the deprivations of Spanish colonialism in the Americas (Anghie, 2007).

It is fitting that Vitoria was born in the same year that Columbus discovered the Americas, since it was his reflections on whether – and how – the Church's laws on war applied to this "new" world context that set him apart from his predecessors and pushed him towards innovation. Vitoria was horrified by what he learnt about the conduct of Spanish colonizers in the New World. In a letter of 1534 to his religious superior, Miguel de Arcos, on the conduct of the conquistadors, Vitoria wrote that, "no business shocks me or embarrasses me more than the corrupt profits and affairs of the Indies. Their very mention freezes the blood in my veins" (Vitoria, 1991, p.331).

Texts

Vitoria published little during his lifetime, limiting himself to short prefaces for volumes, which he edited.[4] The writings that we have are based on notes diligently taken by his students during the lectures he dictated at Salamanca. Vitoria offered a regular series of lectures on Aquinas's *Summa Theologiae* and also an annual lecture to the whole academic community in Salamanca on an issue already covered in the regular series. These were labeled the *relectios* or "re-readings". It is from two of these *relectios* – *Des Indis* ("On the American Indians"), offered in 1539, and *De jure belli* ("On the Law of War"), offered the following year, that we derive Vitoria's thinking on the morality of war and conquest. The first examined the question of whether the Spanish might colonize the American Indians and the second focused on the laws of war. Additionally, Vitoria's *relectio* on dietary laws (cannibalism) also touched on the question of what is today known as humanitarian intervention.[5]

Before considering what Vitoria had to say in these two lectures, it is worth briefly reflecting on his thinking about the state and civil power. For his time, Vitoria had a relatively innovative view of politics and the state, one that would come to underpin the work of jurists from Gentili and Grotius onwards. Vitoria believed that human sociability was derived from nature (as opposed to social contracts as argued by later Enlightenment thinkers) and that nature divided the human community into what he described as "perfect communities". These communities had their own traditions, languages, and cultures and contained within them the means necessary to provide for themselves and the wellbeing of their members. Somewhat radically for his age, Vitoria maintained that different types of states with different religious faiths were capable of being perfect communities. As a manifestation of the natural order, different (non-European, non-Christian) communities enjoyed the same basic rights to dominion and communal life.

Each community required, and gave rise to, a "public power", which was set over them by nature to rule, maintain order and enforce the law (Vitoria, 1991, pp.10–11). These civil powers were bestowed with the natural rights they needed to fulfill their crucial role, such as the right of dominion. As such, no earthly authority was set above the "public power" since they were sovereign (having the exclusive authority to set and enforce the law) and equal among themselves (Reidy, 1959, p.2). This view prompted Vitoria, in his lecture on the American Indians, to flatly reject the idea that either the Pope or Emperor enjoyed universal dominion (Vitoria, 1991, pp.252–264). Vitoria opposed the prevailing idea in Spain at that time that the Emperor (who also happened to be King of Spain) enjoyed dominion over the whole world, a notion with medieval roots in the work of Hostiensis and forcefully presented in the *requirimiento* edited by the jurist Juan López de Palacios Rubios and read to the American Indians upon their subjugation. The *requirimiento* insisted that the American Indians were vassals of the Spanish King and subjects of the Pope. If they chose not to submit themselves to this jurisdiction they would be compelled by force and sent into slavery (Seed, 1995, pp.69–71). Vitoria maintained, however, that as they constituted a theoretically perfect community, the American Indians "were in undisputed possession of their property, both publicly and privately. Therefore, failing proofs to the contrary, they must be held true masters, and may not be dispossessed without due cause" (Vitoria, 1991, p.240).

Vitoria's interest in war was a by-product of his concern about the legitimacy of the Spanish conquest of the Americas. For the sake of space and to avoid repetition in this volume, I point the reader to Daniel Brunstetter's summary of the historical context and controversies that engulfed Spain during this period (see chapter 7), and were the backdrop of Vitoria's thoughts on just war. Most agree that Vitoria attempted to articulate a set of arguments that would constrain what he clearly saw as the excesses of Spanish imperialism. Vitoria wrote disparagingly of the "bloody massacres" and "of individuals pillaged of their possessions and dominions" by the colonizers (*Ibid.*, p.238). Yet Anthony Anghie suggests the opposite: that Vitoria provided a legal justification for colonization (Anghie, 1999). I will examine this issue more closely later, but it is worth saying here that I believe that Anghie does a considerable disservice to Vitoria. Most obviously, perhaps, Anghie downplays the political context that Vitoria operated within, one in which the prevailing view at the time was that the King of Spain needed no legal justification for subjugating the Americas since he enjoyed divine sanction and universal jurisdiction.[6]

Vitoria's lecture *On the American Indians* investigated the Spanish claims to the Americas, first addressing the unfounded claims and then the plausible ones. He rejected the Imperial and Papal claims to universal jurisdiction outlined in the *requirimiento*. He also rejected claims based on the argument that the barbarians could not be true masters of their land, arguing instead that the existence of laws, rulers and rites in the New World meant that the American Indians had dominion since they constituted perfect communities (Vitoria, 1991, pp.239–252). Vitoria went on to reject the "right of discovery" as a legitimate title and the supposed right to forcibly convert non-believers. The barbarians, Vitoria argued, committed no sin through their non-belief prior to being preached the Christian faith. Under no circumstances, therefore, could the Spanish use force to convert the American Indians. As Vitoria put it, "war is no argument for the truth of the Christian faith. Hence the barbarians cannot be moved by war to believe, but only to pretend that they believe" (*Ibid.*, p.272). Vitoria conceded that if Spanish missionaries presented reasonable proofs of the faith "accompanied by manners both decent and observant of the law of nature" the American Indians sinned if they still refused to convert. However, he found that there was no evidence that the Spanish were presenting the faith in a decent fashion and that even if they were, the "sins" of the American Indians did not necessarily provide justifiable grounds for war (*Ibid.*, pp.270–271; Hamilton, 1963, pp.111–113). Vitoria went on to briefly reject three other claims – the sins of the barbarians (because not all sins provide cause for war), the free choice of the barbarians to be ruled by the Spanish (because in reality it would be a coerced not an enlightened choice), and the divine gift of God (because there is no precedent for it and it cannot be proven) (Vitoria, 1991, pp.272–277). Thus, Vitoria expressly ruled out the propositions that the Church and Empire had a universal right to wage wars of conquest (a pivotal idea in the crusades), that wars of Christian conversion were just, and that non-Christian polities held fewer or inferior rights to dominion when compared to the claims of Christian colonizers.

In the second half of the lecture, Vitoria turned to the potentially legitimate Spanish titles over the American Indians. Drawing from numerous authorities, including Gratian and Aquinas but also the *Corpus iuris ciuilis*, he discusses eight possible just titles. First, he argued that the Spanish had a right to travel and dwell in the new lands. This did not amount to a right of dominion, but was predicated on a right to trade that, Vitoria argued, was grounded in natural law. This was a point widely supported by Vitoria's contemporaries and predecessors, but one later criticized by Pufendorf (see chapter 11). For instance, the *Magna Carta* contained a clause expressly protecting the right of foreign merchants to travel in England (Muldoon, 1991, p.74). In certain specific circumstances, this right may lend itself to a just cause for war. But Vitoria required that other conditions, which might today be understood as "last resort" conditions be met first:

> [T]he Spaniards ought first to remove any cause of provocation by reasoning and persuasion, and demonstrate with every argument at their disposal that they have not come to do harm, but wish to dwell in peace and travel without any inconvenience to the barbarians. And they should demonstrate this not merely in words, but with proof …
>
> … Once the Spaniards had demonstrated diligently both in word and deed that for their own part they have every intention of letting the barbarians carry on in peaceful and undisturbed enjoyment of their property, if the barbarians nevertheless persist in their wickedness and strive to destroy the Spaniards, then they may treat them no longer as innocent enemies, but as treacherous foes against whom all rights of war can be exercised.
>
> *(Vitoria, 1991, p.281–283)*

On the basis of the evidence of actual Spanish behavior in the Americas Vitoria argued that this theoretical right could not in fact be exercised because the Spaniards had not fulfilled their obligations. Vitoria was in no doubt that the conquistadors were acting with greed and cruelty towards the American Indians and not out of Christian charity.

Many of the other potentially legitimate titles were predicated on this one. The settlers were permitted to preach the Christian faith and were entitled to wage defensive war if violently prohibited from preaching; they could wage war to protect converts from attack; they might, under certain circumstances, be justified in removing infidel masters and install a Christian mater; they could wage war to protect the innocent from tyranny or to come to the aid of indigenous allies; and a Christian prince may come to power if freely elected by the majority of American Indians (*Ibid.*, pp.278–291).[7] Some of these views – as Las Casas would later argue (see chapter 7) – raised potentially thorny issues in the theatre of the New World.

Vitoria's discussion of the Spanish conquest of the Americas stands as a practical application of just war thinking and – until that point – a rare case in which a public intellectual criticized official policy (Norena, 1997, pp.257–271). Importantly, as an example of applied morality it demonstrates Vitoria's belief that states did not have a *carte blanche* to wage war, even against barbarians. In particular, Vitoria expressly ruled out three potential just causes: religious differences, claims of universal jurisdiction, and the personal ambitions of sovereigns.[8] Moreover, in his lecture on the American Indians, Vitoria offers some of the earliest reflections on whether it is just to wage war for the sake of regime change or as a humanitarian intervention, themes that cut across recent chapters taken up in recent times (see the chapters on Walzer, Elshtain and Johnson, chapters 16, 17, and 18 respectively in this volume).

Vitoria viewed his lecture on the law of war (*de jure belli*) as a continuation of his investigation of the Spanish claims to dominion over the American Indians. This lecture investigated four questions: whether Christians may wage war; who had the authority to wage war; what counted as a just cause and what should happen in times of doubt; and how wars should be conducted. We need not be detained by the first question, because Vitoria offered only a brief explanation based on well-established precepts drawn from Augustine, Gratian and Aquinas, all of whom are discussed in earlier chapters of this volume. Vitoria followed canon law on the question of who had the authority to wage war, arguing that this right belonged only to sovereigns who led perfect communities (Vitoria, 1991, pp.302–303).

Vitoria understood war as a quasi-judicial activity properly resorted to only in cases where there was no judiciary to adjudicate disputes.[9] His direct treatment of just cause was characteristically brief and followed Augustine's basic teaching. Thus, Vitoria argued that the only just cause for war was to right a prior wrong and that difference of religion, enlargement of empire and personal glory or convenience did not constitute just grounds for war.[10] "It follows from this that we must not use the sword against those who have not harmed us. To kill the innocent is prohibited by natural law" (*Ibid.,* 304). These grounds for war he further limited by adding what today we would recognize as a proportionality requirement. "Since all the effects of war are cruel and horrible – slaughter, fire, devastation – it is not lawful to persecute those responsible for trivial offenses by waging war upon them. The wicked man 'shall be beaten according to his fault, by a certain number' (Deut. 25:2) (*Ibid.*)". In other words, war was only justified if the injury it sought to redress was greater than the probable evil it would unleash.

Of course, by this rendition much is left unsaid about what might cause sufficient injury to justify war. Additional specific causes may be inferred from the "just titles" for Spanish rule over the barbarians granted in *De Indis* described earlier. Of particular interest are Vitoria's arguments that just cause could extend to aiding allies, protecting the innocent and installing Christian princes. Citing the Spanish decision to assist the Tlaxcaltecs in their war against the Aztecs, Vitoria commented that "there can be no doubt that fighting on behalf of allies and friends is a just cause of war" since "a commonwealth may call upon foreigners to punish its enemies and fight external malefactors" (*Ibid.*, p.289). We can assume, though Vitoria does not say it explicitly, that this applied only if one's allies were themselves fighting with just cause.

Vitoria also granted that the Spanish might claim title over the barbarians "in lawful defence of the innocent from unjust death" (*Ibid.*, p.288). In these cases, the grounds for war lay specifically in the protection of the innocent and Jesus' injunction that Christians love and help their neighbors. Here again, then, Vitoria was suggesting that the barbarians constituted communities just as European societies did and that these communities were the "neighbors" of the Europeans, deserving their assistance and protection (Davies, 1997, pp.489–490). The presence of tyrannical and oppressive laws against the innocent, such as human sacrifice and killing for cannibalism, therefore provided just grounds for war. Because killing the innocent was an affront to natural law itself, "[i]t makes no difference", Vitoria argued, whether "the barbarians consent to these kinds of rites and sacrifices or that they may refuse to accept the Spaniards as their liberators" (Vitoria, 1991, p.288). This basic proposition, that tyranny affronted natural law granting others a right to wage war to end it and protect the innocent, was accepted by many that followed Vitoria, including Grotius (Grotius, 1925, pp.472–473). Like later scholastics such as Molina, Vitoria argued that failure to act to protect others when one has the ability to do so is as bad as committing the misdeed itself since it was the duty of all Christians to help the innocent (Hamilton, 1963, pp.128–129). Interesting, Las Casas (see chapter 7), arguing a decade after Vitoria's death during the Valladolid debates in 1550, would reject this view.

Another just cause for war that may be inferred from Vitoria's discussion of the legitimate grounds on which the Spaniards may claim title over the American Indians arose in situations where a "good proportion" of the barbarians were converted to Christianity but continued to be ruled by infidel leaders: "the pope might have reasonable grounds for removing their infidel masters and giving them a Christian prince". In such situations, even if they had been converted by threats or other impermissible means, the Pope may have legitimate grounds on which to remove the infidel masters and install a Christian prince – irrespective of whether or not the people asked for this. Vitoria based his judgment on Aquinas' argument that the Church could liberate any Christian from an infidel master in order to prevent that person falling away from the faith into apostasy. Vitoria saw this a war to "liberate" Christians from "obedience and subjugation to infidel masters for the sake of the faith and to forestall danger, provided all provocation is avoided" (Vitoria, 1991, p.287).

It was one thing, Vitoria recognized, to pronounce on the just causes of war in the abstract and another thing entirely to untangle complex claims and counter-claims in practice. In Vitoria's time, European princes waged frequent wars with each other over lands that were plausibly claimed by many given the complexity aristocratic hierarchies and inheritances. Unraveling feudal agreements and inheritance lineages was not an uncomplicated business. For instance, when Henry VIII went to war with France in 1512 claiming inheritance to the French throne he presented a sophisticated legal justification, which demonstrated that his family had a centuries-old claim. The King of France, of course, rejected this claim but both claims had a degree of plausibility (Adams, 1962, pp.62–66). Difficult disputes such as this raised the thorny question of whether a war might be just on both sides and how the justice of each side should be determined.

Vitoria prefaced his answer with the claim that just causes have objective and subjective qualities. Objectively speaking, a war may only be just on one side but only God could know with certainty which side this was. What people *thought* about the war did not affect this "objective justice". "Subjective justice", on the other hand, referred to what people believed. Because humans could never *know* as perfectly as God, they may genuinely believe their actions to be just when in fact they were not. In relation to the just causes of war, "where there is provable ignorance either of fact or of law, the war may be just in itself for the side which has true justice on its side, and also just for the other side, because they wage war in good faith and are hence excused from sin. Invincible error is a valid excuse in every case" (Vitoria, 1991, p.313).[11] James Turner Johnson described this as "simultaneous ostensible justice", the notion that due to the invincible ignorance of humans a war may *appear* just on both sides (Johnson, 1975, pp.20–21). This doctrine carried two consequences. First, because sovereigns needed to make difficult decisions in cases where the truth was veiled by ignorance, it became important to pay more attention to the *process* by which decisions to wage war were taken. Second, if it is conceded that the enemy might have justice on its side, it becomes imperative to conduct the war with maximum restraint.

If a sovereign could never be certain of the justice of his cause, could a war be justified if he merely *believed* his cause just? If the answer to this were affirmative, Vitoria's theory could have been used by clever sovereigns to justify virtually any war. But Vitoria maintained that the sovereign's belief (even if genuinely held) alone did not constitute legitimate grounds for war. The sovereign should test his belief by consulting as widely as possible with good and wise men, and listening to the counsel of those who disagree. Furthermore, the sovereign's deliberations should be informed by wider consultation. All senators, public officials and advisors should consult with the wise so that they may advise their sovereign as well as possible (Vitoria, 1991, pp.235–237; Genovesi, 1981, p.516).

All of this raised the question of whether individual subjects could, or indeed should, refuse to join the army if they doubted the moral grounds for war. Vitoria argued that "lesser folk" were not morally obliged to examine the causes of war. Such people may rely on others to make such judgments and committed no sin when they participated in unjust wars believing them to be otherwise (Norena, 1975, p.130). Pope Adrian VI, a friend of another of Vitoria's successors, Juan Luis Vives, argued that in cases of doubt, individuals should refuse to serve in the army. Vitoria disagreed, arguing that if doubt alone were enough to prevent military service, no state would be able to muster an army to defend itself.[12] When there was *doubt*, Vitoria argued that subjects should trust their sovereign. However, where subjects believed a war to be *manifestly unjust* they should refuse to participate.

This brings us to the question of conduct in war. Vitoria's work stands at a crossroads in the just war tradition. Before Vitoria, the tradition had focused largely on questions of *jus ad bellum*. But by recognizing the fallibility of judgments about the justice of war, Vitoria elevated questions about *jus in bello* – justice in war. On perhaps the central *jus in bello* question, whether it was ever legitimate to kill the innocent, Vitoria offered what has become a standard refrain in the just war tradition based upon the doctrine of double effect first proposed by Aquinas. As a general rule, Vitoria wrote, "it is never lawful in itself intentionally to kill innocent persons" (Vitoria, 1991, p.314). But, in practice, war was never so neat and tidy as to afford simple distinctions between soldiers and civilians, guilty and innocent. In some situations, such as sieges, killing the innocent may be the only means through which the guilty may be attacked. Accordingly, in a turn of argument drawn straight from Thomism:

> It is occasionally lawful to kill the innocent not by mistake, but with full knowledge of what one is doing, if this is an accidental effect … This is proven since it would otherwise be impossible to wage war against the guilty, thereby preventing the just side from fighting … care must be taken to ensure that the evil effects of war do not outweigh the possible benefits sought by waging it.
>
> *(Ibid., p.315)*

Although the innocent may not be deliberately targeted, Vitoria permitted their incidental killing in certain circumstances. For example, the innocent may be killed during a siege when they were inter-mixed with enemy soldiers. Once the siege was over, however, they may not be killed because they are not complicit in any wrong. The victors may judge and slay the guilty but they must let the innocent live unharmed. Once again, however, considerations of proportionality came into play. Vitoria argued that if a besieged city housed so few of the guilty that its taking would not affect the outcome of the war, it could not be considered lawful to attack it (Hartigan, 1973, p.85). Moreover, he argued that it was wrong to kill the innocent pre-emptively to prevent, for instance, the enemy's male children from bolstering its military ranks at some later date. He also maintained that all this be further limited by principles of proportionality: "care must be taken to ensure that the evil effects of the war do not outweigh the possible benefits sought by waging it" (Vitoria, 1991, p.315). If storming a fortress occupied by the innocent (as well as enemy soldiers) is not "of great importance for eventual victory" it may not be undertaken (*Ibid.*, p.316).

Vitoria saw the issue of conduct in war as a matter of distinguishing the innocent from the guilty, not of distinguishing combatants from non-combatants as it is in the modern laws of war. As such, he admitted that there were circumstances in which an army might be justified in executing all the enemy combatants after victory has been gained. Just as individuals may be executed for their crimes, so armies that cause injury may be punished in a similar way since "by the laws of war the prince has the same authority over the enemy as a judge or legitimate prince" (*Ibid.*, p.320). However, such action is not always lawful and expedient. It is only so when "security cannot be obtained without the wholesale destruction of the enemy" as in, for example, wars against the infidels where a negotiated peace can never be hoped for (*Ibid.*, p.321). These dilemmas stemming from these issues were taken up by Vitoria's successors, notably Francisco Suárez, who is the subject of chapter 8.

Controversies

In his own time, Vitoria's thinking was primarily concerned with providing advice to the King on how to act morally. With regards to just war, his reflections marked a significant contribution to the Crown's moral and philosophical deliberations about whether the conquest of the New World was just (see contextual discussion in chapter 7). His thinking also constituted a scholastic challenge to the growing humanist movement led by Erasmus, which rejected the scholastic method and prior Catholic teaching in favor of a combination of early rationalism and direct interpretation of the Bible, and those we would label "realists" today. Vitoria was certainly well schooled in the new humanism and made greater use of classical moral philosophy than his Catholic predecessors. He also introduced the thoroughly modern notion that moral judgments about war made by humans were entirely subjective and therefore fallible. But Vitoria remained staunchly Catholic and scholastic in his worldview, and during his own time focused on defending a broadly traditional view against a range of new challengers. As what he regarded as the Lutheran heresy gained in strength, Vitoria became more dismissive of those, like Erasmus, that he labeled the "new grammerians" (Pagden and Lawrence, 1991, p.xiv). Asked to judge the orthodoxy of Erasmus's writings, Vitoria condemned some sections with "firm moderation as heresy" (Fernandez-Santamaria, 1977, p.62). He reckoned that Erasmus was a "jumped up Grammarian" meddling in affairs he did not understand since he was not properly schooled in Catholic teachings (Pagden and Lawrence, 1991, p.xiv). Against the realists, as we observed earlier, Vitoria held that not all causes of war were just. Indeed, some of those causes most prized by imperial sovereigns and Machiavellian strategists – such as territorial conquest and glory – were expressly ruled out (Vitoria, 1991, p.303). For his defense of scholasticism against the tide of humanism and realism, Vitoria was recognized as a leading authority and a key influence on those who followed: "within the limits of academia, the works of Vitoria and his successors were evidently regarded as conclusive" (Pagden, 1986, p.107). For others, he was "the pride of the Dominican Order ... a distinguished scholar who holds a place of honor in the revival of Spanish theology" (Voegelin, 1998 p.129).

Long after his death, however, Vitoria's work on the American Indians became subject of a major debate, with some charging the Dominican with constructing a normative argument in defense of the colonization and defilement of the New World and its peoples – something that, in his own time, Vitoria consciously railed against. According to Anthony Anghie, Vitoria established the "dynamic of difference" between the new and old worlds through the significance he attached to the cultural differences between the two. Anghie claims that Vitoria suggested that the American Indians could not be fully sovereign because their cultural practices did not correspond with those of the universal (Catholic/Spanish) law. Thus, although he humanized the American Indians, Vitoria subjected them to judgment through European moral values. As such, the Spanish were justified in using war to enforce compliance with natural law whilst the American Indians could not rightfully respond with force. This reasoning, according to Anghie, established the international legal foundations for European colonization by excluding non-Europeans from the protections of sovereignty and creating a moral basis for the subjugation of non-European peoples based on their non-compliance with European cultural values (Anghie, 2007).

Quite whether Vitoria's work influenced colonial thinking in the ways Anghie suggests is open to question. Given that many colonialists at the time – and afterwards – believed that the New World was populated by uncivilized peoples incapable of self-governance or moral lives and that European colonizers needed no special justification for subjugating barbarians, a view roundly disputed by Vitoria, it seems hard to believe that it was the Spaniard's more moderate view that so influenced colonial jurisprudence. Indeed, Vitoria's ideas played a significant role in the promulgation of the "New Laws" of 1542 that protected the rights of the Indians, the weakening of which a few years later provoked the famous Valladolid debates between Bartolomé de las Casas and Juan Gínes de Sepúlveda discussed in the next chapter.[13] Samuel Johnson, an English writer from the 18th century, is credited with commenting, "I love the university of Salamanca; for when the Spaniards were in doubt about the lawfulness of their conquering America, the university of Salamanca gave it as their opinion that it was not lawful" (cf. Boswell, 1839, p.2).

What is more, Anghie's proposition that Vitoria denied sovereignty to the American Indians sits uncomfortably with the text itself. On this question, Vitoria was surprisingly categorical: "before arrival of the Spanish these barbarians possessed true dominion, both in public and private affairs" (Vitoria, 1991, p.251). What is more, each of the seven potential grounds on which the Spanish could claim title over the American Indians constituted a potentially just cause for war as much in the old world as in the new – there is no sense in Vitoria of different legal and moral codes applying to the old and new worlds. We know this in part because Vitoria offered old world examples to exemplify the rules he applied to the new. For example, "it would not be lawful for the French to prohibit Spaniards from travelling or even living in France … therefore it is not lawful for the barbarians either" (*Ibid.*, p.278). For the rest, Vitoria drew his law directly from biblical or canonical teachings developed prior to the discovery of the New World and therefore applicable to the old world. Thus, however else his works might have supported colonization – Vitoria's defense of war against tyranny chief among them – it is hard to support the judgment that he advanced a variegated concept of sovereignty with different rules for the new and old worlds. Rather, his careful argument raise important questions about the link between just war and spreading values, the justice of saving the innocent from tyranny, and the limits of what one can do to win a just war.

Legacies

Beyond these controversies, which continue to rumble today, Vitoria's legacy lies in his reconstitution of scholastic just war thinking. Vitoria directly influenced a significant revival in scholasticism and several subsequent Spanish intellectuals attempted to develop his ideas. The most famous of these was Francisco Suárez, who succeeded Vitoria at Salamanca, following in his footsteps, even if not always in perfect agreement (see chapter 8).[14]

In terms of his longer-term legacy within the just war tradition itself, Vitoria's account captured the main elements of the tradition as it had developed thus far and laid the foundations for its future development and continuing relevance in a secularizing age. His understanding of sovereignty would deeply influence later thinkers, especially Grotius, and those who followed. Moreover, arguably the most significant consequence of Vitoria's discussion of just cause and invincible ignorance was its impact on the position of *jus in bello* within the just war tradition. If, as Vitoria suggested, we can never be entirely sure of our case and there is a chance that our enemy may have a degree of justice of its side, it stands to reason that we should conduct ourselves in a restrained fashion, only targeting those we must to achieve our aims. It was precisely this type of argument that contributed to the shift away from the traditional focus on *jus ad bellum* towards a conception of the just war almost entirely predicated on *jus in bello* in the 19th century. That transformation in thinking about the ethics of war began with Vitoria.

Enduring relevance

Vitoria remains one of the towering figures of the just war tradition and his ideas remain relevant to contemporary debates about the ethics of war. One history of political thought maintained that "we may award Vitoria the distinction of being the first outstanding political intellectual of the modern period" (Voegelin, 1998, p.131). First, and most obviously, his reflections on the American Indians paved the way for the emergence of modern conceptions of sovereignty and statehood – and with them universal rules of war – that applied equally to the Christian and non-Christian worlds. Vitoria was amongst the first thinkers to suggest that the rights of dominion extended to all human grouping, irrespective of their cultural traditions, ethnicity, religion or stance on private property. In the centuries that followed, most Western thinkers distinguished firmly between the sovereign rights of Europeans and the rights of non-Europeans. Vitoria argued that rights to dominion were universal but showed that this did not constitute a right to unfettered tyranny.

Second, Vitoria made a lasting contribution to thinking about humanitarian intervention. Whether it is recognized or not, contemporary debates about the appropriate relationship between sovereignty and human rights were presaged by Vitoria's careful balancing of the rights associated with dominion with the right to protection from tyranny. Third, Vitoria articulated a vision of common humanity that extended beyond culturally similar groups. That is, his whole discussion of the American Indians was premised on the notion of common humanity inasmuch as the American Indians, just like Europeans, were forged in the image of God. "Love thy neighbor as thyself" was the New Testament teaching, and Vitoria maintained that the American Indians "are all our neighbors" who deserve to be defended against "tyranny and oppression" (Vitoria, 1991, p. 288).[15] Finally, Vitoria provided the first insights into the role of reasoning and judgment in the just war tradition and his advice was thoroughly modern. Leaders must consult with the wise before they decide on whether to wage war, for by collecting a plurality of well-informed views there is a greater chance that the final decision will be a just one. This advice remains highly prescient, as Tony Blair's fateful decision to ignore the preponderance of advice and support the invasion Iraq in 2003 shows only too well.

Notes

1   I would like to offer my sincere gratitude to the editors for their insightful comments and advice on this chapter. All errors of fact or interpretation are, of course, my own.
2   This biographical summary is based on (Fernandez-Santamaria, 1977, p.63).
3   That, though, would have to wait until the Enlightenment before it could be fleshed out fully, see (Pagden, 2015); On the in-egalitarian elements of Vitoria's thought, see chapter 3 (Brunstetter, 2012).
4   Excerpts from these texts have been reproduced in Reichberg, Syse, and Begby (2006).
5   All three texts are reproduced in Pagden and Lawrence (eds.), *Vitoria: Political Writings*. All references to Vitoria are taken from this volume.
6   For a good review of the broader literature on Vitoria, especially with regards to the idea of subjective rights, see (Tierney, 1997, p.257).
7   He also explores, for the sake of argument, whether was could be waged against them because of their mental incapacities, an idea with which he seems to disagree, but which hearkens back to the Aristotelian natural slave argument.
8   These points are drawn from (Ballis, 1937, p.80; p.84).
9   Though this role could have been filled by the Papal Court had sovereigns been more willing to subject themselves to its jurisdiction. See (Ullmann, 1971).
10   Thus, "the sole and only just cause for waging war is when harm has been inflicted" (Vitoria, 1991, pp.302–3).
11   This position is discussed further by (Holmes, 1989, p.151) and (Reitan, 2002, p.457).
12   An argument reminiscent of Augustine's in (Norena, 1975, p.130).
13   On Vitoria's influence on the 'New Law' see (Johnson, 1975, p.158). On the Valladolid debates see (Hanke, 1949).
14   The other prominent members of the neo-scholastic movement in Spain were de Soto, Vives, and Molina.
15   For a discussion see (Bain, 2013).

Works cited

Adams, Robert M. 1962. *The Better Part of Valor: More, Erasmus, Colet and Vives on Humanism, War and Peace 1496–1535*. Seattle: University of Washington Press.

Anghie, Anthony. 1999. Francisco de Vitoria and the Colonial Origins of International Law. In Smith, Eve Darian and Fitzpatrick, Peter. eds. *Laws of the Postcolonial*. Ann Arbor: University of Michigan Press, pp.89–108.

Anghie, Anthony. 2007. *Imperialism, Sovereignty and the Making of International Law*. Cambridge: Cambridge University Press.

Bain, William. 2013. Vitoria, the Law of War, Saving the Innocent, and the Image of God. In Recchia, Stefano and Welsh, Jennifer. eds. *Just and Unjust Military Intervention: European Thinkers from Vitoria to Mill*. Cambridge: Cambridge University Press, pp.70–94.

Ballis, William. 1937. *The Legal Position of War: Changes in its Practice and Theory from Plato to Vattel*. The Hague: Martinus Nijhoff.

Boswell, James. 1839. *The Life of Samuel Johnson*. London: John Murray.

Brunstetter, Daniel. 2012. *Tensions of Modernity: Las Casas and His Legacy in the French Enlightenment*. New York: Routledge.

Corbett, Theodore G. 1975. The Cult of Lipsius: A Leading Source of Early Modern Spanish Statecraft. *Journal of the History of Ideas*. **36**(1), pp.139–152.

Davies, G. Scott. 1997. Conscience and Conquest: Francisco de Vitoria on Justice in the New World. *Modern Theology*. **13**(4), pp.475–500.

Erasmus, Desiderius. 1907. *Erasmus Against War*. University of California Press. Fernandez-Santamaria, J. A. 1977. *The State, War and Peace: Spanish Political Thought in the Renaissance 1516–1559* (Cambridge: Cambridge University Press.

Genovesi, V. J. 1981. The Just War Doctrine: A Warrant for Resistance. *Thomist*. **45**(4), pp.503–540.

Grotius, Hugo. 1925. *De Jure Belli ac Pacis*. Oxford: Oxford University Press.

Hamilton, Bernice. 1963. *Political Thought in Sixteenth Century Spain: A Study of the Political Ideas of Vitoria, De Soto, Suárez and Molina*. Oxford: Clarendon Press.

Hanke, Lewis. 1949. *The Spanish Struggle for Justice in the Conquest of America*. Dallas: Southern Methodist University Press.

Hartigan, Richard Shelly. 1973. Francesco de Vitoria and Civilian Immunity. *Political Theory*. **1**(1), pp.79–91.

Holmes, Robert. 1989. *On War and Morality*. Princeton: Princeton University Press.

Johnson, James Turner. 1975. *Ideology, Reason and Limitation of War*. Princeton: Princeton University Press.

Monahan, Arthur P. 1994. *From Personal Duties Towards Personal Rights: Late Medieval and Early Modern Political Thought 1300–1600*. Montreal: McGill-Queen's University Press.

Muldoon, James M. 1991. The Conquest of the Americas: The Spanish Search for Global Order. In Robertson, Roland and Garrett, William R. eds. *Religion and Global Order*. New York: Paragon House Publishers.

Norena, Carlos G. 1975. *Studies in Spanish Renaissance Thought*. The Hague: Martinus Nijhoff.

Norena, Carlos G. 1997. Francisco Suárez on Democracy and International Law. In White, Kevin. ed. *Hispanic Philosophy in the Age of Discovery: Studies in Philosophy and the History of Philosophy*, Volume 29. New York: Catholic University American Press, pp.257–271.

Pagden, Anthony. 1986. *The Fall of Natural Man: The American Indian and the Origins of Comparative Ethnology*. Cambridge: Cambridge University Press.

Pagden, Anthony. 2015. *The Enlightenment and Why it Still Matters*. Oxford: Oxford University Press.

Pagden, Anthony and Lawrence, Jeremy. 1991. Introduction. In *Vitoria: Political Writings*. Cambridge: Cambridge University Press, pp.xiii–xxix.

Reidy, Stephen J 1959. *Civil Authority According to Francis De Vitoria*. River Forest, Ill: The Aquinas Library.

Reitan, Eric. 2002. The Moral Justification of Violence: Epistemic Considerations. *Social Theory and Practice*. **28**(3), pp.445–464

Seed, Patricia. 1995. *Ceremonies of Possession in Europe's Conquest of the New World: 1492–1640*. Cambridge: Cambridge University Press.

Tierney, Brian. 1997. *The Idea of Natural Rights: Studies on Natural Rights, Natural Law and Church Law 1150–1625*. Atlanta: Scholars Press.

Ullmann, Walter. 1971. The Medieval Papal Court as an International Tribunal. *Virginia Journal for International Law*. **11**(2), pp.356–371.

Vitoria, Francisco de. 1991. *Vitoria: Political Writings*. Pagden, Anthony and Lawrence, Jeremy. Eds. Cambridge: Cambridge University Press.

Voegelin, Eric. 1998. *History and Political Ideas: Volume 5 Religion and the Rise of Modernity*. Columbia: University of Missouri Press.

7

BARTOLOMÉ DE LAS CASAS (1484–1566)

Daniel R. Brunstetter

Introduction

Bartolomé de las Casas's strident criticism of the Spanish conquistadors during the better part of the 16th century earned him a place in history as one of the first defenders of human rights. According to one modern scholar, las Casas "unleashed a broad range of arguments against the policies and conduct of his fellow Europeans and has thus earned a much deserved reputation as an important proponent of religious (and also cultural) toleration" (Nederman, 2000, pp.100–101). Once an active participant in the *conquista*, las Casas became the most vocal opponent of Spanish policy and conduct in the Americas. The ideas of the just war tradition held an important place in his struggle to protect the Indians from unjust violence.

Las Casas's place in the tradition has, unfortunately, largely been neglected. Yet, he was, in many ways, the archetypal just war scholar. Steeped in the tradition and fluent in its minutiae, he engaged with pressing political issues of his day, using the authority of the tradition to argue *against* waging what he saw as unjust wars of conquest. This critical edge is a legacy which just war thinking today could benefit from engaging with more deeply.

Contexts

Bartolomé de las Casas's contribution to the just war tradition must be viewed against the backdrop of the Spanish conquest of indigenous populations in the New World. This bloody affair began less than a decade after Columbus's "discovery" of this previously unknown – to Europeans at least – continent. While the Spanish conquistadors, sometimes with the help of indigenous allies, spread across the American continents unloading steel and thunder during the first half of the 16th century, the intellectual milieu back in Spain was shrouded in a fog of uncertainty.

Thus began a prolonged philosophical inquiry initiated by the Crown about whether these wars were just. This period of deep philosophical reflection – what scholars call the Affair of the Indies – began as early as 1504 when a meeting of theologians – a *junta* – was called for by King Ferdinand to discuss the matter of the Indians. The affair became polemical in the ensuing years as theologians disagreed on the nature of the Indians and the justness of the conquest. During a subsequent meeting in 1512, the Junta de Burgos, some theologians justified the conquest by claiming that unbelievers fell under the *dominium* of the Spanish because the Pope had spiritual and temporal power over the entire globe (an idea dating back to Innocent IV and Hostiensis) and by turning to the Aristotelian theory of natural slavery.[1] Francisco de Vitoria's lasting contributions to the just war tradition which challenged these views, discussed in the previous chapter of this volume, were composed during this intellectual and political period of crisis.

The Affair of the Indies engaged thinkers in one of history's most important debates about the relationship between war and justice in an effort to provide guidelines for Spain's political relationship with the "barbarians of the New World, commonly called Indians" (Vitoria, 1991, p.233). Numerous just war scholars probe the Affair of the Indies, but those who examine it closely tend to focus on the important contribution of Vitoria (Johnson, 1981; and chapter 6 of this volume). Others mention it in passing. For example, Brian Orend describes it as "a fertile period" citing Vitoria as having the "deepest theoretical contribution" (2006, p.16); Richard Sorabji suggests it a "case which should impress and inspire us" (2006, p. 18); and Michael Walzer calls it a "heroic moment from the history of the academic world", but goes no further (2004, p.4). And yet one of the chief figures within this movement, las Casas, has been entirely overlooked by scholars of the just war tradition.

Las Casas first came to the New World in 1502 as a member of Governor Nicolas de Ovando's expedition on the island of Hispaniola. During this period he owned land and Indian slaves. He returned to Spain in 1506 and was ordained as a deacon in Seville. He then completed his studies for a degree in canon law at Salamanca, travelling back to Hispaniola around 1510. It was at this point that he began to raise questions about the legitimacy of the Spanish conquest. His famous conversion from a complicit participant in the conquest to a tireless defender of the Indians is well documented (Pagden, 1991). By 1516, he was named "Protector of the Indians" by Spain's Cardinal Francisco Jiménez de Cisneros.

Las Casas's crisis of conscience was no doubt fueled by bearing witness to the injustices committed by the conquistadors during the nearly 50 years he spent living in the New World. This experience inspired his most well-known work, *An Account, Much Abbreviated, of the Destruction of the Indies*, written around 1542. In this work, las Casas lays bare the evils of the Spanish conquest, and his concern with the justice of war is expressed in terms of what we might call today legitimate authority. In the preface dedicated to Prince Philip, who was at that time in charge of matters relating to the Indies, he writes:

> And once Your Highness has seen the deformity of the injustice upon which
> those innocent peoples is done, destroying them and cutting them to pieces
> without cause or just reason for it … I beg Your Highness be kind enough
> to supplicate and persuade His Majesty to deny any man who might propose
> to undertake such noxious and detestable enterprises.
>
> *(las Casas, 2003, p.4)*

This call for justice was a hint of things to come; his most important engagement
with just war occurred at the Valladolid debates in 1550–51.

The context of the Valladolid debates is important to understanding las Casas's
contributions to the just war tradition. After Vitoria's death, Juan Gínes de
Sepúlveda, imperial chronicler to Charles V, attacked the New Laws of 1542,
which, inspired by the arguments of Vitoria, had helped to protect the Indians
from unjust seizure of their lands. Sepúlveda's arguments earned him the wrath of
las Casas, and caused a national controversy. Las Casas feared what might happen if
Sepúlveda's views came to be accepted as the standard of *jus ad bellum*, believing
they would "infect the minds of readers, deceive the unwary, and arm and incite
tyrants to injustice" (*Ibid.*, pp.18–19). In 1550, King Charles V called for the
Valladolid debates to settle the controversy.

Controversies

Las Casas begins his *Argumentum apologiae adversus Genesium Sepúlvedam theologum
cordubensem* (the English version is titled *In Defense of the Indians*), which he
composed for the debates, with a promise to repudiate the four causes of just war
Sepúlveda put forth to justify the conquest of the Indians (las Casas, 1999).[2] To
understand las Casas's contribution to the just war tradition, we need first to revisit
the contribution of Sepúlveda. Sepúlveda's arguments at Valladolid were presented
orally and not transcribed; however, his *Democrates Secundus de justis belli causis*
(*Democrates Secundus, or On the Just Causes of War*) offers a template from which we
can garner his understanding of just war (Sepúlveda, 1984).[3]

Sepúlveda begins by delimiting the "great question" that concerned thinkers of
this time period:

> Whether the war with which the Kings of Spain and our compatriots have
> subdued and look to subdue under their dominion the barbarian peoples
> who live in western and southern region, called communally Indians in
> Spanish is just or unjust, and based on what right can one found an empire
> over these peoples.
>
> *(Sepulveda, 1984, p.1)*

In addressing this dilemma, it is important to note that Sepúlveda clearly knows the
traditional arguments for just war circulating at the time. He turns to Augustine,
St. Isidore and Innocent as his main authorities, explicitly stipulating there is a

difference between waging war for "just causes" compared to war waged for the wrong reasons (*Ibid.*, p.4). Citing Augustine, he asserts war must be waged for the sake of peace (*Ibid.*, p.5). He also recognizes, again citing Augustine, that a just war must be waged with "legitimate authority" (*Ibid.*, p.13), "right intention" (*Ibid.*, pp.13–14) and only if it is formally declared (here he cites St. Isidore) (*Ibid.*, p.13). Among the recognized just causes, he includes: repelling force with force (citing Innocent) (*Ibid.*, p.16), taking back goods wrongfully seized (*Ibid.*, p.17), and punishment for a wrong committed (*Ibid.*). Referring to the collective body of knowledge about just war, Sepúlveda concludes: "these, then, are the 3 just causes of war that St. Isidore enumerated in those few words of his that are recorded and which were passed into the *Decretum* (the *Ecclesiastica Decreta*)". The lasting legacy of Gratian, discussed in chapter 3, as a source of authority can be clearly seen. However, his main argument regarding just war against the New World peoples hinges on four alternatives just causes, "less common", but more directly applicable to the "barbarians" of the New World (*Ibid.*, pp.19–20).

First, the Indians, he submits, are lacking in reason and thus have no concept of good and evil. They therefore have no concept of the rational foundation of human society. Turning to the authority of Aristotle, he then argues that it is just to wage war on those whose natural condition it is to obey others – what Aristotle referred to as the natural slave. It is worth noting that Aristotle was considered an authority on many things, stemming in large part from his incorporation by Aquinas into Christian thought in the 13th century. However, he was not part of the just war conversation per se; one of the first significant references to Aristotle's views on war occurs during the New World controversy in Spain, when theologians at the Junta de Burgos referred to his arguments from Book 1 of the *Politics*. Sepúlveda had translated the *Politics* into Latin, and thus knew it well.[4]

A second just cause applicable to the Indians – for which Sepúlveda finds support in scripture and St. Cyprian – is to eradicate those customs which "distance the [barbarians] from humane and civilized morality, life and culture, and contaminate them with such [nefarious] crimes" – i.e. the practices of human sacrifice and cannibalism that violate the natural law (*Ibid.*, pp.39–45). A third just cause is to save the innocent from "the most unjust of sufferings" and avenge injury to God (*Ibid.*, pp.60–62). Both of these justifications stem, for Sepúlveda, from a reinterpretation of Augustine: while one could argue that the Spanish have no right to wage a just war because they "have not received an injury from the Indians", war is legitimized according to the "definition St. Augustine gives of a just war, that is, war by which one avenges injury" (*Ibid.*, p.60), with the notion of injury open to many interpretations. In this case, the injuries in question are against God and innocents who suffer from barbaric rule. A fourth just cause is to pave the way for the spread of Christianity by removing the barbarians' leaders and instilling Christian rulers (*Ibid.*, pp.64–65). This cause follows from the view that Christianity reflects the natural law, and Christians have a duty to spread the Truth to others.

It is worth noting that, with the exception of the first cause, all these causes were accepted, at least for the sake of argument, by Vitoria. But while Vitoria wavered on whether regime change could be a just cause because it seemed to violate the sovereignty of the Indians, Sepúlveda categorically argues that barbarians who violate the natural law do not have *dominium*.[5] Las Casas, however, disagrees with each of these four causes, and sets out to repudiate them at Valladolid.

Tenets

The arguments of the *Defense*, which las Casas read aloud at Valladolid to a panel of judges over the course of five days, are indicative of early political debates about the rights of the Indians and just war (Hanke, 1974, p.68). They mark an attempt to apply just war principles – at times clarifying their meaning – to a pressing real world problem. Their significance was not, therefore, simply academic. Rather, they were a language of political argument, a critical language used to challenge prevailing views that the conquest was just. Regarding las Casas's *In Defense of the Indians*, Lewis Hanke muses:

> [I]f we could save only one of las Casas's numerous writings, this is the one that would give the world the most universal view of the doctrine that undergirds all the battles he fought as Protector of the Indians. In these pages, the reader sees that combination of legal theory, Christian principles, his special views on the Spanish Conquest, and – especially – his convictions on the capacity of the Indians that endow his words with their enduring vitality
> (Ibid., pp.xiv–xv)

Las Casas believed that war was "a pestilence and an atrocious calamity for the human race". Yet, turning to past authority for support, he recognized that war could sometimes be just. Thus, citing a passage from Augustine quoted in Gratian: "War should be a matter of necessity, so that God may free from need and preserve in peace"; and then referring to Cicero's view from *De Officis*, he recognizes war is unjust unless "unavoidable necessity is so compelling that it cannot be avoided in any way" (las Casas, 1999, p.202). But were the wars against the Indians just?

To answer this question, las Casas begins by rejecting Sepúlveda's first just cause, the view that the Indians were barbarians in the Aristotelian sense, that is, so-called natural slaves against whom a just war could be waged. It is beyond the scope of this chapter to go into the details;[6] however, the thrust of las Casas's arguments is that the Indians are not this kind of a barbarian, but rather, rational beings with sovereignty. And, going a step further than Vitoria, he explicitly states that they have the right to wage a just war against the Spanish in defense of their sovereignty: "Hence every nation, no matter how barbaric, has the right to defend itself against a more civilized one that wants to conquer it and take away its freedom" (las Casas, 1999, p.47, cf. 244–45).

Las Casas then rejects the claim that one can wage a just war to eradicate their barbaric customs (Sepúlveda's second just cause). Such an argument, he clarifies, is applicable only to those who are subject to Christian rulers. This encompassed pagans living in Christian lands and heretics, but not the Indians, who were viewed as in no way living under the jurisdiction of the Crown: "It is not the business of the church to uproot idolatry by force or to punish idolaters, at least if they are not its subjects" (las Casas, 1999, p.65). Note that this argument follows Vitoria, who argued that the Church does not have temporal *dominium* over the entire world, and thus no power to impose rules and punish transgressors. Las Casas writes: "No ruler, whether king or emperor, nor anyone else, can exercise jurisdiction beyond his borders, since borders or limits are so called because they limit, determine, or restrict the property, power, or jurisdiction of someone" (*Ibid.,* p.80). Las Casas even makes a remarkable defense of cannibalism and human sacrifice as rational according to the natural law, at least before Indians come to hear the world of God (*Ibid.,* pp.219–242).

At this point, las Casas begins a long discussion of six possible just causes by which the Spanish could wage a just war against the Indians. He frames his discussion in the context of war as a form of punishment. The first just cause is to take back formerly Christian lands held by unbelievers. Because unbelievers "do continuous injury to us, the Church can actualize the jurisdiction it has over [the lands] in order to regain what belongs to it through force" (*Ibid.,* p.118). The second just cause is to punish pagans who practice idolatry in provinces formerly under Christian control, thus corrupting the region "with evil and hateful vices against nature" (*Ibid.,* p.119). Here, las Casas clarifies the arguments of Hostiensis and Innocent IV, upon whom Sepulveda built his claims; rather than referring to idolatry anywhere in the world, las Casas argues for a more restricted view lest great "absurdities" follow. Both of these just causes have antecedents in previous just war thinking (that it was just to take back by force goods wrongfully seized and to punish those who cause you injury), but are reinterpreted in the context of nascent sovereignty. This restricts the Church's power to punish by war. In the process, las Casas clarifies Gratian (C. 12) and "other canonists" who,

> because they speak generally and without distinctions, confuse matters and darken men's understanding. Because they do not distinguish alien from alien and unbelievers from unbelievers, these men say, with the gloss, that "aliens are under Roman rule [or Empire]". I say that it is stupid to take this in such an absolute case. But since it is incredible that the gloss and those who make similar statements have fallen into this error, we must say that the gloss is to be interrupted as referring to aliens … who live within the provinces of the Church or in the territories of Christian rulers or because they hold lands taken from Christians since those realms are included within the limits of Roman rule that do not go beyond the limits of the Christian people.
>
> *(Ibid., p.151)*

This sort of correction of canonical authorities is important to note. Las Casas recognized the authority of previous thinkers we now consider part of the just war tradition – e.g. Augustine, Aquinas, Gratian, Vitoria who are all discussed in this volume – but he was not afraid to reinterpret their views when he thought they were too vague, and thus liable to being misinterpreted and applied erroneously.

Another key example of this is las Casas's clarification of Vitoria. Las Casas criticizes Sepúlveda for "claiming the very learned Father Francisco de Vitoria approved the war against the Indians" to strengthen his claims. Instead, he points to the "Catholic way [Vitoria] refutes the seven headings by which war against the Indians might seem just" (*Ibid.*, p.340). Las Casas then attempts to clarify the ambiguities in the potentially just causes Vitoria discusses, admitting Vitoria "is a little more careless … regarding some of those titles since he wished to moderate what seemed to the Emperor's party to have been rather harshly put" (*Ibid.*, p.341). As Alex Bellamy shows in his chapter in this volume on Vitoria, las Casas is referring to Vitoria's argument in favor of regime change and saving the innocent, which could be read as justifying humanitarian wars that violated the Indians' sovereignty (Vitoria, 1991, pp.287–289). Yet, las Casas emphasizes that Vitoria speaks "conditionally, fearing that he might suppose or make false statements instead of true ones", meaning that the arguments would not apply "if the circumstances that this learned father supposes are false" (las Casas, 1999, p.341). Las Casas's reinterpretation of the situation, based on his own experience in the New World – Vitoria had never been – attempts to show why the circumstances are indeed false.

A third just cause is to punish certain types of blasphemy: war can be waged against those who are "maliciously, knowingly, and insultingly blasphemous … by speaking out of hatred and contempt for the Christian truth" (*Ibid.*, p.165). The case of blasphemy requires a deeper inquiry because it seems quite open to abuse; however, delving more deeply into las Casas's analysis, we discover some interesting insights. Chief among these is that his first reaction to a potential injury warranting war as a response is introspective. He thus asks his countrymen to inspect their own actions and motives in order to understand the grievances of the Indians, and see if their resistance is warranted:

> So Christians, stop deluding yourself with these pretenses … Let those keep silent who are swollen with foolish learning and who encourage tyrants to persecute innocent sheep by claiming that the latter kill preachers of the faith … they kill those who give them reason for killing … they kill them not because they are preachers but because they are Spaniards, of the same nation, and in the same company of those fierce men who are their enemies.
>
> (*Ibid.*, p.172)

While las Casas has no doubts that the Spanish were culturally superior, this does not provide a moral blanket that denies the Indians the right to self-defense: even if the Indians were to "kill two hundred thousand preachers, and even if they were to kill the Apostle Paul and all the other gospel-preaching followers of Christ", war would not be justified against them if they were provoked or waged a war in self-defense (*Ibid.*). Moreover, if unbelievers "speak blasphemously about the Christian religion not out of contempt and hatred of religion but out of anger toward

Christians by whom they have been maltreated and injured … such persons are not blasphemous" (*Ibid.*, p.165).

Las Casas shows himself open to the possibility that justice may be on the side of the Indians because the conquistadors "slander the Christian religion by their evil lives, their monstrosities, their savagery, and their pride" (*Ibid.*, p.166). There is, however a threshold of toleration, such as the case with the Turks who "have a deep-seated wish that the whole religion of Christ had long ago been blotted out, and generally, in every locality and at all times, they do their utmost to perturb the lives of Christians" (*Ibid.*, p.336). In such cases, just war is vindicated. As las Casas argues elsewhere, the Church can punish, with war, the "infidel Turks and Mores for what they are purposefully doing, mocking, prohibiting and defaming the faith which impedes those who would receive the faith from doing so" (las Casas, 1985, p.232).[7]

A fourth just cause is to punish those who "hinder the spread of the faith deliberately and … attack those who wish to embrace it or already have embraced it" (las Casas, 1999, 168). Referencing Gratian (C.23, q.8), las Casas concludes that "this kind of evil cannot be met with any other remedy" except the recourse to war (*Ibid.*, p.168). Here we should not fail to overlook the deep connection to las Casas's just war arguments and Spain's colonial project (Castro, 2007, p.8).[8] "The Church", he writes, "to which belongs the care of peoples throughout the world as regards the preaching of the truth, can justly wage war upon those who prevent the gospel from being preached within their jurisdiction" (las Casas, 1991, p.170). This argument follows that of Vitoria, and there is significant room for ambiguity as it can easily lead to justifying changing the regime of the "barbarians" to ensure the safety of converts. However, las Casas adds important elements that clarify this ambiguity. First, the truth must be preached in the right manner, i.e. in the absence of arms: "I could dare say that to wage war against Indian rulers could not be just at the very outset – rather, it would be unjust – if, from fear of losing their property, they refuse to receive preachers who are accompanied by fierce and barbarous men" (*Ibid.*, p.172). And second, if the rulers and people do not want to listen because they remain devoted to their own religion, "then, under no circumstances, can they be forced by war to let [preachers] come in" (*Ibid.*, p.173). While las Casas sought the spread of Christianity, his experience in the New World showed him that the use force to vindicate the right to preach the gospel caused more harm than good by hindering the spreading of the faith rather than facilitating it.

A fifth just cause is "natural defense", which las Casas imbues with a sense of what we now call *jus ad bellum* proportionality. Citing Aquinas (ST II–II, q.10) that "it is lawful to repel force with force", las Casas argues:

> By the law of nature, the arms of all peoples throughout the world are raised against their public enemies. So, to crush the insolence of such enemies we take them captive, and by inflicting equal destruction we teach them to fear our men and to avoid injuring us so that they pay for the injuries they have inflicted on us.
>
> (*Ibid.*, p.184)

The notion of self-defense was an accepted element in just war thinking, though in extending this right to non-Christian Indians, as mentioned above, las Casas cuts against the grain of the inherited tradition at the time.

The final just cause is a "new case, not heard of until our times": the Church can wage just war against unbelievers "if they are found to oppress and injure any innocent persons or to kill them in order to sacrifice them to their gods or in order to commit cannibalism" (*Ibid.*, p.186). Sepúlveda (his third just cause), like Vitoria before him, justified war to save the innocent, calling it "an obligation of the just and religious prince" (Sepúlveda, 1984, p.62). For Sepúlveda (and Vitoria), saving the innocent was coeval with removing their tyrannical regimes and installing morally good ones. Las Casas, even though he embraced the Christian ethic of love towards one's neighbor, all but rejects this view. His first-hand experience with war in the New World led him to recognize a twofold danger in positing saving the innocent as a just cause.

First, in terms of physical damage, such wars lead to the death of other innocents. Las Casas recognized the restraining intent of *jus in bello* found in the canonical texts – he cites Gratian as proof that the innocent should be spared (to the extent possible) from the engulfing violence of war. However, he nevertheless worries that war's fury cannot fully be controlled because it is sometimes difficult to distinguish the innocent from oppressors (las Casas, 1999, p.212). This leads him to part ways with Vitoria. Vitoria had also recognized it was unlawful to kill innocents intentionally, but surmised that war could be justified if necessary to remove the obstacles to the faith and if the positive results of war outweighed the evils caused by any subsequent collateral damage (Vitoria, 1991, pp.285–286; 316). Las Casas, however, does not agree with this logic. Rather, when good and evil are intertwined, it is best to avoid the evil of war despite the good it might produce. Thus, where the hardships of the innocent persecuted by the regime "cannot be avoided by any remedy other than war, we are bound by the natural, human, and divine law to tolerate and overlook them lest a countless number perish" (las Casas, 1999, p.213).

Second, las Casas upholds that war will hinder the spreading of the moral good. Rejecting Sepúlveda's fourth just cause (war to pave the way for spreading the Faith), las Casas argues that "anything should be tolerated to avoid waging war, the sea of all evil ... for this is not helpful to the spread of the gospel" (*Ibid.*, p.248). Spreading universal values by war creates hatred for those wielding the power because of the death and destruction war inevitably produces. The problem for las Casas is that this method gives no sense of credibility to the values being spread, but sends instead a message of hypocrisy. He concluded that the result of a war justified by this cause would be that "the Indians will never accept the truth of Christianity if they are hardened [against it]" (*Ibid.*, p.247). Influenced by his experience of the horrors of war in the New World, las Casas brings to our attention that war inevitably tarnishes the image of our values, for those whose ideas are "accompanied by the clatter of arms ... by that very fact are unworthy to have their words believed' (*Ibid.*, p.173). These are powerful statements about the dangers of linking humanitarian goals to just war.

In sum, las Casas did not think the war against the Indians was justified. With passing reference to Aquinas (ST II–II, q. 40) and Augustine quoted in Gratian (C. 23), he concludes:

> Therefore, since war should not be waged unless there has first been a provocation by the person against whom warfare is being prepared toward the one who is waging the war, it follows that war against the Indians is unlawful. This conclusion has also been proved from many arguments that have been offered previously in this work. However, war against them could be just if they committed something found in the six cases we listed above.
>
> *(Ibid., p.355)*

It is important to realize that he did not rule out war altogether, but rather, turned to the just war principles, reinterpreting some of them, to argue that in this specific case war was not justified.

Legacy and enduring relevance

Las Casas's legacy for the development of the just war tradition is largely non-existent. He is not cited by later parts of the tradition as a source of authority or inspiration. That said, I do want to highlight several substantive contributions that showcase his enduring relevance, and then reflect on what the legacy of his struggle to defend the rights of the Indians means for the just war tradition.

The Affair of the Indies was a tumultuous period that was hugely influential on the formation of just war thinking as we understand it today. Like Vitoria, las Casas was at the forefront of an important shift in just war thinking, and his challenge to existing ideas about the legitimacy of war should not be underestimated. Of these, his rejection of war for the sake of religion and his recognition that "barbarians" could wage a just war against Europeans reflect nascent conceptions of sovereignty that shaped the way the West would come to theorize just war in the ensuing centuries. His use of past authorities on just war within the new framework of sovereignty demonstrates the continuity of the tradition as a language to engage pressing political ideas across very different periods of history. His reinterpretation of certain authorities is also significant, supporting the view that just war is a language that needs to be continuously updated; for las Casas, it is significant that his own experience with unjust war as a witness to its negative effects influenced how he reinterpreted the principles of just war. This is something we should always keep in the back of our minds when embroiled in modern day controversies about this or that war.

As for las Casas's legacy, it should come as no surprise that he was not viewed favorably by many of his contemporaries. Las Casas was a controversial figure during his lifetime. His defense of the New World natives was at times provocative, his refusal to give communion to certain conquistadors downright polemical, and some of his political projects questionable. The upshot is that he made himself a fair share of enemies, both intellectually and politically (Comas, 1971). This bad blood, as it were, permeated the historical works in his native Spain that recounted the events of the conquest in the ensuing century. The chronicles that tended to laud the reputation of the conquistadors had, by contrast, a negative, or rather dismissive, view of las Casas. But in time, his legacy grew.

In the French Enlightenment, an era we now associate with the triumph of reason and the belief in progress that informed (European) notions of good government and human rights, Voltaire admired las Casas's defense of the Indians, praising him for "having the courage to plead the case" of the Indians when no one else did. The most staggering portrait of las Casas's legacy is that of the Abbé Raynal:

> He speaks, he acts, he summons his nation to appear in front of the tribunal of the entire universe, he makes both hemispheres shake in horror. Oh las Casas! You were greater in your humanity than all of your compatriots put together in their conquests ... We will see you interposed between the American and the Spaniard, presenting, to save the former, your chest in front of the sword of the latter.
>
> *(Raynal, 1781, pp.480–481)*[9]

What does such praise have to do with the just war tradition? I think it is important to recognize that posterity recorded las Casas as interposed between the swords of the conquistadors and the hearts of the innocent. As the study above has shown, his weapon was the language of just war, which he used to make the case against war. Many contemporary critiques of the just war tradition focus on the manipulability of its language to justify any kind of war (Myers, 1996); however, the example of las Casas highlights the critical power of the just war tradition to make the case for not going to war.

The critical intent is particularly powerful in the case of las Casas's arguments against waging war to save the innocent. In his time, this marked a challenge to the authority of the venerable Vitoria, and the elements of Christian thought (see the historical chapters on Augustine and Aquinas, and the contemporary chapter on Johnson) that saw just war as a transformative means to *tranquillitas ordinis*, the tranquility of a just political order (Johnson, 2005). In the contemporary era where the norm of the Responsibility to Protect draws the link between just war and saving the innocent, las Casas's reflections, shaped by his own terrible experiences with war, offer an alternative critical line of argumentation. It is also pertinent to rethinking the use of force as a vehicle to spread the "best values". His framing of just war as a punitive enterprise – a view of just cause that has largely been eschewed in contemporary thinking, but which he saw a way of restraining the destructiveness of war – invites us to question the relationship between just war and the spread of our moral values, whatever they may be. Ultimately, las Casas reminds us that before striking out against the cruelty of others and using force to try to transform them, we must first of all look deeply inwards to recognize our own barbarism in the midst of war.

Notes

1   For a good general discussion, see (Hanke, 1949)
2   The manuscript was not published in las Casas's lifetime; it only came to print in 1992; All references to this work are from this edition (las Casas, 1999).
3   All references to this work are from the (Sepúlveda, 1984) edition; all translations are my own.
4   It is beyond the scope of this chapter to delve into the details of Sepúlveda's appropriation of Aristotle. I direct the reader to a rich scholarship on what was a very controversial claim. A good starting place is: (Pagden, 1986).
5   In the original manuscript of the *Democratus Secundus*, Sepúlveda makes a note in the margin referring to the mistaken arguments of Vitoria regarding the sovereignty and rights of the "irrational" Indians under the law of nations (p.57).
6   See the discussion in (Brunstetter and Zartner, 2011).
7   My translation.
8   For a complex discussion of las Casas's struggles with the relationship between war, ethics and identity than can be given here, see my own book (Brunstetter, 2012, Ch. 4).
9   My translation.

Works cited

Brunstetter, Daniel. 2012. *Tensions of Modernity: Las Casas and His Legacy in the French Enlightenment*. New York: Routledge.

Brunstetter, Daniel and Zartner, Dana. 2011 Just War Against Barbarians: Revisiting the Valladolid Debates Between Sepúlveda and Las Casas. *Political Studies*. **59**(3), pp.733–752.

Castro, Daniel. 2007. *Another Face of Empire*. Durham: Duke University Press.

Comas, Juan. 1971. Historical reality and the detractors of Father Las Casas. In Friede, Juan and Keen, Benjamin. eds. *Bartolomé de las Casas in History: Toward an nderstanding of the Man and his Work*. DeKalb: Northern Illinois University Press, pp.487–539.

Hanke, Lewis. 1949. *The Spanish Struggle for Justice in the Conquest of America*. Philadelphia: University of Pennsylvania Press.

Hanke, Lewis. 1974. *All Mankind Is One*. DeKalb: Northern Illinois University Press.

Johnson, James Turner. 1981. *Just War Tradition and the Restraint of War*. Princeton: Princeton University Press.

Johnson, James Turner. 2005. Just War, As it Was and Is. *First* **149**(January), pp.14–24.

las Casas, Bartolomé de. 1985. *Obra indigenista*. Franch, José Alcina. Ed. Madrid: Alianza Editoria.

las Casas, Bartolomé de. 1999. *In Defense of the Indians*; Poole, Stafford. trans. DeKalb: Northern Illinois University Press.

las Casas, Bartolomé de. 2003. *An Account, Much Abbreviated, of the Destruction of the Indies*. Indianapolis: Hackett Publishing Company, Inc.

Myers, Robert. 1996. Notes on the Just War Theory: Whose Justice, Which Wars?. *Ethics & International Affairs* **10**(1), pp.115–130.

Nederman, Cary. 2000. *Worlds of Difference: European Discourses of Toleration, 1100–1550*. State College PA: Penn State University Press.

Orend, Brian. 2006. *The Morality of War*. Peterborough, Ontario: Broadview Press.

Pagden, Anthony. 1986. *The Fall of Natural Man*. Cambridge: Cambridge University Press.

Pagden, Anthony. 1991. Text and Experience in the Writings of Bartolomé de las Casas. *Representations* **33,** pp.147–162.

Raynal, Guillaume-Thomas. 1781. *Histoire philosophique et politique des établissemens et du commerce des européens dans les deux Indes*, 10 vols. Genève.

Sepúlveda, Juan Gínes de. 1984. *Democrates Segundo o de las Justas causas de la guerra contra los Indios*. Losada, Angel. Trans. Madrid: Consejo Superior de Investigaciones Científicas.

Sorabji, Richard. 2006. Just War from Ancient Origins to the Conquistadors Debate and its Modern Relevance. In Sorabji, Richard and Rodin, David. Eds. *The Ethics of War: Shared Problems in Different Traditions*. Burlington: Ashgate Publishing Company, pp.13–29.

Vitoria, Francisco de. 1991. *Political Writings*. Pagden, Anthony and Lawrance, Jeremy. Eds. Cambridge: Cambridge University Press.

Walzer, Michael. 2004. *Arguing About War*. New Haven: Yale University Press.

8

FRANCISCO SUÁREZ (1548–1617)

G. Scott Davis

Introduction

Francisco Suárez was born 5 January 1548 to a prosperous family in Granada, the last of the Moorish enclaves of medieval Spain.[1] The city had been returned to Christian rule in 1492. As part of the treaty negotiated between the Catholic rulers, Ferdinand and Isabella, and the Emir of Granada, all Granada's Jews were required either to convert or to leave the country. After early training in Granada, he began reading canon law at Salamanca in 1561 (Scorraille, 1913, vol. I p.30). He was received into the Society of Jesus in 1564, and began his teaching career in 1571, at the age of 23.

In 1564, the Society of Jesus was less than 25 years old. Officially recognized in 1540, the society began to establish schools of its own in the late 1540s. "The Jesuits", as one commentator puts it, "combined the best of different traditions: their lower faculty of languages, literature and rhetoric was largely adopted from the Humanists, while the higher faculties of arts (or philosophy) and theology were modeled on the Aristotelian philosophy and Thomist theology of Paris" (Simmons, 1999, p.522). At Salamanca, in particular, the Jesuits were influenced by "the brilliant revival of Aquinas initiated there earlier in the century by Francisco de Vitoria, Domingo de Soto, and others" (O'Malley, 1993, p.249). It was there that Suárez began his philosophical studies, moved to theology, and then began a peripatetic teaching career that took him from Salamanca to Segovia to the Collegio Romano, where he was Professor of Theology from 1580 to 1585. From there he moved to Alcala and then, at the insistence of the Spanish King Philip II, to the Prime Chair at Coimbra, where he finished his career. Suárez died in Lisbon on 25 September 1617 (Scorraille, 1913, vol. I, pp.xix–xxi). His views on just war hold an important place in the tradition as perhaps the first author to specifically talk about the three phases widely recognized today, the *jus ad bellum*, *jus in bello*, and *jus post bellum.* While a student of Aquinas and Vitoria, both of whom he engages frequently, he was not afraid to depart from their ideas in certain circumstances.

Texts and contexts

Before delving into Suárez's treatment of war, it will be helpful to get a broader understanding of his larger opus. Suárez's first published volume, *On the Incarnate Word*, appeared in 1590. The first of his *Metaphysical Disputations* came out in 1597 and *On Laws and on God the Lawgiver* in 1612. The last volume published during Suárez's life was *On the Defense of the Catholic Faith*, which appeared in 1613 as an answer to James I's attack on English Catholics. Further works, often based on his lectures, began appearing immediately after his death, including *Three Books on Grace* (1619, 1651), his commentary on Aristotle's *De Anima* (1621), and *The Three Theological Virtues: On Faith, Hope, and Charity* (1621). It is in the discussion of charity that we find his explicit discussion of just war.

Suárez was widely read throughout Europe for the next century and a half. Louis Loemker writes of the *Metaphysical Disputations* that they were studied "at most of the universities, Catholic or Protestant, taught to Descartes at La Fleche, [and] read by Leibniz as a boy as if it were a novel (so he says)" (Loemker, 1972, p.20). The first edition of his collected works, however, only appeared between 1740 and 1751, in 23 folio volumes. The Vives edition, which remains the standard, but not critical, edition of Suárez's works, appeared from 1856–78 (see Scorraille, 1913, vol. II, 403ff.).

It is clear that Suárez's publications were often motivated as much by ongoing academic disputes as by his systematic lecturing schedule. It is equally clear, however, that the editors of the Vives edition intended to present Suárez as a systematic thinker in the mode established by Thomas's *Summa theologiae.* Thomas had become a major authority after his death, and such a presentation would not have been surprising. Thus the first three volumes track topics from the first part (Ia) of the *Summa*, while volumes four through nine correspond to the first part of Thomas's second part (IaIIae). In particular, volume four contains *On Man's Ultimate End, On the Will, Goodness and Malice, Virtues, and Vices, or Sins*, a volume that was issued posthumously in 1628 at Lyons. This represents the first 89 questions of Thomas's work. It is followed by *On the Laws, and on God the Lawgiver*, which covers in part question 90–108 of *Summa Theologiae IaIIae*. This, in turn, is followed by three volumes on grace, equivalent to Thomas's last five questions.

The volumes that correspond to the second part of the second part (IIaIIae) – the core of Thomas's moral theology – capture even less of Aquinas's substance (also see chapter 4 of this volume). *On Faith, Hope, and Charity* (1621) brings together material on which Suárez first lectured in 1583–84. It covers roughly questions 1–43, ending with a disputation on war that goes well beyond Thomas's discussion in IIaIIae 40. Four volumes follow this on religion and the religious life, ending with a discussion of the Society of Jesus, expanding on Thomas's questions 80–100 and 183–189. There is no independent discussion of the cardinal virtues, which Thomas treats in more than 100 questions, including such important topics as homicide and self-defense (IIaIIae 64, 7), private property and exigent circumstances (66, 7), truth and deception (109–111), and the kinds of lust (154).

There are several conclusions to be drawn from this, the most obvious being that Suárez never intended, and certainly never achieved, a systematic moral theology along the lines of Thomas Aquinas, although Aquinas was clearly an important figure in shaping his thought. Second, while volume four seems to provide at least the foundations of an ethical theory grounded in Thomas's account of virtue, there is no reason to believe that it is continuous with the account of law that follows immediately in volume five. That account emerged from the perceived need to counter the "Lutherans" and other heretics, and their attacks on the origins of political society. And, finally, it is not clear where Suárez stands in the tradition of moral theology that runs from Thomas to Vitoria and Soto. In terms of just war, this suggests one should read his ideas with one eye towards the authorities of the past, and another towards how Suárez sought to offer innovative answers to classic questions.

Regarding the past, consider the role of Aquinas in shaping Suárez's thought. The moral theology of Thomas Aquinas is grounded firmly in the moral psychology of Aristotle. Understanding virtue and vice meant understanding the nature of human action. Penitents wanted to know exactly how it was that they sinned, and what was necessary to stay on the gospel path. "The ethical analysis found in the *summae confessorum* (compendiums for confessors) … replaced the crude schedules of misdeeds and penances found in the penitential handbooks of earlier centuries" (Chenu, 1968, p.229). There was no finer or more authoritative account of human virtue than Aristotle's, and when Thomas embraced it he was not "baptizing" the Philosopher in order to make him safe for Christians. "Rather", Chenu concludes, "he was giving supreme expression to that Christianity in which a return to the gospel had secured for the believer a presence in the world, for the theologian a mature awareness of nature, and for the apostle an effective appreciation of man" (*Ibid.*, p.238).

As a manual for Dominican brothers, the *Summa theologiae* was designed to train preachers in how to clarify doctrine and search conscience. Two examples should suffice. IIaIIae 64, 7 asks whether or not it is acceptable to kill in self-defense. There is no simple yes or no, because killing is a complex notion. If you are attacked it is reasonable to defend yourself, and in the course of that defense it may happen the attacker dies. But if the defense was proportionate to the attack and if you did not intend to kill, then the death is outside of your intention and no blame attaches to your actions. In 66, 7, Thomas asks whether it is acceptable to steal in cases of necessity. Here the answer is a clear no; theft is an unjust taking and it is never acceptable to commit an evil to achieve even a good end. But, if another party has more than enough to satisfy his needs, and if he refuses to recognize your need, and if the need is truly dire, then it is reasonable to relieve your need by the taking of his goods. In fact, this is not an instance of theft. How do we know whether our defense is proportionate or that it is reasonable to take these particular things from this particular person? Through the exercise of justice and right reason.

This is the approach to practical understanding developed by Vitoria (chapter 6) and Soto, to which Suárez was exposed in his theological training.[2] In the 14th and 15th centuries, the second part of the *Summa theologiae* circulated independently as a manual of ethics. During Vitoria's training in Paris, in the second decade of the 16th century, his teachers had substituted, contrary to official statute, lecturing on the *Summa* instead of *The Sentences* of Peter Lombard, and Vitoria continued this practice when he became first chair at Salamanca. Thus Suárez was fully grounded, early on, in this Thomist tradition often referred to as the "second scholastic". It would appear to be the model for his own moral theology, as brought together in volume four of the Vives edition. Suárez seems, for example, to be following Thomas's account of acts that may be indifferent in themselves, but which are made either good or evil as a result of their circumstances (Suárez, 1878, IV, pp.415–424). And he seems also to be following Aquinas in the origins and division of the virtues (*Ibid.*, pp.455–504). But because there is no exposition of the cardinal virtues it is not clear what role, if any, they play in allowing the agent to recognize and pursue good ends. This work seems to be done by the discussion of law. In fact, Thomas Pink and Terence Irwin, writing in one of the most valuable recent collections on Suárez, take it for granted that his ethics centers on law and obligation in ways that run contrary to the tradition of Thomas and Vitoria (Schwartz, 2012, chaps.6 & 7).

Thomas turns to law in IaIIae 90, immediately after the discussion of vice and sin. Because human virtue is imperfect, the internal motivation it should provide must be supplemented by the external motivation provided first by law (pp.90–108) and subsequently by grace (pp.109–114). Ralph McInerny thinks of natural law as pointing us toward the human ideal, and notes that: "St. Thomas sometimes uses the traditional four cardinal virtues to point to constituents of the human good. Wisdom, justice, temperance, and courage aim at goods that are major constituents of man's ultimate end" (McInerny, 1997, p.47). An alternative would be to say that the natural law comprises the judgments that would be made by the fully informed individual of perfect virtue. Under neither characterization is natural law a book of rules, accessible either through logical analysis or appeal to the innate promptings of conscience. But in Suárez this is beginning to change (Gordley, 2012). And the reasons for this change are closely tied to the religious conflicts of the 16th and early 17th centuries.

Controversies

Quentin Skinner writes that the Thomist tradition, from Vitoria on, "aims to repudiate not merely the Lutheran conception of the Church, but the whole vision of political life associated with the evangelical Reformation" (Skinner, 1978, II, p.138). Among the problematic doctrines are *sola scriptura*, total depravity, the claim that all Christians are fully priests and fully kings, and "the idea that the true Church consists of nothing more than a *congregatio fidelium*" (*Ibid.*, p.146). By rejecting the tradition of biblical interpretation, the Reformers make it impossible to distinguish sound doctrine from whatever some eccentric chooses to maintain. The combination of total depravity and the equality of all Christians portends the fragmentation of the Christian community into contending groups whose claims are only justified by the insistence that they themselves are the community of the saints. From the perspective of Vitoria, Soto, and Suárez (among others), the Lutheran revolution is a challenge to the very possibility of a rational Christian community.

This worry in uppermost in Suárez's mind when he writes that, "the heretics of the present age hold that just men are exempt from the yoke of the law; nor are they speaking simply of human law, as some persons believe, but rather of law in the absolute sense, a fact which may clearly be inferred from the fundamental principles that they uphold" (Suárez, 2015, p.143).[3] Against this, Suárez argues that natural law is "in men, in whose hearts that Lawgiver Himself has written it, as Paul says, and that, by means of the illumination of the mind, as is intimated in Psalm iv" (*Ibid.*, p.205). Because God writes the natural law in the human heart, it follows that the power to establish human law is "a characteristic property resulting from nature", albeit, "this power does not manifest itself in human nature until men gather together into one perfect community and are politically united" (*Ibid.*, p.438). Consequently, it is possible for fallen humans to formulate law that is consistent with God's will for them as political animals. Thus it is false, as the Lutherans contend, "that man is unable, due to his fallen nature, to understand the will of God and so to live his life according to a genuine law" (Skinner, 1978, II, p.166).

Skinner notes the emergence of three related disputes in which Suárez took a leading role. First, there are the teachings of the humanists, in particular Erasmus. Erasmus was involved in re-editing the Latin Bible in the light of the new philology and expanded access to the primary texts. As with Luther's rallying cry of "sola scriptura", this project called into question more than a thousand years of biblical teaching and commentary, thus putting the teaching authority of the Church at risk. "His other error", as Skinner puts it, "lay in his ideal of religious education – his quasi-Lutheran suggestion that the laity should be taught by means of a catechism of faith (a *methodus*), and that the clergy should be further educated by means of compulsory Bible studies" (*Ibid.*, p.141). This risked subverting Church teaching and authority at least as much as the new edition of Scripture.

A second set of humanists were using secular arguments, drawn from Aristotle and the Roman historians, to argue that the natural degeneracy of the newly conquered peoples of the Americas and "reasons of state" licensed what traditional moral theology considered gross violations of justice.[4] "Reasons of state" are associated with the emergence of Machiavelli and the debate over republican virtue and statecraft. "The early Jesuit theorists", Skinner continues, "clearly recognized the pivotal point at which the political theories of Luther and Machiavelli may be said to converge: both of them were equally concerned, for their own very different reasons, to reject the idea of the law of nature as an appropriate moral basis for political life" (*Ibid.*, p.143). A major impetus to grounding all of ethics and politics in the paradigm of law is to thwart the subversion of classical virtue by the self-interest of communities and their leaders.[5]

Finally, Skinner suggests that in the efforts to establish a political theory grounded in the law of nature, the Jesuits in particular are moving toward the notion of human beings in the "state of nature". While Suárez tends to use variations on "power from the very nature of things" (see, for example, 1878, IV, p.173), Skinner notes that "Molina, for example, refers at several points to the condition of mankind '*in statu naturae*' and he imagines the '*status naturae*' as that situation in which all men may be said to have found themselves after the Fall and before the inauguration of political societies" (Skinner, 1978, II, p.155). The inner impetus, after the Fall, to ground political community in the natural law makes perfectly good sense in light of a God who writes that law is in the heart, but Suárez does three things that will cause problems down the line. First, he breaks the continuity between the family and the imperfect community of the village, on the one hand, and the genuinely political community, on the other. Second, he ignores the cardinal virtues, the foundations of which are laid in those imperfect communities. And, third, he now finds it impossible to explain what motivates the creation of a genuine political community. "As Suárez puts it", writes Skinner, "our natural condition is one in which 'each private individual will be concerned only with his own private advantage, which will often be opposed to the common good'"(*Ibid.*, p.160). Without the full panoply of the virtues, as Gordley recognizes, "conclusions about natural law were no longer to be reached by practical reasoning or prudence as Aquinas understood it. Nevertheless, Suárez was unclear as to how they are to be reached instead" (Gordley, 2012, p.220).

These broader controversies are important to grasp when reading Suárez's on just war for they illustrate the intellectual context in which he was writing and teaching. Unlike for Vitoria and Las Casas, no longer were the debates about the *dominium* of the New World peoples and the justice of the conquest the primary controversy that required engaging the question of just war. Rather, Suárez's ideas on just war were situated in a much larger intellectual moment, to be marked by a shift in moral vocabulary away from the virtue driven language found in Aquinas, towards something new.

Tenets

Suárez follows Aquinas in discussing the notion of just war in the context of charity, in his *The Three Theological Virtues: On Faith, Hope, and Charity*. He divides *Disputation XIII,* "On War", into nine parts, covering the traditional topics. On the legitimacy of war, for example, he affirms canonical tradition that war can be just. The content of his teaching follows closely on Aquinas and Vitoria. War, "absolutely speaking, is not intrinsically evil, nor is it forbidden to Christians" (Suárez, 2015, p.911). Here, he distinguishes between defensive (war to repel an ongoing attack) and offensive war (a punitive response to the refusal to redress past wrongful harms), and insists that the latter "is not an evil in itself, but may be right and necessary … in order to ward off acts of injustice and to hold enemies in check. Nor would it be possible, without these wars, for states to be maintained in peace"

(Suárez, 2015, pp.914–915). Without losing sight of protecting the commonwealth, what is becoming important is the ability of the ruler to maintain order.

With the questions of *jus ad bellum*, Suárez begins to forge his own just war ideas. The first two conditions he postulates are indistinguishable from those of Aquinas and his predecessors: "First, the war must be waged by a legitimate power; secondly, the cause itself and the reason must be just". Regarding legitimate authority, Suárez distinguishes between supreme princes and subordinate princes. His concern with the stability of political order and the chain of command leads him to qualify the position of Vitoria on the propriety of inferior princes declaring war. Suárez concludes that when a war is waged without legitimate authority of the supreme prince, it is against both justice and charity (Suárez, 2015, pp.918–919).

In terms of just cause, Suárez takes up questions familiar from the chapters on Gratian and Aquinas regarding self-defense of the commonwealth, taking back goods wrongly seized and responding to *injuria* through punishment. Following Vitoria, he rejects difference in religion, sins against nature, the belief that the Pope was ruler of the world, and that unbelievers are barbarians without *dominium* as just causes (see chapter 6). Suárez observes that just war exists because there is no higher tribunal to administer just punishment for injuries committed. He recognizes instances when the right to war should be abandoned. For example, he argues that offensive war should only be undertaken if there is a reasonable hope of victory: "A prince who declares war is bound to attain the maximum certitude possible regarding victory. Furthermore, he ought to balance the expectation of victory against the risk of loss, and ascertain whether, all things being carefully considered, the expectation is preponderant" (Suárez, 2015, p.937). This criterion seems to apply only to offensive war when the risks associated with war are a matter of choice; for in defensive war, the risks are a necessity.

Suárez follows Vitoria in approving war in defense of the innocent, noting that "there is no ground for war so exclusively reserved to Christian princes that it has not some basis in, or at least some due relation to, natural law, being therefore also applicable to princes who are unbelievers" (*Ibid.*, p.942). While believers and unbelievers alike may justly intervene to save the innocent, Suárez notes that it can be just for a Christian prince to intervene on behalf of those who wish to convert, but are prevented from doing so by infidel princes. This is true only for Christian princes, because preventing someone from embracing "the law of Christ does indeed involve grievous injustice and harm, whereas there is no injury at all in prohibiting the acceptance of another law" (*Ibid.*).[6]

Regarding the third condition, Suárez does mark an important expansion of Aquinas, for where the latter merely demands "right intention" generally, as the condition under which the good is to be pursued, Suárez writes that, "thirdly, the method of [war's] conduct must be proper, and due proportion must be observed at its beginning, during its prosecution, and after victory" (*Ibid.*, p.916). Here Suárez makes explicit what some modern commentators have failed to notice, namely that right intention must define not only the choice to go to war, but must be maintained throughout the prosecution of the war and its aftermath because it is the intention that places an act in its moral species.

When Suárez takes up proper conduct in war (the *jus in bello*), he notes that the prince, his military leaders, and the rank and file soldiers,

> May be considered in certain specific relationships. First, with respect to the enemy, that is to say: how may these classes justly conduct themselves toward the enemy? Secondly, with respect to their mutual relations: how should the king conduct himself toward his soldiers? Thirdly, how should the soldiers conduct themselves toward their kings? Fourthly, how should they conduct themselves toward other persons, for example, those persons in whose houses the soldiers are quartered during the march?
>
> *(Ibid., p.955)*

If proper intention is maintained, "the necessary means to that end are also permissible; and hence it follows that in the whole course, or duration, of the war hardly anything done against the enemy involves injustice, except the slaying of the innocent" (*Ibid.*, p.958–959). This seems clearly to articulate the distinction between enemy soldiers and non-combatants, although he does allow for collateral damage under conditions of necessity.

The implication is that there is no clear distinction between *jus ad bellum* and *jus in bello*; the prosecution of the war is dependent on the continuing right intention of the prince and his army even into the *post bellum* phase. There is, however, a distinction between the non-combatants and their property. Suárez observes that it has become part of the *ius gentium* that "since the soldiers' lives are exposed to dangers so numerous and so grave, they should be allowed something; and the same is true of their prince" (*Ibid.*, p.959).

This centrality of intention is further affirmed in Suárez's discussion of war's end.[7] Not only is the prince allowed "to inflict upon the conquered state such losses as are sufficient for a just punishment and satisfaction, and reimbursement for all losses suffered", but "if all the penalties just enumerated seem insufficient in view of the gravity of the wrong, then, after the war has been entirely ended, certain guilty individuals among the enemy may also, with justice, be put to death" (*Ibid.*, p.959–960). Not only does this reinforce the classical emphasis on retribution (as opposed to reconstruction, which is the favored *jus post bellum* position of today), it also lays the foundations for a concept of war crimes and war trials. And finally, "although the slaying of a great multitude would be permissible only when there was most urgent cause, nevertheless, even such slaughter may sometimes be allowed, in order to terrify the rest" (*Ibid.*, p.960). While this may seem a perverse consequence, it suggests at least a word of restraint against such military leaders as the Duke of Alba, who allowed his unpaid troops to sack the Dutch city of Mechelen in the summer of 1572. "The desolation was so complete", according to one eyewitness, "that not a nail was left in a wall" (Parker, 1994, p.49). In any case, Suárez insists that, "all of these passages must be interpreted in conformity with the rule previously laid down, namely that a just equality must be preserved, and regard must be had for the future peace" (Suárez 2015, 960).

Legacies

If you no longer believe in a natural law, written by God in the heart of each human being, but if you remain wedded to an account of ethics grounded in the legal paradigm, then "why be moral?" becomes a pressing question. Elizabeth Anscombe famously recommended that modern moral philosophy drop the legal paradigm and return to Aristotle (Anscombe, 1981, p.41). Thomas Pink attempts to show that Suárez develops a "force model" of natural law that distinguishes him from what becomes modern moral philosophy, but it is unclear how successful this argument is (Hill & Lagerlund, 2012, chap. 8). What is clear, though, is that Suárez stands on the cusp of a shift in moral vocabulary away from the virtue driven language that Aquinas, Vitoria, and Soto take from Aristotle and toward a legal paradigm that will play out in different ways in Grotius, Hobbes, and the theorists of the social contract. By their insistence on an exclusively legal paradigm, Suárez and his Jesuit followers have unwittingly set the stage for what will become a distinctively modern problem.

Gregory Reichberg, in "Suárez on just war", expands upon this shift by noting the prominence of "jurisdiction" in Suárez, whose analysis has "a distinctive legal coloration" (Schwartz, 2012, 192). Identifying proper jurisdiction, as Reichberg correctly sees, makes it possible to maintain order and to clamp down on warlike inclinations. "A civil authority alone", he writes, "is empowered to administer penalties for wrongdoing, especially when these involve the imposition of physical harm" (*Ibid.*, p.189). Reichberg notes that, "Suárez was aware that an alternative approach could be found in the legal literature" (Schwartz, 2012, p.195). In the emerging notion of sovereignty, which would be codified thirty years after Suárez's death with the Peace of Westphalia, when two princes, neither subordinate to the other, both claimed a serious grievance and there was no higher authority to adjudicate, just war becomes, *de facto*, "an equivalent for public war (*bellum publicum*), a war waged between independent nations or kings, each of which recognizes the sovereignty of the other" (*Ibid.*, p.196). From the Westphalian era on, this view "was in the ascendency and the doctrine of just war in decline" (*Ibid.*, p.203). Reichberg is surely correct that this departs from Suárez's ideal, but he does not, I think, adequately acknowledge Suárez's contribution to this transformation.

When he discusses the law of nations, Suárez concludes that determinations of the substance of our obligations and prohibitions are a matter of natural law and "accordingly, it is from this standpoint that the *ius gentium* is outside the realm of natural law" (Suárez, 2015, p.384). While a detailed reading of Suárez on the law of nations is beyond the scope of this chapter, he seems, in remarks such as this, to be moving away from any idea that the law of nations could have more binding power than pacts and treaties. This will ultimately place sovereign nations in a realm of customary law when it comes to international disputes. Arguments and counter-arguments drawn from the natural law and just war traditions will devolve into what one might call the "checklist" model, where each side counts off its own view of where just cause lies. Suárez's move toward the legal model in his discussion of just war, cut off from the exercise of virtue, drives justification toward the adversarial style of the law court. Disputation XIII, Section 7 – "What Is the Proper Mode of Conducting War?" – illustrates this nicely. "Before the war is begun", writes Suárez, "the [attacking] prince is bound to call the attention of the opposing state the existence of a just cause of war, and to seek adequate reparation therefor" (*Ibid.*, p.956). This having been done, the aggrieved must wait for the response of its adversary, "and if the other state offers such adequate reparation, he is bound to accept it ... If, on the other hand, the opposing prince refuses to give satisfaction, the first prince may begin to make war" (*Ibid.*). The rest of the section lays out rules for what may and may not be done in similar fashion. This would seem to lay the foundations for the "regular war" which Suárez is, as Reichberg notes, at pains to reject.

In 1934, James Brown Scott wrote, with characteristic flourish, that when Grotius encountered the work of Vitoria:

> The great jurist of Holland had at hand – and indeed before his eyes – a system of international law express in its fundamentals and implicit in its consequences: the first sketch, as an architect would say, of the Temple of International Justice to which Grotius was to add with his own hand the details of the completed drawings.
>
> *(Scott, 1934, pp.287–288)*

For half a century or more, Scott's vision of a continuous development, running from Vitoria through Suárez to Grotius, held interpretive sway. By the 1990s, however, Richard Tuck was writing of Grotius that, "far from being an heir to the tradition of Vitoria and Suárez, as was assumed by writers at the beginning of this century, he was in fact an heir to the tradition Vitoria most mistrusted, that of humanist jurisprudence" (Tuck, 1999, p.108). Some hint of why Vitoria mistrusted the lawyers comes out in recent remarks by an international lawyer:

> The laws of armed conflict provide a lexicon for figuring out what will be understood to apply and be legitimate – but only if we think of those rules through the eyes of those we would like to validate our actions ... The transformation of the law in war into a vocabulary of persuasion about legitimacy can erode the sense of professional and ethical responsibility for our decisions.
>
> *(Kennedy, 2006, pp.140–141)*

Lawyers have a fiduciary responsibility to their clients and the adversarial system insures that the client gets the full measure of his lawyer's skill. But, at the level of ethics and moral theology, this can drive a wedge between virtue and professionalism.

The lesson for interpreting the just war tradition seems clear. Even if unintended, adopting the legal paradigm puts justice and charity at risk, and perhaps we should see the breech with Vitoria beginning not, as Tuck would have it, with Grotius, but with Suárez.

Notes

1   All modern biographies of Suárez are dependent on de Scorraille 1913. This includes the popular biography of Joseph Fichter 1940, which may nonetheless be consulted for a quick introduction to Suárez's various controversies. Recent summaries may be found through sydneypenner.ca (see references) and in Schwartz 2012, chap. 1.
2   On Vitoria see Davis 1997; on Soto, Davis 2001. Some background on the distinctively Spanish origins of their discussion of war may be found in Davis 2012. These matters are not beyond controversy. For discussions focusing on the language of rights and its development, see Tierney 1997 and Brett 1997.
3   Originally commissioned by the Carnegie Endowment for International Peace, and published in 1944, this volume contains a substantial, but not complete translation of *De Legibus* (3-752), selections from books III and VI of *Defensio Fidei Catholicae* (755-828) and selections from *De Fidei* and *De Caritate* (831-989). Given that this is the most widely available source for Suárez in English, it seems helpful simply to cite the page numbers of this volume. Excerpts from these texts have also been reproduced in Reichberg, Syse, and Begby (2006).
4   In the chapters on Vitoria (chapter 6) and las Casas (chapter 7) in this volume, we indeed see varied responses in the context of just war that refute the arguments about the degeneracy of New World peoples, with which Suárez largely agrees.
5   On Aristotle and natural slavery, see Davis 1997 & 1999; Suárez endorses Vitoria's position on the illegitimacy of treating unbelievers as natural slaves at Suárez 2015, 941. On republican virtues and reasons of state see Viroli 1992 & the various essays in Skinner 2002.
6   Las Casas, discussed in chapter 7, challenges the points that Vitoria makes here.
7   Note Suárez's views on the ending of war in relation to Kant's (chapter 13), whose views on *jus post bellum* are discussed.

Works cited

All contemporary students of Suárez owe a tremendous debt to Professor Sydney Penner, who has developed a comprehensive website – sydneypenner.ca – with links to Suárez's Latin texts, select translations, introductory material, and a comprehensive bibliography. The following are exclusively titles cited in this essay.

Anscombe, G.E.M. 1981. Modern Moral Philosophy. Reprinted in *The Collected Philosophical Papers of G.E.M. Anscombe, v. 3: Ethics, Religion, and Politics*. Minneapolis, MN: University of Minnesota Press, pp.26–42.
Brett, Annabel S. 1997. *Liberty, Right, and Nature: Individual Rights in Later Scholastic Thought*. Cambridge: Cambridge University Press.

Chenu, Marie-Dominic. 1968. *Nature, Man, and Society in the Twelfth Century: Essays on the New Theological Perspectives in the Latin West.* Taylor & Little. trans. Chicago: University of Chicago Press.

Davis, G. Scott. 1997. Conquest and Conscience: Francisco de Vitoria on Justice in the New World. *Modern Theology.* **13**(4), pp.475–500.

Davis, G. Scott. 1999. Humanist Ethics and Political Justice: Soto, Sepúlveda, and the 'Affair of the Indies'. *Annual of the Society of Christian Ethics.* (19), pp.193–212.

Davis, G. Scott. 2012. Angles of Influence: Jihad and Just War in Medieval and Early Modern Spain. In Hashmi, Sohail. ed. *Just Wars, Holy Wars, and Jihads.* Oxford: Oxford University Press, pp.125–145.

Fichter, Joseph H. 1940. *Man of Spain: Francis Suárez* New York: MacMillan Co.

Gordley, James. 2012. Suárez and Natural Law. In Hill & Lagerlund. eds. *The Philosophy of Francisco Suárez.* Oxford: Oxford University Press, pp.209–229.

Hill, Benjamin & Henrik Lagerlund, eds. 2012. *The Philosophy of Francisco Suárez* Oxford: Oxford University Press.

Hoffman, Tobias, Jorn Muller, & Mattiaas, eds. 2013. *Aquinas and the Nicomachean Ethics.* Cambridge: Cambridge University Press.

Kamen, Henry. 1997. *Philip of Spain.* New Haven: Yale University Press.

Kennedy, David. 2006. *Of War and Law.* Princeton: Princeton University Press.

Loemker, Leroy E. 1972. *Struggle for Synthesis: The Seventeenth Century Background of Leibniz's Synthesis of Order and Freedom.* Cambridge, MA: Harvard University Press.

Lynch, John. 1992. *The Hispanic World in Crisis and Change, 1598–1700.* Oxford: Blackwell
McInerney, Ralph. 1997. *Ethica Thomsitica: The Moral Philosophy of Thomas Aquinas.* rev. ed. Washington, DC: Catholic University of America Press.

O'Brien, T.C., ed. 1974 *Summa Theologiae, vol. 31: Faith* London: Eyre & Spottiswoode.

O'Malley, John W. 1993. *The First Jesuits.* Cambridge, MA: Harvard University Press.

Parker, Geoffrey. 1994. Early Modern Europe. In Howerd, Michael, Andreopoulos, George J. & Shulman, Mark R. eds. *The Laws of War: Constraints of Warfare in the Western World.* New Haven: Yale University Press, pp.40–58.

Schwartz, Daniel. ed. 2012. *Interpreting Suárez: Critical Essays.* Cambridge: Cambridge University Press.

de Scorraille, Raoul 1913. *Francois Suárez, de la Compagnie de Jésus, d'après ses lettres, ses autres écrits inédits et un grand nombre de documents nouveaux,* 2 vols., Paris: Lethielleux, 1912 & 1913 (These volumes have been digitalized, along with the Spanish translation of 1917 and may be accessed through the Hathi Trust website).

Scott, James Brown. 1934. *The Spanish Origins of International Law: Francisco de Vitoria and His Law of Nations.* Oxford: Oxford University Press.

Simmons, Alison. 1999. Jesuit Aristotelian Education: The *De Anima* Commentaries. In O'Malley, John W. et al., eds. *The Jesuits: Cultures, Sciences, and the Arts, 1540–1773.* Toronto: University of Toronto Press, pp.522–537.

Skinner, Quentin. 1978. *The Foundations of Modern Political Thought,* 2 vols. Cambridge: Cambridge University Press.

Skinner, Quentin. 2002. *Visions of Politics, v. II: Renaissance Virtues.* Cambridge: Cambridge University Press.

Suárez, Francisco. 1878. *Opera Omnia.* Andre, A. D. M. et al., eds. 28 vols. Paris: Vives, 1856–1878 (several versions of this may be accessed on line from sydneypenner.ca).

Suárez, Francisco. 2015. *Selections from Three Works.* Pink, Thomas. ed. reprinting the Carnegie text of Williams et al. Indianapolis, IN: Liberty Fund.

Tierney, Brian. 1997. *The Idea of Natural Rights: Studies on Natural Rights, Natural Law, and Church Law, 1150-1625*. Atlanta, GA: Scholars Press.

Tuck, Richard. 1999. *The Rights of War and Peace: Political Thought and the International Order from Grotius to Kant*. Oxford: Oxford University Press.

Viroli, Maurizio. 1992. *From Politics to Reason of State: The Acquisition and Transformation of the Language of Politics, 1250-1600*. Cambridge: Cambridge University Press.

de Vitoria, Francisco. 1932. *Comentarios a la Secunda secundae de Santo Tomas, v. 2: De Caritate et Prudentia (qq. 23–56)*. Heredia, Beltran de. ed.Salamanca: Biblioteca de Teologos Espanoles.

de Vitoria, Francisco, 1991. *Political Writings*. Pagden, Anthony & Lawrence, Jeremy. eds. Trans. Cambridge: Cambridge University Press.

de Vitoria, Francisco. 1997. *On Homicide & Commentary on Summa theologiae IIaIIae, Q 64*. Doyle. ed. & trans. Milwaukee, WI: Marquette University Press.

de Vitoria, Francisco. 2013. *De iustitia/Uber die Gerechtigkeit*, v. 1. Steuben ed. & trans. Stuttgart:frommen-holzboog Verlag.

9

ALBERICO GENTILI (1552–1608)

John Kelsay

Introduction

Of the various contributors to just war thinking in the early modern period, Gentili is probably the least well known. Certainly that is true among Protestant authors. While Grotius acknowledged the work of Gentili in the preface to his own great work – his "Labour has been serviceable to others, and confess it has been to me," he downplayed the importance of his predecessor. He thus writes: "he is often wont to follow either a few examples that are not always to be approved of, or even the Authority of modern Lawyers in their Answers, not a few of which are accommodated to the interest of those that consult them" (Grotius, 2005, p.110). For a variety of reasons, Gentili's most important contribution – the work known as *De Iure Belli Libri Tres* or "The Law of War in Three Volumes" was largely ignored over the next two and a half centuries, when Thomas Erskine Holland, himself a famous scholar of international law, chose Gentili as the subject for his inaugural lecture at Oxford (Holland, 1898, pp.1–9). Even here, however, the focus was on Gentili as a forerunner of Grotius, rather than as an independent thinker in his own right. Only in the 20th century did scholars begin a serious examination of Gentili's work. The number of such studies remains small, however. And this is unfortunate; as we shall see, Gentili's work addresses a number of issues important to our own time – among others, the place of humanitarian intervention or (as many would put it) of the "responsibility to protect" citizens from the "fury" of their own leaders, the matter of preventive or preemptive uses of force, and the proper mode of settlements following the end of conflict (that is, the *jus post bellum*). Gentili's method in addressing such issues is always irenic, focusing on the notion that human beings constitute a kind of universal community, in which differences of religion, ethnicity, and culture ought never cause us to lose sight of the importance of values such as reciprocity, keeping of covenants, and ultimately, of peace.

Context

As a scholar, Gentili was shaped by – and participated in – a number of important social and cultural developments. Of these, three stand out with respect to his work on war: the influence of humanism in the study of law; the religious controversies associated with the Reformation; and the emergence of England, Spain, and other European states as global powers.

A quick summary of Gentili's biography suggests the importance of each of these developments.[1] Born in San Ginesio, a smallish town in the Italian province of Macerata, Alberico was the son of a physician. As a result, he enjoyed a somewhat privileged beginning, especially with respect to opportunities for education. Having mastered the standard curriculum, he obtained the degree of Doctor of Laws at the age of twenty, and began work as a judge.

In Gentili's day, legal studies followed the pattern set by Renaissance humanists: careful study of classic texts – in particular, the Roman code associated with the emperor Justinian I (527–565). Learning to read such texts in Latin (or sometimes, in Greek) and mastering the various commentaries developed by scholars such as Gentili's Italian predecessor and model, Bartolo de Sassoferrato (1313–1357) prepared one to render judgments informed by precedent, as well as to develop arguments intended to persuade others, not least by way of demonstrating one's historical and philological erudition.

Gentili's career was thus off to a good start, beginning with his election as chief judge of Ascoli, followed by work in his home of San Genesio. Religious controversy soon intervened, however. While the Protestant movement never made great inroads in Italy, small numbers of people did become interested, particularly with respect to the teaching of John Calvin (1509–1563) and other leaders of the Reformed wing of the Reformation. By the 1570s, with authorities in Rome keen to root out such heresies, the Inquisition was very much a force, and Gentili came under scrutiny, along with his father and brother. Fearing for their safety, the three left to seek refuge, first in Slovenia, then in the German cities of Tubingen and Heidelberg (the latter in particular being a center of the Reformed movement). Their stay ended abruptly when authorities in Rome announced the excommunication of Alberico and his family, and the court of the Holy Roman Emperor in Austria – in some sense, in control of the German-speaking territories – followed suit by declaring that the Gentilis should leave or face punishment. While his father and brother seem to have ignored the order (the latter, in particular, going on to a distinguished legal career of his own), Alberico fled to England, where he established relations with a community of other Italians in exile for holding Protestant views. When prominent members of this group brought Gentili to the attention of advisers at the court of Elizabeth I, he received opportunities to work, not least by lecturing at St. John's College of Oxford University. There, Gentili excelled, and soon advanced to become the Regius Professor of Civil Law.

During his career at Oxford, Gentili also worked as a legal adviser to the crown. Beginning in the 15th century, Spain's rise to prominence in Europe and the New

World posed a challenge to other emergent states. Along with the Netherlands, England sought increased influence, not least by interfering with Spanish shipping, and in 1583, the complicity of the Spanish ambassador in a plot to assassinate Queen Elizabeth and to restore the Roman Catholic Queen Mary to power led to a great debate regarding the law pertaining to foreign diplomats. Gentili counselled that the law establishing the inviolability of ambassadors pointed in the direction of expulsion, rather than of death. In part because of this advice, the court "merely" sent Bernardino de Mendoza back to Spain, while the English conspirators (along with Queen Mary) were executed. Not long thereafter, the defeat of the Spanish Armada in 1588, and the corresponding defeat of a similar English expedition the next year signaled a confrontation that would continue throughout the remainder of Gentili's life and would require him to present advice on a number of issues pertaining to the law of war. Indeed, in a strange twist of fate, in 1590 Queen Elizabeth appointed Gentili as the legal representative for the Spanish embassy before the High Court of Admiralty, a role he would continue to play under King James.

Texts

Gentili is the author of a number of texts, many of them produced from lectures given at Oxford. *De Iuris Interpretibus Dialogi Sex* ("Dialogues with Six Interpreters of the Law", published in 1582) makes an argument for the "historical" approach associated with Bartolus, as distinguished from the "philological" approach favored by others. *De Legationibus Libri Tres* ("Three Books on [the laws pertaining to] Legates," published 1585) deals with issues related to the standing of diplomats – as we have seen an issue close to Gentili's practice. *De Iure Belli Commentationes Tres* ("Three Commentaries on the Law of War", 1589) provides the background for Gentili's most important work. *De Iure Belli Libri Tres* ("The Law of War in Three Books") would appear in 1598, while a second work specifically on the law of war as understood in ancient Rome (*De Armis romanis Libri Duo*) was published in 1599. A final work related to Gentili's assignment as the legal spokesman for the Spanish embassy (*Hispanicae Advocationis*) appeared posthumously in 1613.[2]

As noted, the work on the law of war is usually regarded as Gentili's most important contribution. Certainly it is the most noteworthy with respect to the purposes of this volume. The work is quite ambitious. The three volumes are intended to cover the entire range of concerns related to the ethics of war. Volume one deals with resort to war, and thus with the standard *jus ad bellum* criteria of right authority, just cause, and right intention. Volume two covers the *jus in bello* or conduct of war, and volume three deals with the *jus post bellum* or post-war arrangements. Despite such a thorough and erudite treatment of issues, however Gentili's book fell into disuse after the appearance of Grotius' much longer work (see chapter 10 of this volume for Grotius). Why read the predecessor, when (as Grotius himself claimed) one has access to something more complete? I have already suggested that one ought not take Grotius at his word. Gentili himself has a lot to offer. Interestingly, when the aforementioned Tomas Erskine Holland called *De Iure*

Belli and other texts to the attention of his contemporaries, the fiercest criticisms of this proposal came through the Italian Catholic Press, which described Gentili as an apostate and noted that as early as 1603, his books had been included in the Index of prohibited works. The Dutch also expressed dismay, on the grounds of Grotius' presumed superiority. The work finally began to receive the attention it deserved only when a critical edition and translation appeared in James Brown Scott's series Classics of International Law in the early 20th century.

Controversies

De Iure Belli begins with a discussion of the very idea of a "law" of war. To some, writes Gentili, the subject seems problematic, not least because it deals with relations between states. When moral or political philosophers discuss good and evil, they do so with respect to norms expressed in the practice of particular communities. When one moves to the international or interstate level, the existence of such norms is less clear – at least, this is a claim advanced by some who hold that to speak of a commonwealth of nations is to commit a category mistake. For such people, there are no global norms, especially when it comes to war, which involves the issue of survival.

Gentili takes a different point of view. The historical record clearly suggests the importance of a few norms that are basic to the behavior of states. The formal practice of making treaties; provisions for the return of prisoners of war; mutual recognition by sovereigns of various states – these and other practices suggest the importance of reciprocity, among other notions. These point to a conception of justice, which, however roughly, involves an intuition that human beings constitute a universal commonwealth. For Gentili, such basic ideas constitute a law of nature, in the sense that they are so ubiquitous as to suggest that knowledge of and respect for notions of justice and equity are more or less "built into" human nature. An account of the law of war proceeds on these general assumptions. The task of interpreters like Gentili then involves an attempt to work out the import of moral intuitions for particular cases. As he describes it, the law of war is a set of practical judgments, in which one tries to understand the historical record as a set of benchmarks, pointing to better and worse ways of approximating the moral law. A competent jurist wants all the help he or she can get, and so draws on a variety of sources. These include codes of Roman law, as noted above. Ultimately, however, an interpreter of the law of war also seeks wisdom from classical literature, the Bible, the behavior of military and political leaders, and the opinions of contemporaries. The scope of the inquiry is vast, and one should understand that very little in the subject can be certain or absolute. Rather, an account of the law of war involves "plausible" conjectures on the basis of previous experience, and the interpreter aims not at the sort of demonstrations expected of mathematicians, but at "persuasive arguments" able to provide instruction (Gentili, 1933, bk.I p.i).

The law of war is thus a matter of controversy, in and of itself. As Gentili proceeds, we understand his work as an intervention in many of the most important issues of his day. His discussions of religion and religious war provide one example, and his arguments regarding the authority of rulers suggest another.

Given Gentili's personal experience, we might expect concerns about religion to occupy an important place in his work. Remember, though, that the issues were not only personal for him. Controversies about religion were endemic to the 16th and 17th centuries, and indeed, throughout the late medieval and early modern periods. One of the great questions involved the legitimacy of fighting in the name of religion, or to advance religious causes. Those advocating for religious or "holy" war laid claim to important examples, not least from the biblical record of Israel's conquest of Canaan. Since Gentili's position is that the scriptures of the Old and New Testaments provide an important source for the law of war, it is natural for him to take up the case. He does not approve of religious war, however. Instead, the idea of *De Iure Belli* is that even in this paradigmatic case the issues that present a just cause of war are human and thus related to ordinary moral or political behaviors, rather than a matter of a special command of God. Violations of rights of safe passage, of trade, and other "secular" concerns make war legitimate – not differences in religious practice.

This is so, Gentili continues, because the nature of religion places it beyond compulsion. "Religion is a matter of the mind and of the will, which is always accomplished by freedom ... the soul has no master save God only ... Religion ought to be free. Religion is a kind of marriage of God with man ..." (*Ibid.*, p.ix). Everyone declares the wars he or she fights to be holy, and thus that the enemy is godless. But "the dispute is about human justice" (*Ibid.*). The "laws of religion do not properly exist between man and man, therefore no man's rights are violated by a difference in religion, nor is it lawful to make war because of religion" (*Ibid.*). This principle applies to the law of nations, so that wars with non-Christian powers like the Ottoman Turks must be justified through secular appeals. It also applies in domestic matters, so that sovereigns are never justified in authorizing force against religious dissenters, unless or until there is evidence of behavior by which the state will suffer harm.

For Gentili, delimiting the role of religion in war is an important part of the jurists' task. Theologians, he writes, only confuse the issue when they argue that war is a matter of divine judgment. While ultimately that may be the case, attempts to guide the behavior of states ought not rest on such matters. "Let the theologians keep silence about a matter that is outside of their province" (*Ibid.*, p.xii).

Gentili's condemnation of the idea that religion constitutes a just cause of war is thus far-reaching, going beyond the dictum of his Roman Catholic predecessor Vitoria, as well as running up against the consensus of many in his day that rulers possess not only the power, but have a duty to ensure conformity to true religion in political affairs. As one might expect from such an historically minded jurist, however, Gentili does cite precedents from canon law and interpretations of Roman codes. As well, his position mirrors a certain account of the Calvinist understanding of Christian faith that informed his own views. On this understanding, the old tradition by which Moses received the Ten Commandments on "two tablets of stone" suggested a distinction between those directives having to do with true worship and those dealing with human relations – if one likes, between religious duties and moral ones. The law of nature (and thus, the law of nations and of war) writes Gentili, is a portion of divine law "which God left us after our sin" (*Ibid.*, p.i). As John Calvin had it, the fall of human beings from their original, created goodness left them with only the barest intuitions regarding spiritual matters. In moral and political matters, however, there is more to build on, so that one cannot imagine a nation anywhere without some notions of justice and equity. While Calvin himself nevertheless found a way to say that sovereigns should see that insults against true religion are discouraged, some of his followers took the doctrine more in the direction of religious liberty (McNeil, 1960).[3] Gentili's arguments for a secular law of war certainly move in this vein.

As to the authority of rulers, Gentili early on provides a definition of war as "a just and public contest of arms". The reference to a "public" contest points to war as a responsibility of authorities charged with protecting the common good. War "is not a broil, a fight, or the hostility of individuals". It is an affair of state, in which "there is a contest for victory between two equal parties" (Gentili, 1933, bk.I p.ii). Along with many other accounts of just war, Gentili's focuses on conflict between sovereigns.

This leads to a number of particular judgments. For example, public war normally requires a declaration of intent, along with a statement of demands. Here, Gentili repeats a point that goes back to antiquity, though he adds an argument that reinforces the notion that war should be a last resort. The right of sovereigns to authorize armed force stems from the need of human beings to order life cooperatively. Under present conditions, this leaves international politics in an imperfect condition, however; if the sovereigns of two or more states understand themselves to have a just cause of war, there is usually no higher court to which they may refer in order to resolve their differences. A statement of demands or offer of terms provides a chance to avoid the costs of war. Indeed, Gentili argues that rulers should think hard and creatively about ways to put their disputes to arbitration, and thus to limit the occasion of armed conflict, not least because it is possible that both sides have some claim to justice.

In cases where one party initiates hostilities, the requirement of a declaration on the part of the state under attack is, of course, mitigated. Nevertheless, the duty of sovereigns to seek a resolution for their dispute remains, so that diplomatic efforts should continue, even as the forces of competing states meet on the plain of battle.

Still other cases involve preemptive or preventive action, in which a sovereign's estimate of the likelihood of attack by a rival power requires that force be utilized while there is still time to head off or deter the enemy's power. In these cases, a formal declaration of war puts the enemy on notice, and presents disadvantages to the cause of justice. Here, Gentili's statements are controversial, and thus it is important to consider the examples he cites. For him, preemptive or preventive war may be justified when the longstanding patterns of an enemy's behavior suggest its leaders "are planning and plotting universal dominion". In such a case, it may be right for a sovereign to initiate armed conflict. Gentili is clear, however – this is not simply to be a matter of suspicion, but rather a response to a situation in which a "just cause for fear is demonstrable". As well, the enemy's drive for universal dominion must involve armed force, say of the type associated with a policy of conquest. A state able to gain even very great power by dint of trade or other means short of war does not come under this heading. For Gentili, the great examples of the day are Turks and the Spaniards, each of which he deems bent on power through conquest (*Ibid.*, p.xiv).

Gentili's emphasis on sovereignty is consistent with the general trend in just war thinking. It leads to negative assessments of individuals or small groups, which claim the right to bear arms. Pirates, for example, are the common enemies of all humankind. Their activities constitute an attack on society as such, and should be suppressed – not as an act of war, but as a kind of law enforcement. Private citizens who consider that they have a grievance against the authorities in their state also do not possess a right of war. Here, however, Gentili takes pains to argue that the prohibition on popular uprisings does not make "sovereigns exempt from the law … bound by no statutes … there must also of necessity be someone to remind them of their duty and to hold them in restraint" (*Ibid.*, p.xvi).

This means that other sovereigns may step in when a ruler behaves in ways suggestive of tyranny – Gentili's term for this is "fury", in the sense of a disproportionate response to complaints or criticisms advanced by citizens. In such situations, the preferred mode of intervention involves diplomatic activity aimed at facilitating a just settlement. Where popular resistance reaches a certain threshold, however, rulers of other states may make use of more forceful means. Part of the problem here is that Gentili holds that all people have a natural right to defend their lives and property when they come under attack. One might put it this way: ordinary citizens do not have a right to make war; but they do have a right to take up arms against an aggressor. In the case Gentili describes, the ruler may be seen as an aggressor. His or her resort to unacceptable levels of force in response to dissent already renders it possible for the rulers of other states to intervene by words. Should the attempt of people to defend themselves reach a certain level, those rulers may consider entering the fray. Once a group possesses power that suggests it is approaching equality with the regular military, the members are more than mere subjects: "they are public characters and on an equality with the sovereign" (*Ibid.*). In such an instance, rulers who intervene on behalf of the people understand that the bonds linking human beings into a global commonwealth are more important than the recognition of a sovereign's right to control his or her territory. There are interesting comparisons to be drawn here with Vitoria's claims about coming to the aid of the innocent or overthrowing barbarian rulers, and how these views may or may not play into colonial discourse.

Legacy and relevance

As noted above, the publication and reception of Grotius' work obscured or elided the important contributions of Gentili. In that sense, talk about the latter's legacy need not take much space. Only in the 20th century did one read accounts in which Gentili is treated in his own right, rather than as a prelude to later authors. In this, the 1968 study by van der Molen still stands as the most complete treatment, so that there remains much to be said (Molen, 1968).

As to relevance, perhaps I have said enough about Gentili's discussions of the issues of his day to point in the right direction. We may begin with the method of *De Iure Belli*. In a time when various forms of realism, idealism, and constructivism present diverse accounts of the nature of international norms, Gentili's account points to something of a middle way. For constructivists, many of whom seem to suggest that justice is more or less a human creation, Gentili's argument that some very basic norms are so ubiquitous as to suggest that they are founded in a common human sociality deserves attention. For idealists who argue that this fact – what one might describe as the un-deniability of normative claims – means that the way forward in law and morality is clear, Gentili's notion that we must search the historical record to discover the most plausible approaches to cases suggests something more complex. For realists who worry that the legal model ignores the ongoing and changing nature of international society, Gentili presents a view of the law of war as responsive to new conditions – as one interpreter puts it, *De Iure Belli* presents the views of an author who "never forgot that a body of rules governing the relations between men or between States is necessarily of an organic nature" (Phillips, 1933, p.51a).

Gentili's approach to religion in international society also seems relevant – for example, in the ongoing conversations regarding jihadist groups. It is worth noting that many contemporary scholars of religion would think that the description of religion as a "matter of the mind and of the will" focuses too much on the individual or subjective aspects of the phenomenon, and overlooks the role of group life in the formation of personal piety. This focus allows Gentili to make some important distinctions, however; and these are echoed in the statements of policymakers who insist that the justification of a military response to al-Qaʿida or the Islamic State group does not rest on the fact that the public statements of jihadist leaders appeal to the Qur'an or other Muslim texts, but rather on the fact that the behavior of these groups violates norms important to international society. If we follow Gentili, this seems a proper move – jihadists may construe the fight as a matter of religion; their opponents in the international community ought not follow suit.

The struggle with jihadist groups also points to the continuing relevance of Gentili's comments about preemptive or preventive strikes and humanitarian intervention. With respect to the former, Mark Totten's 2010 book *First Strike* cites the argument of *De Iure Belli* as an example of the way just war thinking might move from an emphasis on the imminence – in the sense of "liable to occur at any moment" – of a threat as a necessary factor in distinguishing just from unjust preemption to a somewhat more flexible criterion related to the ways an enemy's behavior grounds a well-founded fear of attack (Totten, 2010). While Totten thinks Gentili's treatment leaves the matter too open, so that it is easily abused, he nevertheless argues in ways that build on the historic jurist's work, suggesting the importance of consulting Gentili's work in thinking about one of the great issues of our time.

Similarly with respect to humanitarian intervention, Gentili's account of various modes of intervention ties these to consideration of the nature and scope of conflict within the boundaries of a given state. In one sort of case, the facilitation of negotiations may seem most useful. In others, where the numbers of citizens engaged in efforts against their government suggest that they should be viewed as "public persons" and thus as equal to their rulers with respect to the law of war, military action may be more appropriate, especially if the popular resistance is a response to the ruler's "fury". The contemporary experience with military intervention suggests the need to consider factors that do not come in to Gentili's discussion – for example, the probabilities of success, not least with respect to what happens once fighting ends. *De Iure Belli's* calibration of action to changing conditions on the ground is a good place to start, however, as is putting his ideas into conversation with other thinkers of his time who argued for what we might call humanitarian intervention (Vitoria, chapter 6) and against it (Las Casas, chapter 7).

And that brings us to Gentili's ideas about the end of war. Consideration of the goals of armed force, of how and when to bring wars to an end, the content of a just peace – these are topics contemporary just war thinkers discuss in connection with the *jus post bellum*. As Gentili has it, they are all intrinsic to the law of war, since the aim of any "just and public contest of arms" is peace. In another sense, these topics occupy a distinctive place in the law of war, and deserve a separate treatment. In order to accomplish this, Gentili devotes the entirety of Book III of his work to "the rules of bringing war to an end". His discussion reflects the longstanding emphasis on the role of the victor in setting the terms of peace. Nevertheless, Gentili writes that any just arrangement will take into account the concerns of all sides. Particularly in cases where opposing parties may with some truth claim that their efforts reflected legitimate claims, it will not do for the victorious side to ignore its rival's interests. Looking to the reasons that led to war, victors desire vengeance in the sense of an arrangement that provides redress for harms done, and this, Gentili argues, is legitimate. The matter deserves care, however, since "the nature of victory is itself insatiable ... if the will of the victor controlled everything and the vanquished could lose everything ... there would never be peace, and war would be to the death ..." (Gentili, 1933, bk.III p.ii). To put it another way, those who are victorious in war should keep in mind that their enemies, however misguided, nonetheless remain citizens in the universal commonwealth of human beings.

This means that terms of peace must not only address past harms. They must be crafted with an eye toward the future. What sort of arrangements will make war less likely, and thus preserve what Augustine of Hippo called "ordered harmony"? Gentili is under no illusion that this will be easy. Particularly in cases where one side might be characterized as "barbarians", on the grounds that their actions suggest little if any regard for the norms of war, terms of peace may involve a certain harshness. This is a theme that cuts across several other thinkers in this volume, including Vitoria, Las Casas, and Vattel. One wants to be careful here, however; even an enemy whose fighters violate the criteria of the *jus ad bellum* and/or *jus in bello* nevertheless continues to belong to the commonwealth of nations. Once defeated,

Gentili surmises such a foe should be treated in ways that will prevent the repetition of such wrongs; if possible, through arrangements leading to its reform (*Ibid.*). In other cases, which Gentili seems to regard as more normal, a victor's attempts to display consideration for the honor of defeated forces may well assist the latter to appreciate "the advantages of the peace brought about by their defeat" (*Ibid.*).[4]

Gentili's discussions of the particulars of treaty arrangements, of when it is appropriate to disarm a defeated enemy, and other matters deserve a longer treatment. As well, it seems correct to note that many of the conflicts with which we are currently acquainted are unlikely to issue in the kind of clear victories and defeats he presumes. His statements on the importance of a large vision remain important, however. Let Gentili have the last word:

> … one should ask the question, not what the victor is able to do and what victory may demand, but what befits the character of the victor, as well as that of the vanquished; but in the case of the victor in particular, it should be considered what becomes him and also the nature of the war which is being carried on. But everything must be directed to the purpose of victory, which is the blessing of peace.
>
> *(*Ibid.*)*

Notes

1   See (Grotius, 1898), as well as (Van der Molen, 1968); also the Introduction to Gentili by (Phillips, 1933).
2   Excerpts from these texts have been reproduced in Reichberg, Syse, and Begby (2006).
3   On these aspects of Calvin's thought, see (McNeill, 1960). On the points mentioned, see especially II.vii–viii and III.xix.
4   Here, Gentili is borrowing from Augustine.

Works cited

Gentili, Alberico. 1933. *De Jure Belli, Libri Tres,* (Two Volumes). Rolfe, John C. trans. Philips, Coleman. Ed. Oxford: Clarendon Press.

Grotius, Hugo. 2005. *The Rights of War and Peace.* Indianapolis: Liberty Fund, Inc.

Grotius, Hugo. 1898. *The Law of War in Three Volumes.* Reprinted in Holland, Thomas Erskine *Studies in International Law.* Oxford: Clarendon Press, pp.1–37.

McNeill, John T. ed. 1960. *Institutes of the Christian Religion* (Two Volumes). Lewis Battles, Ford. trans. Philadelphia: The Westminster Press.

Phillips, Coleman. 1933. Introduction to the English translation of Gentili's work: *De Iure Belli Libri Tres.* In Coleman, Philips ed., and Rolfe, John C. trans. Oxford: Clarendon Press, vol. 2, pp.9a–52a.

Totten, Mark. 2010. *First Strike: America, Terrorism, and Moral Tradition.* New Haven: Yale University Press.

Van der Molen, Gesina. 1968. *Alberico Gentili and the Development of International Law: His Life, Work, and Times.* Leyden: A.W.S. Sijthoff.

10

HUGO GROTIUS (1583–1645)

Anthony F. Lang, Jr.

Introduction

Hugo Grotius, the Dutch political and legal theorist of the early 17th century, has long been lauded as a central figure in the just war tradition, largely as a result of his seminal work, *De Jure Belli ac Pacis*, which appeared in 1625.[1] His reputation in the field of international law is equally storied, where he is considered to be one of its founding fathers. Grotius argued that force can be justified on the basis of certain principles that are derived from the nature of the human person. His insights on authority, the just causes for war, and the liability of individuals in wartime are central issues in the conduct of war today.

But not only are his principles still relevant, his way of arguing for those principles speaks to current debates in just war theory and international law. In the Prolegomena of *De Jure Belli ac Pacis*, Grotius cites among the sources he read on just war both Vitoria and Gentili, but downplays the clarity with which they covered the subject (Grotius, 1625 [2005], pp.109–110). Moreover, the evidence he marshals for his arguments was not confined to the Christian scriptures or Church Fathers, which had been the primary sources for previous contributors to thinking about these matters; he also drew on numerous historical examples and Ancient Greek and Roman thought. In so doing, he combined normative and empirical resources to make his arguments. This foreshadowed international legal arguments, which rely on moral principles and the practices of states. Today, questions of legal fragmentation bedevil the discipline of international law (Koskiennemi, 2006). While the just war tradition is faced with contending approaches from revisionists and traditionalists (see chapters 16 and 19 in this volume on Walzer and McMahan respectively), Grotius' way of dealing with the diversity of sources in his day provides an insight into how we might also make arguments about the use of force in the modern world.

This chapter will also acknowledge that while Grotius should continue to be read, there remain controversies around his work. In fact, these controversies are not just unique to Grotius but are at the heart of how we think about the use of force in the current order. Two in particular are worth mentioning. First, based on the diversity of sources on which he drew, scholars of international law and international relations argued that Grotius "secularized" the just war tradition and international law. In recent years, however, this claim has been challenged by scholars who have noted the centrality of theology to Grotius' arguments (Jeffrey, 2006). In his lifetime, he was well known for one text, *De Veritate Religionis Christianae*, or *On the Truth of Christianity*, published in 1627 (Grotius 1627 [2012]); in fact, this text has been translated and reprinted more than *De Jure Belli ac Pacis* (Nellen and Rabbie, 1994, p.vii). His religious beliefs were a crucial part of his ideas, yet his ability to integrate those ideas into a broader natural law framework enabled him to speak across these different traditions. Debates about the role of religious belief in modern discussions of just war remain important, and Grotius' approach to these matters is one from which we may continue to benefit.

A second question raised about Grotius arises from the economic and political context within which he developed his ideas. *De Jure Belli ac Pacis* draws on his earlier work, *De Jure Praedae*, or *The Law of Prize and Booty* (Grotius 1604 [2006]). This text was written by Grotius at the request of his employer, the Dutch East Indies Company, to defend the company's capture of a Portuguese ship near the island of Sumatra in modern day Indonesia. This work links Grotius to a colonial enterprise that, some have argued, implicates not just him but the early modern origins of international law (Keene, 2002; van Ittersum, 2006). This modern day critique is not just about Grotius but about the wider discourse of international law and the just war tradition. That is, are efforts to moderate the use of military force best understood as efforts by powerful colonial actors to ensure that they remain in power within the wider global system? This same question can be posed to thinkers of the late medieval and early modern period, such as Vitoria (chapter 6) and Las Casas (chapter 7), whose writings emerged in the context of the Spanish "discovery" and colonization of the New World.

Thus, even the disagreements about his work point us to the importance of Hugo Grotius. Grotius' ability to bring together a vast range of theological, philosophical, literary, and historical works in support of his attempt to make sense of war provides a model for what just war theorists should do and the difficulties of so doing.

Contexts

Hugo Grotius was born on Easter Sunday, April 10, 1583.[2] He was a child prodigy, reading in Latin and Greek at the age of 8, and soon thereafter composing poetry in Latin. Grotius studied philosophy, classical philology and Oriental languages (Hebrew and Arabic) at Leiden. He did not complete his degree because he was asked to accompany a delegation to France following the issuing of the Edict of

Nantes by Henri IV, the King of France, in 1598, which sought to give rights to French Protestants. Grotius was asked to accompany the delegation in part because of the patronage of Johann van Oldenbarneveldt, the Land's Advocate for Holland, an important political position within the Dutch Republic. When Grotius was presented to the king on their visit, Henry IV famously called him the "miracle of Holland" as a result of his already precocious reputation in philosophy, theology and verse.

In 1598, he obtained a degree in civil and cannon law from the University of Orleans, and was admitted to the bar of Holland in 1599, allowing him to practice law in the Republic. In 1604, he was asked by the Dutch East Indies Company, a quasi-public structure by which the Dutch pursued their trade and colonial enterprises in the East Indies, to write a defense of the company concerning the seizure of a Portuguese ship in the East Indies region. This led to the publication of *De Jure Praedae*, which set out his ideas about natural law and the use of force (Grotius, 1604 [2006]). A small section of this longer book was published in 1608 as *Mare Liberum*, or *The Free Seas*, which defended the right of free trade and movement on the high seas (Grotius, 1608 [2004]). In 1607, he was appointed advocate general in Holland, along with being named the official historian of the Netherlands. Through his association with van Oldenbarneveldt, Grotius became embroiled in a religious controversy that erupted during this time around the issue of predestination in the Calvinist faith of his homeland. His later publication of *The Truth of the Christian Religion* can be read as an intervention not in wider debates about Christian and non-Christian traditions but as arising from this particular conflict with the Dutch Calvinist tradition (Antognazza, 2012, p.x). Van Oldenbarneveldt and Grotius, along with a number of others, fell on the wrong side of the debate and were accused of treason. Van Oldenbarneveldt was executed, while Grotius was sentenced to life in prison in 1619. His confinement, though, was not harsh. His wife was allowed to live with him and he was given access to his books and writing materials, allowing him to continue to write, including material that eventually made its way into *De Jure Belli ac Pacis*.

He escaped prison in 1621 hidden in a box that had been used to bring him books. He fled to France, where King Louis XIII gave him a stipend and the means to continue his scholarship. It was only four years later that he published *De Jure Belli ac Pacis*, translated as either *The Laws of War and Peace* (Grotius 1625 [2012]) or *The Rights of War and Peace* (Grotius, 1625 [2005]). It was dedicated to Louis, undoubtedly in gratitude for being able to live and work unhindered by the theological and political conflicts of his home. In 1635, he was appointed the Swedish ambassador to France. In 1645, on a trip to Sweden to defend himself against concerns about his appointment, he died after his ship wrecked near the city of Rostock on the Baltic Sea. He was buried in Delft, where the Dutch authorities gave him an honorary funeral though they had forced him to flee the city years before.

Before discussing the specific texts for which Grotius is known, it is perhaps worth saying something about the intellectual and political context within which he was educated and worked. First, two broad streams of thought shaped the intellectual context: a classical heritage drawn from Greek and Roman philosophy and the Christian heritage of his Dutch context. These two streams were both in transition in Grotius' lifetime. His education in law, politics and ethics took place in the shadow of Aristotle, the Ancient Greek philosopher. Aristotle's ideas about logic, science (or natural philosophy), ethics and politics were the background condition for scholarship throughout Europe (and the Islamic world to a lesser extent). The influence of Aristotle, however, was leavened by other traditions of thought from the classical era such as the Stoicism of the Roman philosopher Cicero. Indeed, Cicero's influence can be seen in the text of *De Jure Belli ac Pacis*, especially on matters of political community and war. This classical heritage was used by Renaissance figures to create a humanist tradition, which sought to integrate the Christian and classical without drawing on the authority of the Catholic Church. Rather, it brought to life the classical heritage of Greece and Rome through its philosophy, art, and literature.

Alongside of this humanist tradition sat the Christian tradition of theological reflection and Biblical exegesis. Thomas Aquinas, the 13th century theologian and philosopher, had synthesized Aristotle and Christian belief, creating what came to be known as the Scholastic tradition. This tradition influenced Grotius through such individuals as Francisco Vitoria (chapter 6), the 16th century theologian whose reflections on war in the context of discovering the New World shaped the just war tradition. Another important figure from the Scholastic tradition was Francisco Suárez (chapter 8), who overlapped to some extent with Grotius, but whose orientation was much more within the Scholastic tradition. This tradition helped to shape a particular "Spanish" approach to the just war and international law more generally, one that differed from Grotius' use of historical examples and focused more carefully on the normative principles of natural law (Scott, 1934).

As a Protestant, however, Grotius was not tied to the Catholic Church's embrace of the Scholastics. Instead, in his theological writings, Grotius sought to find ways of negotiating the conflicts within the Protestant tradition and between it and Catholicism. Grotius was, in fact, writing during a time of not only intellectual, but also political and even military conflict arising from these differing beliefs. The Thirty Years War (1618–1648) resulted from conflicts between Catholics and Protestants, although these overlapped with political conflicts among dynasties in Europe. In *De Jure Belli ac Pacis*, Grotius argued that war can never be justly fought to promote a particular faith, a position seemingly at odds with the world around him, though one that shares common ground with arguments made by Vitoria a century prior. As noted above, his efforts to find a singular Christian faith were well known and received with the publication of *The Truth of Christian Religion* in 1627. The argument Grotius uses in this text reflects his wider natural law method. The book begins with a proof of the existence of God, and then moves through proofs of the specifics of the Christian religion. From the outset, though, he employs the model of the natural law thinking of the Stoics. He starts by noting that the origin of the world reflects a universal "reason" which is none other than

God (Grotius, 1627 [2012], p.37). His argument does not rely solely on reason but is supported by "evidence" from the different creation stories of which he was familiar; across these different traditions, he finds similar stories with the idea of a "wind across the waters" creating order from chaos, the flood story, and even similar stories of circumcision as are found in the Hebrew scriptures. These claims rely on his wide reading of travellers' accounts along with his ability to read the original Hebrew and Greek scholarship of his day. In fact, such an approach might be seen as parallel to his efforts to combine historical context with moral principles in his reflections on war.

The second context to understand is the political and economic one in which Grotius worked, specifically the political relationship of the United Provinces to each other and to the Spanish Empire; and the economic context of the Dutch East India Company as a quasi-political entity engaged in the use of military force against the Portuguese in the East Indies region.[3] These two contexts shaped the background structure against which Grotius developed his ideas. They are also important to recognize in the context of Grotius' contribution to the just war tradition. What we can see in these two contexts is how Grotius was writing and thinking in the midst of a more complex political environment than theorists of the just war tradition assume. More specifically, Grotius wrote in a context in which the political authority of the Dutch Republic was emerging from the shadow of the Spanish Empire and the power of the Dutch Republic depended on the Dutch East Indies Company.

The first political context is the emergence of the Dutch Republic. In 1551, Philip II of Spain inherited the provinces of the Netherlands, which roughly correspond to the Netherlands and Benelux countries of today. The social and political conditions of the Northern provinces were based on a series of overlapping political structures, with a great deal of power remaining in the cities of the different provinces. As statehood became more centralized in places like Spain, England and France, the provinces retained political structures that were "medieval, political and administratively atomised" (Wilson, 1968 p.8). The Union of Utrecht in 1579 brought together the seven Northern Provinces, led by the wealthiest Holland, into a defensive alliance against the power of Spain.

As a number of historians have emphasized, this union was not one that led to a single unified state (Tracey, 2008; van Geleren, 1993). While there existed the office of Stadholder, originally the lieutenant of the Hapsburgs in the region who became the military leader of the republic after the revolt led by William of Orange in 1566, the true power rested in the States General, or meeting of the delegates of the seven provinces that took place in the Hague. One historian notes that rather than a parliament, this institution was more like a meeting of allies, with the requirement that any decision be unanimous rather than the result of the majority. This structure was even more surprising in light of the vast diversity of economic power between the leading provinces such as Holland and the smaller ones. This constitutional structure gave more power to "local liberties at the expense of central direction" (Haley, 1972, p.67). In other words, Grotius lived in and worked within a political order closer to the early United States or even the current European Union in which sovereignty was not located in a single clearly defined agent but was constituted by overlapping and sometimes conflicting structures and institutions.

The second political context is Grotius' relationship to the mercantile company that dominated the expansion of Dutch trade throughout the world in the 17th century. Dutch economic power emerged in the late 16th century, as they became a pivot in the trade system of Europe, buying goods from the Baltic regions and selling them to Spain, France and England. Not only did they trade in the north, however; the various Dutch republics soon expanded into the Mediterranean as well, again serving as middlemen in the trade system of Europe. Eventually, they expanded to Africa, the Caribbean, and the East Indies (Israel, 1989). It is their expansion into the East Indies that is most relevant for Grotius. In the 1590s, Dutch merchants realized the potential profits to be found in the spice trade from the region. The primary competitor was the Portuguese crown, which controlled most of the economic activity within the region. In contrast, Dutch merchants acted on their own, pursuing profits through investment companies that combined the interests of merchants, investors and the political leadership. After competition among the Dutch merchants for the trade increased in the last years of the 16th century, they turned to the leaders of Holland for help. This resulted in the creation of the United Dutch East India Company in 1602. The company was unlike previous economic organizations, however. As with the Dutch political structure, this mercantile company, which became the engine for Dutch economic expansion in the East Indies, was decentralized. Importantly, as well, it was a quasi-governmental structure. While not controlled by the Dutch republics, it was incorporated by the state of Holland that also invested in it.

Even more important for the purposes of this chapter, the Dutch East India Company used military force in pursuit of its interests in the region. Grotius' patron, van Oldenbarnvelt, encouraged the Company to establish military bases to counter the power of the Portuguese. As one historian puts it, "As far as the States of Holland and Zeeland were concerned, the VOC [the Dutch acronym for the company] was an arm of the state empowered to deploy armies and navies in Asia in the name of the States General and to conduct diplomacy under the States General's flag and seal" (Israel, 1989, p.70).

As described above, Grotius' role in the company was in his capacity as a lawyer who wrote in defense of its use of force in a particular conflict with the Portuguese (van Ittersum, 2006). In 1602, he wrote a legal defense of a Dutch merchant who had captured a Portuguese ship carrying a significant amount of goods from the East Indies. Grotius' defense of this individual became the core of what he called *De Indiis*, but what has become known as *De Jure Pradea*. In 1608, the company requested that Grotius take this text and turn it into a pamphlet in the context of the ongoing dispute between Portugal and the company. This request produced *Mare Liberum*, for which Grotius became quite famous in his day and which many believe influenced the ideas behind his *De Jure Belli ac Pacis*. This text formed the basis of Grotius' ideas about the freedom of the seas, arguing that no state could control them, as the Portuguese claimed, along with important insights into the justification of military force. It is interesting to note that Grotius' conception of what justified the use of force was in defense of a non-state actor, a point that runs counter to the state centrism of modern just war theory (Walzer, 1977). While the Dutch East India Company was one of the first such mercantile companies, it was not the only one to emerge in Europe. As Janice Thomson describes it, these mercantile companies while at first created by states soon needed to be controlled by the state in order that they base their sovereignty on the control of violence, making them an important part of the creation of a sovereign state system (Thomson, 1994).

These two political contexts are important in understanding not just the reasons why Grotius undertook the arguments he did (Tuck, 1999). They are also important in that they speak to concerns and issues that are still with us today. The international political order is formally one of sovereign states with the ability to use force. But it is informally defined by groups and agents, which make claims to be able to use force, from non-state actors to supranational organizations. Grotius may not specifically guide us on whether or not the African Union can undertake military action in defense of human rights, but his arguments and contexts are diverse enough to remind us that simplistic arguments confining the use of force to the modern nation-state may not define the limits of what is possible or morally justified even at the heart of the just war tradition.

Texts

There are a number of texts for which Grotius was known in his lifetime and which continue to deserve our attention. The most important, though, is *De Jure Belli ac Pacis* published in 1625. The core question that Grotius wished to answer in this text is whether or not war can be justified. This is, of course, a question that is still asked today, and it is part of the reason why Grotius' work continues to be referenced and seen as a source of great importance for those working in the fields of the just war tradition and international law.[4]

De Jure Belli ac Pacis is divided into three books along with a Prolegomena or prologue. The Prolegomena provides the basis for the text as a whole, building upon the natural law arguments of his previous works. Book I defines war and political concepts such as justice and sovereignty. Book II explores the reasons for war, with a focus on the three traditional causes of war: self-defense, retaking of property unlawfully taken, and punishment of wrongdoing. Book III examines what may be justly undertaken in war, or what is today called *jus in bello*.

The Prolegomena establishes his understanding of natural law. Grotius' contribution to the natural law tradition was to explore morality in the context of one of the least law-bound human practices, war. Natural law refers to the idea of law that exists prior to any formal law-making process. It is meant to be the source or foundation of laws that are made by people. It is an immutable moral code that is universal for all peoples across all times and places. It is not particular to any religious or moral tradition, but many traditions integrate it into their teachings. While our questions today may be about the reality of this law and its relationship to both analytical philosophy and modern science, the questions of Grotius' day were more about whether or not such laws could be found in religious scriptures or in the use of our reason alone. Grotius argued that there was no clash between natural law and the beliefs of a Christian:

> Natural right is the Rule and Dictate of Right Reason, shewing the Moral Deformity or Moral Necessity there is in any Act, according to its Suitableness or Unsuitableness to a reasonable nature, and consequently that such an Act is either forbid or commanded by GOD, the Author of Nature.
>
> *(Grotius, 1625 [2005], pp.150–151)*

In exploring the relationship of Christian theology to natural law, Grotius also became the subject of some controversy. He wrote the following sentence, which later became known as the Impious Hypothesis: "And, indeed, all we have now said would take place, though we should even grant, what without the greatest Wickedness cannot be granted that there is no God, or that he takes no care in human affairs" (*Ibid.*, p.89). The challenge Grotius presented to the solely Christian conception of natural law did not rely only this sentence, but the fact that he drew upon classical Greek and Roman writers and, most controversially, the practices of states both ancient and contemporary as evidence for the reality of natural law. This controversy, however, may have been constructed by those wishing to tarnish Grotius' legacy in relation to his Christian theological writings or even his political opponents (the two were often interrelated, as noted above). That is, this distinction did not really demonstrate that Grotius failed to believe in the Christian religious tradition, but only that he did not see a conflict between natural law and divine law on matters of central importance to the human condition (Jeffrey, 2006).

Grotius also made an important contribution to the natural law tradition by both differentiating it from but also linking it to the tradition of *ius gentium*, or the law of nations. This concept, as Stephen Neff has argued, was not the positivist tradition of international law, which relies on the unilateral actions of states. Rather, it was the rules of behavior among states that arises from agreements among them and so is located in the actions of individuals rather than the "fabric of the universe" that defines pure natural law (Neff, 2014, p.46). Grotius argued in the Prolegomena that natural law was not the same as the law of nations, but together they reinforced the idea there are rules and laws that govern the conduct of communities when they wage war. He uses both in response to the argument that we should ignore the laws of nature and nations for our own advantage:

> For as he that violates the Laws of his Country for the Sake of some present Advantage to himself, thereby saps the Foundation of his own perpetual Interest, and at the same time that of his Posterity: So that People which violate the Laws of Nature and Nations break down the Bulwarks of their

future Happiness and Tranquillity. But besides, though there were no Profit to be expected from the Observation of Right, yet it would be a Point of Wisdom, not of Folly, to obey the Impulse and Direction of our own Nature.

(Grotius 1625 [2005], pp.94–95)

This relationship between the law of nations and natural law represented a disagreement with his contemporary, Francisco Suárez. Suárez saw the two as distinct, albeit related, while Grotius made a stronger claim for the fact that the law of nations could be derived, at least in part, from the natural law. This was because he made the principle of "consent" more central to the existence of natural law; that is, if we can find the international community agreeing on a set of principles, this is evidence for the fact that it may well correspond to natural law. Suárez, writing from a more scholastic, philosophical perspective, did not see the practice of nations as being as important as Grotius did.

Book I begins with further clarifications about law and war linking the two together to make the point that it can be lawful to wage war according to both natural law and the law of nations. It soon moves onto an extended discussion of authority and sovereignty, beginning with the question of whether or not there can be such a thing as private war. He argues that there can be, especially when an individual wishes to defend himself from harm. He goes on to argue that a public war is defined by the fact that it is undertaken by the sovereign, who is defined as the agent which is not subject to any other power (Grotius, 1625 [2005], p.259). This definition corresponds to that of Jean Bodin, with whom Grotius was familiar, and Thomas Hobbes, who read Grotius as a young man and drew upon his thinking. His reflections on sovereignty and authority appear to reinforce a more traditional understanding. He concludes Book I by arguing against insurrection by subjects of a sovereign, arguing that once they enter into the relationship of a formal community there is a need to ensure that peace is the outcome rather than continued war.

It is worth noting, however, that Grotius qualifies that sovereignty in a way that could have both negative and positive connotations today. While arguing that sovereignty is about the power to act as one wishes, he does point out that in alliances, even unequal ones, sovereignty and authority can be retained by a state even if it must follow the instructions of the "superior" power in the relationship. Grotius argued that superiority does not mean limits on freedom but is can be about "reverence and dignity" (*Ibid.*, pp.320–321). This understanding might be read today as both allowing for belonging to regional and international organizations but also for the justification for an imperial relationship between states and political communities. In addition, when we consider the Dutch political context as described above, it might even allow for more flexible types of political relationships that do not fit into any contemporary pattern.

Book II explores the reasons for which one can wage war, which are the three traditional "just" causes: self-defense, punishment and retaking what has been taken from you. Of these three, only the first remains central in both just war and international law. Because self-defense is so well grounded in international law and the just war tradition, it should not necessarily be seen as Grotius' most important contribution and so receives less attention in this chapter.

However, punishment provides an example of how his particular understanding might have some relevance for today. Grotius does not simply list punishment as a potential cause for war. Rather, he develops a much larger and extensive treatment of the philosophical purpose behind punishment. In Book II, Chapters 20 and 21, "On Punishment" and "On the Sharing of Punishments" Grotius extends the argument that war can be waged for purposes of punishment. Grotius does not assume the necessity of a single community headed by a sovereign who has the responsibility to punish. Rather than argue that the right to punish derives from the inherent dignity or authority of the sovereign, he posits that punishment derives from the character of the violation:

> But the Subject of this Right, that is, the Person to whom the Right of Punishing belongs, is not determined by the Law of Nature. For natural reason informs us, that a Malefactor may be punished, but not who ought to punish him. It suggests indeed so much, that it is the fittest to be done by a Superior, but yet does not shew that to be absolutely necessary, unless by Superior we mean him who is innocent and detrude the Guilty below the Rank of Men, which is the Doctrine of some Divines.
>
> (*Grotius, 1625 [2005], p.955*)

Rather than punishment being defined by the existence of a sovereign, it is instead defined by the objective fact of a criminal violation.

In Section 37 of Chapter 20 Grotius turns to the question of war being waged to inflict punishment. He notes "the Desire for inflicting Punishment is often the Occasion of War" (*Ibid.*, p.1018). This is followed by a discussion of the right to wage war against those who violate the natural law. As discussed in other chapters, this was an argument that Vitoria had rejected a generation earlier, and would be a subject that Pufendorf (chapter 11) would return to in criticism of Grotius' overly expansive view of punishment. He then turns to the question of whether a king whose subjects have not been harmed may launch a war to punish one who has harmed another community, what some might equate with humanitarian intervention (Tuck 2013, pp. 105–07). He argues that yes, those who commit crimes "against nature" may be punished by any sovereign state through war (Grotius, 1625 [2005], p.1021). Grotius' argument that punishment is a just cause for waging war arises from his natural law framework. But, as noted above, his understanding of political authority resulted from a very different political context than we live in today.

We could simply state that punishment is no longer a legitimate cause for war, especially because punishment is illegal in contemporary positivist international law (Gould, 2010). At the same time, the relevance of his justification of punishment might benefit us today. We could, for instance, see efforts to use force in response to a violation of international law, what is called collective security, as a form of punishment. The state that has violated the rules will be subject to harm, an act that maps onto Grotius' judicial understanding of war. While the dangers of punishment becoming vengeance and the lack of a formal authority structure to modify this use of force are always in the background, Grotius' thinking on this point can help us see the use of force as a means to achieve justice in the world rather than as an advancement of one's own interests.[5]

The other justification for force, retaking property that has been stolen, no longer seems as relevant. This might arise from the fact that this justification often relied on the idea that a state was the property of its ruler, so "theft" meant the stealing of one's property from another individual ruler. As states came to be understood as owned by no one but as the political structure through which a community governed itself, this justification for war became less applicable. Yet, one interesting effort to make this aspect of Grotius' insights relevant today comes in the work of Cecile Fabre. Fabre suggests that these arguments can provide justification for what she calls "subsistence wars", or efforts by individuals who are subject to severe poverty to reclaim goods that should be shared by all but because of history have been taken by some over others. She briefly acknowledges that Grotius' understanding of property and labor, similar to John Locke, could lead to colonialism. But, Fabre also notes that according to Grotius "political boundaries are irrelevant to basic entitlements", though of course Grotius' understanding of "basic entitlements" will differ from our modern day understandings thereof (Fabre, 2012, p.105).

Book III is the one in which Grotius explores what is justified in the conduct of war. Here he cites Cicero to reinforce an idea as old as warfare: "There are certain duties to be observed even towards those that have wronged us, for there is a moderation required in revenge and punishment" (Grotius, 1625 [2005], p.1421). This book includes a great deal that is less relevant to the modern day conduct of war, especially if we consider the challenges raised by technological developments in warfare (although it is important to contextualize his arguments about moderation in the norms of his time, and indeed just war thought across time). And yet, the spirit of Grotius' insights retains an important hold on us. Some of his insights are perhaps more historically important than being relevant for today; for instance, his discussions of fraud and lying seem quaint, but they do find their way into the Hague and Geneva Conventions of the 20th century, which include injunctions to "not kill treacherously". Grotius also has extensive discussions of issues such as pillage, rape, and the slaughter of the enemy's populations. While he acknowledges these practices and at times even justifies them, he also sought to moderate them. In reading his text today, we might be drawn more to the fact that he does in fact justify such practices. It is important to acknowledge, though, that he wrote at a time when such practices were normal and broadly understood as being legitimate. So, his extensive discussions of moderation in killing, spoiling, the treatment of captives, and even obtaining an empire, in chapters 11–15 in Book III, are important to acknowledge as a shift in the tradition. To quote James Turner Johnson's important historical study of the just war tradition that singles out the restrictive trend that emerges with Grotius: "In general Grotius' procedure is first to set wide boundaries to what may be done in war, then to narrow them by reference to criteria from nature, *jus gentium*, and charity" (Johnson, 1975, p.223).

One element of Grotius' reflections on what can be done in the context of war, however, has appeared recently in the work of the just war theorist Jeff McMahan (chapter 19). McMahan has famously argued that while soldiers are the ones we think of as being subject to violence in wartime, it might be that civilians who are part of a community that is waging an unjust war will become liable to harm. This argument of the potential liability of civilians stands in stark contrast to the arguments of figures such as Michael Walzer (chapter 16), whose view is that the "war convention" stipulates that only soldiers can be subject to harm (McMahan, 2009; Walzer, 1977).

This controversy is discussed across the chapters devoted to Walzer and McMahan in this volume. Yet, while this appears to be a new controversy for some, in fact it is found in Grotius' work. Indeed, one can find it articulated in his *De Jure Praedae*. In that work, in which he sought to justify the use of force by the Dutch East Indies Company against the Portuguese, Grotius argues that the Portuguese and indeed the Spanish Empire continued to be at war with the Dutch Republic during the time of the attack. While he is defending the economic interests of the Dutch, he argues that the Portuguese in their behavior in the East Indies not only harmed the Dutch sailors but also the native populations in their treatment of them. In so doing, Grotius argues that "the subjects of a state that is shown to have inflicted an injury are liable, as such, to warlike attack; that is to say, every Portuguese person without exception is liable" (Grotius, 1604 [2006], p.379). In Book III, Chapter 18 of *De Jure Belli ac Pacis,* Grotius seems to take up this same point, arguing that while it is good to obey the commander of an army, it may also be justified for a solider in war to use force against those who deserve punishment or to take the goods of the innocent in pursuit of a just war (Grotius, 1625 [2005], p.1529).

And yet, he offers a qualification to this conclusion, one that does not seem available to McMahan. Indeed, it is a conclusion that can be found throughout his work, moderating his "logical" arguments and tempering his enthusiasm for the use of force:

> But it is not enough that we do nothing against the Rules of rigorous Justice, properly so called; we must also take Care that we offend not against Charity, especially Christian Charity. Now this may happen sometimes; when, for Instance, it appears, that such a plundering doth not so much hurt the State, or the King, or those who are culpable themselves, but rather the Innocent, who it may render so extremely miserable, that if we should use the like Extremity to our own private Debtors, it would be judged barbarously cruel.
>
> *(Grotius, 1625 [2005], p.1531)*

It is this Christian charity, or charity more generally, that differentiates Grotius' insights on war from the "rigorous" philosophical insights that shape so much of not only McMahan's work but many 21st century theorists of just war.

Legacies

Grotius' work was not completely "original" in the sense that it introduced radically new ideas into his intellectual context. Rather, his method, the structure of his book, and its vast scope of historical and philosophical learning turned it into an almost instant classic. Prior to its publication, Grotius was better known for his theological writings, literary works, and his short piece on the freedom of the seas, *Mare Libeum*. But with the publication of *De Jure Belli ac Pacis*, Grotius' fame was further established as the European scholarly and political elite saw a work that captured the essence of the natural law idea and made it relevant for what seemed to be the least "law governed" context of all, war.

Following the publication of the work, it immediately saw translation into numerous languages in Europe. It became one of the most well-known and consistently cited works on the laws of war during the 17th and 18th centuries. Thomas Hobbes read Grotius. The German, Samuel Pufendorf (chapter 11), whose contributions to the ideas of natural law were profoundly important, popularized his work. Pufendorf, writing soon after Grotius died, was essential in turning Grotius' into the new representative of not only natural law theory, but natural rights theory. Pufendorf's own work, *The Whole Duty of Man according to the Law of Nature*, which appeared in 1673, drew on Grotius in a number of important ways. The Swiss theorist of international law and international society, Emer de Vattel (chapter 12), also looked to Grotius, though he moved away from the natural law arguments toward what is considered to be a more positivist orientation. The American founders referred to Grotius positively at a number of points in the *Federalist Papers*, particularly as an advocate of a rational and liberal law of nations. While the immediate reception of Grotius was positive, the 18th and 19th century saw more critical responses. Immanuel Kant (chapter 13), Jean-Jacques Rousseau, and Jeremy Bentham all found great fault with Grotius, whom they read as an apologist for the warmongering of European monarchs rather than as a theorist who sought to moderate war. Philosophers today continue to look to Grotius. Jeff McMahan, noted in the discussion of Book III above, argues that Grotius is the most important theorist in the history of the just war tradition (McMahan, 2009). And Larry May, a theorist of both just war and international law, has drawn upon Grotius' ideas about mercy to argue for a greater attention to peace within the tradition (May, 2012).

The impact of Grotius on international law has wavered over the years, but it has been persistent in its influence. In the period when international law came into existence in a formal way, the 19th century, Grotius influence was less important. Henry Wheaton, an American diplomat, produced the first English language textbook on international law, *Elements of International Law* in 1836. It is described by Stephen Neff as being in a "pragmatic Grotian tradition" and became an extremely influential text in the United States and Great Britain (Neff, 2014, p.228). James Brown Scott, the editor of the important Carnegie Endowment translations of classics in international law in the early 20th century, sought to move the tradition away from Grotius and back toward the work of figures such as Vitoria (Neff, 2014, p.350; Brown, 1934). It was not until the mid-20th century, following World War II, that Grotius' reputation returned. Hersch Lauterpacht argued in an influential 1946 article that international law is shaped by a broadly conceived Grotian tradition (Lauterpacht, 1946). Richard Falk, one of the most prominent of international legal theorists still writing today, has argued that the text provides a "Grotian quest" or way of approaching the intersection of law and international politics that is worth emulating (Falk, 1983). With the creation of new international institutions, such as the international criminal tribunals and the International Criminal Court, Grotius' reliance on natural law seems more relevant again, especially his focus on punishing those that violate the laws of war.

Conclusion

Hugo Grotius speaks a language that is very different from ours. His very way of thinking in natural law and Christian theological concepts seems alien to both the analytic philosophy of just war theory and the positivism of international law. But precisely because he sought to combine traditions that did not seem possible to combine, articulate a theory of just war that seemed to stand against the violence of his day, and promote a just and merciful attitude to the most horrible of human practices, he gives us an ideal of what a theorist of just war can do. Even the controversies that his work has generated by postcolonial theorists speak to tensions at the heart of the international moral and legal order. So, whether we agree with him or not, Hugo Grotius continues to deserve our attention when we think about war and peace in the modern world.

Notes

1   Throughout this chapter, I will use the Latin title for this book. It has been translated in two ways into English: *The Rights of War and Peace* (Grotius 1625 [2005]) and *The Laws of War and Peace* (Grotius 1625 [2012]). The translations arise from the fact that the Medieval Latin word "jus" can be translated as either right or law. The modern meaning of those two terms is, of course, different though they are related.
2   For biographical background on Grotius, see Edwards, 1983 and Gellinek, 1983.
3   Some of the following sections are drawn from Lang, 2010.
4   Some of the following sections are drawn from Lang, 2014, pp.146–151.
5   I develop an account of punishment by drawing on Grotius in Lang, 2008, pp.35–39.

Works cited

Antognazza, Maria Rosa. 2012. Introduction to Hugo Grotius *The Truth of the Christian Religion* [1627] with Jean le Clerc's Notes and Additions. Clarke, John. ed. trans. Indianapolis: Liberty Fund.

Edwards, Charles. 1983. *Hugo Grotius: The Miracle of Holland: A Study in Legal and Political Thought*. Chicago: Nelsen-Hall.

Fabre, Cecile. 2012. *Cosmopolitan War*. Oxford: Oxford University Press,

Falk, Richard. 1983. The Grotian Quest: Preface to Charles Edwards, *Hugo Grotius: The Miracle of Holland: A Study in Legal and Political Thought*. Chicago: Nelsen-Hall.

Gellineck, Christian. 1983. *Hugo Grotius*. Boston: Twayne Publishers.

Gould, Harry. 2010. *The Legacy of Punishment in International Law*. New York: Palgrave.

Grotius, Hugo. 1604 [2006]. *Commentary on the Law of Prize and Booty*. van Ittersum, Marine, Julia. Ed. Indianapolis: Liberty Fund.

Grotius, Hugo. 1608 [2004]. *The Free Sea*. Armitage, David. ed. Indianapolis: Liberty Fund.

Grotius, Hugo. 1625 [2005]. *The Rights of War and Peace*. Tuck, Richard. ed. Indianapolis: Liberty Fund.

Grotius, Hugo. 1625 [2012]. *On the Law of War and Peace: Student Edition*. Neff, Stephen C. ed. Cambridge: Cambridge University Press.

Grotius, Hugo. 1627 [2012]. *The Truth of the Christian Religion*, with Jean le Clerc's Notes and Additions. Clarke, John. trans. Antognazza, Maria Rosa. ed. Indianapolis: Liberty Fund.

Haley, K.D.H. 1972. *The Dutch in the Seventeenth Century*. London: Thames and Hudson.

Israel, Jonathan. 1989. *Dutch Primacy in World Trade, 1585–1740* Oxford: Clarendon Press.

Jeffrey, Rene. 2006. *Hugo Grotius in International Thought*. London: Palgrave Macmillan.

Johnson, James Turner. 1975. *Ideology, Reason, and the Limitation of War: Religious and Secular Concepts 1200–1740*. Princeton: Princeton University Press.

Keene, Edward. 2002. *Beyond the Anarchical Society: Grotius, Colonialism and Order in World Politics*. Cambridge: Cambridge University Press.

Koskenniemi, Martii. 2006. *Fragmentation of International Law: Difficulties Arising from the Diversification and Expansion of International Law*. Report for the International Law Commission. Geneva: United Nations, available at: www.helsinki.fi/eci/Publications/A%20CN4%20L682[1].pdf.

Lang, Jr. Anthony F. 2008. *Punishment, Justice and International Relations: Ethics and Order after the Cold War*. London: Routledge.

Lang, Jr. Anthony F. 2010. Authority and the Problem of Non-State Actors. In Heinze, Eric and Steele, Brent. eds. *Just War and Non-State Actors*. London: Routledge, pp.47–71.

Lang, Jr. Anthony F. 2014. *International Political Theory: An Introduction*. London: Palgrave Macmillan.

Lauterpacht, Hersch. 1946. The Grotian Tradition in International Law. *British Yearbook of International Law*. **23**, pp.1–53.

May, Larry. 2012. *After War Ends: A Philosophical Perspective*. Cambridge: Cambridge University Press.

Neff, Stephen. 2014. *Justice among Nations: A History of International Law*. Cambridge MA: Harvard University Press.

Nellen, Henk J. and Edwin Rabbie, eds., 1994. *Hugo Grotius: Theologian*. Leiden: Brill Publishers.

Scott, James Brown. 1934. *The Spanish Origin of International Law: Francisco de Vitoria and His Law of Nations*. Oxford: Clarendon Press.

Thomson, Janice. 1994. *Mercenaries, Pirates and Sovereigns*. Princeton: Princeton University Press.

Tracey, James D. 2008. *The Founding of the Dutch Republic: War, Finance, and Politics in Holland, 1572–1588*. Oxford: Oxford University Press.

Tuck, Richard. 1999. *The Rights of War and Peace: Political Order and International Order from Grotius to Kant*. Oxford: Oxford University Press.

Van Geleren, Martin. ed. 1993. *The Dutch Revolt*. Cambridge: Cambridge University Press.

Van Ittersum, Martine. 2006. *Profit and Principle: Hugo Grotius, Natural Rights Theories and the Rise of Dutch Power in the East Indies, 1595–1615*. Leiden: Brill Publishers.

Walzer, Michael. 1977. *Just and Unjust Wars: A Moral Argument with Historical Illustrations.* New York: Basic Books.

Wilson, Charles. 1968. *The Dutch Republic and the Civilisation of the Seventeenth Century.* London: Weidenfeld and Nicolson.

11

SAMUEL PUFENDORF (1632–1694)

Luke Glanville

Introduction

Samuel Pufendorf had several powerful reasons for wanting to place limits on the recourse to war. Born in Saxony in 1632 during the Thirty Years' War (1618–1648) which brought such devastation upon Europe, he experienced the horrors of war first-hand when, as a seven-year-old, he was forced to briefly flee his home with his family. After the Peace of Westphalia brought the war to an end, he spent several years at the Universities of Leipzig and Jena studying theology and law before securing employment as tutor to the family of Sweden's special envoy to Copenhagen. Here he was affected by another war, being imprisoned for eight months upon the outbreak of conflict between Sweden and Denmark in 1658. Over the next few decades he worked as a professor of the law of nature and nations at the Universities of Heidelberg and Lund and a historiographer in Stockholm and Brandenburg until his death in 1694.[1] In various writings on the history of the states of Europe and their present-day politics, he displayed an acute awareness of the vulnerability of the German princely states in which he lived. These states, which after 1648 included Sweden, were delicately held together in the form of the Holy Roman Empire by the Westphalian settlement. Pufendorf worried about how they might best work together to preserve their liberties against both the meddling and predations of the strongest among them as well as the interference and encroachment of even stronger external powers (Pufendorf, 2007; 2013). He had good reasons, then, to seek to limit wars between European states. He also had good reasons to reject prevailing justifications for imperial conquests beyond Europe, given that the Holy Roman Empire's European rivals had grown so powerful from their colonial enterprises and Sweden's brief attempt at establishing its own colony in the Americas had been crushed by the Dutch (Tuck, 1999, pp.143–144).[2]

It is little wonder, then, that when he came to treat the law of war in his profoundly influential studies of the law of nature and nations, Pufendorf sought to place much more stringent limits on the just resort to war than earlier Protestant natural law theorists, such as Alberico Gentili (chapter 9), Hugo Grotius (chapter 10), Francis Bacon, and Thomas Hobbes. As Richard Tuck has summarized: "Pufendorf lived in the group of European states which felt themselves most at risk from the kind of militarist and imperialist expansion in which the Dutch and English writers gloried" (1999, p.142). He was therefore motivated to reject many of the extensive rights of war that these writers had embraced and instead offered a remarkably statist interpretation of the principles of just war that prioritized and defended the rights and liberties of the territorial sovereign state.

Texts

Before delving into Pufendorf's treatment of the law of war, it is worth briefly explicating his understanding of the fundamental principles of natural jurisprudence upon which he sought to base this law. He spelt this out in his landmark work, *The Law of Nature and Nations* (*De Jure Naturae et Gentium*) (1672), and then in an abridged version of that work that he wrote for students, *On the Duty of Man and Citizen According to Natural Law* (*De Officio Hominis et Civis Juxta Legem Naturalem*) (1673). Like other Protestant natural law theorists before him, Pufendorf attributed much of the civil and interstate violence that had plagued Europe in the 16th and 17th centuries to confessional disputes between Catholics and Protestants. His response was to seek to articulate grounds for morality that did not depend on divine revelation or the doctrines of any particular confession and thus could command the consent of all people. The hope was to establish conditions for peace and security in the context of religious diversity both within and between states. He later observed that one of his purposes in writing *The Law of Nature and Nations* had been "to abolish in natural law all theological controversies, and adapt it to the understanding of the whole of mankind, who disagreed in many different ways over religion" (Pufendorf, "The Origin and Progress of the Discipline of Natural Law" (1677), quoted in Hochstrasser, 2000 p.70). Pufendorf conceived of his religiously neutral theory of natural law as a contribution to a new science of morality that had been inaugurated by Grotius and developed by Hobbes. However, wary of charges of impiety and even atheism that his predecessors had met, he distanced himself from both on certain matters.

Grotius had built his system of natural law in *The Law of War and Peace* (1625) on the premise that man has a natural desire for society: "But among the traits characteristic of man is an impelling desire for society [*appetitus societatis*], that is, for the social life – not of any and every sort, but peaceful, and organized according to the measure of his intelligence". From this natural desire, Grotius infamously suggested, we can derive fundamental precepts of the law of nature that "would have a degree of validity even if we should concede that which cannot be conceded without the utmost wickedness, that there is no God, or that the affairs of men are of no concern to Him" (Grotius, 1925, *Prol.* 6, 11, pp.11, 13). These precepts required that actors refrain from harming each other while pursuing their own interests and provided a universal right to punish those who violate the law. The law of nature was said to be applicable to ungoverned individuals who existed in what Hobbes would soon label a "state of nature" and, by extension, to states who, in the absence of a world government, existed in their own international state of nature. Upon these grounds, Grotius justified what Pufendorf saw as overly expansive rights to war, declaring that war was rightly waged in response to a wide range of injuries. These included failure to provide hospitality or innocent passage, and in response to grave violations of natural law wherever they occur.

In contrast to Grotius, Hobbes (1997, I.2n, p.25) had bluntly declared that, even if men were naturally desirous of society, they were not capable of it. In the absence of a common power to restrain individuals, he claimed in *Leviathan* (1651), human nature provides three causes of quarrel: competition, diffidence, and glory. These three causes lead individuals to behave violently toward each other for purposes of gain, safety, and reputation. He painted a bleak picture of the state of nature as a condition of war "of every man, against every man", in which there is "continual fear, and danger of violent death; and the life of man, solitary, poor, nasty, brutish, and short". This natural condition of war, he claimed, could be recognized in the posture of sovereigns to one another: "in all times, kings, and persons of sovereign authority, because of their independency, are in continual jealousies, and in the state and posture of gladiators ... which is a posture of war" (Hobbes, 1996: XIII.6–12, pp.83–85). In such a condition, he claimed, individuals, and by extension states, were at liberty to do whatever was conducive to their preservation. The law of nature that he derived from this condition of nature was derived not from the desire or capacity of actors for society but from considerations of utility. Individuals should refrain from harming others because to do otherwise would only create enmity. States should likewise refrain from unnecessary wars and excessive cruelty because to do otherwise would only undermine their own security. But actors in the state of nature should never rely on the good faith of others for their security: "Even when the fighting between [commonwealths] stops, it should not be called Peace, but an intermission during which each watches the motion and aspect of its enemy and gauges its security not on the basis of agreements but by the strength and designs of the adversary" (Hobbes, 1997: XIII.7, pp.144–45).

When Pufendorf came to formulate his own system of the law of nature, he combined Grotius' emphasis on sociability with Hobbes' emphasis on utility.[3] Wary of the charges of anti-Aristotelianism and impiety that had met Hobbes' rejection of natural sociability, Pufendorf made sure to embrace man's capacity for sociability. However, in contrast to Grotius (chapter 10), he grounded his system not in man's natural desire for social life but in the utility to be derived from sociable behavior.[4] He shared Hobbes' belief that life in the state of nature is unstable and dangerous, but he firmly rejected the suggestion that it is akin to a condition of war. For evidence, he pointed to the peaceful relationships that are often found between states joined together by treaties and by friendship. The natural condition is not one of war but of peace, he declared. This is so because actors in a state of nature recognize that they stand to benefit from practices of mutual assistance. Certainly, they are fiercely protective of their own preservation. But they recognize that they cannot secure such preservation without the assistance of others. This in turn gives them reason to extend assistance to others in time of need in order to gain their trust and favor and to be free from enmity and harm. Rather than being a natural characteristic of man, as it was for Grotius, sociability is an imperative produced by the need and desire for self-preservation. And, as such, it is a fundamental law of nature:

> And so it will be a fundamental law of nature, that "Every man, so far as in him lies, should cultivate and preserve towards others a sociable attitude [*socialitatem*], which is peaceful and agreeable at all times to the nature and end of the human race" … [B]y a sociable attitude we mean an attitude of each man towards every other man, by which each is understood to be bound to the other by kindness, peace, and love, and therefore by a mutual obligation.
>
> *(Pufendorf, 1934: II.3.15, p.208)[5]*

Pufendorf explained that, when actors in the state of nature seek their advantage only, to the exclusion of others, their desires tend to clash with the desires of others. This leads only to conflict and insecurity. Actors who hope to secure themselves should not disregard the needs and interests of others but instead cultivate a sociable attitude and seek to contribute to the mutual advantage of all (II.3.16, pp.209–211). Every ungoverned individual and, by extension, state thus has a self-interest in seeking to "willingly advance the interests of others, so far as he is not bound by more pressing obligations … [I]t is for his advantage to conduct himself in such a way as to profit from their friendly attitude rather than incur their anger" (II.2.9, p. 172; see generally II.2–3, pp. 154–230).

Some scholars have suggested that Pufendorf's duty of sociability generated cosmopolitan duties of mutual aid and assistance among states. Anthony Pagden, for example, claims that Pufendorf's law of nations "involves an obligation on the part of one social group not merely not to harm, but actively to promote the welfare of all others" (2000, p.12). However, such claims are too strong. In the hands of Grotius, and Vitoria before him, the obligation to sociability generated "perfect" rights to engage in commerce with others and to receive hospitality and passage through their lands. Violation of those rights generated rights to wage war. It also generated a right to punish grave violations of natural law wherever they may be found. In the hands of Pufendorf, however, the obligation to sociability generated merely "imperfect" rights to commerce, hospitality, and passage – rights that could not be justifiably enforced by war – and it certainly did not generate a universal right to punish violations of natural law. As we will see in the next section, Pufendorf drew from the foundational principle of sociability laws of war that protected the rights and liberties of the territorial sovereign state.

Controversies

Pufendorf began his treatment of the law of war in *The Law of Nature and Nations* by claiming that human interactions should ordinarily be peaceful. Indeed, he suggested, one of the chief reasons why the law of nature has been placed in the hearts of individuals was so that they may preserve peaceful relations with each other. However, he conceded that under certain conditions it is lawful and sometimes even necessary to resort to war. The just causes for war that he outlined echoed those that had been spelt out by many before him: to preserve ourselves and our possessions against injury; to claim from others those things that are rightfully ours if they refuse to provide them; and to obtain reparations for past injuries and guarantees that they will not be repeated (VIII.6.2–3, pp.1292–1294). Each of these just causes for war depended on there being an injury done. In the absence of injury, there were no grounds for war. Lust for fame, domination, and riches, he bluntly declared, ought never to be considered just causes for war. He admitted that war may be justly waged to overcome an enemy that was openly preparing to do an injury even if the injury had not yet been done, but insisted that "the mere fear of the strength and power of a neighbour" provided no grounds for war (VIII.6.5, pp. 1295–1296). To put it in today's terminology, he allowed pre-emptive but not preventive war. Moreover, he cautioned that any doubts about the justice of a war should be taken very seriously. We should be wary about misreading the actions and intentions of potential enemies or miscalculating the balance of consequences that would result from war with them. And even if we believe the cause to be just, we should not rashly resort to arms. Rather, wherever possible we should first seek a conference with the other party, or appeal to third parties for arbitration, or do both (VIII.6.4, pp. 1294–1295).

Rejection of key arguments for colonial conquest

Pufendorf's emphasis on the necessity of injury enabled him to reject some particularly lamentable arguments that had been developed in recent centuries to justify the conquest and colonization of the Americas by European powers. One such argument, articulated in various forms by Francisco de Vitoria (1991, 3.1, pp. 278–84), Gentili (1933, I.17, 19, pp.79–82, 86–92), Grotius (1925, II.2, pp.186–205), and others, was that people have rights to trade with others, to innocently pass through their lands, to receive hospitality from them, and to settle in vacant lands. A refusal to satisfy one of those rights, so the argument went, constituted an injury and therefore just grounds for war. Pufendorf responded by claiming that rights to commerce, passage, hospitality, and settlement were appropriately conceived as "imperfect" rights and the duty of others to satisfy those rights were likewise "imperfect" duties. While it is always a good thing to discharge "imperfect" duties and to satisfy "imperfect" rights where safe to do so, such action should always be subject to the discretion of the duty-bearer and should never be enforced with arms. The right to be free from attack is a "perfect" right that is appropriately subject to enforcement, but the right to receive a benefit from others in the form of trade, passage, hospitality, or settlement is "imperfect" and should not be considered subject to enforcement since "it is foolish to prescribe a medicine far more troublesome and dangerous than the disease" (I.7.7, p.118). If a state believes that it has reasonable grounds to fear others who wish to enter their territory, even if that fear is misguided, it should not be compelled to let them in (III.3, pp.346–378). Property-holders must always have the final decision regarding whether they wish to share with others the use of their property, and it would be crude to say otherwise without regard to "the numbers in which they come, their purpose in coming, as well as of the question whether, in passing through without harm and visiting a foreign land, they propose to stay but a short time, or to settle among us permanently, as if upon some right of theirs". Of course, it would be barbarous for a state to show "indiscriminate hostility to those who come on a peaceful mission", he noted, but no state should be compelled to behave otherwise by force of arms (III.3.9, pp.364–65).

It seems that Pufendorf's primary intention in making this argument was to reject a justification for conquest and occupation in the New World that he regarded as particularly spurious. He singled out Vitoria for special attention, mistakenly charging the 16th-century theologian with developing this justification in order to justify the Spanish conquests of the Indies (III.3.9, p.364).[6] However, Tuck (1999, pp.143–144) has usefully noted that Pufendorf may have also had European affairs in mind. His denial of a "perfect" right of passage through the territory of another power, for example, may have been prompted by fear of the threats to Sweden's security if the great powers of Europe were to be allowed free passage through the Sound.

A second argument that had been used to justify colonial conquests and which Pufendorf bluntly rejected was the argument for a universal right to punish grave violations of natural law. This argument had been most famously formulated by Grotius, who claimed that the natural liberty to punish any persons for grievous violations of the law of nature, wherever they occurred, was retained by all sovereign rulers, not because they were in authority over those deserving punishment but because they were in subjection to none, just as individuals were in a state of nature. Just as ancient heroes such as Hercules were to be praised for punishing grievous violations of the law of nature, Grotius claimed,

> So we do not doubt that wars are justly waged against those who act with impiety towards their parents, like the Sogdianians before Alexander taught them to abandon this form of barbarity; against those who feed on human flesh, from which custom according to Diodorus, Hercules compelled the ancient Gauls to abstain; and against those who practice piracy. … Regarding such barbarians, wild beasts rather than men, … war against them [is] sanctioned by nature.

> *(Grotius, 1925, II.20.40, pp.504–506)*

Pufendorf firmly rejected this notion of a universal right of punishment. "the power to exact penalties is a part of sovereignty", he insisted, "and so no one can impose upon another a penalty, properly speaking, unless he have sovereignty over him". He warned against accepting the notion that "every sin so lowers the dignity of a man, that he must immediately upon its performance be classed among the beasts". An individual was free in a state of nature to punish those who injured him, he claimed, "[b]ut if the sin was against another, whose defense has not been laid upon me as a special charge, I can no more take upon myself to avenge him, unless bound to him by a treaty, than to pronounce laws to such as are not subject to me" (VIII.3.7, pp.1170–1171). Revisiting themes addressed by Vitoria (chapter 6) and Las Casas (chapter 7), Pufendorf, on these grounds, rejected the argument that war could be justly waged against the Indians of the Americas on the mere grounds that they had violated natural law by practicing human sacrifice and cannibalism. The only exception that he allowed was when the victims of such cruel practices were the warring prince's own citizens, and only if they had come upon the Indians not as enemies and robbers but as innocent guests or driven by storms (VIII.6.5, p.1297).

Nevertheless, Pufendorf did accept that there were some just occasions for war beyond instances of injury to oneself. He agreed with Grotius, for example, that all men had a right to punish those persons who placed themselves beyond the jurisdiction of any courts of justice: "For against pirates and freebooters, inasmuch as they are enemies of all mankind, every man is a soldier in defence of his country" (VIII.3.13, p.1182). And, in a claim that was later echoed by Vattel (chapter 12), he suggested that the same could be said for those states who behave as if they are the enemies of all others, "conducting themselves, without just cause, in opposition to the law of nature". Such states rightly suffer the following consequences:

> That unless they go about to renounce that fierce and bloody manner of life, others must show no more mercy on them than on wolves and other savage animals. And when they have been apprehended they are usually treated more cruelly than other enemies, even though the latter also threatened us with utter destruction. They are also held unworthy to receive any office even of simple humanity, since they are bent upon the injury of others.
>
> *(VIII.4.5, pp.1232–1233)*

While Pufendorf did not say which particular states he had in mind here, the language echoed justifications by earlier thinkers, including Vitoria and Las Casas, for the right of Christians to take up arms in response to Turkish incursions into Christendom (Tuck, 1999, p.162; Brunstetter, 2012, 43–44; 79–81).

A right to wage war in defense of others

A further just cause for war that Pufendorf allowed that did not require an injury being done to oneself was the right to take up arms in defense of injured others, today known as collective security. Here he stuck closely to the opinion of Grotius (see Grotius, 1925, II.25, pp. 578–586). He declared that states were primarily obligated to defend their own subjects. But they should also defend their allies to whom they are bound by treaty, so long as they can do so without impairing their primary obligation. "After allies come friends", Pufendorf continued, "or such as we are joined to by reason of some kindness or favour". The development of mutual friendship, he explained, "is understood to imply a promise that the safety of the one will be the other's care, so far as more binding obligations permit". Furthermore, he added, mutual humanity alone "can be sufficient to make a man undertake another's defence against the manifest injuries of his enemies, especially since it can very easily be our highest interest, and in fact redound to the general good of mankind, to prevent a man from injuring and insulting others with impunity" (VIII.6.14, pp. 1305–1306).

However, repeating his earlier rejection of Grotius' universal right of punishment, Pufendorf cautioned against anyone forcing himself upon the world as a decider of controversies:

> Nay, for a person to thrust himself forward as a kind of arbitrator of human affairs, is opposed even to the equality granted by nature, not to mention the fact that such a thing could easily lead to great abuse, since there is scarcely a man living against whom this could not serve as an excuse for war.
>
> *(VIII.6.14, p. 1307)*

Therefore, he insisted, a state must only come to the defense of an injured party when such aid is requested. In this way, the intervening party would be acting not on their own authority but on the authority of the victim of injustice. As Tuck (1999, p.160) rightly suggests, Pufendorf no doubt had in mind the horrors of the Thirty Years' War in which the involvement of non-German powers in the affairs of the German princely states had wrought such devastation.

As Vitoria and Grotius had done, Pufendorf extended this right to wage war in defense of others to include not only the defense of other states but also the defense of the subjects of those states if they were victims of grave injuries at the hands of their sovereign. Such arguments find parallels in today's concepts of humanitarian intervention and the Responsibility to Protect. Grotius had articulated such a right to intervene to defend the oppressed despite his insistence that the oppressed themselves had no right to resist their sovereign. In contrast, Pufendorf suggested that the right to intervene followed from the oppressed subjects' right of resistance: "the safest principle to go on is, that we cannot lawfully undertake the defence of another's subjects, for any other reason than they themselves can rightfully advance, for taking up arms to protect themselves against the barbarous savagery of their superiors" (VIII.6.14, p.1307).[7]

In later years, Pufendorf applied such arguments to particular European cases. In response to increasing persecution of Protestant Huguenots within France, sanctioned by Louis XIV's Revocation of the Edict of Nantes in 1685, he suggested a need for Protestant princes to take action in defense of the oppressed Protestant subjects of tyrannical Catholic rulers and he attached this right to a broader need to defend the "Protestant interest" in Europe against Louis' aspirations to universal monarchy (see Pufendorf, 2002, §54, pp.120–121). He then applied such ideas directly to William of Orange's invasion of England in 1688–1689. Michael Seidler (1996, p.103) has shown that Pufendorf justified the expedition of William as a necessary action generated by the Dutchman's "personal ties to England, and his duty to protect the Dutch in particular and Protestantism in general against Anglo-French collusion". Such concern for the "Protestant interest" was arguably consistent with his long-standing desire to secure the rights and liberties of territorial sovereign states against threats from predatory powers, albeit now colored in a religious hue.

Just conduct in war

While Pufendorf refuted Grotius on several matters of *jus ad bellum*, his treatment of *jus in bello* largely constituted a brief summary and endorsement of the principles laid down by the Dutchman. In the absence of positive international laws that could bind states and their soldiers to certain rules of war and render them effectively enforceable, Pufendorf simply laid out what justice allows and then supplemented this with what the "law of humanity" recommends, just as Grotius had done in the third book of *The Law of War and Peace*. When an enemy gives me just grounds for war against him, Pufendorf claimed, "he allows me to use force against him to any degree, or so far as I may think desirable". Not only may I use force against my enemy until I have warded off the present peril with which I am threatened, or to secure reparations for injuries, but also I may proceed so far as to secure guarantees for my future security. My concern is not with inflicting proportionate punishment or reforming the guilty party, as is the task of a civil tribunal. Rather, my concern is "the defence and assertion of my safety, my property, and my rights". In order to secure these ends, I am permitted "to use whatever means I think will best prevail" against the enemy. However, Pufendorf emphasized, the "law of humanity" asks those on the just side in war to consider not only what they may rightly do to the enemy, but also "what should be the deeds of a humane and, above all, a generous victor". Therefore, as far as possible, I should inflict harm on the enemy only in a manner that is proportionate to the harm done to me. As well as being recommended by the "law of humanity", this was prudent policy. Belligerents ought to temper their treatment of the enemy lest their savagery motivates present or future enemies to act in kind (VIII.6.7, pp.1298–1299). But Pufendorf made clear that this "law of humanity" was not enforceable. No third party should pass judgment on the actions of belligerents, he claimed, "especially since the belligerents have agreed by a tacit pact either to increase or temper the savagery of the war at their own pleasure" (VIII.6.16, pp.1307–1308).

Legacy and enduring relevance

Pufendorf's writings on the law of nature and nations were profoundly influential throughout the 18th century, but they have gone largely unread since then.[8] At the end of that century, Immanuel Kant listed him alongside Grotius and Emer de Vattel as a "sorry comforter", claiming that their writings were "still dutifully quoted in *justification* of military aggression, although their philosophically or diplomatically formulated codes do not and cannot have the slightest *legal* force, since states as such are not subject to a common external constraint" (Kant, 1970, p.103). While they may have outlined clear principles on the use of military force, he suggested, "there is no instance of a state ever having been moved to desist from its purpose by arguments supported by the testimonies of such notable men" (*Ibid.*) The 19th and 20th centuries saw increasing emphasis placed on the development of positive law that was supposed to more effectively constrain states than natural law. The natural law tradition by no means fell into disuse. The writings of Grotius and Vattel have remained popular through to today. But Pufendorf is one of many whose contributions to natural law theorizing about the justice of war were influential at the time only to be subsequently neglected.

This neglect is regrettable for Pufendorf's contribution to the development of thinking about just war was pivotal. He provided a distinctly modern rendering of the laws of war that justified and prioritized the liberty and security of the territorial sovereign state. Whereas earlier theorists such as Vitoria and even Grotius had been able to conceive of the world in terms of a global commonwealth of humankind, Pufendorf tended to perceive a world of sovereigns driven by rivalry and competition. He sought to set limits to the conflict and violence that marked that world by rejecting several of the more reckless and politically convenient rights to war that many before him had sought to justify. While he did not know the concept of non-intervention that would be developed by Christian Wolff and Vattel in the mid-18th century, Pufendorf's was a firmly statist rendering of the principles of justice that restricted the rights of war primarily to defensive wars waged in response to injuries to oneself or to others. Wolff and Vattel would repeat his rejection of earlier arguments for a right to wage war in response to denial of hospitality, passage, and commerce and to punish grave violations of the law of nature. Those justifications for colonial conquest would be largely abandoned by imperial powers, although, of course, colonialism itself did not come to an end. Rather, alternative justifications were found, including most notoriously the notion that civilized peoples have a right and a duty to subject barbaric peoples to their rule for their own benefit and improvement. It was not until the second half of the 20th century that justifications for colonialism finally gave way to a universal principle of self-determination.

It is worth noting that, while Pufendorf's statism generated anti-imperialist conclusions that may be appealing to many readers today, it also generated other conclusions that many will find troubling. Most concerning is that, despite his appeals to sociability, he justified a kind of national selfishness, contributing to an understanding of sovereignty that not only protected states against the predations of external powers, but that also allowed states to ignore the suffering of strangers and foreigners. He drew some remarkably callous principles from his statist reasoning, including the claim that states could justly expel foreigners in time of famine for the sake of their own citizens (III.3.9, pp.365–366).

Nevertheless, there is much in his statist vision of international justice that remains compelling today. Perhaps the key insight of Pufendorf for us is his warning against powerful states setting themselves up as judges of weaker others. While he encouraged states to be hospitable and generous towards others, he championed the rights of the weak to decide for themselves what they can afford to do for the interests of the strong. And while he cautiously accepted the permissibility of the resort to arms to rescue oppressed peoples, he recognized the danger of abuse and set firm restrictions, including insisting that such wars must only be waged with the consent of the victims. If only some powerful states would adhere to such principles more consistently today.

Notes

1   For useful overviews of Pufendorf's life, see Simons (1934) and Tully (1991).
2   It should be noted, however, that Pufendorf seems not to have devoted much attention to the Dutch capture of the colony of New Sweden, referring to it only in passing in a single work, *de Rebus a Carolo Gustavo Sueciæ rege gestis commentariorum* (Pufendorf, 1696, I.85/120, VI.58).
3   It is worth noting, however, that he distanced himself from Grotius' "impious and idiotic theory" that these laws would hold true even if God did not exist, claiming that "the obligation of natural law is of God, the creator and final governor of mankind, who by His authority has bound men, His creatures, to observe it" (Pufendorf, 1934, II.3.19–20, pp. 215–18).
4   In a response to his critics, published in 1686, Pufendorf claimed that "the basic premise from which I draw the law of nature stands in direct opposition to the theory of Hobbes. For I come very close to the reasonable theory of the Stoics, whereas Hobbes serves up a *rechauffé* of Epicurean theories" (quoted in Pagden, 2013, p.58). However, some scholars charge that Pufendorf's efforts to distance himself from Hobbes were insincere and that his theory was fundamentally much closer to that of Hobbes than he was willing to admit (see Palladini, 2008).
5   Hereafter, citations to Pufendorf's *The Law of Nature and Nations* will be made simply with section and page references.
6   As discussed in chapter 6 of this volume in more detail, while Vitoria did develop and defend this justification for war, he remained unconvinced that the conditions that he laid out had been satisfied in the case of the Spanish conquests (see Vitoria, 1991, 3.1, pp. 278–84).
7   For Pufendorf's cautious defense of the right of a people to "defend itself against the extreme and unjust violence of its prince" and, if successful, to not put themselves under his yoke again, see VII.8.6–7, pp.1109–12. For Grotius' treatment of war to rescue oppressed peoples, see Grotius (1925, II.25.8, pp.583–84).
8   On Pufendorf's reception and legacy, see Seidler (2015).

Works cited

Brunstetter, Daniel. 2012. *Tensions of Modernity: Las Casas and His Legacy in the French Enlightenment*. New York: Routledge.

Gentili, Alberico. 1933. *De Iure Belli Libri Tres*, vol. 2. Rolfe, John C. trans. Oxford: Clarendon Press.

Grotius, Hugo. 1925. *De Jure Belli ac Pacis Libris Tres*, vol. 2. Kelsey, Francis W. ed. Oxford: Clarendon Press.

Hobbes, Thomas. 1996. *Leviathan*. Gaskin, G.C.A. ed. Oxford: Oxford University Press.

Hobbes, Thomas. 1997. *On the Citizen*. Tuck, Richard and Silverthorne, Michael. eds. Cambridge: Cambridge University Press.

Hochstrasser, T.J. 2000. *Natural Law Theories in the Early Enlightenment*. Cambridge: Cambridge University Press.

Kant, Immanuel. 1970. Perpetual Peace. In Reiss, Hans. Ed. *Political Writings*. Cambridge: Cambridge University Press.

Pagden, Anthony. 2000. Stoicism, Cosmopolitanism, and the Legacy of European Imperialism. *Constellations*. 7(1), pp.3–22.

Pagden, Anthony. 2013. *The Enlightenment and Why It Still Matters* (Oxford: Oxford University Press.

Palladini, Fiammetta. 2008. Pufendorf Disciple of Hobbes: The Nature of Man and the State of Nature: The Doctrine of *Socialitas*. *History of European Ideas*. **34**(1), pp.26–60.

Pufendorf, Samuel. 1696. *de Rebus a Carolo Gustavo Sueciæ rege gestis commentariorum*. Norimbergoe.

Pufendorf, Samuel. 1934. *De Jure Naturae et Gentium Libri Octo,* vol. 2. Oldfather, C.H. and Oldfather, W.A. eds. Oxford: Clarendon Press.

Pufendorf, Samuel. 2002. *Of the Nature and Qualification of Religion in Reference to Civil Society*. Zurbuchen, Simone. ed. Indianapolis, IN: Liberty Fund.

Pufendorf, Samuel. 2007. *The Present State of Germany*, Seidler, Michael J. ed. Indianapolis, IN: Liberty Fund.

Pufendorf, Samuel. 2013. *An Introduction to the History of the Principal Kingdoms and States of Europe*, Seidler, Michael J. ed. Indianapolis, IN: Liberty Fund.

Seidler, Michael J. 1996. 'Turkish Judgment' and the English Revolution: Pufendorf on the Right of Resistance. In Palladini, Fiammetta and Hartung, Gerald. eds. *Pufendorf und die europäische Fruhaufklärung*. Berlin: Akademie Verlag.

Seidler, Michael J. 2015. Pufendorf's Moral and Political Philosophy. *Stanford Encyclopedia of Philosophy*. November 3, 2015. Available from: http://plato.stanford.edu/entries/pufendorf-moral/#Inf.

Simons, Walter. 1934. Introduction. In Pufendorf, Samuel. *De Jure Naturae et Gentium Libri Octo*, vol. 2. Oldfather, C.H. and Oldfather, W.A. eds. Oxford: Clarendon Press.

Tuck, Richard. 1999. *The Rights of War and Peace: Political Thought and the International Order from Grotius to Kant*. Oxford: Oxford University Press.

Tully, James. 1991. Introduction. In Pufendorf, Samuel. *On the Duty of Man and Citizen According to Natural Law*. Tully, James. Ed. Cambridge: Cambridge University Press.

Vitoria, Francisco de. On the American Indians. In Pagden, Anthony and Lawrance, Jeremy. eds. *Political Writings*. Cambridge: Cambridge University Press.

12

EMER DE VATTEL (1714–1767)

Theodore Christov

Introduction

Born in 1714 in the Swiss canton of Neuchatel, Emer de Vattel came from a privileged background: his father was a high-ranking clergyman in the Reformed Church, while his mother was the daughter of the treasurer of the Prussian King. His passion for philosophy came from his father, who had a deep interest in theology, while he acquired an interest in politics from his mother's side of the family. Unique among many of his contemporary philosophy writers, he was both an imaginary thinker and a talented diplomat. As customary at the time, he was trained in the humanist tradition of the ancient Greek and Roman classics, especially perspectives on human nature and the rights of war and peace. As his career developed, he wrote on the laws and rights of war and peace in the tradition of Grotius, Pufendorf, and Wolff. He was not, however, deferent to these authoritative figures. Rather he discounted elements of their work as deficient and posited his own writings as an advancement on them (Vattel, 2008, pp.7–8; 9; 12–13). His principal work, *Le droit des gens ou principes de la loi naturelle appliques a la conduite et aux affaires des nations et des souverains* (1758), [*The Law of Nations, or, Principles of the Law of Nature, Applied to the Conduct and Affairs of Nations and Sovereigns*] set out to provide a definitive study of the law of nations – "the science which teaches the rights subsisting between nations or states, and the obligations correspondent to those rights" (*Ibid.*, p.67).

The *Law of Nations* became an instant classic and a guidebook on how to conduct international relations in the 18th century. It was, for example, referenced as a source of authority during the American Revolution, the French Revolution and the Napoleonic wars, and remained important well into the 19th century (Fenewick, 1913). Constitutive of the modern natural law tradition, Vattel's *Law of Nations* had profound ramifications for just war thinking: it provided a blueprint for international conduct and diplomacy as we have come to know it today. By focusing on the rights and obligations of citizens and states, it established the golden rule of sovereigns – one should be treated as one treats others, whether a person or a state. This view of sovereignty set a general principle of non-intervention, as each state holds the right to govern itself, with no other state having a say in its internal affairs (Beaulac, 2003). This view of sovereignty marks a stark departure from the classical just war tradition – the view that sovereigns had a moral obligation to secure justice in the world at large, and especially in the case of tyranny, and was the final step in the secularization of just war thinking (Johnson, 2014, p.97). Indeed, we are in many ways the heirs to the legacy of Vattelian sovereignty (at least in its ideal form), which remains pivotal in understanding international affairs today, while his arguments about just war – preventive war in particular – hold renewed significance (Pitts, 2013).

Contexts

Vattel was born a year after the conclusion of the Treaty of Utrecht (1713), which established the Peace of Utrecht after the War of the Spanish Succession. The *Law of Nations* appeared right in the middle of the Seven Years' War (1756–1763). Even though the major actors in these international wars were European empires, their battle over ideology, power, and influence took place both within European boundaries and extended further into the colonized spaces of the New World.

The War of the Spanish Succession (1700–1714) revealed widespread 18th-century sentiments that universal monarchy would disrupt the venerable balance of power key to peace among states (Oseander, 1994). These were, deep down, existential fears about what would happen if a rival power became too powerful. When King Charles II of Spain died without a direct heir in 1700, he was succeeded by French prince Philip of Anjou (also known as Philip V). This raised the possibility of a union of the French and Spanish crowns that would put other powers at great risk. The ensuing War of the Spanish Succession was fought to prevent French dominion on mainland Europe, with the Austrians, English, and Dutch favoring Archduke Charles of Austria (Holy Roman Emperor 1711–1740) as the alternative to succeed Charles II. The war was arguably a classic example of what we would call today preventive war, fought to stave off the looming danger of France becoming too powerful.

Lurking in the background was, of course, the specter of Louis XIV of France, or "the Sun King", who fueled fears of a universal monarchy by establishing hegemony over Europe. Any aspirations to universal dominion in a world that was beginning to be organized along national, if not state, lines raised security suspicions. A ruler as aggrandizing as Louis XIV was a threat, not only to the national interest of other countries, but also to Europe's balance of power and international order itself.

> If Charles the Second, king of Spain, instead of settling the succession on the duke of Anjou, had appointed for his heir Louis XIV … [it would] have

> been nothing less than delivering up all Europe to servitude, or at least reducing it to the most critical and precarious situation.
>
> *(Vattel, 2008, p.493)*

Had the French ruler actually ascended the throne, he would have most certainly raised alarms of a continent-wide danger.

The fourteen years of war that followed the death of Charles II in 1700 were certainly on Vattel's mind as he incorporated this period of warfare that had engulfed most of Western Europe into his own thinking about just war. Most European states were fearful of any possible French reign over Spain and its possessions. The preliminaries of peace between France and Great Britain, signed in 1711, tacitly accepted the partition of Spain's possessions in Europe. The prolonged peace negotiations included the question of how to provide guarantees that the crowns of France and Spain would be kept separate, which was subsequently addressed in the summer of 1712, when Philip signed a renunciation. At stake in these negotiations was the nature of hegemony in international relations, and Vattel was sensitive to these developments. The final treaty effectively ended any French ambitions of hegemony in Europe (at least until the Napoleonic Wars) and restored the European system based on the balance of power. The question of how to treat French hegemony, however, would remain central to Vattel's thinking about justice among states.

The peace established between European powers with the conclusion of the Treaty of Utrecht would endure for several decades until the onset of the Seven Years' War. While the War of the Spanish Succession was fought exclusively for dominion within Europe itself, the Seven Years' War transplanted great power rivalry across the Atlantic to lands they competed to claim. The contention between Britain and France, traditionally limited to claims for land-based rule in the Old Continent, now found a new battleground in North America. Because of his knowledge about the workings of foreign relations, Vattel was asked to be involved in public affairs by Augustus III, who was the King of Poland as well as Elector of Saxony in the Holy Roman Empire. Vattel was appointed a Privy Councilor of Augustus III's Cabinet. His ideas about the rights and wrongs of warfare would ultimately be shaped in an environment of active political duties.

The Seven Years' War ended with the Treaty of Paris between France, Spain and Great Britain, and the Treaty of Hubertusburg between Saxony, Austria and Prussia, in 1763 – five years after the publication of *Law of Nations*. The peace treaty transformed the European political order for generations to come by opening the way for Britain's global hegemony throughout the nineteenth century, the rise of Prussia, and the independence of America's colonies. The main protagonists in these events – diplomats, statesmen, and officials – held a deep familiarity with the works of Vattel and, for many from the mid-18th century onwards, his *Law of Nations* served as a guidebook in formulating foreign policy (Lang and Russell, 1990; Gould, 2003). As the very first recognizably modern treatise of international law, the book enjoyed tremendous success for generations, not least because it was written in the vernacular French (rather than Latin), but especially because it was intended for "cabinet politicians" and not academicians (Vattel, 2008, p.259).

While Grotius's work is generally considered groundbreaking in establishing the conduct of states as sovereign actors – especially his views that the seas are open to all – Vattel's treatise was far more expansive in its scope and detailed in affirming the rules of engagement not only in times of war but also in times of peace. Vattel considered the observance of universal justice among nations not as an obscure and contestable scholarly endeavor, but pre-eminently as an applicable principle that practicing statesmen should turn to for consultation. Without denying that the "principles of the law of nature and of nations" are "sacred", he effectively linked the domain of rightfulness with that of politics, for "it is an invariable truth that justice is inseparable from sound policy" (Vattel, 2008, p.491). Justice and statesmanship went hand in hand, and Vattel's *Law of Nations* was meant to lay out practical standards for sovereigns to follow in international dealings.

Tenets

To understand the justice of war for Vattel, one must begin with the general ties that bind states together – the law of nations. James Turner Johnson notes that Vattel marks an important point in the secularization of just war in so far as he derives his principles from nature as opposed to grace (Johnson, 1975, p.253). His thought thus breaks from the classic just war doctrine found in thinkers such as Aquinas (chapter 4), Vitoria (chapter 6), and even Suárez (chapter 8).

Vattel's thought was influenced especially by Cicero and Grotius (both of whom are covered in this volume), as well as Christian Wolff's *Ius naturae et ius gentium*:

> Nations, being obliged by nature reciprocally to cultivate human society are bound to observe towards each other all the duties which the safety and advantage of that society require ... now the laws of nature being no less obligatory on nations than on individuals, whatever duties each man owes to other men, the same does each nation, in its way, owe to other nations. Such is the foundation of those common duties – of those offices of humanity – to which nations are reciprocally bound towards each other.
>
> *(Vattel, 2008, p.261)*

The essential analogy between natural individuals and sovereign states determines the scope of what is morally permissible and universally just in international conduct.[1] When the law of nature is applied to states, it is then commonly called the law of nations and consists of precepts recognizable by the light of reason ("necessary law of nations") and the general customs regulating relations between states ("voluntary law of nations"). Both of these kinds of laws are:

> established by nature, but each in a different manner; the former as a sacred law which nations and sovereigns are bound to respect and follow in all their

actions; the latter, as a rule which the general welfare and safety oblige them to admit in their transactions with each other.

(Vattel, 2008, p.17)

Vattel also admits that some nations might fall outside these bounds. "If there were a people", he wrote, "who made open profession of trampling justice under foot, – who despised and violated the rights of others whenever they found an opportunity, – the interest of human society would authorize all the other nations to form a confederacy in order to humble and chastise the delinquents … the safety of the human race requires that [such a nation] should be repressed" *(Ibid.,* p.297).

The law of nations is based on notions of common reciprocity, "founded on certain and invariable principles" *(Ibid.,* p.16). Justice among nations is both universal, with respect to its observance, and rectificatory, in its remedy to restore losses and obtain an equal distribution of gain and loss. To remedy claims of injury and restore losses, recourse to force may sometimes be necessary: "But if, from particular conjectures, and from the obstinacy of an unjust adversary, neither reprisals, nor any of the methods of which we have been treating [compromise, mediation, arbitration], should prove sufficient for our defense and for the protection of our rights, there remains only the wretched and melancholy alternative of war" *(Ibid.,* p.467).[2]

Vattel's discussion of just war occurs in Book III of *Law of Nations.* After explaining the concept of the nation (Book I) and the duties between nations and states, including ways of terminating disputes short of war (Book II), Vattel then turns to war. Relevant to our purposes, Book III covers the different kinds of war, the just causes of war, the importance of declaring war, the nature of the enemy, the rights of nations in war, and the difference between the necessary and voluntary law of nations, along with a host of other topics statesmen at the time would find useful. Although we won't discuss it here, it is important to note that Book IV discusses the restoration of peace, suggesting that Vattel, as with many other thinkers covered in this volume, saw a clear link between just war and a return to peace.

Vattel defines war as "that state in which we prosecute our right by force" (2008, p.469). Wars can be either defensive or offensive depending on the object of what is to be obtained. A defensive war is carried out "to repel the attack of an enemy" for "no other [purpose] than self-defense", whereas the case of offensive wars "relates either to the prosecution of some rights, or safety" *(Ibid.,* p.471). Vattel clearly distinguishes between legal war, or "regular warfare", and illegal war, which would include "conquest, or the desire of invading the property of others" *(Ibid.,* p.471).

For Vattel, the "cause of every just war is injury, either already done or threatened" *(Ibid.,* p.483). Thus, he lays out three just causes:

1. To recover what belongs or is due to us. 2. To provide for our future safety by punishing the aggressor or offender. 3. To defend ourselves, or

protect ourselves from injury by repelling unjust violence. The first two are the objects of an offensive, the third that of a defensive war.

(Ibid., p.484)

Armed hostilities should only be approached in the last extremity, rather than treated as an immediately available resort. "Humanity revolts against a sovereign", Vattel warns, "who, without necessity or without very powerful reasons, lavishes the blood of his most faithful subjects, and exposes his people to the calamities of war, when he has it in his power to maintain them in the enjoyment of an honorable and salutary peace" *(Ibid.,* p.482). The "destructive and unhappy consequences of war" should be endured only on condition that they have been endorsed by the people of the nation, so that they do not feel forced to fight an unwanted war *(Ibid.,* pp.482–3).

Only the sovereign power "possesses the authority to make war" *(Ibid.,* p.471), and war must be undertaken with "proper and commendable motives" *(Ibid.,* p.485). Because he is accountable to his citizens, a skilled statesman will ordinarily settle controversies with another nation by any peaceful means possible and only rarely choose to use force. Vattel warns that "bare suspicions" can never "serve as sufficient authority" to wage war and he expressly denounces any false "abundance of pretexts to give a color of justice" that a state may contrive to advance its own vain ambitions, for by doing so it would be "sapping every foundation on which rests the security of nations" *(Ibid.,* pp.455–56). While the maintenance and cultivation of peace should be the goal of each leader, the waging of war is morally permissible.

Much of the responsibility for determining whether all pacific measures have been exhausted rests on the shoulders of individual states "in virtue of their natural liberty", so that "each one is free to judge in her own conscience how she ought to act, and has a right to make her own judgment the sole guide of her conduct with respect to her duties in every thing that is not determined by the perfect rights of another" *(Ibid.,* p.456). The decision to act constitutes an internal duty in consulting one's own conscience, rather than an external obligation, and no state may presume to judge the necessity of waging a war on behalf of another state.

At the heart of Vattel's reflections on the rights and wrongs of warfare lies the question of injury and the aim is to describe its proper meaning, nature, and scope. On the one hand, because justice is rectificatory and consequently demands the equalization of what has been lost or injured, hostilities can be initiated for the purpose of obtaining such restoration. This is consistent with much of the Medieval or classic just war tradition found in Augustine, as well as Vattel's immediate predecessor Grotius. On the other hand, Vattel admits that the meaning of "injury" is rather open to a wider interpretation, and could be linked to the perception of a future threat: "it is not always necessary that every conciliatory measure be first expressly rejected". Rather, if a state has "every reason to believe that the enemy would not enter into those measures with sincerity…and that the intervening delay would only expose [the state] to greater danger of being overpowered", then it can take up arms (2008, p.455). Vattel thus inquires: In a world of no superior judge, where nations do not recognize an ultimate arbiter to decide on controversies, how does a nation respond to the "celebrated question" of "whether the aggrandizement of a neighboring power … be a sufficient reason for making war against him" (*Ibid.*, p.491)? This is the question of preventive war.

Vattel was not the first to theorize this question – Gentili (chapter 9) also defended preventive war (Colonomos, 2013).[3] Vattel's argument is that power alone does not threaten, but when combined with the will to use it, then a threatened state has the right to act preventively against its enemy (Vattel, 2008, p.492). A prudent ruler can read the signs of the times and choose not to wait until it is too late: "Are we to allow of the aggrandizement of a neighbor, and quietly wait till he makes his preparations to enslave us? Will it be a time to defend ourselves when we are deprived of the means?" (*Ibid.*, p.491) In asking these questions, Vattel clearly distinguishes preventive war (a threat in the distant future) from pre-emptive war (against an immediate threat).

While one could ascribe something of a balance of power element to Vattel's view of preventive war, this should be done with caution. On the one hand, the just cause of preventive war is tightly linked to *jus ad bellum*, as opposed to purely utilitarian pursuit. As one scholar puts it: "Restoring the balance of power by force of arms was only justified when a weaker nation was actually injured, or when it could be established with certainty that the hegemonic power entertained designs of oppression and conquest" (Zurbuchen, 1979, p.414).[4] On the other hand, Vattel's system of thought, into which his view of preventive war must be placed, sought to strip countries of their national zeal for aggrandizement and safeguard the general liberties of all states. This was especially the case for his own Europe, which provided him with lived experiences of such threats from which he drew upon.[5]

The prudent ruler will be able to judge the behavior of an enemy state, and recognize the brewing threat based on a history of injustice "that gives rise to suspicion" (Vattel, 2008, p.492). But even then, not all threats warrant preventive war; only existential threats do: "If the evil in question be of a supportable nature – if it be only some slight loss – matters are not to be precipitated: there is no great danger in delaying our opposition to it, till there be certainty of our being threatened. But if the safety of the state lies at stake, our precaution and foresight cannot be extended too far" (*Ibid.*, p.493). Vattel concludes that absolute certainty of a looming threat is not needed; rather, when it is "impossible or too dangerous to wait … we may justly act on a reasonable presumption" (*Ibid.*p.493).

Once a ruler declares war, whether offensive or defensive, against another sovereign, "it is understood that the whole nation declares war against another nation: for the sovereign represents the nation, and acts in the name of the whole society" (*Ibid.*, p.509). At this point, the two nations become enemies and all their subjects, including soldiers, women and children, are to be accounted enemies. That being said, there are limits on what states can do in war, which Vattel discusses with regards to persons and things.

Concerning Vattel's ideas about *jus in bello* – "the rights which are to be respected during the war itself … and the rules which nations should reciprocally observe" – these derive from the "object of a just war: for, when the end is lawful, he who has a right to pursue that end, has, of course, a right to employ all the means which are necessary for its attainment" (*Ibid.*, p.541). Included in these is the right to kill enemy soldiers: "The enemy who attacks me unjustly, gives me an undoubted right to repel his violence; and he who takes up arms to oppose me when I demand only my right, becomes himself the real aggressor by his unjust resistance" (*Ibid.*, p.543). Also included is the right to destroy property being used to fight, and seize property of the enemy state, albeit in moderation and only with the aim of victory (and reparations for an injury received) in mind. Importantly, these rights exist *independent of whether one is fighting for a just cause*: "If the enemy observes all the rules of regular warfare, we are not entitled to see him as a violator of the law of nations" (*Ibid.*, p.591). We find here something akin to what Walzer (2015, ch.3), calls the moral equality of soldiers. For Vattel, "this is absolutely necessary … if people wish to introduce any order, any regularity, into so violent an operation as that of arms, or to set any bounds to the calamities of which it is productive, or leave a door constantly open for peace" (Vattel, 2008, p.591).

Regarding what one can do against people, Vattel rejects methods that are "of an odious kind", those that are "unjustifiable in themselves", or "prohibited by natural law" (*Ibid.*, p.543). These include poisoning wells and assassination. Among the other limits that Vattel recognizes: the unlawfulness of killing those who cease to fight and sparing woman, children, the sick, men of letters and peasants who do not take up arms from the ravages of war. The underlying reason lies in the function of these people: the former, soldiers who lay down their arms, are no longer capable of committing injury; while the latter are not part of the armed forces. Of course, were women, for example, to interfere in military actions, then the clemency they ought to receive would be rescinded.

Regarding objects, Vattel permits laying waste to an enemy's land, but only in cases of necessity. If done wantonly, those who do so "are looked upon as savage barbarians" (*Ibid.*, p.570). The crux here is, again, a matter of function – if the objects do not serve the war effort of the enemy, they should be spared. Vattel also argues that certain buildings "which do honor to human society and do not contribute to increase the enemy's strength – such as temples, tombs, public building and works of remarkable beauty" ought to be spared as well, except for cases of extreme necessity (*Ibid.*, pp.571–72). Thus, he provides the following maxim: "All damage done to the enemy unnecessarily, every act of hostility which does not tend to procure victory and bring the war to a conclusion, is a licentiousness condemned by the law of nature" (*Ibid.*, p.573).

Lurking is the background of his discussion is a tension between necessity – doing what is necessary to achieve the end of the war – and recognizing the humanity of the enemy. The former permits a broad array of actions and sometimes caveats to the above mentioned restrictions, while the latter coaxes those fighting to act with restraint:

Let us not forget that our enemies are men. Though reduced to the disagreeable necessity of prosecuting our right by force of arms, let us not divest ourselves that charity which connects us with all mankind. Thus we shall courageously defend our country's rights without violating those of human nature. Let our valour preserve itself from every stain of cruelty, and the lustre of victory will not be tarnished by inhuman and brutal actions.

(Ibid., pp.563–64)

Recognizing the common humanity even of one's enemy is essential to Vattel's just war theory because it reflects the reciprocal duty nations owe to each other. These "sentiments of humanity" form the essence of the law of nations and the prospect of peace because nations that maintain them "will never seek to promote their own advantage at the expense and detriment of other nations: however intent they may be on their own happiness, they will ever be careful to combine it with that of others, and with justice and equity" (*Ibid.*, p.652). This is why war must be fought with moderation and justice in mind.

There is, however, an implicit caveat to discuss. In several passages in *Law of Nations*, Vattel suggests that against some enemies, the limits may not apply: "When we are at war with a savage nation, who observe no rules, and never give quarter, we may punish them in the persons of any of their people whom we take … and endeavor … to force them to respect the laws of humanity" (*Ibid.*, p.544). The existence of "savage nations" points to a potential contradiction that undermines his view of equal sovereignty for all nations. Those who make war without any justifiable reason or apparent motives, Vattel writes, including "the barbarians who destroyed Rome … the Turks and other Tartars, – Genghis-khan, Timur-Bec or Tamerlane", present an affront to civilization "as enemies to the human race". As enemies to humanity, "all nations have a right to join in a confederacy for the purpose of punishing and even exterminating those savage nations" (*Ibid.*, p.487). The clear implication here is that the *jus in bello* rules may not apply in such wars – indeed, in wars of extermination, how could they?

Vattel does not really explore who defines the natural law in the first place, perhaps assuming that humanity's laws are automatically in line with broader European values. But he was very clear that the reciprocal duty that holds between so-called civilized nations does not hold between the civilized and the savages. After discussing the restraints that reciprocity between civilized states demands, Vattel raises an exception that illustrates this point:

There is, however, one case, in which we may refuse to spare the life of an enemy who surrenders, or to allow any capitulation to a town reduced to the last extremity. It is when that enemy has been guilty of some enormous breach of the law of nations, and particularly when he has violated the laws of war.

(Ibid., p.544)

Vattel, of course, is not alone in positing caveats to his general principles; rather, it bears keeping in mind that this seems to be a perennial theme that runs across the just war tradition, and continues to concern us even today (Brunstetter and Zartner, 2011). Reminiscent of Cicero, what is significant about Vattel is where he draws the line between mere punishment against enemies with whom we (the civilized) can cohabit the earth, and wars of annihilation against those with whom cohabitation is impossible.

Legacy and enduring relevance

Vattel has frequently been placed in the larger tradition of the history of international relations and seen as a major voice in the construction of the discipline that eventually came to be known as international law. Along with Vitoria and Grotius, he is widely regarded as a foundational figure in the study of the law of nations, in which the discourse of war and politics of enmity occupied a central position. Thus, one of his major legacies is his contribution to the modern understanding of sovereignty. James Turner Johnson puts it succinctly:

> [Vattel's] conception of the international order as composed of independent and juridically equal states, with each state having the right to make its own determination of what is just and no other state having the right to challenge this unless it poses a threat, is essentially the conception that solidified in the years after him. Convention calls this "the Westphalian system" but it might be called the Vattel system.
>
> *(Johnson, 2015, p.98)*[6]

And yet, as part of this inheritance we find his defense of preventive war – a view that is quite controversial in modern times (Chatterjee, 2013), but no mention of humanitarian intervention that occupied the minds of some of the authorities he cited (Pufendorf and Grotius, for example). Vattel, in fact, ridicules those who defended the conquest of the New World on such false precepts (presumably Vitoria), and explicitly challenges Grotius: "it is strange to hear the learned Grotius assert that a sovereign may take up arms to chastise nations which are guilty of enormous transgressions of the law of nations" (Vattel, 2008, p.265).[7]

His intellectual concerns, however, were far broader, in their appeal to a political outlook in which moral principles and ethical scrutiny were made central. Inasmuch as he established the pre-eminence of justice among nations by laying out the principles that regulate states' conduct during times of war and times of peace, he is trapped in a worldview that allowed a clear distinction between the civilized, who uphold the law of nations, and the savages, who fall outside of it. This too captures something import of the international sphere that we have inherited. His just war theory remains Janus-faced: it affirms what is most common and noble to all humans, while it simultaneously excludes some of them on potentially dubious grounds. It is this legacy of Vattel's thought that we, in the present, continue to grapple with as we face the dilemmas associated with the Responsibility to Protect doctrine and humanitarian intervention (Welsh, 2004; Welsh, 2010), as well as wars against barbaric non-state actors such as the so-called Islamic State group that threaten international peace and security based in Vattelian sovereignty.

A return to Vattel's moral grapplings, forged at a time when the notions of sovereignty we have arguably inherited were coming into being, provides fertile ground for thinking about how to use force to maintain international peace and security among nations.

Notes

1   As a side note, an interesting comparison can be drawn between Vattel's claim and the reductive individualist arguments made by McMahan, covered in chapter 19 of this volume.
2   For a broader discussion of Vattel and the variations of natural law, see: (Zurbuchen, 2009, pp.409–411).
3   Compare Vattel with Medieval counterparts in: (Reichberg, 2007).
4   For a discussion on Vattel's contemporaries and the balance of power, see: (Vagts and Vagts, 1979).
5   For a broader discussion, see chapter 8 "Vattel the Sorry Comforter" in (Christov, 2015).
6   For a counter view, see: (Pitts, 2013).
7   For a discussion of this issue, see: (Christov, 2015, p.247).

Works cited

Beaulac, Stéphane. 2003. Emer de Vattel and the Externalization of Sovereignty. *Journal of the History of International Law*. **5**, pp. 237–92.

Brunstetter, Daniel and Zartner, Dana. 2011. Just War Against Barbarians: Revisiting the Valladolid Debates Between Sepúlveda and Las Casas. *Political Studies*. **59**(3), pp. 733–52.

Chatterjee, Deen K. ed. 2013. *The Ethics of Preventive War*. Cambridge: Cambridge University Press, pp.1–14.

Christov, Theodore. 2015. *Before Anarchy: Hobbes and His Critics in Modern International Thought*. Cambridge: Cambridge University Press.

Colonomos, Ariel. 2013. War in the Face of Doubt: Early Modern Classics and the Preventive Use of Force. In Recchia, Stefano and Welsh Jennifer M. eds. *Just and Unjust Military Intervention: European Thinkers for Vitoria to Mill*. Cambridge: Cambridge University Press, pp.48–69.

Fenewick, Charles G. 1913. The Authority of Vattel. *American Political Science Review*. **7**(3), pp. 395–410.

Gould, Eliga H. 2003. Zones of Law, Zones of Violence: The Legal Geography of the British Atlantic, circa 1772. *William and Mary Quarterly*. **60**(3), pp. 471–510.

Johnson, James Turner. 1975. *Ideology, Reason and the Limitation of War: Religious and Secular Concepts, 1200–1740*. Princeton: Princeton University Press.

Johnson, James Turner. 2014. *Sovereignty: Moral and Historical Perspective*. Washington D.C.: Georgetown University Press.

Lang, Daniel G. and Russell, Greg. 1990. The Ethics of Power in American Diplomacy: The Statecraft of John Quincy Adams, *The Review of Politics*. **52**(1), pp. 3–31.

Oseander, Andreas. 1994. *The State System of Europe, 1640–1990: Peacemaking and the Conditions of International Society*. Oxford: Oxford University Press.

Pitts, Jennifer. 2013. Intervention and Sovereign Equality: Legacies of Vattel. In Recchia, Stefano and Welsh Jennifer M. eds. *Just and Unjust Military Intervention: European Thinkers for Vitoria to Mill*. Cambridge: Cambridge University Press, pp. 132–53.

Reichberg, Gregory. 2007. Preventive War in Classical Just War Theory. *Journal of the History of International Law*. **9**(1), pp.5–34.

Vagts, Alfred and Vagts, Detlev F. 1979. The Balance of Power in International Law: A History of an Idea. *The American Journal of International Law*. **73**(4), pp.555–80.

Vattel, Emer de. 2008. *The Law of Nations*. Indianapolis, IN: Liberty Fund.

Walzer, Michael. 2015. *Just and Unjust Wars: A Moral Argument With Historical Illustrations*. New York: Basic Books.

Welsh Jennifer M. ed. 2004. *Humanitarian Intervention and International Relations*. Oxford: Oxford University Press.

Welsh, Jennifer M. 2010. Implementing the Responsibility to Protect: Where Expectations Meet Reality. *Ethics & International Affairs*. **24**(4),pp. 415–430.

Zurbuchen, Simone. 2009. Vattel's Law of Nations and Just War Theory. *History of European Ideas*. **35**(4), pp. 408–17.

13

IMMANUEL KANT (1724–1804)

Brian Orend

Introduction

Immanuel Kant (1724–1804) is renowned as one of the most comprehensive and influential philosophers in the history of Western – if not world – thought. His name is commonly placed alongside that of Plato, Aristotle, Descartes, and Hume for the depth, breadth, and impact of his writings, which dealt with everything from aesthetics to metaphysics, from geography to morality, and from science and theories of knowledge and education to law and theories of domestic and international justice (Cassirer, 2009).

Perhaps because of this stature, some readers may be surprised to find Kant included in this volume, shoe-horned (as it were) inside of a "mere" tradition of thought, like just war theory, whereas a philosophical colossus such as Kant surely transcends such a thing, and develops a *sui generis* account of war and peace that must leave others embarrassed, or in his conceptual dust.

It must be admitted, in reply, that Kant did not *explicitly* identify with the just war tradition, for two reasons. First, it remained mainly concerned (at the time) with wars *between* countries, and thus seemed out of touch with the burning issue of his era, which was violent revolution *within* a country (or empire). Second, the just war tradition was then, culturally, associated with Catholicism – the intellectual line of thought from Aquinas to Vitoria, for example; and Kant, as someone brought up in Prussia within a firmly Protestant family, did not want to align himself overtly with just war understandings. Indeed, he mocked some of the then-prominent just war theorists: labelling Grotius, Pufendorf, Vattel ("and the rest") as mere "tiresome comforters". After reading the chapters on each of these, the reader may wish to challenge Kant's views. But Kant felt that the just war theories of his day were like a mere Band-Aid over the bigger problem of ending war as such (Kant, 2015, p.67). Thus, to include Kant within the just war tradition is controversial. Yet, we'll see he *does* share many of the exact same understandings of *jus ad bellum* (justice of the start of war) and *jus in bello* (justice of conduct during war) as does the tradition. Further, the argument will be made that Kant is probably the creator of what many today have come to see as the third category of just war thinking, *jus post bellum* (justice after war). If true, Kant may actually turn out to be *one of the most historically important* members of the just war tradition, in spite of some of his hasty rhetorical declarations (Orend, 1999).

Contexts

When Kant wrote about war and peace, Western society was being convulsed by two world-historic revolutions: the American (1775–83) and the French (1789–99). These revolutions signalled the end of absolute monarchy as a legitimate form of governance, and heralded the first pro-rights republican societies. These events had a massive impact on Kant's political thinking, and there's no doubt that – though he personally preferred gradual reform over sudden violence – in his heart of hearts, he was a profound supporter of the liberal ideals (*"Liberté! Egalité! Fraternité!"*) of both these revolutions (Armitage and Subrahmanyan, 2010).

At the least, Kant felt that the conservative structures of *"ancien régime"* society needed to be transformed utterly. Kant was an ardent supporter of the Enlightenment: i.e., the broad cultural shift in European intellectual life *away* from religion, tradition, and authority *towards* science, reform, and an individual's human rights, and capacity for critical thought. Kant hoped that the American and French Revolutions would extend Enlightenment attitudes into political and social domains. (He even penned a spirited short essay entitled "What is Enlightenment?" His answer: "Man's emergence from his own self-imposed immaturity". The related slogan that Kant believed to best capture the ethos of the Enlightenment? "*Sapere Aude!*" or "Dare to Know!") (Kant, 1983a, pp.41–47; Pagden, 2013).

Inspired by the Enlightenment, many thinkers before Kant crafted proposals for solving the problem of war. After all, if critical rationality could create empirical science, and dispel superstitious tradition, then perhaps reason could also finally solve the age-old problem of armed conflict. Many proposals for "ending war", in this systematic fashion, were crafted in the century leading up to Kant, notably including those of the Abbé de Saint-Pierre and Jean-Jacques Rousseau. Kant follows in this tradition, no doubt inspired by Rousseau, of whom he thought very highly (vague references to Rousseau's famous concept of "the general will" abound throughout Kant's political writings). Indeed, Kant's most famous essay on armed conflict is entitled *"Perpetual Peace"*, and includes Kant's own proposals in this regard.[1]

By chapter's end, we may come to see Kant's reflections on war and peace as being particularly profound: uniting the just war tradition *with* the perpetual peace tradition; and *bringing together* Enlightenment optimism and liberal idealism in the committed reformist (or even, revolutionary) project of a better and more peaceful world.

Texts

Consider Kant's thoughts in terms of *jus ad bellum, jus in bello,* and *jus post bellum.*

Jus ad bellum

Kant is, quite commonly, considered a pacifist. This is probably because people tend only to have heard of, and read, his famous essay "*Perpetual Peace*" (1795). It is also owing to some "purple prose" in that idealistic manifesto and elsewhere, such as the 1797 work, *The Doctrine of Right* (or "*Rechtslehre*") when Kant practically shouts in italics that: "*There shall be no war*" (Kant, 1995, p.174). But the crucial word there is "*shall*", and it does *not* refer to an absolute prohibition. It refers, rather, to Kant's understanding of a long-term process of both domestic and international reform, whose end-state, *at some point in the future*, will be a world without war. But, until we arrive at such an end-state, Kant explicitly allows countries moral permission to resort to armed force under certain conditions, such as when he (also) declares in the *Rechtslehre*: "[T]he right to make war … is the permitted means by which one state prosecutes its rights against another" (*Ibid.*, p.167).

Such a clear statement allows us to label Kant meaningfully as *some kind* of just war theorist, as the three basic logical options, on the ethics of war and peace, are: 1) *pacifism*, which says that no war can ever be morally justified (there's always some superior, hopefully non-violent, alternative); 2) *realism,* which asserts that war and morality have nothing to do with each other, and countries should only tend to their own prudential self-interests in warfare; and 3) *just war thinking*, whose core notion is precisely that, sometimes, it can be morally permissible for states to go to war (Orend, 2013; Walzer, 1977).

On top of this core, crucial proposition, Kant adds further explanation. *A state may resort to armed force if and only if its rights have been violated.* Which rights do states have? Kant's very standard reply is political sovereignty and territorial integrity: i.e., the right of a people to live on a piece of land and govern themselves in a manner of their own choosing (provided they violate no other people's rights in doing so). But states have these rights, morally, because such rights are needed to realize the human rights of their individual citizens. The key principle here, in Kant's just cause principle, is *the defence, protection, and vindication of the fundamental rights of political communities and their citizens.* Kant says that a state can resort to war either in response to "actively inflicted injury" (particularly an invasion or attack) or to "threats" (presumably the credible and imminent threat of such an invasion or attack). So, the right to go to war is, for Kant, not purely or literally defensive; provided there is a serious enough threat, "the right of anticipatory attack" can also be legitimate (Kant, 1995, p.167). (*Note that this is quite far, indeed, from pacifism*). Like earlier just war thinkers, Kant is not insistent that just wars be purely defensive, as so many thinkers of our time have been, at least until the 9/11 attacks and the resurgence of severe terrorist threats and the attending desire to thwart them pre-emptively (Orend, 2013, pp.9–32; 78–86).

That being said, the main thrust of Kant's justification for armed conflict remains defensive. What exactly, for Kant, grounds the right of armed self-defence on the part of a state? His main argument is perhaps best understood as the following chain of propositions:

1. All states have moral rights (to political sovereignty and territorial integrity) and moral duties (not to violate other states' rights). The function of these rights and duties is to enable state governments to help secure the human rights of their individual citizens. (The very essence of political legitimacy, for Kant as for John Locke and the American and French revolutionaries, is the realization of individual rights to life, liberty, equality, property, and the pursuit of happiness) (Orend, 2013, pp.19–21; Boucher, 1998). States' rights and duties are the bedrock, and most fundamental priority, of international justice.
2. These rights entitle states to employ reliable measures necessary to secure the objects of these rights and protect them from violation.
3.   There is no reliable or effective international authority, which can currently assure states in the possession of the objects of their rights. Thus, states *are on their own* with regard to such assurance.
4. Currently, the most effective and reliable form of such self-help assurance with regard to rights-protection, at least in the last resort, is the use of armed force.
5. Thus, faced with serious violation of their rights, such as armed aggression, states are entitled to employ armed force and war in order to repeal the aggression of the rights-violator, to vindicate their rights, and to re-secure their objects and those of their citizens' human rights (Orend, 2000).

It's important to understand that, on Kant's reasoning, states *do no wrong* in responding to rights-violating aggression with armed force. A war in such a case, for Kant, is not merely one of evil compounding evil (as many a pacifist might say). It is, rather, a matter of repealing the wrong of aggression and of asserting and defending, in an effective fashion, one's own status as a rights-bearer. The pith and substance of Kant's justification, then, is two-fold and intertwined: a state may resort to war both *to defend itself* and *to repeal the aggression* that made the defence imperative. "Thus", Kant says, "if a state believes that it has been injured by another state, it is entitled to resort to violence, for it cannot in the state of nature gain satisfaction through legal proceedings …" In the international arena, "the right to make war … is the permitted means by which one state prosecutes its rights against another" (Kant, 1995, p.167; Orend, 1999).

Another way of making this important point, at the most fundamental level of Kant's influential moral philosophy, is to show how wars of self-defence against aggression do *not* violate the categorical imperative. The categorical imperative – the foremost command of morality for Kant – mandates that all rational agents act in such a way that: 1) all rational agents could (also) act on the exact same principle of action; and 2) in acting, full respect is paid to the rational agency that is the hallmark of our humanity (Kant, 1983b; O'Neil, 1989).

It is clear we can universalize the following maxim or policy: "When faced with rights-violating aggression, I reserve the right to employ those measures, including armed force, necessary for self-defence". Arguably, every rational agent, whether individual or collective, can endorse such a maxim of permissible self-protection. Of note, some contemporary just war scholars reject this view (see chapter 19 on McMahan). However, a system of international law allowing all states to defend themselves from aggression, with force if need be, is thus entirely consistent and universal: the course of action in question is open to all who fulfil its conditions. Secondly, we do not disrespect rational agency when we respond with armed force to aggression because: 1) we hold the aggressor state responsible for its actions (and thus treat it as a fully deliberative agent); and 2) we are, in doing so, actually vindicating the system of rules and laws designed to secure for everyone the elements of their rational agency, notably law and order and human rights. *We are thus resisting and punishing a rogue state which has violated the fundamental ground-rules needed for a just and well-functioning international system.* We are, so to speak, hindering a hindrance to our freedom as rational agents. And, in his domestic theory of justice, Kant precisely defines a just use of force as one, which "hinders a hindrance to freedom" (Kant, 1995, p.134; Orend, 2000, pp.15–88).

Jus in bello

Drawing upon, and interconnecting with, these understandings of *jus ad bellum*, Kant frames a small series of rules regarding just conduct in war. First, and crucially, he makes mention of the major *jus in bello* principle of discrimination/non-combatant immunity: "[T]o force individual persons [in a conquered state] to part with their belongings ... would be robbery, since it was not the conquered people who waged the war, but the state of which they were subjects that waged it through them" (Kant, 1995, pp.168–169). Unfortunately, this is not a terribly precise, or suggestively robust, account of the familiar rule of discrimination in targeting, as developed throughout the just war tradition. This is quite disappointing, given the importance of the principle (Walzer, 1977, pp.127–233), but it seems that we can safely infer that Kant must have *some* such rule in mind because: 1) the quote just mentioned *does* enumerate an immunity of a kind on the non-combatant civilian population; and 2) nowhere does Kant mention a right to deliberately kill innocent people, which non-combatant civilians are presumed by just war thinking to be. It is only rational actors (whether states or individuals) who either actually attack, or are imminently about to attack, who may be responded to with lethal armed force.

Kant also endorses restrictions on means *"mala in se"* (or "evil-in-themselves") (Orend, 2013, p.130). For Kant, this rather vague and sweeping criterion rules out any wars of "extermination", "subjugation", and "annihilation". Civilian populations cannot be massacred or enslaved. It also means that states cannot employ "assassins or poisoners", or even spies (Kant, 2015, p.57). In sum, he declares: "The attacked state is allowed to use any means of defence except those whose use would render its subjects unfit to be citizens. For if it did not observe this condition, it would render itself unfit in the eyes of international right to function as a person in relation to other states and to share equal rights with them" (Kant, 1995, pp.168–169). Such a state would, in effect, be an outlaw and unjust state. So it is clear that, for Kant, the end does *not* justify the use of any unjust means to attain it. Kant asserts this quite clearly when he says: "The rights of a state against an unjust enemy are unlimited in quantity or degree, although they do have limits in relation to quality. In other words, while the threatened state may not employ *every* means to assert its own rights, it may employ any intrinsically permissible means to whatever degree its own strength allows" (*Ibid.*, pp.170–171, emphasis original).

Kant scholar Arthur Ripstein has impressed upon me the difference and significance of what he calls "the inward-looking nature" of Kant's *jus in bello* (Ripstein, 2009, pp.123–167). Most just war theorists seem to frame *jus in bello* in outward-looking terms: what do you owe the enemy in wartime? Which restraints on your dealings with the enemy ought you to accept? Hence, such rules as non-combatant immunity and no means *mala in se* (Orend, 2013, pp.111–152). But we have just seen that, while Kant *does* endorse such rules, his development of them seems diffuse, disappointing, half-hearted and, in any event, nowhere near as detailed and action-guiding as other accounts of *jus in bello*, including those – such as Grotius, who is seen as a key figure in the emergence of *jus in bello* rules (see chapter 10) – prominently on offer in Kant's time (Johnson, 1981). Ripstein has persuaded me, and Dan Zupan concurs (Zupan, 2004, pp.43–85), that Kant is less interested in the standard, outward-looking rules – resulting in such things as literally hundreds of legal restrictions on prohibited kinds of weapon (Boothby, 2009) – and more concerned with developing an inward-looking conception of *jus in bello*: *how should I restrain my own conduct in war, so that I can avoid moral corruption and maintain my fitness as a decent individual, or political community, moving forward into the future?* If everyone observed this rule – as clearly inspired by the categorical imperative – then the outward-looking rules might even be unnecessary: soldiers, generals, and belligerents would restrain their own conduct in the appropriate way. The result of this would be the absence of atrocity, the avoidance of searing shame, and the maintenance of a non-poisoned atmosphere, in which negotiations about peace can succeed.

I think this is a profound insight, especially in terms of Kant scholarship. It rings true as an account of what Kant probably most wished for, in terms of the conduct of actors in wartime. It also has the happy consequence that Kant's account of *jus in bello* starts to look much more rich and practical than his very quick, sweeping, and highly theoretical remarks above. On this reading, what we actually have on offer is a rule directly applicable to *every* wartime action, regardless of circumstance.

Jus in bello rules are not just "external", but "internal", too. The rules are not only, or even mainly, about how you should treat the enemy. They are also about getting you to reflect critically and morally upon your own choices, and to restrain your own conduct. In particular: *Act always in such a way to avoid the kind of rights-violating moral corruption which would not only render oneself unfit to be an upstanding citizen in a just community but would render the securing of a just and enduring peace impossible afterwards.*

Truly, this command is something like what we might call "Kant's Categorical Imperative, or Golden Rule, of War-Planning and War-Fighting" (Orend, 2015).

Jus post bellum

One of the most creative things about Kant's reflections on warfare deals with peace treaties, or the proper endings of wars. This is totally *unlike* thinkers both before and after him, obsessed as they have been with the outbreak of wars, and then conduct within wars (as above). But, Kant sharply asks: what about justice *after* war? What makes for a just peace treaty? This is, e.g., the very first thing he says in *Perpetual Peace* (Kant, 2015, p.54).[2] In other words, he argues that traditional thinking about war and peace is, at the least, incomplete in so far as it leaves out one whole phase of war! Since there are, generally speaking, three phases of any given war – beginning, middle, and end – we cannot only have rules that deal with the first two. We need to think about a just ending to war. And not merely for the sake of completeness – though reason alone would demand such – but also because Kant believes wars that are wrapped up badly sow the seeds of future wars. (Reflection on the connection between the ending of the First World War (1914–18) and the outbreak of the Second World War (1939–45) gives evidence in favour of this view. The same could be said for the two recent "Serb wars" in the 1990s, and the two recent armed conflicts in Iraq in 1991 and 2003). Kant probably deserves credit for inventing *jus post bellum*, which has recently witnessed tremendous interest and fresh development in our own time (Orend, 2013, pp.285–250; Orend, 2002; May, 2012; Easterday, 2014).

We can distinguish between short-term *jus post bellum* and long-term *jus post bellum*, and it's fair to say that Kant's major interest in, and contribution to, concerns the latter. Of the former, which concerns how to end particular wars, it comes as little surprise that Kant says such things as: there needs to be a peace treaty that formally ends the war in question; such a treaty must be clear and public, with no secret provisions; and the former belligerents need to have fought, and continue to conduct themselves (in the often-delicate transition from war to peace), in such a way as to build confidence in each other and to prevent poisonous, ruinous back-sliding into armed conflict (Kant, 2015, pp.54–60).

Long-term *jus post bellum* essentially concerns Kant's own "recipe" for the achievement of perpetual peace. It is based on an important speculative thesis, namely, that *republics will never go to war against each other.*[3] Why not? Well, a Kantian republic respects and realizes the human rights of its individual citizens. It is a limited government with no tyrannical designs, either against its own citizens' freedoms, or against the territory or authority of any foreign government. It has a free economy, urges its citizens to excel culturally and economically, and it shows foreign visitors warm hospitality (Kant, 2015, pp.11–44; Williams, 1983). Kant reasons that *a country like this would never start a war against another, similarly-structured, country*. It would not be domineering and tyrannical, and thus not a conquering force; and – since its people would have freedom and control – they would never authorize such wars in the first place. Kant thinks that people are basically rational, and they do not want to start wars, as such are so destructive and do not seem to forward anyone's self-interest. Moreover, people living in a free and open society have all kinds of ways to spend their time, to seek satisfaction, and to quench any competitive striving they may have: arts; business; culture; education; the professions; personal romance; sports; you name it. These things would occupy their time and thoughts, as opposed to political conquest and territorial expansion (Kant, 2015, pp.60–73; Rosen, 1991).

Here is how Kant sees this step-by-step dynamic, moving forward:

> Several countries, themselves peaceful, prosperous, free, and rights-respecting, ought to form a club or "cosmopolitan federation". This club is totally voluntary and has, as its main terms, the following: 1) you have to agree to these values to join; 2) you agree to defend anyone in the club if and when it gets attacked by countries from outside of the club; and 3) you allow for free trade, science and technology, and the free movement of peoples within the borders of the club.
>
> *(Kant, 2015, pp.11–44; 60–73)*

Kant predicted that such a club, or federation, would be a spectacular success. So much so that other countries would experience envy. The envy, or jealousy, would produce one of two responses: 1) irritation and attack; or 2) the desire to join. Kant said the club should freely allow other countries to join, so long as they keep to the above terms of the deal. They might have to reform their own societies, so that they could be "fit" to join the club. So be it, and only then would they get in. But if the envy provoked attack, the republican federation would have the right to defend itself, and war would be on. Kant said that, if and when the federation beats back such an aggressor and defeats it in war (which he apparently assumed would always happen), the federation could and should forcibly transform the institutions in the aggressor state to republican, rights-respecting ones. The federation can essentially create, by force, a new member for the club – *but only if first attacked* (Kant, 1995, pp.166–171).

Over time – that is, *centuries, not merely decades* – Kant predicted that the republican club would grow and grow, until a truly *global* cosmopolitan federation developed. Not a binding, institutionalized world government but a voluntary club of decent, rights-respecting countries who could and would offer their people: security and justice; peace and prosperity; and the freedom to pursue their own skills, interests, and happiness (Kant, 2015, pp.60–73; Kant, 1995, pp.166–177).

Many people see this as the beating heart of Kant's forward-thinking, extremely progressive international philosophy. They've seen in his proposal of the 1790s the philosophical seeds of what became, 200 years later, the European Union (EU) in Western Europe. (The EU is indeed a voluntary club of rights-respecting societies that is committed to mutual defence and free trade, and has grown and grown ever since its creation in 1950, to the point where it now includes 27 countries and 500 million people, and is understood to be one of the three biggest economic units in the world, alongside the United States and China).[4]

Controversies

A focused consideration of some controversies commonly found with Kant's thoughts about war and peace would include, first, the already-mentioned issue of *where exactly to locate his thinking*, especially in connection with the just war tradition.

Second, we have shown that Kant is not a pacifist. Putting forward a proposal for perpetual peace is not the same thing as being a pacifist. Indeed, Kant at times has a rather bold authorization for the use of force: beyond mere self-defence to include *anticipatory attack* and even *the forcible transformation of defeated societies, post-war, in the direction of liberal republicanism*. The latter two options are, of course, very controversial even within the just war tradition; and the bite of such controversy has been keenly felt with such recent wars as those in Iraq and Afghanistan (Orend, 2013, pp.185–250).

At the time, Kant's proposal for a purely *voluntary* global federation was blasted by such contemporary critics as Hegel for being completely impractical, as they argued that, to be effective, any such world government would actually require powers of coercion over its members. Kant saw the need for the federation to use coercion in defence against outsiders, but is here seen as being naïve for not supposing that, to ensure the faithful following of club rules, some tools of coercion might be needed even within the club itself (Hegel, 1991, pp.368–369).

Perhaps relatedly, Kant's thoughts on war and peace *have always been accused of excess optimism and idealism*, especially by realists. Regardless of what one believes in this regard, it's probably true that such distinctive, unapologetic idealism is the main reason why Kant's "*Perpetual Peace*" is still read today at all.

Lastly, many commentators discern a tension between the pro-rights liberal aspirations of Kant's political thinking, and his residual, conservative inclinations in favour of gradual change, and adherence to law and order all the while the process of liberal reform occurs. This seems accurate, though one may say in Kant's favour that, in sporting such a tension, he merely mirrors the complex realities of his momentous era, with massive forces of conservative inertia pitted against the break-out energies of liberal revolution (Pogge, 1998).

Legacies (to the just war tradition)

As argued for, in a sustained way, throughout this chapter, Kant's main legacy to the just war tradition is his creation and development of the third just war category of *jus post bellum*. As such, this arguably makes him one of the most significant and original just war theorists. Comparing his views to thinkers such as Suárez (chapter 8) and Vattel (chapter 12), offers for interesting comparisons. When talking about *post bellum*, these thinkers permit considerable more victor's justice than his model designed with perpetual peace in mind would.

Less accepted, though quite interesting, is the claim by such thinkers as Ripstein and Zupan that Kant has an importantly different understanding of the *jus in bello* as well: less concerned with conduct towards the enemy, and huge lists of "external" rules specifying such, and more concerned with "internal" reflection on the permissibility of one's actions, tactics, and strategies.

Perhaps ironically – given how often he's labelled a "pacifist" – Kant actually provides substantial ammunition for the just war tradition *against* the pacifist. First, he gives deep philosophical rationale (from one of the most acclaimed and influential moral theorists) as to why defensive violence is morally permissible. Second, in creating and detailing *jus post bellum*, he takes away one major and sharp complaint of the pacifist against just war theory, namely, that the latter is too complacent and accepting of war and does nothing to concern itself with the creation of a more peaceful and just world order over time.

Enduring relevance to our time and world

We have noted how Kant's permission for anticipatory attack and forcible post-war regime change are extremely topical, and controversial, for our world.

We also noted how many fans of Kant believe that his vision of a cosmopolitan federation was a direct philosophical inspiration for the founding and development of the European Union, one of the most important political, social, and economic associations in the world today. More generally, Kant is often mentioned in any discussions about global governance more broadly, whether in reference to its historical growth from the now-defunct League of Nations to today's United Nations, or to new plans for more specialized global governance agencies and treaties, whether dealing with climate change, human rights, cyber-security, or armed conflict.

Another impressive contemporary impact of Kant's thinking is this: American political scientist Michael Doyle, very recently, has taken over Kant's early conjectures and put out a so-called "democratic peace thesis", suggesting that *democracies have never gone to war against each other, nor will they ever do so*, for reasons very similar to what Kant first suggested (Doyle, 1983). Doyle enumerates compelling facts. Counting all major wars of the modern era – since 1750 (when Kant was 26) – the three countries most frequently involved in armed conflict have been America, Britain, and France. But, these countries – since becoming true democracies after WWI (once slavery ended, and women got the vote) – *have never gone to war against each other*. And ditto for all the other democracies. Doyle's democratic peace thesis has received much careful scrutiny. Many have tried to prove him wrong, offering up possible counter-examples. But these have all been questioned, and there's now widespread consensus that the democratic peace thesis is at least compelling, if not full on correct (Doyle, 2011; Brown et al., 1996). If so, it points one substantial way towards Kant's dream of perpetual peace: *if democracies never go to war against each other, we need to increase the number of democracies, and then we will have more and more peace.* Theoretically, if every country were to become a democracy, we would then have a true and enduring solution to the problem of war. This underlines one of Kant's central insights: the profound connection between internal domestic reform in a rights-respecting direction, and the achievement of external, stable, international peace.

Indeed, in many ways the "democratic peace thesis" can be seen as a robust revival of (or, at least, continuous with) the old perpetual peace tradition of Kant's time, discussed in the first section.[5] It is important to note how the democratic peace thesis exists alongside current just war thinking and international law, and they can even be seen to dovetail, in a way that expresses much of Kant's essential vision on war and peace: we can have an end-state goal like the global spread of peaceful, rights-respecting, democratic governance but, until we get there, we can admit that there may be exceptional circumstances where we may need to consider the use of force as a tool for resisting aggression and defending people's lives and freedoms. To the extent that the dream of Kant's legacy might lead us to justify war for the sake of democratic regime change – a controversial view of just cause that cuts across the spectrum of recent just war thinkers including Walzer (chapter 16), Elshtain (chapter 17) and Johnson (chapter 18) – then a careful rereading of Kant, with particular attention to his internal *jus in bello* and *post bellum* ideals, is all the more warranted.

Notes

1   The (Kant, 2015) volume includes the famous essay (pp.51–102) as well the perpetual peace plans of St. Pierre, Leibniz, Rousseau, and such unexpected others as William Penn and Jeremy Bentham (pp.103–17).
2   "Very first" as in the first so-called "preliminary article" of perpetual peace.
3   He had thought of this as early as his 1784 essay, "Universal History", and stuck with it all the way until his final political writings in the *Rechtslehre* of 1797. See: (Kant, 2015, pp.117–122) for the exact, and original, sections.
4   This chapter was written just as Britain's "Brexit" vote happened in late June 2016, with unclear and complex implications for the future of the EU. See in general: D. Dinan, *Ever Closer Union: An Introduction to European Integration* (London: Lynne Rienner, 4th ed., 2010); B. Orend, *Introduction to International Studies* (Oxford: Oxford University Press, 2014), 125–53 & 333–44.
5   Thanks for this insight, and more broadly, to Cian O'Driscoll and Daniel Brunstetter.

Works cited

Armitage, D. and Subrahmanyan, S. 2010. eds. *The Age of Revolutions in Global Context*. London: Palgrave Macmillan.

Boothby, W. 2009. *Weapons and The Laws of Armed Conflict*. Oxford: Oxford University Press.

Boucher, D. 1998. *Political Theories of International Relations*. Oxford: Oxford University Press.

Brown, M. *et al*. eds. 1996. *Debating the Democratic Peace*. Cambridge, MA: MIT Press.

Cassirer, E. 2009. *Kant's Life and Thought* (revised ed.). Haden, J. trans. New Haven, CT: Yale University Press.

Doyle, M. 1983. Kant, Liberal Legacies, and Foreign Affairs. *Philosophy and Public Affairs*. **12**(3–4) pp.205–235; 323–353.

Doyle, M. 2011. *Liberal Peace*. New York: Routledge.

Easterday, J.S. *et al*., eds. 2014. *Jus Post Bellum*. Oxford: Oxford University Press.

Hegel, G. 1991. *Elements of the Philosophy of Right*. Wood, A. ed. Nisbet, H. trans. Cambridge: Cambridge University Press.

Johnson, J.T. 1981. *The Just War Tradition and The Restraint of War*. Princeton: Princeton University Press.

Kant, I. 1983a. An Answer to the Question: "What is Enlightenment?". In Kant, I *Perpetual Peace and Other Essays*. Humphrey, T. trans. Indianapolis: Hackett, pp.41–47.

Kant, I. 1983b. *Groundwork for the Metaphysics of Morals*. Ellington, J. trans. Indianapolis: Hackett.

Kant, I. 1995. *The Metaphysics of Morals (Part One: The Doctrine of Right)*. In Reiss, H. ed. *Kant: Political Writings*. Nisbet, H.B. trans. Cambridge: Cambridge University Press.

Kant, I. 2015. *On Perpetual Peace*. Orend, B. ed. Johnston, I. trans. Peterborough, ON: Broadview Press.

May, L. 2012. *After War Ends: A Philosophical Perspective*. Cambridge: Cambridge University Press.

O'Neill, O. 1989. *Constructions of Reason: Explorations of Kant's Practical Philosophy*. Cambridge: Cambridge University Press.

Orend, B. 1999. Kant's Just War Theory. *Journal of the History of Philosophy*. 37(2), pp.323–347.

Orend, B. 2000. *War and International Justice: A Kantian Perspective*. Waterloo, ON: Wilfrid Laurier University Press.

Orend, B. 2002. Justice After War. *Ethics & International Affairs* **16**(1), pp.43–57.

Orend, B. 2013. *The Morality of War* (2nd ed.). Peterborough, ON: Broadview Press.

Orend, B. 2015. Framing the Moral Issues, II: The Kantian Perspective on *Jus in Bello*. In Johnson, J. T. & Patterson, E.D. eds. *The Ashgate Research Companion to Military Ethics*. London: Ashgate, pp.131–143.

Pagden, A. 2013. *The Enlightenment, and Why It Still Matters*. New York: Random House.

Pogge, T. 1988. Kant's Theory of Justice. *Kant-Studien*, pp.408–433.

Ripstein, A. 2009. *Force and Freedom: Kant's Legal and Political Philosophy*. Cambridge, MA: Harvard University Press.

Rosen, A. 1991. *Kant's Theory of Justice*. Ithaca, NY: Cornell University Press.

Walzer, M. 1977. *Just and Unjust Wars: A Moral Argument with Historical Illustrations*. New York: Basic Books.

Williams, H. 1983. *Kant's Political Philosophy*. Oxford: Oxford University Press.

Zupan, D. 2004. *War, Morality and Autonomy*. London: Ashgate Press.

14

FRANCIS LIEBER (1798–1872)

Stephanie Carvin

Introduction

Francis Lieber, often described as the father of the modern laws of war, led a fascinating life. He was frequently in communication with many of the 19th century's leading thinkers on two continents including Alexis de Toqueville, Johann Caspar Bluntschli, Richard Cobden, and many of the leading figures of the Lincoln administration including Edward Bates, Edwin H. Stanton, and William H. Seward. He also excelled in mathematics, political science, economics, history and international law. Furthermore, Lieber wrote on some of the most pressing issues of the day, including free trade and prison reform as well as political theory.

Nevertheless, Lieber is somewhat of an odd fit with the rest of the just war thinkers in this book. First, unlike the other theorists, Lieber was a soldier who understood battle after fighting in two wars and played an important role in a third. Further, his writings make clear that he genuinely valued war and believed it could bring about positive change. Thirdly, Lieber's contribution to how we understand justice in conflict is firmly in the *jus in bello* as opposed to *jus ad bellum* tradition, although the later influenced his views on the former. In particular he believed that states had a duty to conduct vigorous wars so as to end them as quickly as possible.

Today, jurists and publicists largely remember Lieber for being the first to collect and write down the various ideas and theories that had been posited for centuries in a convenient and comprehensible way. This provided commanders in the field easily accessible guidance for the dilemmas that emerged during the American Civil War; a conflict that saw the use of guerillas, land mines, the abuse of prisoners of war, among other crimes. Indeed, his pamphlet would go on to have a major impact on discussions about the restraints on the use of force in Europe and play a major role in the development of the laws of war and the development of national military manuals.

Contexts

Francis Lieber was born on March 18, 1798 as the French Revolutionary Wars spread across Europe. His biographers often recount the tale of the six-year-old Lieber crying at a window in his house as he watched Napoleon's troops parade through the streets (Freidel, 1947, p.1; Thayer, 1880 p.16). The ninth child of 11, he reportedly had a happy childhood, and would grow up to be a fierce patriot not just of Prussia, but of Germany (Freidel, 1947, p.12). He would see two of his brothers leave to fight Napoleon in 1813 and would do so himself in March 1815 when Napoleon returned from Elba.

Lieber's first experience on the battlefield was formative. On his first day his company was reduced from 150 to 20 or 30 men. Battles were followed by endless marching, with little time to rest or eat. He was seriously wounded at the battle of Waterloo and left on the battlefield for dead where he was subject to pain, thirst, and peasants stealing his personal effects and clothes. Following his miraculous recovery, Lieber returned to his regiment as part of an occupying force where he had to deal with trouble with the peasants, sickness and cold (Freidel, 1947, pp.13–17; Lieber 1880). Returning home in 1816, he felt that "In one year I had grown older many years" (1880, p.174).

And yet these experiences seem to have only inspired the young Lieber in his liberal nationalism. He enrolled in a gymnasium in Berlin that sought to create strong bodies and nationalist minds that would reform Prussia and quickly became a star pupil. Unfortunately, this brought him to the attention of the conservative reactionaries in government and he was arrested. For the next decade Lieber would fall under the suspicion of the Prussian government, which continuously restricted where he could study and work. In 1821 Lieber managed to sneak out of the country to join the War of Greek Independence, but soon lost faith in the cause after his arrival. Finding himself back in Prussia after a brief respite in Rome, he once again came under the scrutiny of authorities and back in jail. Having finished his Ph.D. in mathematics at Jena, Lieber fled to England in 1826 where he stayed for a year before travelling to America in 1827.

In his new homeland, Lieber sought to obtain a teaching position in the North, but was ultimately unsuccessful. Although he met with great success in creating the first American encyclopedia (a project that brought him into contact with many of the great minds of the age), he eventually took a job at South Carolina College. Feeling himself cut off from intellectual stimulation in the North and the "art and science" of Europe that he loved, Lieber hoped this measure would be temporary. Unfortunately for him, Lieber would find himself in the slave-holding South for two decades.[1]

Tenets

Although he was not thrilled with his lot, Lieber was determined to make his time in the South productive. He used this period to write three works of political theory, *A Manual of Political Ethics* (1838), *Legal and Political Hermeneutics, or Principles of Interpretation and Construction in Law and Politics* (1838), *and On Civil Liberty and Self-Government* (1853). It is in one of the final chapters of the second volume of *Political Ethics* that Lieber's first thoughts on just war can be found. It is not surprising that Lieber, who had fought in two wars, and writing at the time of heightened tensions with Mexico, had thought about warfare. However, placing his thoughts where he did in this volume, suggests that it may not have been central to his thinking and political theory at this time.

Indeed, Lieber's thoughts on just war are not particularly innovative and his criteria are similar to the other writers in this book. He notes that just wars must be undertaken on just grounds: to repel or revert a wrong, that it must be the last resort, necessary, "wise" (there must be a likelihood of success) and that the good achieved will outweigh the evil caused (1881, p.446). Somewhat more novel is his list of the kinds of just wars that can be fought: wars of insurrection to gain or regain liberty, wars of independence, wars to quell armed factions, wars to unite distracted states of the same nation to form one political society, wars of defense and wars of chastisements. Although this list may be contradictory (how does one reconcile the justness of a war of insurrection versus a war to quell armed factions?), it is not discussed by Lieber. However, it is interesting to note that Lieber did not assume a single form of warfare, but recognized its empirical diversity and incorporated this into his ethical reasoning.

Further, and unfortunately for the modern reader, Lieber is not always clear about the sources that he found influential. In many of his works he prefers to cite history rather than abstract arguments as evidence. (And in the Lieber Code discussed below, he cites no sources at all). We know that Lieber read Grotius, Cornelius van Bynkershoek and Samuel Pufendorf but looked down upon the writings of Vattel, who he calls "Father Namby-Pamby" (Freidel, 1947, p.333 n.38). It is certain that Vattel's ideas about limited war did not resonate or appeal to the Prussian soldier and ardent liberal nationalist who had fought the armies of Napoleon.

However, as noted in the introduction, what makes Lieber unique is his love of war and belief that it is normal, even healthy, and brings benefits to a nation even though it causes suffering. One might draw interesting comparisons with Cicero, for whom war also served the cause of glory and virtue, or Augustine, for whom war was part of a fallen world but could be a means to remake the world order for the better; this perspective being in sharp contrast to the arguably more dominant elements of the tradition that focus on the tragic side of war. These benefits go beyond preserving territory and way of life or righting a wrong to actually improving the moral wellbeing of citizens and spreading civilization around the world.

Lieber starts his defense of war by listing objections to it: that men should not behave as animals, those who suffer are not responsible for the war, that war causes the cessation of morality, that any positive result is outweighed by the evil it is trying to fix and that differences between states should be decided by principles of justice (1881, pp.435–436). Lieber then sets out to demonstrate what while there may be some truth in these arguments, they are inherently flawed. First, men are not rational and we cannot expect all states to abide by reason. Even if states went to a court to solve their differences, "an unjust adversary would not do the bidding of the court and abide by its decision were it not supported by public force".

> I am bound to protect my life, for my Creator has given it to me for various solemn purposes. Were I not to protect it, brute force would rule, and the most sacred ends of humanity would be set at naught. Man is a reasonable being indeed, but he is not ordered to act by reason alone … In brief, the ancient "vim vi repellere licet" is not only justifiable, but is one of the principles of God's whole creation and the abolition of it would create universal moral and physical disorder.
>
> *(1881, pp.435–436)*[2]

He acknowledges that those who suffer in war are usually the least cause of wrong. However, he offers two responses to this point. First, we should not assume that one's own state is actually responsible for the evils of war – it may simply be protecting itself against an act of aggression. Second, reflecting a Germanic emphasis on the state as historical organism rather than product of rational human choice, he argues that the connection between people and the state renders suffering "not as great as is often supposed" (Watson, 2001, p.307; Lieber, 1881, p.438):

> For it is the plan of the Creator that government and people should be closely united in weal and woe: no state of political civilization, no high standard of national liberty and general morality, is possible where this is not the case.
>
> *(1881, pp.438–439)*

Lieber notes, for example, that when a criminal is punished it is not just the individual who suffers but many innocent individuals as well: mothers, children who depend upon him, his wife and his friends (1881, p.439).

Finally, on the idea that war is immoral and begets immorality, Lieber agrees that unjust wars are "one of the greatest crimes – murder on a large scale". These include wars for plunder and/or compelling men in their belief. Lieber argues that these wars create immorality and crime, annihilate the "fixed standard of morality and pure justice" and therefore are destructive to civil liberty which governs law and right (*Ibid.*).

However, Lieber argues that just wars are not demoralizing and returns to his own experience fighting the French as proof:

> … the German nation was greatly raised by their struggle for national independence against the French in 1812–14 – a moral elevation which showed itself in all spheres and all branches; and it was universally observed at the time that the soldiers had returned from those wars with high and elevated tone of moral feeling.
>
> *(1881, p.440)*

And he brings the issue back to his adopted homeland, "The Americans certainly came out of their revolutionary struggle none the worse in their morals" (*Ibid.*).

Essentially, Lieber believes that, "Many nations have been morally rescued by wars, which imparted new vigor to them". A just war can help bring a nation together and cement bonds between fellow citizens. He asks, "Is this not an act eminently moral in its character?" (*Ibid.*) Further, Lieber argues that "in the hands of Providence" just wars can be the means of disseminating "civilization if carried on by civilized peoples" and gives the example of Alexander the Great. "Frequently we find in history that the ruler and victorious tribe is make to revise, civilization as it were already on the wane, in a refined nation" (*Ibid.*, p.442–443).

In this sense, it cannot be denied in Lieber's thoughts that war is not only something to be endured, but something that can bring about morality and positive change. His views on the positive side to war, though, differ from those of, say Augustine or Aquinas discussed in this volume (chapters 2 and 4 respectively), as well as contemporary thinkers such as Johnson and Elshtain who turn to the just war tradition for moral force. "War is indeed a state of suffering, but it is often one of those periods of struggle without which no great and essential good ever falls to the share of man. Suffering, merely as suffering, is not an evil" (Lieber, 1881, p.444). And it is this that schemes for perpetual peace by Abbé St. Pierre, Bentham and Kant overlook. Describing Kant's scheme as one of the "weaker productions of that philosopher", he argues that their schemes would be no less absolutist than a world state. "A congress on the banks of the Po, or on the Bosphorus, for Asia, Europe and America, would make galling decisions for people near the Rocky Mountains" (*Ibid.*, p.445).

What are we to make of these views in a volume on the just war tradition? First, when it comes to warfare, it cannot be denied that Lieber is a man of his times, who uses his understanding of history rather than rational principles as evidence to support his arguments. Certainly he was not alone in believing that warfare could promote morality of the state and bring civilization to the world. In this volume, one could look to the context in which Vitoria's claims (chapter 6) were set. Closer to Lieber's time, one need only think of the justifications offered for colonialism throughout the 19th century as benefiting those who were being colonized. We can also trace similar ideas in other 19th century liberals such as John Stuart Mill, who famously argues:

> it is during an arduous struggle to become free by their own efforts that these feelings and virtues have the best chance of springing up. Men become attached to that which they have long fought for and made sacrifices for; they learned to appreciate that on which their thoughts have been much engaged; and a contest in which many have been called on to devote themselves for their country, is a school in which they learn to value their country's interest above their own.
>
> (Mill, 2002, p.491)

Or as Giuseppe Mazzini writes:

> Do not abandon the banner which God has given you. Wherever you may
> be, into the midst of whatever people circumstances may have driven you,
> fight for the liberty of that people if the moment calls for it; but fight as
> Italians, so that the blood which you shed may win honour and live, not for
> you only but for your country.
>
> *(Mazzini, 2002, p.482)*

While it cannot be denied that Lieber's fondness of warfare sets him apart from
many Liberal thinkers of the age, it would be wrong to describe Lieber as a
"warmonger". Instead, as John Fabian Witt notes, Lieber held justice, not peace,
as the highest ideal (2012, pp.178–179). For example, while he was tempted to
enlist in the Mexican-American war, Lieber ultimately opposed the conflict
because he felt it would bring another slave state into the Union.

Finally, what is crucial here is that Lieber believes that war, as a moral act, must
be fought in a moral way. On the surface, it does not seem much of a concern for
Lieber:

> … it is my duty to inflict on my enemy, as such, the most serious injury I
> can, in order to obtain my end, whether this be protection or whatever else.
> The more actively this rule is followed out, the better for humanity, because
> intense wars are of short duration. If destruction of the enemy is my object,
> it is not only my right, but my duty to resort to the most destructive means
> … When nations are aggressed in their good rights, and threatened with the
> moral and physical calamities of conquest, they are bound to resort to all
> means of destruction, for they only want to repel.
>
> *(1881, pp.451–452)*

This has raised the ire of modern critics, such as James Turner Johnson, who argue
that Lieber is basically arguing for unrestricted warfare. For Johnson, Lieber's
experiences in the era of the Napoleonic wars and *levée en masse* means that he
relegates the laws of war to the age of chivalry and "limited" wars of an earlier
period (Johnson, 1981, p.301).

And yet it is clear that Lieber puts emphasis on the fact that the justice of a cause
does not free its defenders from obligations to the other side, "War does not
absolve us from all obligations to the enemy" and:

> We do not injure in war in order to injure, but to obtain the object of war.
> All unnecessary infliction of suffering, therefore, remains cruelty as among
> private individuals. All suffering inflicted upon persons who do not impede
> my way, for instance upon surgeons or other inoffensive persons, if it can
> possibly be avoided, is criminal.
>
> *(1881, pp.449–450)*

Indeed, nowhere does Lieber suggest that war somehow produces anarchy or a situation ungoverned by morality (Baxter, 1963, p.176). Although Lieber believes that war can produce good, he is keenly aware that it can produce evil. In this sense, there is nothing in Lieber that suggests that might makes right, including in warfare. This reflects a principle that Lieber was keen to stress throughout his career, "No Right without its Duty; no Duty without its Right". Where there is only a right, there is despotism; where there is only duty, there is slavery. For Lieber, duty helps to complete a right – in this case, the right to wage war. As James F. Childress argues, for Lieber a nation does not have the right to wage war without also being subject to the duties and obligations that constitute the laws of war. They are "inter-completing" (Childress, 1976, pp.47–48).[3]

Texts

As contemporary biographies make clear, during his life (and for a short while after his death) Lieber was known more for his political theory than his contribution to the laws of war.[4] And yet today, there can be little doubt that Lieber's greatest legacy is his eponymous "Code", otherwise known as "General Orders No. 100: Instructions for the Government of Armies of the United States in the Field".

The origins of the document lay with certain challenges the Northern (or Union) forces were facing in the battle with the Southern (or Confederate) forces. If the North applied the laws of war to the South, did that confer legitimacy and/or recognition of the South as a legitimate belligerent? How should Union forces deal with guerrilla warfare by Confederate forces? And how should forces distinguish between a legitimate soldier and an opportunistic thief in uniform? And when Confederate forces "paroled" Union soldiers (the practice of letting soldiers go upon promising that they would not return to the conflict for the remainder of its duration) in order to burden the North with large numbers of men who had to be paid but could not fight, how could the Union respond?

By this time Lieber had escaped the South and accepted a position as the first professor of "history and political science" in the US at Columbia College (later University) in 1857. In the years before the war, Lieber's attention turned to the laws of war and he considered teaching a course on the subject at West Point. Instead, he delivered the course at Columbia during the winter of 1861–1862 that drew upon his work on just war and international law in *Political Ethics* (Friedel, 1947, p.324).

While Lieber was never one to miss an opportunity to promote his own work, he was a strong supporter of the North and eagerly sought to lend his knowledge to supporting the Union.[5] His intense dislike of slavery and love of the United States meant that he was keen to see the preservation of the Union through a determined, "vigorous" campaign. However, in keeping with his earlier writings on war and his political theory, he recognized that a war to preserve the US Constitution would have to be fought in accordance with its principles (Carnahan, 1998, p.220). For Lieber, and many Americans, this must not be a conflict fought on the basis of revenge, but on just principles.

But Lieber also had a personal reason for wanting the conflict to be fought justly: his son Oscar, raised in the South, had decided to join with the Confederate Army. His other sons, Hamilton and Norman fought with the Union Army, the former being grievously wounded in battle. Eventually, Oscar was killed at Williamsburg. Lieber, the old soldier who had twice fought in Europe, had his family torn apart by war in his adopted homeland.

Whatever torment Lieber felt, he turned his efforts to providing guidance for the Union forces in a series of articles and essays to address some of the key challenges that had emerged. He wrote letters to New York City newspapers arguing that Union leaders could abide by the laws of war without extending recognition to the South (Dilbeck. 2015, p.237). And in response to the guerrilla question, Lieber wrote a 6,000-word essay that, in plain language, identified ten different types of irregular combatants and how the Union forces should wage war against them (Dilbeck, 2015, p.239). The essay was widely regarded by Union officers, including Major General Henry Halleck who was also known as an expert in the laws of war.

Following the success of these efforts, and wanting to turn his attention to the question of parole, Lieber approached Halleck with a proposal to draft a useable guide to the laws of war that would be flexible, comprehensive and clearly written so that its guidance would be clear for all soldiers to follow (Dilbeck, 2015, p.241). This latter point is key – the Union army comprised thousands of men who had never before seen battle and were largely or entirely ignorant of the laws of war. What was needed was a guide on how a soldier was expected to behave, treat the enemy, conduct himself on captured territory, duties and obligations towards enemy citizens and property and the prohibited means of warfare. Although it took some persuading, eventually Halleck agreed to Lieber's plan and a committee was formed to produce the new Code. Lieber finished his draft by February 1863, which was edited lightly over the next few weeks and then published on April 24, 1863.

Composed of 157 Articles, the Lieber Code makes it clear that war is a means to an end, not an end in and of itself, and therefore limited. The object of war is not killing, but to achieve a political end, normally the return to peace. This has two important corollaries that reflect Lieber's writings on just war and are present throughout the document. First, that war must be pursued vigorously. As he argues in Article 29, "The ultimate object of all modern war is a renewed state of peace. The more vigorously wars are pursued, the better it is for humanity. Sharp wars are brief".

However, this did not mean that wars are an invitation for unrestricted slaughter. Lieber is clear that what governs the use of force in these conflicts is the principle of military necessity: states may only engage in activities that help them achieve the object of war, anything else is superfluous and prohibited. In this sense, actions carried out for the purpose of revenge are not allowed, including the seizure of private property not required to support the army (Article 37), or the destruction of art, libraries, collections or instruments belonging to hostile nations (Articles 35 and 36). Actions not "indispensable for securing the ends of the war" (Article 14) were prohibited.[6]

In this sense, there is continuity between Lieber's *jus in bello* views and the arguments found in Vitoria, Suárez, and Grotius, who also argue for some form of moderation. We can also find in the Code the main principles of the laws of war that have guided it ever since: proportionality, necessity, distinction, and humanity:

> **Article 15:** *Military necessity* admits of all direct destruction of life or limb of armed enemies, and of other persons whose destruction is *incidentally unavoidable* in the armed contests of the war; it allows of the capturing of every armed enemy, and every enemy of importance to the hostile government, or of peculiar danger to the captor; it allows of all destruction of property, and obstruction of the ways and channels of traffic, travel, or communication, and of all withholding of sustenance or means of life from the enemy; of the appropriation of whatever an enemy's country affords necessary for the subsistence and safety of the army, and of such deception as does not involve the breaking of good faith either positively pledged, regarding agreements entered into during the war, or supposed by the modern law of war to exist. *Men who take up arms against one another in public war do not cease on this account to be moral beings, responsible to one another and to God.*
>
> **Article 16:** *Military necessity does not admit of cruelty* – that is, the infliction of suffering for the sake of suffering or for revenge, nor of maiming or wounding except in fight, nor of torture to extort confessions. It does not admit of the use of poison in any way, nor of the wanton devastation of a district. It admits of deception, but disclaims acts of perfidy; and, in general, military necessity does not include any act of hostility which makes the return to peace unnecessarily difficult.[7]

Further, it is possible to find in the Lieber Code many of the provisions that would make themselves into future national and international documents on the laws of war, including bans on slavery (Articles 41–44), not giving quarter (Article 60), poison (Article 70), unnecessary suffering (Article 71), and torture (Article 16). He argued that prisoners of war (Articles 72–78) and captured enemy wounded (Article 79) must be treated humanely.

Legacy

Despite Lieber's careful neutrality (except, perhaps, for the clauses about slavery), the Code was immediately condemned by Confederate officials upon its release, including President Jefferson Davis who described it as "inhuman" compared to the "moral character" of the South's soldiers (Witt, 2012, p.339). While Confederate leaders were relentless in their criticism, they did actually have some legitimate points. Lieber's analysis might have been sober, intended for those on the battlefield, but it was very vague, leaving a lot of discretion in the hands of officers who had to apply it to a variety of different situations and circumstances (*Ibid.*, p.195).

There were other controversial issues that arose after the war as well. The victorious North sought to try many officials in the South for war crimes based on General Orders 100, particularly in the wake of President Abraham Lincoln's assassination in 1865 and on the discovery of certain Confederate atrocities, such as the prison at Andersonville where thousands of Union prisoners of war died from maltreatment (Friedel, 1947, p.362; Witt, 2012, p.294). The US government asked Lieber to investigate Confederate President Jefferson Davis for complicity in the assassination and war crimes, although no evidence deemed worthy emerged (Friedel, 1947, pp.370–374). Although Lieber was eager to see his Code used to prosecute war crimes, a desire to achieve reconciliation over prosecution prevailed.

Enduring relevance

Today, the Lieber Code lives on in two important ways: since its publication in 1863 the United States would always have a military manual on the laws of war that guided its actions. After Lieber died in 1872, his son, Norman Lieber (by this time a veteran of the Civil Wars and several battles against the Blackfeet and Sioux tribes) had taken up his father's legacy, teaching the laws of war at West Point. In 1884 he was appointed the Judge Advocate General for the Army and would see the implementation of the Code and subsequent developments of the laws of war in several US conflicts (Witt, 2012, p.328).[8] As such, the Lieber Code was very influential in shaping how the US government, soldiers and civilians understood warfare – for good and sometimes ill. For example, some of the harsher language in the Code was used to defend war crimes committed during the Philippines. This included the clauses about military necessity justifying the use of torture against the Filipino insurrectionists. While the US military courts did not accept this argument, finding that the Code did not allow for such conduct, the sentences given to officers involved in these activities were very light (Carvin, 2010, p.76–83; Witt, 2012, pp.253–361). As a military manual, the Code remained in place until an update was drafted in 1914, although this too would quote many of the passages of its predecessor.[9]

The second way the Lieber Code lives on is through its influence on what might be described as the "humanitarian moment" that emerged in the second half of the 19th century. It was during this period that Henri Dunant published his *Memory of Solferino*, which called for nations "in time of peace and quiet, to form relief societies for the purpose of having care given to the wounded in wartime by zealous, devoted and thoroughly qualified volunteers?" (Dunant, 1986, p.115) This was similar to the work being done by the US Sanitary Commission established in 1861, and two women on two different continents: Clara Barton during the US Civil War and Florence Nightingale's work in the Crimean War.

During this period, it was increasingly recognized by humanitarians that war might be inevitable, but this did not mean it required unrestricted slaughter. Instead, some of its more harsh aspects might be tamed in a way such that neutral parties and those *hors de combat* (such as the captured, sick and wounded) might be spared further suffering. This idea was codified into the 1864 Geneva Convention that led to the foundation of the International Committee of the Red Cross.

Lieber's Code fit directly into this sentiment. And as General Orders 100 came to Europe, it had an immediate impact on the humanitarian movement taking place. Championed by international lawyers such as Johann Caspar Bluntschli, portions of the Code made it into the humanitarian treaties and documents of the day, including the 1899 Hague Regulations of Land Warfare, which directly copied from it. In addition, recognizing the usefulness of the Code, several countries would go on to publish their own military manuals. In this way, Lieber's work influenced the codification of international humanitarian law that still plays a role, despite inherent tensions, in placing restraints on warfare today.

Notes

1   Lieber's relationship with slavery is complicated. His biographers are unanimous in that he detested slavery and believed the institution to be as toxic as it was immoral. However, while he was in the South he had several slaves and never spoke out about the issue. Some attribute this action to Lieber's pragmatism – needing to provide for his family, Lieber recognized that he would certainly lose his job had he spoken out against the institution. Nevertheless, it is also clear that Lieber continued to look out for slaves and bought more, "accepting and applying typical slave owners' standards in the process" (Keil 2008). Nevertheless, once back in the North, he publically returned to his abolitionist views, offending his former friends and students in the South. Lieber's own views on slavery are reflected in his Code in articles 42 and 43.

2   Roughly translated, "vim vi repellere licet" means, "it is legitimate to repel force with force". It is an ancient Roman law cited throughout history as a justification for self-defense.

3   On Lieber's maxim, "No right without its duties, no duty without its rights", see: (Harley, 1970, p.154).

4   Lieber's contemporary biographers spend considerable time discussing his contributions to political theory rather than the Lieber Code. See, for example, Thayer (1880b), and Harley (1970). A later biographer noted, Lieber died convinced of his own greatness and placed his own political theory in merit beside Grotius, Montesquieu and Tocqueville (Freidel 1947:324).

5   As one scholar notes, "The Columbia professor never required prodding from others to bring attention to his achievements" (Mancini, 2011, p.331).

6   For a discussion of military necessity as a restraint on the use of force in the Civil War see: (Carnahan, 1998).

7   Italics added for emphasis. Text from the Avalon Project. Available online: http://avalon.law.yale.edu/19th_century/lieber.asp

8   Norman Lieber retired in 1901 and remains the longest-serving Judge Advocate General in the United States.

9   The person chosen to update the Lieber Code was Edwin F. Glenn who had been convicted of torture in the Philippines. This would seem to undermine the very rules he was charged with updating, but as Witt notes, "the manual bore few traces of its author's terrible past" (Witt, 2012, p.364). The 1914 update was roundly praised and

most of the text stayed in place for several decades, into the post-Second World War occupation of Germany.

Works cited

Baxter, R.R. 1963. The First Modern Codification of the Laws of War: Francis Lieber and General Orders No. 100. *International Review of the Red* Cross. **3**(25), pp.171–189.

Carnahan, Burrus M. 1998. Lincoln, Lieber and the Laws of War: The Origins and Limits of the Principle of Military Necessity. *The American Journal of International Law* **92**(2), pp.213–231.

Carvin, Stephanie. 2002. *Prisoners of America's Wars: From the Early Republic to Guantanamo.* New York: Columbia University Press.

Childress, James F. 1976. Francis Lieber's Interpretation of the Laws of War: General Orders No. 100 in the Context of His Life and Thought. *American Journal of Jurisprudence.* **21**, pp.34–70.

Dilbeck, D.H. 2015. 'The Genesis of This Little Tablet With My Name:' Francis Lieber and the Wartime Origins of General Orders No. 100. *The Journal of the Civil War Era.* **5**(2), pp.231–253.

Dunant, Henry. 1986. *A Memory of Solferino.* Geneva: International Committee of the Red Cross.

Freidel, Frank. 1947. *Francis Lieber: Nineteenth-Century Liberal.* Baton Rouge: Louisiana State University Press.

Harley, Lewis R. 1970. *Francis Lieber: His Life and Political Philosophy.* New York: AMS Press.

Johnson, James Turner. 1981. *Just War Tradition and the Restraint of War: A Moral and Historical Inquiry.* Princeton: Princeton University Press.

Keil, Hartmut. 2008. Francis Lieber's Attitudes on Race, Slavery and Abolition. *Journal of American Ethnic History.* **28**(1), pp.13–33.

Lieber, Francis. 1880. Personal Reminiscences of the Battle of Waterloo. In Lieber, Francis. *Reminiscences, Addresses and Essays*, Vol 1. Philadelphia and London: J.B. Lippincott Company, pp.149–175.

Lieber, Francis. 1881. Manual of *Political Ethics Designed Chiefly for the Use of Colleges and Students at Law*, Vol. II. Second Edition Revised. Woolsey, Theodore D. ed. Philadelphia and London: J.B. Lippincott Company.

Mancini, Matthew J. 2011. Francis Lieber, Slavery and the 'Genesis of the Laws of War.' *The Journal of Southern History.* **LXXVII**(2), pp.325–348.

Mazzini, Giuseppe. 2002. On the Duties of Man. Cited in Brown, Chris, Nardin, Terry and Rengger, Nicholas. eds. *International Relations in Political Thought: Texts from the Ancient Greeks to the First World War.* Cambridge: Cambridge University Press.

Mill, John Stuart. 2002. A Few Words on Non-Intervention. Cited in Brown, Chris, Nardin, Terry and Rengger, Nicholas. eds. *International Relations in Political Thought: Texts from the Ancient Greeks to the First World War.* Cambridge: Cambridge University Press.

Thayer, M.R. 1880a. Biographical Discourse. In Lieber, Francis. *Reminiscences, Addresses and Essays*, Vol 1, Philadelphia and London: J.B. Lippincott Company.

Thayer, M. Russell. 1880b. The Life, Character and Writings of Francis Lieber: A Discourse Delivered Before the Historical Society of Pennsylvania, January 13, 1873. In Lieber,

Francis. *Reminiscences, Addresses and Essays: Volume I,* Gilman, Daniel C. ed. Philadelphia: J.B. Lippincott Company, pp.13–44.

Watson, Bradley C.S. 2001. Who was Francis Lieber?. *Modern Age,* **43**(4), pp.304–310.

Witt, John Fabian. 2012. *Lincoln's Code: The Law of War in American History.* New York: Free Press.

15

PAUL RAMSEY (1913–1988)

Adam Hollowell

Contexts

Matters of war and international conflict were constants in Paul Ramsey's life. He was born in Mendenhall, Mississippi, in 1913, nearly eight months before the onset of World War I. He graduated from Millsaps College in Jackson, Mississippi, in 1935 during the buildup to World War II. After completing his Ph.D. at Yale University, Ramsey began teaching at Princeton University in fall of 1944, shortly before US troops began a full-scale attack on the German "West Wall". He was appointed Harrington Spear Paine Professor at Princeton in 1957, the same year President Dwight Eisenhower pledged his support of Ngô Đình Diệm and South Vietnam. Throughout the 1960s and 1970s he wrote widely on pressing issues of justice and war, from the conflict in Vietnam to the morality of nuclear deterrence in the Cold War. After four decades of teaching and writing at Princeton, he retired in 1982 and became a member of the Center for Theological Inquiry. Within a few years of his death in 1988, US operations would begin for the first Iraq War.

It would be difficult to overstate the influence of war, as well as the politics of international relations, on Paul Ramsey's life. Still, he served neither in war nor political office. In fact, on August 10, 1940, the Commission on World Peace of the Methodist Church confirmed his registration as a conscientious objector on religious grounds (Commission, 1940).

It would also be difficult to overstate Ramsey's influence on the recovery of the just war tradition in the wake of military atrocities conducted in the 20th century. Profoundly influenced by Augustine, and in particular Reinhold Niebuhr's brand of Augustinian moral realism, Ramsey argued that violent resistance against the evildoer may be a form of Christian love of neighbor. His writings on war and politics reanimated just war reasoning and applied it to the emerging challenges of nuclear deterrence, adaptive guerilla tactics in contemporary war, and the politics of global conflict. He also rooted his thinking in deeply theological convictions, offering to the just war tradition a 20th century example of religious moral reasoning that aims to serve the common good and contribute to public discourse beyond the confines of the church.

A few years after Ramsey's death, Princeton philosopher and political theorist Jeffrey Stout wrote in the *Journal of Religious Ethics* of an encounter he had with professor Ramsey while a young undergraduate at Brown University. Stout recalled, "First comes a moral awakening, with its youthful attachments to great causes or charismatic heroes; next an initial encounter with Ramsey; and then an unending and ambivalent struggle with his arguments ... Ramsey did not win you over all the way, he just changed your life forever" (Stout, 1991, p.210). In the context of this collection of just war thinkers, Ramsey's particular arguments on issues of deterrence or the direct targeting of noncombatants may not "win you over all the way". But his work searches for answers to questions at the heart of political theory and international relations: What is the essence of political authority? To what ends, and under what limitations, might force be justified? How might power be used prudently, and what are its appropriate moral limitations? In his answers to these questions, Ramsey's relentless concern for precision and clarity has had a monumental impact on contemporary just war thinking.

Texts

Ramsey's earliest writings on political authority focus less on technical aspects of just war and more on the broader theological commitments that ground his understanding of human agency and moral obligation. For Ramsey, the social contract philosophies of Hobbes, Locke, and Rousseau locate moral obligation in the individual self. A contractual approach to ethics can only make sense when individuals are freely acting agents who freely choose to enter into political obligation. This dissatisfies Ramsey, who argues in *Basic Christian Ethics* (1950) and *Christian Ethics and the Sit-In* (1961a) that all human agents are instead born into myriad forms of dependence and relationship, from mother and child to Creator and creature. Thus, Ramsey argues that an account of human agency and moral obligation must begin with God's loving act of creation, the covenant relationship between Yahweh and Israel, and the embodied fulfillment of that covenant in Jesus Christ (1950, p.388). By emphasizing the embeddedness of agency in covenant relationships, Ramsey establishes the theological foundations of his political ethics and points to the external rather than internal nature of moral obligation. (This is sometimes called moral realism). He also outlines covenant love as that which motivates protection of the "neighbor", which can include violent resistance to the perpetrator of injustice.

War and the Christian Conscience (1961b) is Ramsey's first book-length exploration of the possibility of justified war as a form of neighbor-love. Here he attempts to chart, as so many just war thinkers do, a *via media* between a pacifism which neglects the obligation to protect the innocent neighbor and strict political realism where "might is right". This forces him to confront what is often called "the problem of dirty hands" (Walzer, 1973), although he does not use that term directly. For Ramsey, stepping into political office cannot simply involve an intentional embrace of wrongdoing or an inevitable submission to evil practices. He fights to preserve an account of faithful obedience in the form of constructive and purposive political action, while maintaining an adherence to the "Pauline prohibition" never to do evil that good may result.[1] As explored in detail in James Turner Johnson's chapter in this volume on interpretations of Augustine (chapter 2), Ramsey uses Book XIX of Augustine's *The City of God* (1998) when making these arguments in *War and the Christian Conscience*. In Ramsey's understanding of Augustinian theological realism, forceful resistance to an evildoer should take place only when the action meets the criteria of *justification* (i.e., the action is morally permissible), *obligation* (i.e., the action is morally necessary), and *limitation* (i.e., the action is morally restrained).

Under the heading of moral limitations on justified war Ramsey develops his commitment to two crucial principles: discrimination and proportionality. The principle of discrimination indicates that force exercised in protection of an unjustly wronged neighbor must not directly intend the killing of noncombatants. This placed Ramsey at odds with the realists who justified the use of nuclear weapons and obliteration bombing in WWII on grounds that, such attacks shortened the length of the war. Ramsey was no nuclear pacifist, and he was clear that serious moral reasoning could not rule out justifiable use of nuclear weapons altogether. Still, the bombings of Hiroshima and Nagasaki were morally atrocious acts, and he cautioned against any attempt to rationalize indiscriminate use of nuclear weapons. For Ramsey, there can be no utilitarian justification for violating the principle of discrimination between combatants and noncombatants in war, "On this distinction hangs the discrimination between war and murder, between limited and unlimited war, between barely civilized and wholly uncivilized, even if technically efficient, military action" (1968a, p.160). Instead, according to Ramsey, the just war theory must articulate "*right* doing that good may come of it, not wrong doing quixotically alleged to be warranted solely by consequences expected to follow" (1968b, p.21).

The principle of proportionality indicates that use of force in resistance to a perpetrator of injustice may render justice, but must not be done out of mere retaliation. The resistance force must be proportionate to the offending force. Commitment to proportionate use of force placed Ramsey significantly at odds with the growing effort in the 1960s and 1970s to deter global warfare by stockpiling nuclear weapons. Again, he keeps open the genuine possibility that targeted nuclear weapons could be used in proportionate and discriminate ways, or held with deterrent effect for possible future use in such ways. But nuclear stockpiling for the purpose of threatening large-scale population destruction is a moral failure on grounds of proportionality. Ramsey writes, "If deterrence rests upon genuinely intending massive retaliation, it is clearly wrong no matter how much peace results" (1968a, p.250).

Ramsey extends these s in his most significant political text, *The Just War: Force and Political Responsibility* (1968a). In addition to his reiteration of the significance of discrimination and proportionality, two broader conclusions about the nature of political agency from this later work are particularly important. The first comes in Ramsey's essay "The Uses of Power". There he declares, first,

> The proposition that the use of power, and possibly the use of force, belongs to the *esse* of politics (its *act of being*) and is inseparable from the *bene esse* of politics (its *proper act of being*, or its act of being *proper* politics) is denied by two views of the state, or of political community.
>
> *(1968a, p.5)*

He adds later,

> Power, which is of the *esse* of political agency, may be a conditional value only; but order and justice, which are ever in tension yet in inter-relation, both are values that comprise the well-being, the *bene esse*, of political affairs and the common good which is the goal of political action.
>
> *(1968a, p.11)*

Notice that, for Ramsey, power is not a good in itself; power finds its place as the external basis for order and justice, which comprise the internal "well-being" of the common good. One common misinterpretation of Ramsey's work is the suggestion that he views the exercise of force as the essence of political agency. But power has a technical (read: provisional) function in this account, a "conditional value only". Power is not the *bene esse* of politics – that belongs to the "terminal goals" of order and justice (1968a, p.29). Yet power is the medium by which the one who holds political office moves the community with purpose toward the good. Thus, Ramsey insists that, "a political action is always an exercise of power and an exercise of purpose. Power without purpose and purpose without power are both equally nonpolitical" (1968a, p.8; see also Hollowell, 2015).

With regard to the role of just war thinking in international relations, Ramsey was especially attuned to the difficulty of relating definite just war principles to the contingent and ever-changing "international system" (1988). Nowhere is this more evident than in his crucially important essay "A Political Ethics Context for Strategic Thinking", which originally appeared in a volume titled *Strategic Thinking and Its Moral Implications* (1973) and was later reprinted at the end of Ramsey's final book, *Speak Up for Just War or Pacifism* (1988). There he describes the realities of the "law of move and countermove" (1988, p.186). Because there are a variety agents in the political realm, governmental action is always anticipatory, reactive, and responsive to the changing landscape of international relations. No legislation, movement, or leader can escape the contingencies of political life, including matters of timing, expediency, and patience. Ramsey is equally suspicious of those who abandon political relations to moral chaos or conflicts of unrestrained power as he is of those who believe they can be controlled by "technical reason" (1988, p.194). Rather, he argues that the difficult task of judgment is inescapable for those who take the mantle of political office. This is why, in an essay titled "Force and Political Responsibility", he suggests that political judgment is "not primarily a matter of social engineering, of building institutions; it is rather a system of interacting *doings*" (1972, p.50).

Controversies

Ramsey was deeply embedded in the theological, philosophical, and political debates of his day, two of which I want to highlight here. The first concerns his defense of US military action in Vietnam. In 1966 Ramsey published "Vietnam: Dissent from Dissent" in *Christian Century* and in 1967 he published "Is Vietnam a Just War?" in *Dialog*. The essays incensed several of his critics, and subsequent issues of both journals featured responses from various theological perspectives (for example, Hoyer, 1967; Dahl, 1967). Later that year Ramsey published a response in *Dialog* under the heading "Two Extremes: Ramsey Replies to His Critics" (1967b).

At issue in the debate is Ramsey's refusal to condemn US participation in Vietnam as immoral and the call from his critics for a public apology. Robert Hoyer observes, "the sadness lies in the fact that [Ramsey has] left no room for Christian ambivalence and doubt, no room for repentance" (Hoyer, 1967, p.142). Philip Wogaman criticizes Ramsey's defense of US military action as "a strange invitation to self-righteousness" (Wogaman, 1967, p.294). Ramsey resists these calls for repentance because he hears behind them a call to abandon the realm of political authority to a politics of "evil military necessity" (1967b, p.219). Instead, he insists, stubbornly, that a theological account of just war theory must attempt to "prolong Christian moral judgments into life and show that life-situations are corrigible to Christian ethical analysis" (*Ibid.*).

What is at stake in these debates, and in the calls for Ramsey to repent of his judgments of the justice of the US intervention in Vietnam? For Ramsey, it was a matter of whether Christian theology is capable of rendering political judgments, while maintaining a belief in the sovereignty of divine judgment. In an essay written the following year, he observes that:

> theologically speaking, we grasp something of God's *overruling* of man's [*sic*] ruling and self-ruling.[2] To use this notion in our analysis of *present* experience, however, to introduce it into our analysis of the prospective shape of things to come or (hopefully) to be given to experience ahead is always a category mistake.
>
> *(1968b, p.18)*

His point is that while ostensible political judgments surely do not justify an individual before God, neither does the universal need for forgiveness "level" all earthly distinctions nor permit an abandonment of the urgent moral task of political judgment. Though it may seem counterintuitive, Ramsey insists that "an ethics grounded in justification in Christ has no … urgent need to avoid making judgments of right and wrong in politics" (1961b, p.13).

Only later in his career does Ramsey admit the error of his judgments (and, to some extent, his silence) on Vietnam, saying that, "I freely grant that in the fury and fog of the verbal wars I failed to keep my agenda for reasoning morally about insurgency and counterinsurgency warfare entirely distinct from my own conviction that we were in Vietnam honorably" (1983, p.21). But Ramsey's intense commitment to debates about Vietnam during the 1960s and '70s had little to do with his own judgment; in fact, Ramsey's main goal was to sustain a functional account of the principles of discrimination and proportionality for those responsible for making material political judgments while in office. As a point of contrast, Michael Walzer, discussed in chapter 16, remained committed to his anti-war stance throughout US intervention in Vietnam and staunchly rejected political realism, even as his classic text, *Just and Unjust Wars* (1977), also highlighted discrimination and proportionality as essential to justifiable war.

The second controversy of particular interest in Ramsey's work concerns the debate between pacifists and just war theorists and his attempt to address this debate in his final book, *Speak Up for Just War or Pacifism* (1988). Ramsey initiates the discussion with reference to a common topic of discussion among political ethicists in the 1970s, the idea that pacifists and just war theorists share a "presumption against violence". Simply stated, Ramsey remains unconvinced that the logic of that "presumption" is a helpful starting point for a discussion aimed at transcending these "two options for Christian conscience" (1988, p.51). It is worth noting that Johnson also rejected this presumption against violence, though as discussed in chapter 18, he anchored his views in the principles found in classical just war theory.

Ramsey suggests that "the one thing Christian pacifists and just warriors have in common is that if anything is shown to be *per se* a moral atrocity, or to have no 'just cause' *now*, it should be given Christian endorsement *no moment more*" (1988, p.52). He maintains, as indicated in his work from the 1960s, that no anticipation or calculation of justice or peace can justify the perpetration of moral atrocity. Such calculation would patently violate the "Pauline prohibition", mentioned earlier. Pacifists and just war thinkers are thus united under the prohibition by a presumption against moral atrocity (rather than a presumption against violence *per se*).

Ramsey is at pains in *Speak Up* to reject the idea that just-war criteria can be applied as "a thoughtless, legalistic way of condemning all wars at one time, and any war test-by-test" (1988, p.71). His refusal to identify all acts of violence as moral atrocities may frustrate pacifists, but Ramsey is trying to clarify the conceptual ground that pacifists and just war theorists can share, even as they disagree. His just war theory relies on a category of violence that is morally ambiguous – i.e., that "risks" conceivable (unintended) evil in pursuit of more proportionate, probable and achievable (intended) good. Where there is a clear choice between right and wrong *per se*, then a Christian of any ethical persuasion is obligated to choose that which is so clearly right. But Ramsey believes that political choices are more frequently unclear and indeterminate. His establishment of the upper limit – where the Christian says, "no moment more" – means that inviolable rules of conduct always restrict his account of how one resists evil.

Under the limits of the prohibition of moral atrocity, Ramsey's theory of justified war cannot support a situation where inherently wrong actions serve some greater or preferred good (i.e., a kind of sinister utilitarianism). Rather, just war theory must operate within the reality that those who hold political offices trade in a number of currencies that are unavoidably ambiguous in their potential for moral good or evil. The most fundamental point of agreement between pacifists and just war thinkers, for Ramsey, should be a promise to consider inherently immoral acts no moment more. Beyond that promise is a realm of actions with intended (but not guaranteed) consequences, purposive (but not unassailable) decisions, and desired (but nevertheless contingent) outcomes. In Ramsey's mind, what to do amid these contextual ambiguities and uncertainties represents the true point of contention in the pacifist/just war debate.

What is also at stake in *Speak Up* is whether these points of contention between pacifists and just war theorists have anything to do with theology. It is a debate about who can lay claim to a political ethic modeled after Jesus Christ, and here he enters directly into a conflict with one of the most influential pacifist Christian theologians of the twentieth century, John Howard Yoder. In 1972 Yoder drew new attention to Christian pacifism with his book, *The Politics of Jesus*.[3] As the field of Christian ethics increasingly flocked to this non-violent vision of discipleship, Ramsey refused to sit comfortably with Yoder's supposed pacifist monopoly on the political significance of the life, teachings, death, and resurrection of Christ. To Yoder, he writes in *Speak Up*, "My point there, however, is simply to say that there is nothing to be gained from [saying] … 'We all participate in Jesus; you in your way, I in *his*'" (Ramsey, 1988, p.114). While there is significant emphasis on the principles of proportionality and discrimination in Ramsey's just war theory, he does not, as one critic has suggested, indicate that waging a justified war is "merely a matter of following rules or principles" (Bell, 2010, p.118). Ramsey consistently emphasizes the way his just war principles reflect obligations of faithfulness toward the neighbor, derived from our creation in covenant. For Ramsey, justified war is ultimately a pursuit of justice, and justice, ultimately, is a form of discipleship, a form of participation in Christ.

Legacies

Ramsey was particularly fond of describing the unique challenges of political leadership with a line from former U.S. Secretary of State Dean Acheson. Acheson, who was also a furniture-making hobbyist, said, "a chair is made to sit in: when you've made it you can tell whether you made it right; there is no such definitive test of the rightfulness of a political policy-decision" (Ramsey, 1972, p.49). For Ramsey, one central feature of political theory should be the recognition that all moral judgment is difficult, due to contingency, and political judgments are particularly difficult, due to the ambiguity and complexity of international relations. There are no chairs "made to sit in" in international relations. Instead, there are complex configurations of power and authority, as well as exigencies of time and place.

While Ramsey focuses on principles of discrimination and proportionality as central governing features of justified war, he also situates principles and rules within a broader account of virtue. If we lived in a world with determinate choices – Ramsey spoke of this earlier as a choice between right and wrong "*per se*" – then we would have no need of virtue (1988, p.52). But Ramsey is an Augustinian, and the business of politics is obscure, ambiguous, and indeterminate, as is evident in his insistence that judgment is the foremost task of political authority. Thus, alongside the theological virtues of faith, hope, and love, Ramsey insists that justified war will require prudence, temperance, and courage.

Ramsey's work aims to develop discrimination and proportionality as inviolable moral principles, while at the same time maintaining a broader theory of community and virtue that can sustain those principles and hold leaders to account for them. His abiding legacy for the development of just war thinking thus contains both strands of thought, though they are not always held together. For instance, Ramsey's resuscitation of the importance of discrimination and proportionality heavily impacts Michael Walzer's *Just and Unjust Wars* (1977), while his underlying virtue theory shapes G. Scott Davis' *Warcraft and the Fragility of Virtue* (1992). Other efforts, such as John Howard Yoder's *When War is Unjust* (1984) and Daniel Bell's *Just War as Christian Discipleship* (2009), use criticisms of Ramsey as starting points for charting new directions in theories of pacifism and justified war. In this way, Ramsey's legacy is as much as a figure to negotiate with rather than an authority to accept. As one commenter wrote, Ramsey's work has a keen ability to "define the conceptual space within which other thinkers [have] to move even when they have not been persuaded to accept his conclusions" (Stout, 1991, p.210). His writings establish several crucial conceptual spaces on issues such as nuclear deterrence, protection of the neighbor, and the ways of political judgment.

Ramsey's legacy also includes his role as a Christian writing and speaking about the role of theological belief and the Christian community in broader efforts to secure the common good. He is neither a neoconservative nor an apologist for Christian exceptionalism, though he is accused by critics of being both. In fact, Ramsey sets an important example for those who would follow him by writing as a Christian who refuses to grant priority to those who also write within the Christian tradition. As he writes in "The Case of the Curious Exception": "It ought not to be surprising if there are philosophical analyses that are useful in repairing some of the worst aspects of theological ethics, and Christian ethical understanding that may improve some of the best philosophy" (1968c, p.70). Ramsey did not care if his unapologetic Christianity made him unpopular with secular thinkers, and he enjoyed the fact that his concessions to secular theorists infuriated his colleagues in theological ethics. One aspect of his legacy is his enduring insistence that all can, and must, contribute to the common good, if it is to be truly common and truly good.

Enduring relevance

By the late 1960s, Ramsey took great interest in the question of the "justifiable exception", with regard to both just war principles and the broader place of rules within moral and practical reasoning (1968c, p.77). He wonders, if there are no "relevant moral warrants" for an action, then how can it be morally justifiable? At the same time, if such moral warrants exist, by what criteria can that action be described as permissibly exceptional? These questions suggest that a justifiable exception is a contradiction in terms, precisely because moral justifications operate as "generic" claims (1968c, p.78). This begs the question, if morality itself is generic, what is the relationship between general moral rules and particular actions? Or, in other words, how are we to give an account of practical reasoning in connection with moral justifications?

These questions are particularly important for those who would embrace theories of justified war as sources of regulating limitations on the use of force in international conflict, and they were central to Ramsey's reflections on war as something that should involve both power and purpose. It remains a central task of just war theorizing to address the temptation to appeal to justifiable exceptions in war, thereby bypassing the limitations of discrimination and proportionality. This controversial theme is famously taken up by Michael's Walzer's exploration of supreme emergency, but let me point to one contemporary example.

In the wake of the release of "torture memos" from the George W. Bush administration (beginning in 2002) and the subsequent passing of the Detainee Treatment Act of 2005 (introduced by Senator John McCain), the issue of categorical prohibitions of torture emerged as a matter of significant and continuing public debate. Advocates of the moral permissibility of torture in emergency situations frequently invoke the utilitarian language of justifiable exceptions. For instance, conservative commentator Charles Krauthammer wrote in *The Weekly Standard*, "the problem" with a categorical legal prohibition of torture is that "it is going to be very difficult to publicly carve out exceptions" (Krauthammer, 2005). Jeremy Waldron wrote shortly thereafter about attempts by lawyers working in the White House and Departments of Justice and Defense in 2002 and 2003 to "narrow the definition of torture … so the prohibition would cover much less than most people supposed" (Waldron, 2006, p.33). Even former president Bill Clinton contributed to the debate, saying on NBC's Meet the Press in 2007, "if you have any kind of formal exception [to a prohibition against torture], people just drive a truck through it, and they'll say, 'Well, I thought it was covered by the exception.'" But Clinton refused to make the legal prohibition a categorical moral prohibition: if someone finds themselves in an emergency situation – "and it was six hours to the bomb or whatever … you'll do whatever you do and you should be prepared to take the consequences" (Clinton, 2007).

At the center of the torture debate are questions about the use of exceptions to uphold the creativity and sensitivity of the law in emergency situations. Ramsey warned that the most enticing of those escape clauses would emerge in the language of consequentialism. This is nowhere more apparent than in suggestions that, when it comes to the moral permissibility of torture, "all that's left to haggle about is the price" (Krauthammer, 2005). One significant way that Ramsey's writings remain relevant is that we continue to need rigorous, thoughtful reflection on the inviolability of moral norms in war. The torture debate is evidence that we still face the same erosion of moral deliberation by a reliance on escape clauses and exceptions in the logic of international relations. This points to the continued liveliness of Ramsey's insistence that the source of true creativity and sensitivity in the moral law will be found in commitments to rigid moral obligations, rather than exceptions to them.

The challenge, for contemporary international relations, is how to establish binding moral obligations that are rooted in the common good. For Ramsey, of course, a deepening of our moral commitments always involves sustained reflection on the source of those commitments, which for him is the love of God making possible the love of neighbor. His wrestling with the place of rules and exceptions in theological ethics presents a lively challenge that remains relevant: amid the knottiest international conflicts, will Christians mimic the creativity and resilience exhibited in God's faithfulness with all creation? In broader, more secular terms (though not, as Ramsey would add, in necessary conflict with Christian commitment to public good), can the international community probe the depths of its collective responsibilities and avoid temptations to abandon its moral obligations when the consequentialist siren calls? These are enduring questions, and Ramsey's work is an enduring resource for those who wish to answer them.

Lastly, Ramsey employs the theological language of covenant to honor the place of rules of conduct in war, all the while promoting deepening moral commitments and the rejection of utilitarian exceptionalism. Against many of the cultural and intellectual trends of his era, Ramsey insists that theological language can illuminate the structure of political agency and public goods. He steadfastly believes that Christians can (and should) explore the unique contours of political authority, even as they uphold the stringency of moral norms and limitations. This includes a commitment to the cultivation of virtue and the significance of political judgment, which find their place in the bonds of covenant love. The enduring relevance of Ramsey's work to the tradition of just war thinking will partly depend on the role faith communities play in the future of local politics, state governance, and international relations. Ramsey refuses to compromise the theological ground of his arguments about war, yet he refuses to shield Christians from the correction and reproof of secular and non-Christian voices. His work stands as one example of moral reasoning within a theological tradition that aims to secure public goods shared by participants across many traditions. One question his work puts to those who follow him is whether the just war tradition can serve international relations in a way that sustains its moral rigidity while welcoming, rather than excluding, diversity of conviction in common pursuit of common goods.

Notes

1   'And why not say (as some people slander us by saying that we say), "Let us do evil so that good may come"? Their condemnation is deserved!' Romans 3:8 (NRSV)
2   Throughout his career Ramsey used "man" and "mankind" to refer generally to humankind. He wrote in a period where the universality of these terms was assumed, and he did not intend them to be gender exclusive. Where possible I avoid these terms in preference for gender-neutral expressions.
3   It is now widely known within the field that Yoder emotionally manipulated and sexually violated numerous women while employed by what is now called Anabaptist Mennonite Biblical Seminary (AMBS). For one consideration of how to approach Yoder's pacifist writings in light of these realities, see "Scandalizing John Howard Yoder" (Cramer, *et. al.*, 2014).

Works cited

Augustine, Saint. 1998. *The City of God Against the Pagans*. Dyson, R.W. ed. trans. Cambridge Texts in the History of Political Thought. Cambridge: Cambridge University Press.

Bell, Daniel M. 2009. *Just War as Christian Discipleship*. Grand Rapids, MI: Brazos Press.

Bell, Daniel M. 2010. The Way of God with the World: Hauerwas on War. In Pinches, Charles R., Johnson, Kelly S., and Collier, Charles M. eds. *Unsettling Arguments: A Festschrift on the Occasion of Stanley Hauerwas's 70th Birthday*. Eugene, OR: Wipf and Stock, pp.112–131.

Clinton, Bill. (2007) Interview with Tim Russert. *Meet the Press*, NBC, September 30.

Commission on World Peace of the Methodist Church to Paul Ramsey. August 10, 1940, Box 3, The Paul Ramsey Papers, David M. Rubenstein Rare Book & Manuscript Library, Duke University.

Cramer, David, Howell, Jenny, Tran, Jonathan, and Paul Martens. 2014. Scandalizing John Howard Yoder. *The Other Journal*. July 7.

Dahl, Gordon J. 1967. Repentance Rather Than Rationalization. *Dialog* **6**(2), pp.144–145.

Davis, Grady Scott. (1992) *Warcraft and the Fragility of Virtue*. Moscow, Idaho: University of Idaho Press.

Hollowell, Adam Edward. (2015) *Power and Purpose: Paul Ramsey and Contemporary Christian Political Theology*. Grand Rapids, MI: Wm. B. Eerdmans Publishing Co.

Hoyer, Robert. 1967. Sad Self-Justification. *Dialog* **6**(2), pp.142–144.

Krauthammer, Charles. 2005. The Truth about Torture: It's Time to Be Honest about Doing Terrible Things. *Weekly Standard*. December 5.

Ramsey, Paul. 1950. *Basic Christian Ethics*. New York: Charles Scribner's Sons.

Ramsey, Paul. 1961a. *Christian Ethics and the Sit-In*. New York: Association Press.

Ramsey, Paul. 1961b. *War and the Christian Conscience: How Shall Modern War Be Conducted Justly?* Durham, NC: Duke University Press.

Ramsey, Paul. 1966. Vietnam: Dissent from Dissent. *Christian Century*. **83**(29), pp.909–913.

Ramsey, Paul. 1967a. Is Vietnam a Just War?. *Dialog*. **6**(1), pp.19–29.

Ramsey, Paul. 1967b. Two Extremes: Ramsey Replies to His Critics. *Dialog*. **6**(3), pp.218–219.

Ramsey, Paul. 1968a; 1983. *The Just War: Force and Political Responsibility*. New York: Charles Scribner's Sons; Lanham, MD: Rowman & Littlefield Publishers, Inc.

Ramsey, Paul. 1968b. Politics as Science, Not Prophecy. *Worldview.* **11**(1), pp.18–21.

Ramsey, Paul. 1968c. The Case of the Curious Exception. In Outka, Gene H. and Ramsey, Paul. ed. *Norm and Context in Christian Ethics.* London: SCM Press Ltd, pp. 67–135.

Ramsey, Paul. 1972. Force and Political Responsibility. In Lefever, Ernest W. ed. *Ethics and World Politics: Four Perspectives.* Baltimore and London: The Johns Hopkins University Press, pp. 43–73.

Ramsey, Paul. 1973. A Political Ethics Context for Strategic Thinking. In Kaplan, Morton A. ed. *Strategic Thinking and Its Moral Implications.* Chicago: University of Chicago Center for Policy Study, pp. 101–147.

Ramsey, Paul. 1983. Response. In Neuhaus, Richard John. *Speaking to the World: Four Protestant Perspectives.* Washington, D.C.: Ethics and Public Policy Center.

Ramsey, Paul. 1988. *Speak Up for Just War or Pacifism.* University Park, PA: The Pennsylvania State University Press.

Stout, Jeffrey. 1991. Ramsey and Others on Nuclear Ethics. *Journal of Religious Ethics* **19**(2), pp. 209–237.

Waldron, Jeremy. 2006. What Can Christian Teaching Add to the Debate about Torture. *Theology Today.* **63**(3), pp.330–343.

Walzer, Michael. 1973. Political Action: The Problem of Dirty Hands. *Philosophy and Public Affairs.* **2**(2), pp.160–180.

Walzer, Michael. 1977, 5th ed. 2015. *Just and Unjust Wars.* New York: Basic Books.

Wogaman, Philip. 1967. The Vietnam War and Paul Ramsey's Conscience. *Dialog.* **6**(4), pp.292–298.

Yoder, John Howard. 1972. *The Politics of Jesus.* Grand Rapids, MI: Wm. B. Eerdmans Publishing Co.

Yoder, John Howard. 1984. *When War is Unjust.* Minneapolis: Augsburg Publishing House.

16

MICHAEL WALZER
(1935–PRESENT)

Chris Brown

Introduction

Grasping Michael Walzer's standing as a just war thinker presents real difficulties. He is, on most people's reckoning, the single most influential just war thinker of the last hundred years; theologians might look to Paul Ramsey, historians of the tradition to James Turner Johnson, but, for political theorists and philosophers, scholars of international relations, military educators and the general reader, Walzer's *Just and Unjust Wars* is the single most important modern work in the field (Johnson, 1975 & 1981: Ramsey, 1968: Walzer, 1977/2015, Nardin *et al.*, 1997). First published in the immediate aftermath of the Vietnam War in 1977, it has never been out of print, nor has it required revision – the five editions of the book have different prefaces or afterwords addressing the issues of the day, but the text itself remains unchanged, still relevant, a genuine classic in the full sense of the term. So, where is the problem? It lies in the fact that, set in the context of the tradition, he is not, in any considered sense of the term, a just war thinker at all. From a historical point of view, the just war tradition has deep Christian roots, while Walzer is a secular Jew, a political philosopher whose democratic socialist beliefs have few points of contact with Augustine, Aquinas and their successors and, as a result, whose account of the just war ignores, or sometimes actually rejects, many features of the tradition. His approach to the tradition is *à la carte* – he takes from it what he needs, what makes sense to him, and leaves the rest: historical examples for their moral exemplarity. Whence the aforementioned difficulty. In the 21st century, just war thinkers can generally be divided into "traditionalists" whose work follows on from Augustine, Aquinas *et al*, or "revisionists", whose arguments conform to the norms of analytical philosophy; Walzer falls into neither camp – he is *sui generis*, a law unto himself, and yet arguably more influential than all the other just war thinkers put together. To explore this paradox, we need to place *Just and Unjust Wars* in the context of its times, and Walzer's life.

Texts and contexts

Born in 1935 in New York City, Walzer was educated at Brandeis University, Cambridge, UK, and Harvard, where he was awarded his Ph.D. in 1961 for a thesis, subsequently published as *The Revolution of the Saints: A Study in the Origins of Revolutionary Politics* (1965). This was an examination of the thought of seventeenth century Puritanism in England; it highlighted an interest in the theme of religion and politics that persists to the present day, as witnessed by his work on the *Jewish Political Traditions* (2000, 2003), and by his most recent book, *The Paradox of Liberation: Secular Revolutions and Religious Counterrevolutions* (2015a). But as well as writing and thinking as a political philosopher, Walzer was in the 1950s and '60s, and is now, a political activist, a participant in the politics of the democratic left in the United States, a contributor to, and, for thirty years until recently, a co-editor of the democratic socialist journal *Dissent*. To participate in American politics in the 1960s necessarily involved adopting a position on the Vietnam War; Walzer, by then a teacher at first Princeton and then Harvard was, predictably, an active member of the anti-war movement, and his academic focus shifted as a result of this engagement. The first product of this shift was his collection of essays, *Obligations: Essays on Disobedience, War and Citizenship* (1970), but by far the most substantial work this new engagement stimulated was the aforementioned *Just and Unjust Wars*, which appeared in 1977 after the end of the war, and drew from that conflict only a few of the many practical examples of moral dilemmas in war which make it such an attractive read, but which is clearly still steeped in the politics of the era.

Part 1 of *Just and Unjust Wars* focuses on the moral reality of war, arguing against realism. Walzer's opposition to the Vietnam War quite naturally ruled out the adoption of a political realist, Clausewitzian understanding of war as simply an act of policy, with no particular moral freight attached to the choice of violence. For Walzer, the default setting is that to wage war is to commit a crime. However, unlike many members of the anti-war movement, he did not adopt a pacifist stance, opposing all wars, nor did he espouse the ultra-radical position of supporting only wars of national liberation. The dedication of the book, drawn from the Pillar of Heroism at the *Yad Vashem* Memorial in Jerusalem, signals his belief in the legitimacy of the Allied cause in World War II; equally, he supported Israel's action in the Seven Days War of 1967, which he understood as a war of self-defense, albeit one begun by a, in his view justified, pre-emptive strike. These commitments ruled out both the pacifist and the ultra-radical position and suggest that there are circumstances under which the waging of war is not criminal. His goal is to find a philosophically defensible way of way of distinguishing those circumstances where inter-state violence might be legitimate and those where it would not be; within the Western canon of political philosophy it is the just war tradition that attempts to make this distinction, and this is where he found part – though only part – of the inspiration for *Just and Unjust Wars*.

It is fair to say that prior to Walzer's book, the just war tradition had been understood largely in Christian terms, even though the roots extend back to Cicero's Rome. Aquinas, in particular, systematized the doctrine, arguing that God intended us to live together in peace with justice and without violence, but that violence might sometimes be necessary to right a wrong and thereby restore the peace that had been broken by injustice (Finnis, 1996). For a war to be just (in fact, just is not really the right term here, "justified" fits the situation better) a number of criteria need to be met – there should be a just cause, a wrong that must be righted, those who wage war should do so with right intention, war should only be declared by a proper public authority, as a last resort, the violence employed should be proportional to the offence, the innocent should be protected, and there should be a reasonable prospect that violence would make things better rather than worse. These last four criteria (last resort, proportionality, protection of the innocent, prospect of victory) it should be noted, were derived by Aquinas from the "golden rule" ("do unto others as you would be done by") that governs moral conduct in general, rather than from any features of moral reasoning specific to war – strictly speaking, it is the first three criteria (just cause, right intention and right authority) that address what is distinctive about war.

In the deep tradition of medieval moral philosophy, these criteria were to be understood as a package that could not be disaggregated; all must be satisfied for a war to be considered "just", although this was not a "box-ticking" exercise, but rather one that called for the exercise of different kinds of judgment – not for nothing was Aquinas an Aristotelian as well as a Christian, and Aristotle's *phronesis*, practical judgment, was central to his thinking. However, within the later tradition in the era of Vitoria and Grotius, and with the rise of the modern state the canonical criteria were gradually separated into two categories, recently characterized as *ius ad bellum* and *ius in bello*, which dealt respectively with the justice of resort to war, and with right conduct in war. This latter distinction provided the framework for Walzer's book – on his account *ius ad bellum* becomes the theory of aggression derived from the "legalist paradigm" described in Part 2, and *ius in bello* becomes the "war convention" set out in Part 3. To complete the story, Part 4 explores "Dilemmas of War" focusing *inter alia* on "supreme emergency" (on which see below) and nuclear deterrence, while Part 5 straddles both *ius ad bellum* and *ius in bello* considerations by exploring the question of responsibility, as applied to both political leaders, commanders and ordinary soldiers.

Tenets and controversies

Ius ad bellum is presented in terms of a theory of aggression. The "legalist paradigm" governs here – it is based on the proposition that there exists a society of states whose members possess political sovereignty and territorial integrity; attacks on the latter are acts of aggression which the victim is entitled to resist, to enlist the aid of others in so doing, and later to punish the aggressor. With one or two very limited exceptions, the only "just cause" that can be recognized under modern conditions is self-defense, and all members of the society of states may defend themselves from external assault on their autonomy and territory. The aforementioned exceptions concern pre-emptive war (to be distinguished carefully from preventive war) and a very restrictive doctrine of humanitarian intervention that would give outsiders the right (though not the duty) to intervene in cases of extreme human rights violations – genocide and mass enslavement are mentioned in this context.

The "war convention" concerns the rights of combatants and non-combatants, *ius in bello*. On his account the justice of a war (*ius ad bellum*) does not affect who may, or may not, be killed or how they may be killed (*ius in bello*). Soldiers should not be understood as simply individuals – they are representatives of a political community, but, nonetheless, they do have rights, which govern the circumstances under which they may kill, or be killed, and the ways in which they kill or are killed. The "moral equality of combatants" implies that all combatants are legitimate targets whether fighting in a just cause or not and subject to the same limitations on the weapons that may be employed. Non-combatants should not be intentional targets in any circumstances – though, controversially, he does allow in Part 4 that a "supreme emergency" might justify waiving this rule if thereby a greater moral disaster can be avoided (Walzer 1977, pp.34–47). Thus, for example, the bombing campaign against German cities in World War II might have been justified had this been the only way to prevent the disaster of a Nazi victory – although he argues that it was not, and the campaign was therefore illegitimate.

The subtitle of *Just and Unjust Wars* is "A moral argument with historical illustrations" and in Parts 3, 4 and 5 Walzer offers a wide range of such historical illustrations, covering such matters as non-combatant immunity and military necessity, sieges and blockades, guerrilla war, terrorism, reprisals and war crimes. One of the attractive features of the book is the way in which Walzer is determined at every stage to anchor his moral arguments in real-world situations, whether drawn from the siege of Jerusalem in 72 AD, submarine warfare in World War I or the rules of engagement for American forces in Vietnam. He turns to historical examples for their moral exemplarity, that is, because they can provide some "particularly illuminating or forceful argument" pertinent to the present character of the world (Walzer 1977, p.xxii). Walzer has expressed elsewhere his impatience and dissatisfaction with the kind of political theory that involves the "playful extension of hypothetical cases, moving farther and farther away from the world we all lived in" and the way in which he develops the arguments in *Just and Unjust Wars* exemplifies his determination to remain at all times focused on real people and real issues (Walzer, 2003). It is perhaps misleading to describe the many cases he examines as "illustrations" – the historical examples he employs do not simply *illustrate* his arguments, they actually *are* the way in which he argues. In any event, the present author can testify that the mini-case studies Walzer offers make the book immensely attractive to students at all levels, and it is not implausible to argue that part of the longevity of the book rests on its sheer readability and utility as a teaching text as well as on the depth of its argument.

The positions Walzer adopts on aggression and the rules of war are broadly compatible with the contemporary legal regime governing the use of force in international relations. The UN Charter recognizes self-defense as the only legitimate use of force (although only until the Security Council has taken the measures necessary to ensure international peace and security, Article 51). Walzer's willingness to allow for intervention in the case of mass enslavement and genocide corresponds to various anti-slavery conventions, and the Genocide Convention of 1948. As far as the War Convention is concerned, the Law of Armed Conflict (also known as International Humanitarian Law), that is, the Geneva and Hague Treaties and the accompanying Protocols, is clear that the same rules of war apply to all combatants, and the same protections to all non-combatants.

One area where Walzer departs from the modern legal regime is with respect to "supreme emergency", which is not recognized by lawyers as a legitimate basis for suspending the rules of war. Indeed, it is not simply lawyers who find disturbing the notion that supreme emergency can provide a "get out of jail" card. The problem lies in the difficulty of deciding which emergencies are supreme and which are, as it were, normal – most would probably agree that a potential victory for Nazism would qualify as a supreme emergency, but some might argue that any defeat in war could be seen in the same terms, with the result that the qualifications that Walzer wishes to attach to the term go by the board. Still, one suspects that most actual decision-makers have in the back of their minds the thought that some such provision may be necessary *in extremis*. Walzer's thinking on this subject is akin to the position laid out in his essay on "Political Action: The Problem of Dirty Hands" (1973, anthologized in *Thinking Politically,* 2007) where he argues that there are times when, all things considered, it can be right to do something that is morally wrong – a position that applies to a range of situations, from the supreme emergencies discussed in *Just and Unjust Wars* to the dubious tactics employed in the so-called War on Terror. In an interview in 2003, in the context of the post-9/11 debates on torture, Walzer comments on the issue of dirty hands:

> [But] extreme cases make bad law. Yes, I would do whatever was necessary to extract information in the ticking bomb case – that is, I would make the same argument after 9/11 that I made 30 years before. But I don't want to generalize from cases like that; I don't want to rewrite the rule against torture to incorporate this exception. Rules are rules, and exceptions are exceptions. I want political leaders to accept the rule, to understand its reasons, even to internalize it. I also want them to be smart enough to know when to break it. And finally, because they believe in the rule, I want them to feel guilty about breaking it – which is the only guarantee they can offer us that they won't break it too often.
>
> *(Walzer, 2003)*

As with supreme emergency, his thinking on this subject probably corresponds to the intuitions of most political leaders, albeit that they less rarely acknowledge the essential proviso that those who dirty their hands in this way must acknowledge that they have done so and bear the guilt that attaches to their acts.

Returning to the more general point, Walzer's position could be seen as a defense of the current legal framework governing the use of force – but it departs radically from what had previously been understood to be the just war tradition. In the tradition – here one can look at the formulations of just cause enumerated from Augustine all the way through at least Vattel explored in detail in the preceding chapters – a "just cause" is understood in general terms as righting a wrong, and is certainly not restricted to self-defense. The right to defend oneself is an important feature of the aforementioned "golden rule", and the tradition is not hostile to the notion, but while self-defense may be *a* just cause it is not generally understood to be the *only* just cause. Again, "right intention", the notion that what is important is not just doing the right thing, but doing it for the right reason, is crucial in the tradition but plays no part in Walzer's account – for Walzer, a just war is a response to a crime, and the state of mind of the respondent is relevant only in so far as if it is inappropriate it may prejudice or distort his or her actions. The medieval concern with the state of the soul of the individual, crucial to Aquinas, plays no part in Walzer's thinking, understandably enough, given his relentlessly secular approach to the just war. The criterion of "right authority" poses many interesting questions in the modern age – for example, does the UN Security Council alone possess the authority to legitimate force? Or can we simply accept the state as the appropriate authority? – but is barely touched upon by Walzer; as with right intention, his legalism points him away from the tradition (and modern thinkers such as Johnson and Elshtain who draw force from the tradition) and towards an examination of authority in terms of command responsibility. And finally, with respect to the War Convention, the moral equality of combatants central to Walzer's account, is a principle that the tradition would not recognize; wrongdoers do not, could not, have the same moral standing as those who would reverse a wrong – although admittedly medieval thinkers saw the assignment of right and wrong as ultimately a matter for God, unlike modern analytical philosophers who are confident that they themselves can do the job (McMahan, 2009). Having said all that, it should perhaps also be noted that Walzer's opposition to the notion of nuclear deterrence, as set out in chapter 17 of *Just and Unjust Wars*, is based on reasoning that is much closer to the tradition than the defense of deterrence offered by the theologian Paul Ramsey (on whom see chapter 15 of this volume). Walzer argues that deterrence may be a necessary strategy – c.f. a "supreme emergency" – but it is morally unacceptable and alternatives should be sought; in an illuminating aside he remarks "supreme emergency is never a stable position" (Walzer, 1977/2015, p.282).

Legacies and enduring relevance

Put all this together and it is easy to see why Walzer's legacy as a just war thinker is so complex. Although he uses the term "just war" to describe what he is doing, in practice the secular, legalistic version of the just war that he presents bears little relation to the way the tradition has understood the term. The driving force of his analysis actually lies elsewhere, in his account of the rights of the individual and of the political community. His focus on self-defense stems from the belief that in defending the right of political communities to resist aggression, he is actually defending the rights of the individuals who make up these communities – political communities are worth defending because of the shared understandings and common life they promote, and, crucially, this may be true even if their institutions of government are non-democratic. Autonomy is to be valued in its own terms, and not simply if it leads to democratic self-government. As Walzer puts in,

> The moral standing of any particular state depends on the reality of the common life it protects and the extent to which the sacrifices required by that protection are willingly accepted and thought worthwhile. If no common life exists, or if the state doesn't defend the common life that does exist, its own defence may have no moral justification.
>
> *(Walzer, 1977/2015, p.54)*

This is why his thinking leads to only a very limited doctrine of humanitarian intervention, in contrast to the willingness of many just war theorists steeped in the authority of the tradition to embrace much more radical ideas (Johnson, 2005). As a social democrat, Walzer naturally hopes that communities will choose democracy, but outsiders are obliged to assume that whatever form of government exists reflects the wishes of the people concerned; even if pro-democracy movements are suppressed, as long as the society has not collapsed into civil war and insurrection it has to be presumed that there is a "fit" between government and people. Short of such a collapse, the only real circumstances in which outsiders would be entitled (although not obliged) to intervene would be in the case of genocide or mass enslavement – in such circumstances the fit between governed and governors has clearly broken down, but otherwise the presumption of *international* legitimacy must hold, whatever we think of the internal politics of the country in question. This position is very clearly at odds with the wider just war tradition, and, of course, with the cosmopolitanism set out by Charles Beitz and David Luban in the influential collection *International Ethics* (Beitz et al., 1985). For pragmatic reasons, traditionalists and cosmopolitans may come to the same conclusion about the need to embrace similar anti-interventionist politics as Walzer, although they get there from very different starting points.

Would Walzer be concerned to be told that his work departed radically from the just war tradition? Almost certainly, he would not. In recent years his approach has come under attack from the so-called "revisionist" just war theorists – see chapter

19 in this volume on Jeff McMahan – and he has responded with some force, most particularly in the "Afterword" to the 2015 edition of *Just and Unjust Wars*. As against McMahan's insistence that soldiers fighting in an unjust cause lose the rights we might assign to just combatants, Walzer defends the division between *ius ad bellum* and *ius in bello*, arguing that the justice of a war should not determine the rights of combatants; his attitude to the revisionists is that their theories are divorced from the actual practice of war, a position nicely caught in a 2012 online interview with Nancy Rosenblum where he sets out the basis for his differences with them – he remarks that for the revisionists "the subject of just war theory is just war theory [whereas] I think the subject matter of just war theory is war" (Rosenblum, 2012). This is, I think, an answer that he would give with equal force to critics who uphold the traditionalist account of just war. In fact, as an answer, it is actually more effective when given to traditionalists as opposed to revisionists. *Pace* his focus on war rather than theory, the way in which he sets up the argument does depend quite heavily on a theory of rights, which leaves him vulnerable to those, such as the revisionists, who also begin with rights, but offer a different version of the theoretical relationship between the individual and the community. Interestingly, this point was picked up in one of the first reviews of *Just and Unjust Wars*, by Richard Wasserstrom in the *Harvard Law Review* (Wasserstrom, 1978). Wasserstrom suggests, rather harshly, that Walzer's presents an "uninspiring, constricted theory of individual rights" (p.542), and that a more fully worked out account of the rights of individuals would undermine his position that, extreme oppression aside, states are entitled to defend their political sovereignty even when non-democratic. Whether this criticism is justified or not is a matter that individual readers of Walzer's book will form their own opinions on, but it is worth noting that his position does oblige him to fight a war on two fronts – on the one hand, with those who are unhappy with the idea of basing a conception of the just war on the notion of individual rights, and, on the other, with those who are happy to take this step but offer a different conception of rights.

Walzer is a political philosopher who since producing *Just and Unjust Wars* has written on a great many topics, such as, the nature of justice (Walzer, 1983), the nature of moral argumentation and social criticism (Walzer, 1987; 1995a), what it means to be an American (Walzer, 1992; 2003) and the Jewish political tradition (Walzer et al., 2000; 2003), but while he has never abandoned an interest in war, he has equally not felt it necessary to address the subject at anything like the length he did in *Just and Unjust Wars*. It is predominantly as a commentator on public affairs – which he sees as wholly consistent with the vocation of political philosophy – that he has returned to the issue of war via contributions to *Dissent* and other radical and liberal journals, the most important of which are anthologized in two collections, *Arguing About War* (2004) and *Thinking Politically* (2007). In the process he has modified somewhat the positions he adopted in his earlier writings. In a *Dissent* essay of 1995, "The Politics of Rescue" (anthologized in *Arguing about War*), written in response to the events of the immediate Post-Cold War era, he widens the range of situations in which intervention might be justifiable, and anticipates a longer engagement with post-intervention politics than was envisaged in his earlier work. His earlier position involved returning control to local populations as soon as possible after an intervention, but he now recognizes that such a policy may simply lead to a replication of the circumstances that led to intervention in the first place. His views on humanitarian intervention have also evolved over time.

Still, his essential position remains anti-interventionist, and he maintained this stance even in the aftermath of 9/11, although he supported the US intervention in Afghanistan in 2001 as an example of self-defense, and joined with just war theorists Jean Bethke Elshtain and James Turner Johnson in signing the Manifesto "What We Are Fighting For" (Elshtain, 2003). This letter was directed against those elements on the left in the United States who were inclined to blame American foreign policy for the attacks on New York and Washington and Walzer reiterated his resistance to this argument in an interview in 2003, identifying himself as in opposition to the Bush Administration, but criticizing "the idiocy of many of my fellow oppositionists: knee-jerk anti-Americanism, old left dogmatism, and the rejection of any fellowship larger than the sect of the politically correct and the morally pure" (Walzer, 2003). Still, he parted company with Elshtain and Johnson over the Iraq War, and, in general, in his opposition to regime change as a motive for intervention. On similar grounds he opposed the NATO-led intervention in Libya in 2011, thus confirming that he still operates a quite restrictive understanding of when "rescue" is appropriate – although it should be said that many people who were surprised by his opposition at the time, including the present author, now feel that subsequent events have vindicated his caution (Walzer, 2011). More recently, his refusal to see action against the so-called Islamic State in Syria as justifiable in accordance with just war criteria is striking, especially since the leading just war revisionist, Jeff McMahan, has come out in favor of action (Walzer, 2015b; McMahan, 2015). Walzer's argument here is that there is no reasonable prospect of success and therefore military action cannot be justified. This position follows on from a series of articles Walzer has written in *Dissent* over the last five years, in which his position on intervention has shifted, from an initial stance against "a half-assed intervention" (Walzer, 2012), via a defense of Obama's "dithering over Syria" (Walzer, 2013a), to an admission that US intervention earlier in the conflict could not, in fact, have made things worse and might have made things better (Walzer, 2013b). These short blog posts are actually very revealing about the way in Walzer thinks about war and justice; some at least of the classic just war criteria lurk in the background of his arguments – last resort, proportionality, a reasonable prospect of success – but the foreground is always a kind of principled pragmatism, an engagement with the facts, a willingness to change his mind when the circumstances demand it. As against the dogmatism of some just warriors of both traditionalist and revisionist disposition, Walzer might well deploy the formulation attributed, probably wrongly, to John Maynard Keynes – "When the facts change, I change my mind. What do you do sir?"

Walzer's distaste for an approach to political theory that relies on high levels of abstraction and fanciful hypothetical examples has been noted above, and adherents of that kind of theory have often responded in kind, as witnessed by some of the essays collected in *Pluralism, Justice and Equality* (Walzer & Miller, 1995). In another context, a master of abstract political theory – Jon Elster – once referred to Walzer as "a phenomenologist of the moral life" (Elster, 1992, p.14). This was not, I think, intended as a compliment, but it seems to me to encapsulate perfectly Walzer's project over the last sixty years, and to point us towards understanding why *Just and Unjust Wars* continues to be a source of inspiration for scholars and students. His concern always is with how life is actually lived – in this case, with how and why wars are actually fought. He brings out the moral dilemmas of war with a clarity that few other contemporary writers have achieved, and encourages us to use our wits to think about those dilemmas; he employs some of the concepts made available to him by the just war tradition, but is never afraid to discard parts of the tradition, or adapt other parts to make them more amenable to contemporary conditions. In a world where new forms of warfare abound – asymmetric, hybrid, cyber – this flexibility is obviously called for, but it is crucially important that it be accompanied by a moral compass that will tell us if we are straying into dangerous ground. It is because he possesses such a compass that Walzer's work remains relevant and his commentaries on current affairs, international and domestic, have such force. He may or may not be a "just war thinker" in the full sense of the term, but he certainly is the most accomplished moral phenomenologist of war of our age.

Works cited

Beitz, C., Cohen, M., Scanlon, T. and Simmons, J.A. eds. 1985. *International Ethics*. Princeton NJ: Princeton University Press.

Elster, J. 1992. *Local Justice*. New York: Russell Sage Foundation.

Elshtain, J.B. 2003. *Just War Against Terror: The Burden of American Power in a Violent World*. New York: Basic Books.

Finnis J. 1996. The Ethics of War and Peace in the Catholic Natural Law Tradition. In: Nardin T. ed. *The Ethics of War and Peace*. Princeton: Princeton University Press.

Johnson, J.T. 1975. *Ideology, Reason and the Limitation of War*. Princeton, NJ: Princeton University Press.

Johnson, J.T. 1981. *Just War Tradition and the Restraint of War*. Princeton, NJ: Princeton University Press.

Johnson, J.T. 2005. *The War to Oust Saddam Hussein: Just War and the New Face of Conflict*. Lanham, MD: Rowman and Littlefield.

McMahan, J. 2009. *Killing in War*. Oxford: Oxford University Press.

McMahan, J. 2015. Syria is a Modern Day Holocaust: We Must Act. *Washington Post* in Theory: Opinion November 30, 2015. www.washingtonpost.com/news/in-theory/wp/2015/11/30/syria-is-a-modern-day-holocaust-we-must-act

Nardin, T., Smith, M.J., Hendrickson, D.C., Koontz, T.J., Boyle, J. and Walzer, M. 1997. Special Section: Twenty Years of Michael Walzer's *Just and Unjust Wars*. *Ethics and International Affairs*. **11**, pp.3–104.

Ramsey, P. 1968. *The Just War: Force and Political Responsibility.* New York: Charles Scribner's Sons.

Rosenblum, Nancy. 2012. A Conversation with Michael Walzer. *You Tube* www.youtube.com/watch?v=TvpnmmLoO38, accessed May 18, 2015.

Walzer, M. 1965. *The Revolution of the Saints: A Study in the Origins of Revolutionary Politics.* Cambridge, MA: Harvard University Press.

Walzer, M. 1970. *Obligations: Essays on Disobedience, War and Citizenship.* Cambridge, MA: Harvard University Press.

Walzer, M. 1973. Political Action: The Problem of Dirty Hands. *Philosophy and Public Affairs* **2**(2), pp.160–180

Walzer, M. 1977, 5th ed. 2015. *Just and Unjust Wars.* New York: Basic Books.

Walzer, M. 1983. *Spheres of Justice.* New York: Basic Books.

Walzer, M. 1987. *Interpretation and Social Criticism.* Cambridge MA: Harvard University Press.

Walzer, M. 1988, 2nd ed. 2002. *The Company of Critics.* New York: Basic Books.

Walzer, M. 1992. *What It Means to Be an American.* New York: Marsilio.

Walzer, M. 1995a. *Thick and Thin: Moral Argument at Home and Abroad.* Notre Dame: Notre Dame Press.

Walzer, M. 1995b. The Politics of Rescue. *Dissent* (Winter), pp.35–41.

Walzer, M. 2003. The United States in the World – Just Wars and Just Societies: An Interview with Michael Walzer. *Imprints: A Journal of Analytical Socialism* **7**(1), pp.4–19.

Walzer, M. 2004. *Arguing about War.* New Haven: Yale University Press.

Walzer, M. 2005. *Politics and Passion: Towards a More Egalitarian Liberalism.* New Haven: Yale University Press.

Walzer, M. 2007. *Thinking Politically: Essays in Political Theory*, New Haven: Yale University Press.

Walzer, M. 2011. The Case Against our Attack on Libya. *The New Republic.* March 20, 2011 www.tnr.com/article/world/85509/the-case-against-our-attack-libya

Walzer, M. 2012. Syria. *Dissent* March 9, 2012 www.dissentmagazine.org/blog/syria

Walzer, M. 2013a. Syria: What ought to be done?. *Dissent* May 14, 2013. www.dissentmagazine.org/blog/syria-what-ought-to-be-done

Walzer, M. 2013b. Were we wrong about Syria?. *Dissent.* October 30, 2013. www.dissentmagazine.org/blog/were-we-wrong-about-syria

Walzer, M. 2015a. *The Paradox of Liberation: Secular Revolutions and Religious Counterrevolutions.* New Haven: Yale University Press.

Walzer, M. 2015b. What Kind of a War Is This? *Dissent* December 3, 2015. www.dissentmagazine.org/blog/france-us-uk-air-strikes-isis-just-war-theory

Walzer, M. and Miller, D. 1995. *Pluralism, Justice and Equality.* Oxford: Oxford University Press.

Walzer, M., Lorberbaum, M., Zohar, N. and Ackerman, A. Eds. 2000. *The Jewish Political Tradition:* Volume 1*, Authority.* New Haven: Yale University Press.

Walzer, M. Lorberbaum, M., Zohar, N. and Ackerman, A. Eds. 2003. *The Jewish Political Tradition.* Volume 2. *Membership.* New Haven: Yale University Press.

Wasserstrom, R. 1978. Review of *Just and Unjust Wars* in *Harvard Law Review.* **92**(2) pp.536–545.

17

JEAN BETHKE ELSHTAIN
(1941–2013)

Nicholas Rengger

Introduction

Jean Bethke Elshtain was a phenomenon. A scholar who wore her (very real) learning lightly, a wonderful teacher, a committed and engaged public intellectual and a lover, as she herself once put it, of "Crazy Horse and Augustine",[1] of that blend of high culture and popular culture that is so very American and so difficult to pull off with real success – but every time she did. She wrote about, and lectured on, a bewilderingly wide variety of topics, from feminism to terrorism, from democracy to sovereignty, from the family to the problem of dirty hands. But an abiding concern – and the reason for her inclusion in this volume – was with the morality and practice of war, and in particular, the vicissitudes of the just war tradition. And that, of course, is what will concern us here, though as we will see it is not always easy to separate out the various different themes that permeate her work.

Contexts

Jean Bethke was born on January 6, 1941, in Timnath, Colorado (population 185), a farming town north of Denver, the oldest of five children of Paul and Helen Bethke, and grew up in nearby Fort Collins, Colorado, where her father, a schoolteacher, principal and later school superintendent, had moved the family. Their religious background was Lutheran. At the age of 10, the young Jean contracted polio and spent much of the next few years confounding her doctor's prediction that she would never walk again. As she said herself many years later, as a teenager with polio, and then someone who had her first child at 19, bodies and embodiment played a very powerful role in her thought from very early on. She walked with a slight limp for the rest of her life, but never let her physical difficulties get in the way. At conferences, meetings, seminars and indeed in the local bar or coffee house she was always a fount of energy.[2]

After graduating from Colorado State University in 1963 and earning a master's degree in history as a Woodrow Wilson Fellow, Elshtain received her Ph.D. in political science from Brandeis University in 1973 (where she was taught, amongst others, by Kenneth Waltz, a debt she repaid many years later in *Women and War*). She was on the faculty at the University of Massachusetts, Amherst, from 1973 to 1988, when she moved to Vanderbilt University in Nashville, becoming the first woman to hold an endowed professorship there. She and her husband Errol, had three daughters and a son and on her death in 2013, she was survived by them, two sisters, two brothers and four grandchildren.

In 1995, Elshtain moved from Vanderbilt (though she continued to maintain a home in Nashville) to become Laura Spellman Rockefeller Professor in Social and Political Ethics at the Divinity School at the University of Chicago, with cross appointments in the Department of Political Science and the Committee on International Relations. Such an appointment was very unusual, given the increasing compartmentalization of the modern university – and the hostility to "divinity" of much mainstream social science – but it suited Elshtain's interests perfectly: "I do political theory", she would say, "with ethics at its heart". She identified, very strongly, with the Christian Realism of the likes of Rheinhold Niebuhr and Paul Tillich and sought, in her own times, to do as they did in theirs. Her friend William Schweiker emphasized that her work was marked by "a hard-nosed realism, [but] with a very humane heart".[3]

Her published work is, as indicated above, extraordinarily wide ranging. Amongst her major books that we will really not discuss in what follows, one should surely flag up her first – *Public Man/Private Woman* (1981) – a path-breaking study of the public face of gender roles and *Democracy on Trial* (1993) – a major intervention about the crisis facing contemporary democracy and, perhaps most important of all, the published version of her 2006 Gifford lectures at Edinburgh, *Sovereignty* (2008). But as she herself acknowledged, she had become best known, perhaps, for writing about war. "It has become my topic by default", she admitted. "If we lived in less tumultuous times, I would write about it less".[4] Thus, in this chapter we will focus especially on three books that display her engagement with the just war tradition most directly, *Women and War* (1987), *Augustine and the Limits of Politics* (1995) and *Just War Against Terror* (2003a).

Texts

The text, which, more than any other sets up the parameters of Elshtain's engagement with the just war tradition, is *Women and War*. At one level this was a direct continuation of the trajectory explored in *Public Man/Private Woman*, in that it is concerned with the way in which, as she puts it in the preface, the roles men and women play in war are represented and narrated in the stories we tell about ourselves. But, as she also says, the story *Women and War* tells becomes a more complicated one. "*Women and War*", she tells us, "is the result of overlapping recognitions of the complexity hiding behind many of our simple, rigid ideas and formulations" (Elshtain, 1987, p.xi).

Written after a year of leave at the Institute for Advanced Study at Princeton and aided also by a period at the Bellagio Centre of the Rockefeller Foundation on Lake Como, the book argues that the central narrative spine of the Western imaginary of war is the dichotomous one of "Beautiful souls" and "just warriors", with women being largely confined to the former and men to the latter. But the reality, Elshtain argues, is far more ambiguous and complex. Following a very personal narrative of her own responses to the lived experience of war in her own life, in her family, community and in the wider culture around her – a very Elshtainean weaving together of the personal, political and the cultural – she turns to the meat of the argument. This is simply that the evolution of the ideas and practices implicated in the notion of "armed civic virtue" from the Greeks to the present reveals a much more nuanced and complicated story than one might think if one mixes up the categories that congealed as beautiful souls and just warriors. In part, it also shows that the attempt to disarm civic virtue (by, for example, the early Church) produces the just war tradition. And it is here, in the central chapter of *Women and War* (chapter 4 "The Attempt to Disarm Civic Virtue") that we meet the just war tradition in Elshtain's hands for the first time and also the basic inspiration for her reading of it, Augustine. Indeed, after surveying the evolution of just war thinking in the modern period and criticizing it (in particular in the thought of Michael Walzer – see chapter 16), the leading secular just war thinker of her day (and a friend of hers) and, like James Turner Johnson (see chapter 18) the famous pastoral letter issues by the American Catholic Bishops in 1983 – she contends that it is Augustine's reading that does most justice to the fragmented and disputable character of our experiences of war and peace. The astute reader will compare Elshtain's thoughts to what Augustine actually has to say across his life (see chapter 2), but here are her thoughts on the matter:

> To make more secure contact on the level of the lived life, to enter into the fray from the ground up rather than descending from the lofty pinnacle of a "morality system", just war thinkers would do well (she writes) to retrieve Augustine's way of thinking as part of an effort to capture the loving textures within which limited human beings think and act. Augustine deflates rather than builds up the possibility that we might one day control events … inviting neither total relativism nor despairing withdrawal, Augustine's tragic recognitions point to modes of moral thinking stripped of the demand for triumphant moral heroism. He seeks to limit the damage done by oneself and others, rather than to preach an unattainable counsel of perfection that invites smugness and despair.
>
> *(Elshtain, 1987, p.158)*

The rest of the book continues to problematize simplistic narratives of gender and war and does so very powerfully indeed, but for our purposes, her course has been set. Elshtain sees herself as a champion of an armed civic virtue chastened and illuminated by an Augustinian just war sensibility that is alert to the fragile and contested character of ourselves as agents and thinkers. As she puts it in the last paragraph of *Woman and War*:

> For the political embodiment of the attitude I here suggest, I return to the chastened patriot. He or she has no illusions: recognizing the limiting conditions internal to international politics, this civic being does not embrace utopian fantasies of world government or total disarmament … this citizen is skeptical about the forms and claims of the sovereign state; recognizes the (phony) parity in the notion of "equally" sovereign states and is thereby alert to the many forms hegemony can take; and deflates fantasies of control.
>
> *(Elshtain, 1987, p.258)*

While, of course, concerned with many other topics during the late 1980s and 1990s, Elshtain continued her engagement with both Augustine and the just war tradition.

In 1991, for example, just after the first Gulf War, she published an edited collection on *Just War Theory*[5] and her 1992 book *Meditations on Modern Political Thought* contained a long and important essay on discourses of war from Machiavelli to Arendt. But her next extended piece of writing relevant to our concerns in this volume was occasioned by the invitation to deliver the Frank M. Covey Jr. Loyola Lectures in Political Analysis at Loyola University, Chicago in 1995. The published version of her lectures, *Augustine and the Limits of Politics* (1996), marked her most detailed treatment of the thinker who, as we have seen, has been a major influence on her in general and also on her treatment of the just war tradition.

What Elshtain tries to do, as Mary Ann Glendon remarks in a perceptive review of the book, is to reveal the Augustine who:

> is a man of paradoxes. She evokes his delight in "the world" together with his vivid sense of its brokenness; his dedication to the life of the mind along with his awareness of the limits of reason; his ease amidst cultural pluralism and multiple interpretations; his understanding of choice as always constitutive and often tragic; his struggles with temptation and doubt.
>
> *(Glendon, 1996)*

In other words, Elshtain fills out and elaborates the Augustine she evoked so powerfully in *Women and War*. Not a pessimist, nor a misogynist, but rather someone only too aware of the frailties and ambivalences of our nature and our condition. Not someone – unlike some of his political descendants in the Medieval period – who ever equated Christianity with any temporal polity in any shape or form, but recognized it had things of huge importance to say to all regimes. For

Elshtain, Augustine's crucial significance lies in his recognition that the fallen and pluralistic nature of the world "should usher into a rueful recognition of limits, not a will to dominion that requires others for one to conquer" (Elshtain, 1996), and his recognition that action takes place on a field of moral danger and ambiguity. And while Augustine's skepticism of the temporal power is real, he is also "respectful of the social and civic arrangements that sinful man has created" (Elshtain, 1996) for social life "on all levels is full of ills and yet to be cherished" (Elshtain, 1998).

There is little discussion of the just war directly in *Augustine and the Limits of Politics*, but its evocation of an Augustinian sensibility informs all of Elshtain's writing on war and civic life up to and including her Gifford lectures on "Sovereign God, Sovereign State, Sovereign Self" in 2005–06 and, indeed, the work she was pursuing towards the end of her life. There is, however, one other text that we should look at closely in the current context, since it seems to throw doubt onto that claim. That is perhaps her most controversial book (in an intellectual life that had not up till then exactly been a stranger to controversy): *Just War Against Terror* (2003a).

Just War Against Terror: The Burden of American Power in a Violent World, to give it its full title, was published in 2003, more than a year after the 9/11 attacks on Washington and New York that frame the book and Elshtain's concerns in it. I will defer discussion of the controversies the book provoked (declaration of interest: I was a party to one part of this controversy) until the next section of this essay. For now, let me just outline the context of the book and its argument.

Elshtain opens the book with citations of two writers that she had also discussed in *Augustine and the Limits of Politics*: Albert Camus and Hannah Arendt (both powerful influences on Elshtain). She refers to Camus's *The Plague* and in particular to those one of the protagonists refers to as the "humanists",

> people who see themselves as living in a reasonable world in which everything is up for negotiation … in modernity, it simply must be the case that all human purposes and the means deployed to achieve them are open to adjudication and judgement. Just get the aggrieved parties to *talk* to one another, because that is the way *reasonable* people do things … Camus's humanists are unwilling or unable to peer into the heart of darkness … confronted by people who mean to kill them and to destroy their society, these well-meaning people deny the enormity of what is going on. To such arguments, the late political theorist Hannah Arendt would have had a sharp retort. "Politics is not the nursery", she liked to say.
>
> *(Elshtain, 2003a, pp. 1–2)*

Arendt's retort is also, of course, Elshtain's. She frames her essay by arguing that those who launched the 9/11 attacks cannot be reasoned with, in the manner the "humanists" would like – and that no change in US policy would have that effect – for the simple reason that:

they loathe us because of who we are and what our society represents … Bin Laden and his followers mean it when they call us infidels. To Islamists, infidels are those who believe in the separation of Church and state. Infidels profess the wrong religion or the wrong version of a religion, or no religion at all. Infidels believe in civic and personal freedom. Infidels educate women and give them a public presence and role. Infidels intermarry across lines of religion. Infidels believe that all people have human rights. Whatever else the United States might do on the world scene to allay the concerns of its opponents, it cannot repeal its founding constitutional principles, which condemn it in the eyes of such fundamentalists.

(Elshtain, 2003a, pp.3–4)

From this starting point, Elshtain goes on to outline an account of what happened on 9/11, what was at stake (in her view) in the conflict and, crucially for the argument of this book, she offers an account of what a just war is – repeating and to some extent simplifying the accounts she had given elsewhere, especially in *Women and War* – and why the US war against terrorism is an example of one. She then engages some critics of the kinds of position she is supporting (both in the US academy and elsewhere) before moving on to identify herself with the Christian Realism of Rheinhold Niebuhr and Paul Tillich (and by implication criticizing those who do not) before closing with two chapters detailing the problems of defense and self-defense in a dangerous world and, especially, the role the United States should play in such a world. Essentially, she argues, the United States must take the lead – not alone, to be sure – but it must take the lead in defending human dignity. "As the world's superpower", she argues in chapter 12,

America bears the responsibility to help guarantee … [the world's] international stability, whether much of the world wants it or not … We, the powerful, must respond to attacks against persons who cannot defend themselves because they, like us, are members of states, or would be states, whose primary obligation is to protect the lives of those citizens who inhabit their polities.

(Elshtain, 2002, pp.169–170)

Controversies

As I remarked above, Elshtain was hardly a stranger to intellectual controversy. Her earlier work, on feminism and the like, attracted its fair share of academic critics, as one would expect in a notoriously contentious field such as political theory, and she was involved in a number of more general debates, particularly over her strong support of family (and implicit, and sometimes explicit, criticisms of some feminist arguments in this context – a topic to which she returned in the latter part of *Sovereignty: God, State and Self*) and more recently over her criticism of some aspects of the gay marriage debate. But all of these were dwarfed by the controversies that engulfed her after the publication of *Just War Against Terror*, and some of her writings and lectures that followed on from that. It is therefore on these controversies that I will dwell here.

It is fair to say, I think, that Elshtain expected (indeed, perhaps to some extent intended) the argument of *Just War Against Terror* to be controversial. The book had its roots in an earlier controversy occasioned by the issuing of a public letter signed by 60 prominent US intellectuals (including Elshtain, who had a large role in drafting the letter) entitled "What We Are Fighting For". This letter had prompted 200 Saudi intellectuals to publish a response claiming a causal relationship between the actions of the US government and the rise of Al-Qaida, a claim Elshtain roundly rejected in *Just War Against Terror*.

The arguments of *Just War Against Terror* were controversial enough in themselves, of course, but what really sent the controversy into overdrive was the invasion of Iraq in 2003, and Elshtain's take on it. Of course, *Just War Against Terror* had been written in advance of the Iraq invasion – in the original edition of the book Iraq is not even mentioned – but in the run-up to the invasion and, indeed in its aftermath representatives of the US government seemed to be repeating arguments that Elshtain had made in the book. And Elshtain herself, to add insult to injury, supported the decision to invade Iraq, advised the Bush administration and contributed to a range of public debates about the fallout from the Iraq war, including the (extremely) heated debates over whether the administration's – how shall we call it? – relaxed attitude towards "enhanced interrogation techniques" amounted, in practice, to torture (and thus to a violation of the US commitment to uphold international norms).

Her position on Iraq, and the arguments of *Just War Against Terror* in general, brought her into conflict with people to whom she had previously been close. The Christian ethicist and theologian Stanley Hauerwas, for example, had been a friend of Elshtain's for many years and had praised many of her writings in very strong terms. But on this he was incandescent, a disagreement that led to a bad-tempered debate in the pages of the journal *First Things* in October 2003.

The temperature of the controversy heated up still further when Elshtain contributed an essay to a collection edited by Sanford Levinson on the topic of torture and, in the course of it, asked the following set of questions:

> Is a shouted insult a form of torture? A slap in the face? Sleep deprivation? A beating to within an inch of one's life? Electric prods on the male genitals, inside a woman's vagina, or in a person's anus? Pulling out fingernails? Cutting off an ear or a breast? All of us, surely, would place every violation on this list beginning with the beating and ending with severing a body part as forms of torture and thus forbidden. No argument there. But let's turn to sleep deprivation and a slap in the face. Do these belong in the same torture category as bodily amputations and sexual assaults? There are even those who would add the shouted insult to the category of torture. But, surely, this makes mincemeat of the category.
>
> (*Elshtain, 2004*)

Many saw this as, effectively, opening the door to forms of behavior that many others would routinely describe as torture and also asserted that this seemed oddly "unrealistic" coming from a self-proclaimed realist. Here is Corey Robin, one of Elshtain's most persistent critics on this:

> Distinguishing the awful from the acceptable, Elshtain never mentions the details of Abu Ghraib or the Taguba Report, making her list of dos and don'ts as unreal as the ticking time bomb itself. Even her list of taboos is stylized, omitting actually committed crimes for the sake of repudiating hypothetical ones. Elshtain rejects stuffing electric cattle prods up someone's ass. What about a banana? She rejects cutting off ears and breasts. What about "breaking chemical lights and pouring the phosphoric liquid on detainees?" She condemns sexual assault. What about forcing men to masturbate or wear women's underwear on their heads? She endorses "solitary confinement and sensory deprivation". What about the "bitch in the box", where prisoners are stuffed in a car trunk and driven around Baghdad in 120° heat? She supports "psychological pressure", quoting from an article that "the threat of coercion usually weakens or destroys resistance more effectively than coercion itself". What about threatening prisoners with rape?
>
> *(Robin, 2011)*

One could repeat instances of this endlessly, and the controversies swirled on; about whether the US should exit from Iraq (Elshtain thought it shouldn't) about torture and the so called "ticking bomb scenario" (she still thought an absolute prohibition problematic) and, perhaps most of all about the limits (or lack thereof) of the legitimate exercise of power by sovereign states in general (part of the concerns of her Gifford lectures) and by the United States in particular. Towards the end of her life she was rumored to be working on a book rethinking aspects of all these issues: apparently it was to be called, *Torture and Terror in a Time of Troubles.*[6]

But if these were the specifics of the political controversies her position on the just war in general – and on contemporary wars in particular – generated, what, we might ask, was *intellectually* at stake in them? I want to suggest that what was intellectually at stake was the status of her "Christian Realism" both in general and in connection with war specifically: and in particular what was at stake was her reading of the *Augustinian* roots of Christian Realism, what it permitted and what it eschewed.

In this respect, Elshtain was fighting a war on at least two fronts: chiding on the one hand the "humanists" (to use Camus's idiom) – the apostles of liberal (or indeed postmodern) progressivism who seem to think all is a matter of individual choice and that everything will be fine if men and women of goodwill just get around a table and talk – and on the other, Realists of a non-Christian sort who see the international order simply as a struggle for power and interest. It is significant, for example, that Elshtain disagreed profoundly with her Chicago colleague – and leading political Realist – John Mearsheimer on this. She helped to write a public letter saying "What

We Are Fighting For"; he organized one to the *New York Times*, signed by virtually all significant political (and non-Christian) Realists in the US (aside from Henry Kissinger), arguing that the US should not be fighting in Iraq at all.

One might, I think, see a tension in Elshtain's thought in this context, directly occasioned, and perhaps made starker, by the events surrounding 9/11, and then by the controversies into which she was sucked after that, but perhaps present from the beginning. In my own contribution to the controversy over *Just War Against Terror*, I put it like this:

> But in the power of her witness – and I use that Christian term as a compliment to her – it is easy to forget the problem with her argument. As the Augustine of whom she is such a great admirer would have told her, as she herself as interpreter of that self-same Augustine knows very well, any instance of the use of force, however just, runs the risk of bringing all kinds of strife in its train. In her book on Augustine, Elshtain had emphasised, rightly on my reading, that Augustine is a firm believer in limits; "In this world of discontinuities, of profound yearnings, of sometimes terrible necessities", she says, "a human being can yet strive to maintain or create an order that approximates justice, to prevent the worse from happening *and to resist the seductive lure of imperial grandiosity*".
>
> (Rengger, 2004, pp.114–115, emphasis added)

Yet surely there is more than a touch of "imperial grandiosity" in her belief that we noted above, to wit that the United States is the only guarantor of human dignity in the contemporary world and that it is the special responsibility of the United States, both because of its political character and the temper of the times, to act as the "indispensable nation". "We, the powerful", as she puts it, have first, perhaps, to examine the sources of our own power rather than merely assuming that it is "ours" to deploy in the service of justice as we wish. As Augustine recognized very well, part of the "seductive lure" of "imperial grandiosity" is the belief that we can do great good with our great power; but the reality is likely to be that, as always, power will simply corrupt.

This tension between her civic engagement with America and her valorization of the United States – though recognizing its blemishes, contradictions and iniquities as well – alongside the Augustinian skepticism of *all* states and the claims they make, is an enduring dissonance in her work, I think. In her early work, the problems with America are foregrounded and so the tension is less stark; in much of (though to be sure not all) of her later work they are recessed and so the tension rises to the surface. The tension surfaces again in her Gifford lectures, written, of course as the controversies generated by her stance on the Iraq war were at their height. I am not sure she ever fully resolved the tension. Perhaps, given her multiple and overlapping loyalties, it was really not resolvable at all.

Legacies and enduring relevance

After her death in 2013, there were many tributes to Elshtain from across the political and intellectual spectrum. Most were laudatory, even if recognizing disagreements, sometimes strong ones. A few were more critical – Corey Robin's post on the blog *The Crooked Timber of Humanity* perhaps unusually so.[7] Many attempted to suggest where her main legacies would lie. A favorite was praise for her record of public and civic engagement; another was her commitment to her students despite the increasingly strenuous schedule she pursued. Both of these claims are manifestly true and warrant high praise.

Elshtain was not afraid of controversy and thought it important that academics and intellectuals talk not just to each other or to their students but play a part in the wider conversation of the societies of which they were a part. That might mean disagreement – sometimes strident disagreement – but that in itself was important.[8] Part of her argument in *Democracy on Trial* was that democracy is in large part about, as she put it, *reaching* disagreement and thus compromising. Compromise, for Elshtain, was in a way the *essence* of democratic politics because it had to recognize principled disagreement and live with it. That recognition was a hallmark of her "realism".

Equally, however, an academic *is*, perhaps first and foremost, a teacher. Tribute after tribute from former students testified to the seriousness with which Elshtain took this responsibility, but while serious she was never solemn. But perhaps beyond even these rightly lauded attributes, I think her enduring relevance for the just war tradition, and perhaps her greatest legacy in that context, is her painstaking insistence that thinking about the use of force requires a multi-layered understanding of power *and* ethics, of the fragility of our capacities *and* of the importance of our attempts to exceed them, of our responsibility to ourselves as people and as citizens *and* our responsibilities to others, people themselves and citizens of somewhere else. There was never any suggestion that these multiple engagements were easy, or always clear. Mistakes would be made. Judgments would err. This is the human condition, as she read it, tutored by her reading of Augustine, Niebuhr, Arendt, Camus and many others. She herself might sometimes, under the pressure of events or of controversy, veer some way away from this position – as did, I think, in *Just War Against Terror* – but she never abandoned it. It was the core of her understanding, not just of just war, but of politics itself and it is, I submit, her greatest legacy for the tradition today. In a world where the attempts to make the tradition ever more abstract and legalistic grow greater and more influential by the day (see chapter 19 on McMahan) – the relevance of her engagement with these ideas has never been greater.

Perhaps we should leave the last words to Elshtain herself and to the Augustine to whom she was devoted throughout her career:

> Augustine urges that one must reflect on even justifiable wars, not with vainglory, but with great sorrow. There are no victory parades in Augustine's world. However just the cause, war stirs up temptations to ravish and devour

often in order to ensure peace. For Augustine, just war is a cautionary tale, not an incautious and reckless call to arms. Peace is a great good – so good that "no word ever falls more gratefully upon the ear, nothing is desired with greater longing, in fact, nothing better can be found". Peace, for Augustine, is delightful and "dear to the heart of all mankind".

(Elshtain, 2003b)

Notes

1 See *Augustine and the Limits of Politics*.
2 I can vouch for this from personal experience.
3 See https://divinity.uchicago.edu/jean-bethke-elshtain-scholar-religion-and-political-philosophy-1941-2013
4 See www.nytimes.com/2013/08/16/us/jean-bethke-elshtain-a-guiding-light-for-policy-makers-after-9-11-dies-at-72.html?_r=0
5 This was reprinted in 2003 in a new edition, this time co-edited with Lauri Umansky.
6 See: http://magazine.uchicago.edu/1006/investigations/just-war.shtml.
7 See: http://crookedtimber.org/2013/08/15/when-it-came-to-torture-and-much-else-jean-bethke-elshtain-was-no-realist).
8 See, for example the forum, with contributors including Cian O'Driscoll, Michael Walzer, Maja Zehfuss, and Elshtain herself on *Just War Against Terror* published in *International Relations*. **21**(4), 2007.

Works cited

Elshtain, Jean Bethke. 1981. *Public Man/Private Woman: Women in Social and Political Thought*. Princeton: Princeton University Press.
Elshtain, Jean Bethke. 1987. *Women and War*. New York: Basic Books.
Elshtain, Jean Bethke. ed. 1991. *Just War Theory*. New York: New York University Press.
Elshtain, Jean Bethke. 1992. *Meditations of Modern Political Thought: Masculine/Feminine Themes from Luther to Arendt*. University Park: Penn State University Press.
Elshtain, Jean Bethke. 1995. *Democracy on Trial*. New York: Basic Books.
Elshtain, Jean Bethke. 1996. *Augustine and the Limits of Politics*. South Bend: Notre Dame University Press.
Elshtain, Jean Bethke. 2003a. *Just War Against Terror: The Burden of American Power in a Violent World*. New York: Basic Books.
Elshtain, Jean Bethke. 2003b. Why Augustine? Why Now?. *Catholic University Law Review*. **52**(2), pp.283–300.
Elshtain, Jean Bethke. 2004. Reflections on the Problem of Dirty Hands. In Levinson, Sanford. ed. *Torture: A Collection*. Oxford: Oxford University Press, pp. 77–89.
Elhstain, Jean Bethke. 2008. *Sovereignty: God, State, and Self*. New York: Basic Books.
Glendon, Mary Ann. 1996. A Saint for our Time. *First Things*. November 1, 1996. Available at: https://www.firstthings.com/article/1996/11/005-a-saint-for-our-times
Rengger, Nicholas. 2004. Just a War Against Terror? Jean Bethke Elshtain's Burden and American Power. *International Affairs*. **80**(1), pp.107–116.
Robin, Corey. 2011. *The Reactionary Mind: Conservatism from Edmund Burke to Sarah Palin*. New York: Oxford University Press.

18

JAMES TURNER JOHNSON (1938–PRESENT)

Nahed Artoul Zehr

Introduction

James Turner Johnson is a foundational historian, theorist, and moralist of contemporary just war thinking. By bringing historical expertise to present issues and problems, Johnson has provided critical insight to the values and commitments of Western thinking on the just use of force. Through his historical work, Johnson has demonstrated the outlines of how Western civilization has thought about the just use of force. In addition, he has demonstrated the continuing significance and relevance of the historical materials by constructing a moral and ethical framework by which we can evaluate the use of force today. This framework is based on the assumption that violence and injustice are an inherent part of the human story and that any peace that is achieved is, in light of human limits, temporary. As such, it supposes that force is a necessary and legitimate tool in a world prone to injustice, but also one that must always advance justice and be subject to appropriate restraints. It is the mandate of the just war tradition – which Johnson describes as the "fundamental way we in the West think about the justification and limitation of violence" – to provide guidance in this regard (Johnson, 1981, pp.4–10). In this way, Johnson understands both the just war tradition and his contribution to its recovery in the 20th and 21st centuries as a retort to, on the one hand, pacifists, who are unrealistic about human beings and their limits, and, on the other, realists, who fail to see the existence and import of cultural and historic values to international affairs.

Contexts

Johnson's work took shape during the contemporary recovery of the just war tradition, which began in the early 1960s. He cites as important personal influences on the development of his thought: Paul Ramsey, Michael Walzer, and William V. O'Brian. More broadly, his engagement with the just war tradition and his quest for a practical ethics of just war have been informed by his deep knowledge of the history of Christian thought, gleaned while a divinity student, as well as his ongoing engagement with leading Catholic thinkers and military practitioners.

His intellectual development came during the throes of the Cold War, in which the hitherto unconceivable horrors of nuclear destruction were at the forefront of American political and moral discussions regarding the use of force (Johnson, 2009, pp.248–49). These developments in warfare were greeted by a chorus of voices contending that war, with its newfound ability to cause categorical destruction, could no longer serve as an appropriate means of responding to international conflict. Others, though, approached the problem of nuclear warfare from a different direction. Challenging absolute pacifists, these scholars argued that the revival of the concept of just war could help us to navigate the moral and ethical problems associated with modern war. Perhaps the paradigmatic statement on this comes from Protestant theologian Paul Ramsey (see chapter 15), who, in 1966, urged a return to what he referred to as the "most uninterrupted, longest-continuing study of moral decision-making known in the Western World, the just war theory" (Ramsey, 1961, p.xxiii). While Ramsey – who was Johnson's teacher – was at the forefront of this initial revival, it was Johnson who recovered and developed the historical core of just war thinking. Certainly others have followed Johnson into the arena of just war thinking from a variety of methodological and theoretical perspectives. One could, for example, make the case that Walzer is also a foundational figure given the importance of his work, but his work comes from a very different starting point (see chapter 16). In terms of reviving the traditional form of just war thinking, Johnson remains the principle intellectual figure.

Texts

Johnson's work is founded on the idea that ethics is a "history-conscious" discipline. This is in opposition to what he calls the "moral principles approach", in which principles such as "do not murder", "turn the other cheek", or "Christian charity" are used in a schematic manner to order how we think about justice in war (Johnson, 1981, p.4). The moral principles approach is problematic, according to Johnson, because, in attempting to understand the just war tradition by holding up one or a combination of these principles as primary while ignoring others that have been significant at other points in history, it "misinterprets by truncation" (*Ibid.*, pp.4–10). In much the same vain, he argues that Kantian or Utilitarian approaches to ethics fail to take adequate note of the "historical sources of moral values" (Johnson, 1979, p.99). Rather, they purport to "have to do with universal values" that are "understood and applied by an ahistorical reasoning process" (*Ibid.*, p.100). This is not to paint Johnson as a monist. He finds merit in other approaches, such as, for instance, cross-cultural and comparative efforts to think about the ethics of war.[1] It is, however, important to note that, for Johnson, the best way to think clearly about the ethics of war today is to equip oneself with a working knowledge of the moral values that have undergirded and informed historical just war thinking – and one cannot achieve this without noting that morality and ethics are rooted in the reciprocal relationship between historical reflection and moral valuing, with one shaping the other in turn (Johnson, 1979, pp.109–10).

Johnson developed these positions on the importance of history early in his career, particularly in his landmark books on the just war tradition: *Ideology, Reason, and the Limitation of War: Religious and Secular Concepts, 1200–1740* (1975) and *Just War Tradition and the Restraint of War: A Moral and Historical Inquiry* (1981). Explaining the assumptions underlying the arguments he develops in these books, Johnson writes:

> My own understanding of the nature of moral values is that they are known through identification with historical communities, while moral traditions represent the continuity through time of such communal identification. This implies that moral life means … keeping faith with such traditions; it also requires, more fundamentally, that moral decision making be understood as essentially historical in character, an attempt to find continuity between present and past, and not an ahistorical activity of the rational mind ….
>
> (Johnson, 1981, p.x)

One of Johnson's main tasks is thus uncovering the historical nature of the just war tradition, that is, the way in which ideas about just war evolved over time, how they developed into a set of authoritative guiding principles, and the potential utility of these ideas in the contemporary setting.

Johnson's early work offers a rich and textured account of the just war tradition from the Middle Ages to the early modern period and beyond. While many attribute the beginning of the just war tradition to Augustine, Johnson's account demonstrates that it was not until the close of the Middle Ages that a just war "doctrine" fully emerged. And, while it was in "rough and preliminary form", it nonetheless contained the "elements that today would be cited as characteristic of just war doctrine" (Johnson, 1975, p.75). As we will see below, Johnson will return to these "classic" tenets of just war to inform his later engagement with contemporary problems.[2]

The historical "benchmark" of just war is attributed to two sources: the code of canon law – of particular importance is Gratian's *Decretum* and its interpretive history – and what Johnson refers to as the "theological tradition" of which Thomas Aquinas's *Summa Theologica* plays a critical role (see chapters 3 and 4 respectively on Gratian's and Aquinas' work in this volume) (Johnson, 1975, p.33–43). These sources focused primarily on *jus as bellum* concerns, providing three requirements for a just war – right authority, just cause, and right intention. The other *jus ad bellum* criteria – last resort, probability of success and proportionality – would come later. While the religious sources were less concerned with *jus in bello* issues, they did begin to set limits on war, such as those derived from the Peace of God and the

Truce of God movements. The former specified days in which fighting was prohibited and the latter attempted to designate a set of groups (initially clergy but latterly extending to other categories of person) as protected from the use of force (Johnson, 1981, pp.124–30).

Johnson's historical approach reveals *changes* in just war thinking over time. Perhaps the most critical of these was the move from the Medieval to the Modern era, in which the foundation of the tradition's moral values shifted from Christian thought and theology to natural law (Johnson, 1975, pp.150–54). Here, Johnson singles out Francisco de Vitoria as among the most important contributors (see chapter 6 in this volume for a discussion of Vitoria). Vitoria's primary contribution was his insistence that the limits imposed on the use of force in the just war tradition are rooted in natural law. Moreover, he rejected the idea that difference of religion was just cause for war. Furthermore, in using natural law as the foundation of restraint, Vitoria argued that just war limits were not only binding on Christians in their wars with other Christians, but, at least theoretically, could be invoked in conflicts with non-Christians. Importantly then, for Vitoria, although natural law was a derivation of divine law, his language and thinking could be used and adapted by others that came after him without, as Johnson puts it, "having to trouble themselves with his theological presuppositions" such that, effectively, Vitoria, "made it possible for just war thought to be adapted to the modern age" (Johnson, 1981, p.176).

This shift was continued by Grotius, who, writing at the end of the Thirty Years War, helped to "complete the secularization of just war theory already begun, but not accomplished by Victoria [sic]" (*Ibid.*, p.178). While Vitoria's conception of natural law derived from divine law, Grotius argued that Christian doctrine on just war was a "perfection of the natural law ... a result of the progressive working out of the implications of natural law" such that "*Christian* morality was thus made over into highly developed *natural* morality" (*Ibid.*). It was this emphasis, then, that opened the door for the growth of international law as an "expression" of just war thinking and shifted much of the development of the just war tradition in the modern era to the secular sphere (*Ibid.*, p.188).

Johnson's emphasis on change across time is important. While initially referring to just war thinking as a "doctrine" or "theory", he eventually drops these terms, preferring the term "tradition". This is intentional on his part. On the one hand, he contends that conceiving of just war thinking as a doctrine or theory is unhelpful: it is, he writes, "ambiguous because of the variety of contexts out of which the just war idea has arisen; because of the metamorphosis of the concept of just war over time, because of the existence at any one time of *numerous* theories; because of the imprecision of language" (*Ibid.*, p.xxi). On the other hand, conceiving of just war thinking as a form of tradition acknowledges that it comprises "a multifaceted and various unity of moral insights and practices reflecting the experience and judgments of historical persons across the whole breadth of cultural institutions" (Johnson, 1984, p.13). On this view, uncovering the history of just war tradition can help to clarify the ways that moral and ethical reflection on war has retained relevance and what Johnson would call "authority". More specifically, then, while Johnson demonstrates shifts and developments, he is also keen to establish the point that just war thinking, as a historical *tradition,* is the carrier of a set of ideas, values, and commitments that have been sustained through time (Johnson, 1981, p.xxii).

Johnson is not, however, simply an historian of ideas; he is also as a moralist.[3] His recovery and reconstruction of the norms and values of historical just war thinking is not merely an effort to provide clarity and organization to a historical, intellectual, theological, and material tradition; it has also served to provide the basis for how, in his view, the moral wisdom of this tradition should be used to help guide decision-making on the use of force today. In *Can Modern War be Just* (1984) and *Morality and Contemporary Warfare* (1999), Johnson employs the wisdom from the tradition to contemporary problems, exploring the purpose of modern just war and its limits. In the former, he rejects the notion, informed by the fear of mutual assured destruction by nuclear weapons, that modern just war is necessarily unjust. He then sets out to apply the wisdom of the tradition to inform practical debates about modern war, examining a myriad of *jus ad bellum* and *jus in bello* concerns that defined the 1980s. In the latter, Johnson continues in a similar vein by investigating the morality of what he calls local, low-level and limited wars (including civil wars and ethnic conflicts) that pose distinct challenges compared to previous conflicts. The common thread across these books is his use of the just war tradition to help us think pragmatically and morally about the ethical challenges war poses in a given – and changing – historical context, for the 1980s and '90s were very different in terms of international relations.

Regardless of the time period, the world, Johnson argues, is beset by circumstances that *require* moral deliberation about just war. Assuming that we continue to live in a world in which, at times, "force may be all that remains to protect and preserve values" it is imperative that we insist on "present human capabilities to control and limit the force available to nations so as to keep it subservient to higher values and principles" (Johnson, 1984, p.viii). This is especially important considering the cataclysmic destructive power of contemporary weapons. To put it plainly, for Johnson, "to conceive of the use of force in this totalistic, unlimited way is to put the world in enormous danger" (*Ibid.,* p.2). For this reason, "we have the greater responsibility to recover those lessons in a time when the only restraints on the destructiveness of war can be those set by purposeful human choice" (*Ibid.*).

What form should that recovery take? Johnson's argument is that it must take the form of a deliberative engagement with the historical tradition, which seeks to extrapolate norms of conduct from the principles, precedent, and moral wisdom embodied in both *jus ad bellum* and *jus in bello* principles (Johnson, 1999, p.40). While new questions require that moralists subject the just war criteria to ongoing scrutiny to ensure they remain capable of responding to contemporary issues and problems, there are also certain boundaries that circumscribe just war reasoning. The tradition is not "free floating" in the sense that it may be "given whatever content one may think appropriate in whatever context" (Johnson, 2005b, p.35). Rather, it demonstrates values that have been carried forward throughout the Western history of ethical reflection on the proper use of force. While these "take various specific forms over time", they, just as importantly, "remain fundamentally stable" (Johnson, 1999, p.51). Thus, even though the just war tradition is marked by change and development, it also demonstrates a commitment to a set of "core values carried by the tradition", that, while not categorical, carry authority that ought to be given its proper due (*Ibid.*).[4] For Johnson, the core values are those that coalesced by the end of the Middle Ages, what he refers to as the classic just war doctrine. This doctrine

> [W]as focused on the problems of good government, not on individual morality. It developed within a set of assumptions about such government expressed as the three ends of politics: order, justice, and peace, with justice understood by reference to historical precedents, context, and natural law, and peace defined as what Augustine had called the "tranquility" of an order ruled by the doing of justice.
>
> *(Johnson, 2013, p.41)*

Understanding the "meaning" of the just war tradition – both historically and in its contemporary applications, requires "engagement with the tradition out of which it comes and entering into dialog with the *classical* statement of the just war idea within the tradition" (Johnson, 2005b, p.35, emphasis mine). Such engagement is critical to "discipline just war thinking and keep it true to itself". It allows us to "get at the values that underlie it and the lasting concerns about human life in political community on which just war thinking is based and which it expresses" (*Ibid.*). But as with any moral framework, its application to real-world problems inevitably courts with controversy.

Controversies

Johnson's recovery of classical just war thinking, when applied to contemporary concerns, certainly made its mark. Johnson did not shy away from the moral challenges that erupted across his career, but rather, faced them head on. Two specific controversies deserve our attention. His interpretation of the just war tradition challenged orthodox thinking about Christian just war in the 1980s and proffered what many consider to be controversial responses to new threats in the post-9/11 era.

In 1983, the US National Conference of Catholic Bishops penned "A Pastoral Letter on War and Peace – *The Challenge of Peace: God's Promise and Our Response*". The letter was addressed to the Catholic community in the US, but also had the aim of contributing to wider debates about war and peace. The US Catholic Bishops argued that, "Catholic teaching begins in every case with a presumption against war and for peaceful settlement of disputes. In exceptional cases, determined by the moral principles of the just war tradition, some uses of force are permitted" (National Conference, 1983, p.iii–iv). They go on to argue that:

[O]nly if war cannot be rationally avoided, does the teaching then seek to restrict and reduce its horrors. It does this by establishing a set of rigorous conditions which must be met if the decision to go to war is to be morally permissible. Such a decision, especially today, requires extraordinarily strong reasons for overriding the presumption in favor of peace and against war.

(Ibid., *38*)

Johnson famously takes issues with both the US Catholic bishops' starting point and the way they portray just war tradition. While he identifies the letter as a "benchmark" in "contemporary conceptions of just war", he argues that it departs from the classic understanding of just war in important ways. By ascribing to the just war tradition a "presumption against violence", the US Catholic bishops align it with a pacifist vision (Johnson, 2013, p.28). Following their logic, because the catastrophic nature of modern weapons is such that war cannot be fought discriminately or proportionately, this all but renders modern war unjust (Johnson and Weigel, 1991, p.6). He goes on making the argument that the idea that "just war begins with a presumption against war" or "that the function of the just war criteria is to override this general negative assumption" is to make just war thinking "into something very different from what it properly is" (Johnson, 2005b, p.35).

Importantly, Johnson sees the use of force through a different lens, emphasizing what he sees as the "deontological" criteria – i.e. those that express moral duties – of just cause, legitimate authority, and right intention that form the core of the classical *jus ad bellum*. The "classic" just war tradition, which he uncovered in his previous work, represents the normative mold against which other expressions of just war thinking ought to be compared and tested for it captures the essential moral purpose of just war thinking that lies at the heart of the tradition – responding to injustice in the world. While certainly the prudential *jus ad bellum* criteria (last resort, proportionality, probability of success) can serve as a check against imprudent or foolhardy decision-making, they are not meant to override the point that when justice is lacking, so indeed is real peace.

The contemporary relevance of classic just war tradition is especially prominent in his views on the controversial US-led war against Iraq in 2003. Johnson was joined by a chorus of just war thinkers who analyzed the decision to invade Iraq, as well as the decision to stay the course of that campaign, through the just war tradition. In particular, Michael Walzer (chapter 16) and Jean Bethke Elshtain (chapter 17) were vocal about the need to provide a multifaceted analysis of what was at stake. In his richly argued book, *The War to Oust Saddam Hussein* (2005b), Johnson takes on this task, analyzing the run up to, and prosecution of, the Iraq war. It is not a polemical book in the same vein of Elshtain's *Just War Against Terror* (2003), but rather, a profound analysis of real-world moral dilemmas in the contemporary world. A key part of his analysis is the observation that something important has been lost in contemporary discussions of the just use of force, namely the foundational idea that the just war tradition aims at the achievement of international peace, defined as a "conception of life in political community oriented to a just and peaceful order" (2005b, p.36). According to the just war tradition "rightly understood", the "fundamental moral problems" surrounding this political order are "injustice and the threat of injustice". This is because "in the absence of justice, the political community is not rightly ordered, and there is no real peace either in that community or in its relations to other political communities" (*Ibid.*).

Taking the classical framework as his lens of analysis, Johnson argues that the war against Saddam Hussein may have been justified. He notes that the "traditional just war idea" allows for "the use of force to punish evil", and that "surely applied in the case of Saddam Hussein and his regime" (*Ibid.*, p.63). Importantly, he makes this point to counter those who were arguing that the invasion would violate Iraq's right to sovereignty; rather, just war thinking, as he understands it, holds a different view of sovereignty.[5] The sovereign does not have a blank check for rule. Rather, "failure to discharge the sovereign's obligations" of creating and maintaining a rightly ordered political community removes the "right of sovereignty" (*Ibid.*, p.62). Moreover, it may be the case that a different sovereign identifies a moral duty to use force against such communities if they threaten the stability of international order required for good governments to thrive. The reader will no doubt be aware of the debates that Iraq war generated in just war circles, and one can agree or disagree with Johnson's arguments. But the overarching point is to recognize the extent to which Johnson's application of the classical just war framework helped to analyze the situation, and adjudicate the moral decisions of statecraft.

Johnson has been critiqued for his insistence that the "classic" just war tradition represents *the* lens through which just war thinking ought to be viewed. Critics argue that there is no logical reason why Johnson should assert the authority of a historical snapshot of the just war tradition in the way that he does, and, furthermore, that doing so widens the gulf between the just war tradition and international law.[6] Despite this, however, Johnson continues to insist on the importance of the just war tradition as it was "classically" construed, as this understanding of the tradition contains the values and norms that he sees as integral to the tradition as a practical source of wisdom for statecraft today. "Diversity", he concedes, is important, as it provides "openings for new ideas and new developments of old ones" (Johnson, 2013, p.40). In fact, he contends, this is why it is preferable to speak of a *tradition,* when describing just war thinking. Yet, "a tradition needs sufficient commonality, a coherence of basic conceptions and agreements as to meaning and purpose" such that "speakers may differ broadly as to vocabulary, pronunciation, syntax, intonation" yet still allow them to be recognizable to others who speak the same language (*Ibid.*). In so far as just war is a kind of moral language, then this need for continuity holds as well (O'Driscoll, 2007). Otherwise, he writes, taking aim at both Elshtain's Augustinian paradigm (see chapter 17) and McMahan's revisionist just war philosophy (see chapter 19), "at some point a local version of a language may become so different, so unintelligible to persons from different localities, that it has to be recognized as a different language" (Johnson, 2013, 40).

Legacy

Johnson has created an approach for thinking about moral values in history, as they relate specifically to the just use of force. Perhaps the most obvious legacy is the foundational historical work Johnson undertook in excavating and framing the historical tradition of just war. This work is a valuable source – a necessary starting point of engagement – for all those charting their own course through the history of the just war tradition. Here, his attention to methodology and recovery of the ideas in their historical context, and the journey of ideas across time to other contexts, serve as an example of how read texts and uncover moral meaning. Moreover, Johnson's work has not only provided an enhanced understanding of Western thinking on the just use of force, but has also initiated a method for thinking about these questions comparatively across cultures and traditions.

For Johnson, though, there is more to the story. His historical work produced a normative framework that, he asserts, ought to continue to guide deliberative ethical reasoning and decision-making on the use of force. And so a second legacy is his engagement with the most crucial use of force questions of the day, across a timeframe that spans decades of historical and technological change. Indeed, his continued engagement with the world's most pressing war-related issues through the lens of classic just war has been a driving force in ongoing debates in the field of military ethics throughout the course of his career.

A final legacy is his quest for a just war ethics that can inform the responsible exercise of governance and address the challenges of injustice in the world. If just war thinking is to have meaning, then it must be able to play a role in statecraft for the creation of a better world. We see this sentiment throughout Johnson's work – from his recovery of the classic core of the tradition to his application of the tradition to contemporary problems. Let us allow Johnson to have the last word:

> As traditionally understood, the ethics of just war is a practical art, not a science; the responsible party makes a decision, following the guidelines laid out but also attempting to discharge the responsibility given him or her to pursue justice and peace and thus serve the common good. This is a conception that corresponds to the Greek notion of ethics as having to do with arête, excellence achieved through practice (which includes the possibility of making mistakes and learning from them). Rules are important for this praxis, but they do not themselves yield the right and the wrong.
>
> (Johnson, 2013, p.43)

Notes

1   Johnson has been at the forefront of the comparative study of the ethics of war: Johnson and Kelsay (1990); Kelsay and Johnson (1991); and Johnson (1997).

2   For a tightly argued discussion of the classical core of just war thought see (Johnson, 2005a); also insightful is: (Johnson, 2006); for a more critical discussion than is possible here, see also (Zehr, 2009).

3 For a deeper discussion than is possible here, see (Kelsay, 2009).
4 For a discussion of Johnson's historical methodology, see O'Driscoll (2007; 2009).
5 Johnson develops his views on sovereignty elsewhere (2014).
6 These arguments have been put forward by, among others, Lang (2009) and Zehr (2009).

Works cited

Elshtain, Jean Bethke. 2003. *Just War Against Terror: The Burden of American Power in a Violent World*. New York: Basic Books.

Johnson, James Turner. 1975. *Ideology, Reason, and the Limitation of War: Religious and Secular Concepts, 1200–1740*. Princeton: Princeton University Press.

Johnson, James Turner. 1979. On Keeping Faith: The Use of History for Religious Ethics. *The Journal of Religious Ethics*. **7**(1), pp.98–116.

Johnson, James Turner. 1981. *Just War Tradition and the Restraint of War: A Moral and Historical Inquiry*. New Jersey: Princeton University Press.

Johnson, James Turner. 1984. *Can Modern War be Just?*. New Haven: Yale University Press.

Johnson, James Turner. 1997. *The Holy War Idea in Western and Islamic Traditions*. University Park: Pennsylvania State University Press.

Johnson, James Turner. 1999. *Morality and Contemporary Warfare*. New Haven: Yale University Press.

Johnson, James Turner. 2005a. Just War, as It Was and Is. *First Things*. January **149**, pp.14–24.

Johnson, James Turner. 2005b. *The War to Oust Saddam Hussein: Just War and the New Face of Conflict*. Lanham: Rowman and Littlefield.

Johnson, James Turner. 2006. The Just War Idea: The State of the Question. *Social Philosophy and Policy*. **23**(1), pp.167–95.

Johnson, James Turner. 2009. Thinking Historically about Just War. *Journal of Military Ethics*. **8**(3), pp.246–259.

Johnson, James Turner. 2013. Contemporary Just War Thinking: Which is Worse, to Have Friends or Critics?. *Ethics & International Affairs*. **17**(1), pp.25–45.

Johnson, James Turner. 2014. *Sovereignty: Moral and Historical Perspectives*. Washington D.C.: Georgetown University Press.

Johnson, James Turner and Kelsay, John. eds. 1990. *Cross, Crescent, and Sword: The Justification and Limitation of War in Western and Islamic Tradition*. Westport: Greenwood Press.

Johnson, James Turner and Weigel, George. 1991. *Just War and the Gulf War*. Lanham: University Press of America, Inc.

Kelsay, John. 2009. James Turner Johnson, Just War Tradition, and Forms of Practical Reasoning. *Journal of Military Ethics*. **8**(3), pp.179–189.

Kelsay, John and Johnson, James Turner. eds. 1991. *Just War and Jihad: Historical and Theoretical Perspectives on War and Peace in Western and Islamic Traditions*. Westport: Greenwood Press.

Lang, Jr., Anthony F. 2009. The Just War Tradition and the Question of Authority. *Journal of Military Ethics*. **8**(3), pp.202–16.

National Conference of Catholic Bishops. 1983. *The Challenge of Peace*. Washington, D.C.: United States Catholic Conference.

O'Driscoll, Cian. 2007. Learning the Language of Just War Theory: The Value of Engagement. *Journal of Military Ethics*. **6**(2), pp.107–116.

O'Driscoll, Cian. 2009. Hedgehog or Fox? An Essay on James Turner Johnson's View of History. *Journal of Military Ethics*. 8(3), pp.165–178.

Ramsey, Paul. 1961. *War and the Christian Conscience: How Shall Modern War be Conducted Justly?* Durham, Duke University Press.

Zehr, Nahed Artoul. 2009. James Turner Johnson and the "Classic" Just War Tradition. *Journal of Military Ethics* **3**(8), pp.190–201.

19

JEFF MCMAHAN (1954–PRESENT)

Heather M. Roff

Introduction

Jeff McMahan's contributions to contemporary just war theory have opened new horizons of debate amongst moral philosophers, political theorists and legal scholars. His criticisms of "traditional" just war theory, embodied most prominently in Michael Walzer's *Just and Unjust Wars* (1977), have not only sparked new lines of research in military ethics, but have also changed policies and viewpoints within governments and militaries. Indeed, McMahan's theory of "reductive individualism" as the foundation for the morality of war, as opposed to a theory that prioritizes the rights and privileges of states, is seen by some as providing the most coherent account of just war principles to date. As part of a larger historical tradition, his main philosophical tenets offer a link to the notion of punishment that once formed the linchpin of thinking about *jus ad bellum* from Augustine to Vattel. And in keeping with the theme of this volume – that a key part of the tradition is challenging inherited ideas to offer new insights to contemporary ethical dilemmas – McMahan has brought his innovative just war thinking to bear on the most pressing issues related to war today, from preventive war to drone strikes, to push the ethics of war in new directions.

Contexts

Jeff McMahan's body of work cannot be fully appreciated unless one understands how he approaches the study of ethics. McMahan's education in philosophy took place mostly in the United Kingdom at the University of Oxford and the University of Cambridge, in the late 1970s through the early 1980s. Though he is an American, McMahan's training in moral philosophy abroad more than likely expanded his viewpoints of the world and one's place in it. His early work engaged with problems in moral and political philosophy, particularly practical ethics, such as population ethics and the ethics of nuclear war, defense and deterrence.[1]

Population ethics approaches ethical problems concerning populations, such as how the number of people in the world may adversely affect the welfare of the whole. Thinking through the kind of ethical dilemmas associated with nuclear war, fallout and deterrence, one can immediately see that these are, in a sense, perfect cases for the population ethicist to consider. Yet if one considers dilemmas associated with nuclear war, one cannot but help to read *about* war.

Enter here McMahan's first foray with traditional just war theory. As he explains:

> I first read *Just and Unjust Wars* in 1980, about a year after I had begun my graduate work in philosophy. I was then, and have remained, greatly influenced by it. Over the years I have reread various chapters, some on several occasions. [...] I have written pieces that have been critical of various claims made in the book, and I have often stated my own views about the morality of war by contrast with or in opposition to those claims. But I nevertheless find much to admire in this book, and much to agree with, particularly in Walzer's judgments about issues of practice, such as preemptive war, the demand for unconditional surrender, siege warfare, reprisals, terrorism, and the responsibility for war crimes.
>
> *(McMahan, 2007, p.91)*

What is important to note here is that McMahan does not believe that Walzer's work is insufficient, or that Walzer is necessarily incorrect on all fronts. Rather, McMahan's interest is in what he calls *the deep morality of war* and not with the prudential, practical or conventional ways in which people fight or believe they ought to fight war. McMahan's interest comes from a deep-seated belief in moral realism, grounded in commonsense morality and liberalism.

It is important to note how McMahan's early training influences his present day work on the morality of war, and thus explains where he sees need for deeper philosophical reflection. For as "a pacifist, a philosopher, a socialist, a southerner, a vegetarian, a ruralist, a belletrist, a squash player, or all these at once" he is, in addition to his concern for philosophical rigor, undoubtedly a nuanced thinker that sees the world in degrees and shades rather than in crude absolutes (McMahan, 1997, p.121).[2] All this to say that he is also concerned with the "real world", and aware of how his works may (adversely) affect the way wars are fought and the rights of innocent people. He hopes that his work on the ethics of war prompts "a reconsideration of certain beliefs that have hardened into unquestioned orthodoxies" and that tend to encourage "complacency about killing in war", ultimately making it "easier for governments to lead their countries into unjust wars" (McMahan, 2009a, p.vii). While there is, he asserts, "a general presumption that the law should be congruent with morality – that is, that the prohibitions and permissions in the law should correspond to the prohibitions and permissions of morality", McMahan argues the case that "this correspondence with morality does not and, at present, cannot hold in the case of the international law of war. For various reasons, largely pragmatic in nature, the law of war must be substantially divergent from the morality of war" (McMahan, 2008b, p.19). Yet the goal of McMahan's blend of revisionist just war theory is ultimately to bring the two closer together: "What revisionists hope is that their work can be a source of guidance in establishing new international institutions that will eventually make it possible to reform the law of armed conflict in ways that will bring it into closer congruence with the morality of war" (McMahan, 2012b). To this end, his primary interest lays in the foundations of morality and how these guide the permissions and obligations of individuals fighting in armed conflict.

Texts and controversies

McMahan's landmark book, *Killing in War* "is a sustained assault on the linchpin of Walzerian just war theory, the moral equality of combatants" (Lazar, 2010, p.181). The main argument of the book is that killing in war should not be subject to a separate set of justifications than those that govern in interpersonal contexts. The book works through the key tenet of McMahan's just war thinking – the notion of liability – and draws implications regarding the moral obligations of combatants and the rights of non-combatants. As we will see in the course of this chapter, his arguments challenge key assumptions about just war, with the moral implications of his philosophical investigations leading to provocative claims about who may or may not be permissibly killed in war. The book, however, is the result of a sustained effort to think through the complete account of Walzarian just war theory, as is so much of McMahan's thinking developed before and alongside the book in articles ranging from: the doctrine of double effect (1994a), debates about the preventive war in Iraq (2005b), the moral equality of combatants (2007), the laws of war (2008b), terrorism (2009b), the moral distinction between combatants and non-combatants (2010a), humanitarian intervention (2010b), and targeted killing (2012c).

McMahan takes serious issue with the claim that there is a logical division between *jus ad bellum* (the just resort to force) and *jus in bello* (the just use of force.) As the reader will recall from chapter 16 on Walzer, Walzer argues that *jus ad bellum* and *jus in bello* are disconnected moral categories – that is, one can wage a just war unjustly, and, vice-versa. The *jus ad bellum* provides a potential belligerent party with a permission to fight. This framework, governed by the "legalist paradigm", takes states as the agents of war, where each resides in a somewhat loosely governed international society. This legalist paradigm uses what Walzer calls the "domestic analogy" to argue that states are analogous to individuals residing in domestic society. The rules that govern when it is permissible to use defensive force there apply to states in a more anarchic international society, too. The legalist paradigm thus admits that self-defense, and in some instances, other-defense, is a key justifying condition to go to war.

Jus in bello, contrarily, governs the conduct of those agents who actually do the fighting of war: the combatants. Famously, Walzer writes:

> The moral reality of war can be summed up in this way: when soldiers fight freely, choosing one another as enemies and designing their own battles, their war is not a crime; when they fight without freedom, their war is not their crime. In both cases, military conduct is governed by rules; but in the first the rules rest on mutuality and consent, in the second on shared servitude.
>
> *(Walzer, 1977, p.37)*

In essence, Walzer believes that because the reasons that govern going to war take place at the level of states, individuals cannot be held accountable for state or government-level decisions. In international relations parlance, we may call this a level of analysis problem. *Jus ad bellum* applies to a different level of analysis than *jus in bello.* Moreover, in most instances, those who fight in wars do so for a myriad of reasons (false beliefs, passion, duty, coercion, ignorance), but they are all in some way morally equivalent in that they are not there by their own design. Walzer refers to this condition as the Moral Equality of Soldiers. They are not responsible for the war itself, but only for their actions during war. The rules that govern their actions comprise the "war convention" (discrimination, proportionality, necessity), and if any combatant violates these rules they can be charged with war crimes. However, if they comply with them – say by using necessary and proportionate lethal force to kill only enemy combatants and not civilians – then they cannot be charged with wrongful killing (i.e. murder), for their actions are not immoral or unlawful. Both just and unjust sides of a war receive these permissions.

It is here that McMahan takes issue with Walzer's theory of just war (McMahan, 2006a). His position is perhaps best summarized here:

> The revisionist approach treats war as morally continuous with other forms of violent conflict and therefore rejects the idea that a different morality comes into effect in conditions of war. It asserts that the principles of *jus ad bellum* apply not only to governments but also to individual soldiers, who in general ought not to fight in wars that are unjust. It denies that *jus in bello* can be independent of *jus ad bellum* and therefore concludes that in general it is not possible to fight in a way that is objectively permissible in an unjust war.
>
> *(McMahan, 2012a)*

Tenets

The revisionist or "reductive individualism" approach attempts to clarify the difficult questions of complex relations in war into a simpler format: that which justifies lethal action and that which does not by way of interpersonal relations. McMahan thinks that if one takes an interpersonal and common morality approach to justifying the use of lethal force, such as the thinking espoused in the "domestic analogy", then one cannot permit the killing of innocent people by unjust ones.

If one is posing an unjust lethal threat to another, say by wielding a loaded gun and threatening to shoot, then the innocent person is justified, all things considered, in using lethal defensive force to thwart the unjust attack. This is the foundational assumption of just war *and* individual self-defense: that both situations possess the same justification. Indeed, as some would argue too, defending others also acts equally as a justification. In other words, being morally justified means that it is *morally right* – that is, it precludes wrongfulness – to use lethal defensive harm in those instances. In more concrete terms, Helen Frowe explains, "what may be done in the name of a group is nothing more or less than [what] may be done by the individuals who compose that group. So, in order to establish what a nation may do to defend itself during war, we must establish what it is permissible for individuals to do in self-defense" (Frowe, 2011, p.690).

If one's state is justified in going to war, this is because it has satisfied at least the conditions of just cause and proportionality, along with perhaps the other *jus ad bellum* criteria such as right intention, proper authority, last resort and reasonable chance of success. The just cause, however, is always seen as self or other-defense. If one grants this, then it is hard to see how one could ever condone an unjust side's combatants having an equal right to kill any innocent combatants on the other side. McMahan thus argues,

> against the view that unjust combatants act permissibly when they fight within the constraints of the traditional rules of *jus in bello* … with a few exceptions, they cannot satisfy the constraints of *jus in bello*, even in principle, when those constraints are properly understood.
>
> *(McMahan, 2009a, p.6)*

In essence, if we admit of the domestic analogy that states possess rights and are "more or less like individuals" and it is self- and other-defense that justifies harmful action, then one *cannot* separate *jus ad bellum* from *jus in bello*. An even more provocative conclusion that cuts against the grain of the Walzerian understanding of just war, as well as much of its historical grounding, follows: those who fight unjust wars are not given moral license to kill combatants on the just side merely because those just combatants wear a uniform. Thus, contrary to conventional approaches to just war and international law, McMahan challenges that: "Unless they fight by wrongful means, just combatants do nothing to make themselves morally liable to attack. They neither waive nor forfeit their right not to be attacked. They are not, therefore, legitimate targets" (*Ibid.*, p.205).

From this simple analytic framework, McMahan builds a very powerful theory and critique of traditional just war thinking. One that takes consideration of: innocent attackers, that is agents who are morally innocent but still causally contributing to the threat another innocent agent faces (1994b); the limits of associative duties (2006b); the limits of national partiality (1997); as well as, how one cannot rely on a one-time judgment of when it is permissible to fight, but how the decision to use force is intertwined with different temporal periods and empirical realties (2015). By rejecting the initial assumption of the division between the two regulating frameworks of *jus ad bellum* and *jus in bello*, McMahan can examine in greater detail all of the conclusions that follow it.

Let us, then, look deeper into the specifics to appreciate the greater analytic detail of McMahan's theory of the just war and how *liability to harm* is its keystone concept. If everyday common-sense morality claims that individuals have rights against harm, and when one is subject to unjust lethal harm one is permitted to act in one's self- or other-defense, then questions still remain as to the limitations of this defense. For example, in the case of the innocent attacker, say someone who is brainwashed, sleeping, or drugged, we would say that she is not morally responsible for the unjust threats her physical body is posing. Put another way, we could say that the "threatening action is morally unjustified but nevertheless excused or nonculpable" (McMahan, 1994b, p.263). From here we could identify a series of different types of innocent attackers, such as those who are excused or nonculpable depending upon a variety of reasons (such as: inadvertent/accidental; mistaken; insane; or compelled). Moreover, we could also identify other relevant actors in the moral calculus such as bystanders and culpable attackers, culpable threats or culpable causes (whose action is the ultimate or proximate cause of an unjust threat).

Each of these subclasses of individuals pulls on something in our moral intuitions, leading us think more deeply about who it is right or permissible to inflict harm upon. Take for instance a case where one may permissibly act in self-defense, but by doing so one must grab an innocent bystander to use her as a human shield to block the attacker's bullet. The bystander has done nothing to render herself liable to attack, she is wholly innocent. We would all, I think, recoil at the thought that such an action is justifiable or even merely permissible. Yet, if McMahan is correct, this intuition that regulates our behavior in everyday interpersonal relations ought also to regulate our intuition about the same behavior during war. For using the innocent shield ought to be morally repugnant in the same way in everyday relations as it is in war. Yet traditional just war thinking does sometimes justify something akin to, morally speaking, this sort of act if we couch the killing of bystanders in the Doctrine of Double Effect.

The Doctrine of Double Effect (DDE) holds that it is permissible to kill an innocent (or non-combatant depending upon versions) if doing so is the foreseen but unintended consequence of an otherwise permissible act, subject to constraints of proportionality. By way of example, if a justified combatant flying at 30,000ft calculates that dropping a 500lb warhead on a weapons depot located next to a hospital will more than likely kill ten civilians in the neighboring hospital, the DDE claims this is a permissible act. The value of the military objective (destroying the weapons depot) outweighs the foreseen but unintended harm of killing the ten civilians.

Walzer recognizes, however, the over-extensive nature of the traditional DDE and claims in his work that it is far too expansive and should be revised to what he calls a "Doctrine of Double Intention" whereby combatants take on additional risks to themselves to mitigate the foreseeable harms to non-combatants (Walzer, 1977, p.155). Double intention requires that the combatant "aims narrowly at the acceptable effect; [that] the evil effect is not one of his ends, nor as a means to his ends" (*Ibid.*). Yet, if one grants that one cannot permissibly kill any number of bystanders in pursuit of an unjust aim, such as prosecuting an aggressive unjust war, then the traditional way of thinking about DDE, or even Walzer's revised Double Intention version, begins to collapse. For it does not matter that one "aims narrowly" or takes on additional risk to oneself when one is not justified, or even merely permitted, to use lethal force in the first place.

One may, of course, object that the DDE is different than the innocent shield argument because the agent defending him or herself intends to use the innocent shield as a means of defense, and this is clearly not what the DDE permits (McMahan, 1994a). The DDE says only that it is permissible to kill a non-combatant if doing so is foreseeable but unintended. The shield is clearly intended. While I cannot resolve the debate here about whether innocent shields and innocent bystanders are morally distinct categories, or whether the intentional use of an innocent by an equally innocent person in defense is permissible, the point that McMahan raises is that one cannot really understand the nexus of what is and is not morally permissible or required without reference to the initial or proximate conditions that place them in particular categories (just vs. unjust). The combatant's and non-combatant's individual actions cannot be divorced from the larger state structures that encompass them.

This leads to McMahan's concept of liability. "To say that a person is liable to be attacked", he writes, "is [...] to say that he would not be *wronged* by being attacked, given certain conditions, though perhaps only in a particular way or by a particular agent" (McMahan, 2005a, p.15, emphasis original). Important for this volume is that McMahan recognizes the following:

> The connection I am claiming between just cause and liability may be found, though not altogether explicitly, in the work of some of the earlier jurists writing in the just war tradition. These writers typically insisted that just cause is founded in an injury, by which they meant a wrong or a violation of rights.
>
> *(Ibid., p.8)*

McMahan references Vitoria, Suárez, Grotius, and Vattel. Now, McMahan is not an historian of the just war tradition like James Turner Johnson (chapter 18), but it is important to recognize that the tradition itself is not inimical to the concept of liability. As the chronological flow of this volume reveals, the moral weight of punishment has tended to fall out of the list of just causes after Vattel. Yet McMahan offers a compelling case for rethinking the justness of punishment by linking it to the notion of defense and liability. "We could", he argues later, "have a practice of punishment that would have as its sole aim the defense of innocent people against those who, by violating the laws, had shown themselves to be presumptively dangerous and simultaneously made themselves liable to preventive action" (McMahan, 2008a, p.81). While this would certainly be different from the way Vitoria, Suárez, Grotius or Vattel (all of whom engaged the question who is liable to harm in their own historical context and from alternative intellectual starting points) envisioned it, McMahan's take offers renewed avenues of inquiry that those interested in the history of the tradition ought to find appealing.[3]

Liability to harm acts as the primary determinant as to who may or may not be justifiably harmed, and this liability cannot be based on mere membership in a group (such as combatant). Rather, liability to harm means that one would not be *wronged* and would "have no justified complaint" about being harmed if attacked (McMahan, 2009a, p.8). In this framework, liability is internal to some other goal, such as achieving a just cause or aim. A person becomes liable to attack because he or she has acted in some manner that forfeits or diminishes the right not to be attacked. This could be because: the person has knowingly and unjustly wronged someone else, thereby forfeiting his or her right; the person has waived his or her rights; or in some instances attacking the person is justified as a lesser evil (*Ibid.*, pp.9–10).

As McMahan explains:

> The principle condition of a person's being liable to be harmed in the pursuit of the goal is that he or she be implicated in some way in the existence of the problem [to be resolved]. If a person is implicated in the existence of the problem in such a way that harming him in a certain way in the course of solving the problem would not wrong him, then he is liable to that harm.
>
> *(*Ibid.*, p.19)*

If McMahan is correct, then liability to harm during war means that one has had to be "implicated" in some way in the unjust war. Unpacking what exactly that means, then, is the basis for much of the present work in just war theory.

Legacy and enduring relevance

McMahan's legacy and enduring relevance to the just war tradition cannot be overstated, but it should also come with some very clear nuanced distinctions. First, McMahan's arguments are from an analytic philosophical approach to war. He begins with some foundational assumptions and then scales the argument up from there, thinking that if one can find cases with the same or similar premises the same conclusions ought to hold as well. This is a logical point. However, logic rarely follows from principles to practice.

For instance, McMahan is not concerned with how international law, particularly the law of armed conflict, yields different conclusions than his "deep morality" of war. As his liability framework cashes out, some civilians can be liable to attack because they can be "implicated" in the right way to link them to an unjust war. This means that attacking them would be morally permissible. However, this conclusion is in stark contradiction to the laws of war that treats all civilians as a protected class. Thus the morality of war says x, while the laws of war say y. This is not to say, however, that McMahan thinks they should say the same thing. Rather he thinks that:

> In current conditions, the law of war cannot aspire to congruence with the morality of war. It must be formulated with a pragmatic concern for the consequences of its implementation. And pragmatic considerations argue decisively for an absolute, exceptionless legal prohibition of intentional military attacks against civilians.
>
> *(McMahan, 2009a, p.234)*[4]

Nevertheless, his rejection of the Walzerian theory of just war has had its philosophical objections as well. Second, then, much depends on one's assumptions about the importance of factors such as uncertainty, duress, agency, and group membership. By way of example, Seth Lazar identifies what he calls the "responsibility dilemma" in McMahan's works. This dilemma, he explains commits McMahan to "choose between two unpalatable options: either adopt a contingent form of pacifism, or concede that many more non-combatants may be killed than is currently thought defensible" (Lazar, 2010, p.181). The contingent pacifist position is the logical conclusion one must adopt, he argues, if one admits that even some unjust combatants are not "sufficiently responsible to be liable [to attack]", and that just combatants must then "discriminate between those who are and are not sufficiently responsible" (*Ibid.*, p.187). Yet such a judgment is impossible because one cannot know the context, personal histories or reasons for fighting for an unjust side. The just combatant not being able to distinguish between those who he can or cannot attack is left committed to not fighting back, something that it seems McMahan would not endorse.

Thus if one considers uncertainty a crucially important factor to consider when making a moral judgment about the right action, one may be committed to privileging inaction (or omission) rather than action (commission). Or, one may think that not possessing the requisite knowledge about a situation excuses one from moral responsibility through ignorance. Duress too may exculpate someone from moral condemnation because they were forced to take up arms. However one examines the reasons for fighting, undoubtedly there will be differences of opinion about which ones matter more or less in justifying or excusing one's actions.

The liability framework, however, has another tenet of relevance in that it has generated a wide range of interest in just war theory from different academic disciplines but unified in a similar method: analytic philosophy. Instead of viewing the just war tradition as a historical exercise, a case review of international law, or even from the perspective of political theory, which takes perhaps a more robust account of the empirical world into its constructs, analytic philosophy's method is to engage in rigorous logical analysis of the foundations. Premises must follow from one another and their conclusions must cohere.

Indirectly, then, McMahan's writings on just war from this perspective attracted the attention of more analytic philosophers and jurists who had up until that point been placing their attentions elsewhere. He wanted to draw their knowledge into the debates as much as to examine these problems from his own perspective.[5] Arguing from McMahan's perspective, Helen Frowe, for instance, builds the most complete and systematic theory of the morality of war based on individual rights, filling out much of what it means for someone to be implicated in an unjust war. Her foray into this domain complements McMahan's initial exercise, further explaining the thresholds for responsibility (Frowe, 2014). Additionally, Cécile Fabre's work on liability extends McMahan's framework to cases he has not considered (Fabre, 2009; 2012). Victor Tadros likewise takes up the liability account but identifies areas in McMahan's theory that are deficient. For instance, Tadros claims that McMahan does not identify all potential ways to justify harming someone, and indeed that he fails to consider cases when there is a person who possesses an enforceable duty to suffer harm, or ought to suffer a harm even though they are not causally responsible for the immediate harm (Tadros, 2016; 2011).

Conclusion

In widening the lens of just war debates, McMahan has thus influenced many contemporary just war theorists, military ethicists, and legal scholars over the past 20 years. His work has engendered a lively and timely debate that does not take as unproblematic the Walzerian framework, thereby enriching our reflections about the morality of armed conflict. Whether one is committed more to a Walzerian framework; whether one thinks that theory cannot be wholly divorced from practice, or if one is concerned only with the normative truths and not the empirical realities, McMahan's contributions cannot be ignored. He has forced us all to examine the assumptions we bring to an argument, and he has thought carefully and considerately about the reasons we fight. In doing so he has – either intentionally or not – made us all better theorists, jurists or philosophers because we have had to craft coherent, robust and forceful responses to his work.

Notes

1   McMahan's doctoral thesis was on practical ethics.
2   While this is a small passage from one of his essays, it is in fact a very tidy description of many of his attributes.

3 Francisco de Vitoria, *On the Law of War* [Questions 2 and 3]; Francisco Suárez, *The Three Theological Virtues: On Faith, Hope, and Charity* [Disputation 13 'On Charity', Section VI]; Hugo Grotius, *The Rights of War and Peace* [Book 3, Chapter XI, Emer de Vattel, *The Law of Nations* [Book 3, chapters 8, 11].

4 It should also be noted that in personal discussions with Henry Shue during workshops at Oxford's Center for the Ethics of Law and Armed Conflict (ELAC), McMahan softened his positions to accept the premise that practice of armed conflict cannot admit of exceptions to the rules of protection. Author's private correspondence with Henry Shue.

5 According to conversations with Jeff, he was unsatisfied with the philosophical rigor of Walzer's work and that he did not see any analytic philosophers placing much focus on it. He had thus written a few articles in various outlets that did not receive much public attention, though the arguments were, even in their infancy, there from some of his earliest writings. When others in the philosophical community turned their attention to the issue more fully, there was quite lively debate in the United States and the United Kingdom drawing in some of the best minds and institutions in the world. Personal correspondence with Jeff McMahan.

Works cited

Fabre, Cécile. 2009. Guns, Food, and Liability to Attack in War. *Ethics.* **120**(1), pp.36–63.

Fabre, Cécile. 2012. *Cosmopolitan War.* Oxford: Oxford University Press.

Frowe, Helen. 2011. Jeff McMahan. In Chaterjee, Deen. ed. *Encyclopedia of Global Justice.* New York: Springer, pp.690–93.

Frowe, Helen. 2014. *Defensive Killing.* Oxford: Oxford University Press.

Lazar, Seth. 2010. The Responsibility Dilemma for Killing in War: A Review Essay. *Philosophy and Public Affairs.* **30**(2), pp.180–213.

McMahan, Jeff. 1994a. Revising the Doctrine of Double Effect. *The Journal of Applied Philosophy* **11**(2), pp.201–212.

McMahan, Jeff. 1994b. Self-Defense and the Problem of the Innocent Attacker. *Ethics.* **104**(2), pp.252–290.

McMahan, Jeff. 1997. The Limits of National Partiality. In McKim, Robert and McMahan, Jeff. eds. The Morality of Nationalism. New York and Oxford: Oxford University Press, pp.107–138.

McMahan, Jeff. eds. *The Morality of Nationalism.* New York and Oxford: Oxford University Press, pp.107–38.

McMahan, Jeff. 2005a. Just Cause for War. *Ethics & International Affairs.* **19**(3), pp.1–21.

McMahan, Jeff. 2005b. Preventive War and the Killing of the Innocent. In Rodin, David and Sorabji, Richard. eds. *The Ethics of War: Shared Problems in Different Traditions.* Aldershot, UK: Ashgate Publishing, pp.169–90.

McMahan, Jeff. 2006a. Killing in War: A Reply to Walzer. *Philosophia* **34**, pp.47–51.

McMahan, Jeff. 2006b. On the Moral Equality of Combatants. *Journal of Political Philosophy.* **14**(4), pp.337–393.

McMahan, Jeff. 2007. The Sources and Status of Just War Principles. *Journal of Military Ethics.* **6**(2), pp.91–106.

McMahan, Jeff. 2008a. Aggression and Punishment. In May, Larry. ed. *War: Philosophical Perspectives.* Cambridge: Cambridge University Press, pp.67–84.

McMahan, Jeff. 2008b. The Morality of War and the Law of War. In Rodin, David and Shue, Henry. eds. *Just and Unjust Warriors: The Legal and Moral Status of Soldiers*. Oxford: Clarendon Press, pp.19–43.

McMahan, Jeff. 2009a. *Killing in War*. Oxford: Oxford University Press.

McMahan, Jeff. 2009b. War, Terrorism, and "The War on Terror". In Miller, Christopher. ed. *War on Terror: The Oxford Amnesty Lectures 2006*. Manchester: Manchester University Press.

McMahan, Jeff. 2010a. The Just Distribution of Harm Between Combatants and Noncombatants. *Philosophy and Public Affairs* **38**(4), pp342–379.

McMahan, Jeff. 2010b. Humanitarian Intervention, Consent, & Proportionality. In Davis, N. Ann, Keshen, Richard and McMahan, Jeff. eds. *Ethics and Humanity: Themes from the Philosophy of Jonathan Glover*. New York: Oxford University Press, pp.44–72.

McMahan, Jeff. 2012a. Rethinking the "Just War", Part 1. *The Stone: The Opinionator, New York Times*, 12 November. [Accessed 11 March 2016]. Available from: http://opinionator.blogs.nytimes.com/2012/11/11/rethinking-the-just-war-part-1

McMahan, Jeff. 2012b. Rethinking the "Just War", Part 2. *The Stone: The Opinionator, New York Times*, 12 November. [Accessed 11 March 2016]. Available from: http://opinionator.blogs.nytimes.com/2012/11/12/rethinking-the-just-war-part-2

McMahan, Jeff. 2012c. Targeted Killing: Murder, Combat, or Law Enforcement?. In Altman, Andrew, Finkelstein, Claire and Ohlin, Jens David. eds. *Targeted Killings: Law and Morality in an Asymmetrical World*. New York: Oxford University Press, pp.135–155.

McMahan, Jeff. 2015. Proportionality and Time. *Ethics* **125**(April), pp.1–24.

Tadros, Victor. 2011. *The Ends of Harm: The Moral Foundations of Criminal Law*. Oxford: Oxford University Press.

Tadros, Victor. 2016. Causation, Culpability, and Liability. In Coons, Christian and Weber, Michael. eds. *The Ethics of Self-Defense*. Oxford: Oxford University Press.

Walzer, Michael. 1977. *Just and Unjust Wars: A Moral Argument with Historical Illustrations*. New York: Basic Books.

CONCLUSION

Daniel R. Brunstetter and Cian O'Driscoll

Introduction

The nineteen substantive chapters of this volume have covered roughly 2,000 years of intellectual history. We started in ancient Rome with Cicero, traversed the Middle Ages, the period of early modernity and then the Wesphalian era, to arrive at the just war revival in the 20th century. One could tell many narratives about the just war tradition across these periods; indeed, there are excellent books that do just that – the reader could start with those described in the chapter on James Turner Johnson. But the purpose of this volume is different. By focusing on individual thinkers instead of the ebb and flow of ideas across the millennia, the reader sees the subject of just war from the vantage point of a multitude of snapshots embedded within specific historical contexts. Each of the individual chapters has focused on key thinkers who, in the context of a specific moment in history, made a mark on the tradition. We hope the reader will be intrigued to explore the primary sources of the thinkers themselves, and mine the bibliographies at the end of each chapter for key secondary sources.[1] In doing so, our hope is that the reader will begin the process of piecing together his or her own narrative of the just war tradition, with the aspiration that this may provide insight in their analysis of the conflicts of tomorrow. To this end, we want to highlight several points to guide the reader's reflection.

Turning points

First, let us identify the major turning points that occur within the tradition. One way of thinking about change in the tradition is in linear temporal terms – Pagan Rome, the Christian Middle Ages, the secularization in early modernity, and the modern day revival. But this is only part of the story: within each of these periods there are significant milestones of change. In classical Rome, for instance, the writings of Cicero reflected the process by which ancient Greek and Hellenic philosophical traditions were modified and formalized to meet new political realities. In the Christian Middle Ages, the contribution of Gratian as the first to solidify the just war doctrine is significant, for his compilation of just war maxims would influence all Christian thinkers to the dawn of early modernity. Aquinas would make his mark on the tradition, in part via his reintegration of Aristotelian ethics, but also by centering his thoughts on just war in the context of Christian charity – a framing that would have a major impact on Suárez. Christine de Pizan followed these developments by opening the discourse as it had developed to this point to include insights gleaned from the knightly class and the code of chivalry to which they subscribed. The period of secularization begins with Vitoria, who was also arguing in the intellectual shadows of the Middle Ages. Then Grotius and Vattel work to frame the tradition in greater and greater secular terms. And by the time we reach Lieber, religion is all but thoroughly removed. But, religion would be the doorway to the 20th century revival as Ramsey and then Johnson recovered the idea of just war by returning to its Christian roots.

Change and continuity

Another way of thinking about change across the tradition is by identifying when certain ideas crystalized and charting their trajectory across time. The reader who wishes to follow this course might, for instance, observe the ebb and flow of the classic just war doctrine centered on the *jus ad bellum* criteria of legitimate authority, just cause and right intention. This is a story of both continuity and change. On the one hand, while the "*jus ad bellum*" label and its current schematization is a relatively recent development, it is also apparent that ideas homologous to the principles that we usually list under its rubric are discernible throughout the entirety of the period under discussion. On the other hand, one cannot ignore the protean character of these same principles. Viewed in this light, it is possible to trace how changes in the meaning of sovereignty and the constitution of international society over time have had a knock-on effect upon how the right to war has been understood. The period from Vitoria (whose arguments were couched in debates about the sovereignty of "barbarians") to Vattel (whose thoughts were formed in the crucible of the Westphalian "peace" that saw Europe's empires vie for power and survival), furnishes a neat study in this regard. It offers us a clear view of how questions pertaining to what counts as a just grounds for warfare have remained constant over time – especially in respect of a recurring interest in the legitimacy of preventive war, regime change, and humanitarian intervention – while the way of addressing those questions, and the exact nature of the answers they have elicited, have arguably shifted quite dramatically.

Additionally, the emergence of *jus in bello* norms offers insight into how, as the destructive power of war increased with new technologies, new rules emerged to moderate what was regarded as an acceptable level or form of violence in war. One might be tempted to view this in evolutionary terms – i.e. that just war thinking with each new generation has included more and more protections and limits, but this would betray a much more complex story (Linklater, 2016). It is clear that over time more limits have indeed emerged, but they have also been flanked by caveats, qualifications, and indeed permissions. Most interesting in this respect is arguably the ubiquity of the belief that *jus in bello* restraints may (and perhaps even should) be set aside in times of military necessity. One discerns this conviction already in Cicero; it can be found in all early modern thinkers who explore *jus in bello* in depth (e.g. Vitoria, Grotius, and Vattel), and later in Lieber, whose impact on contemporary *jus in bello* norms is substantial. Of course, what necessity itself means is a matter of debate.

Looking beyond the easily recognizable categories of the *jus ad bellum* and the *jus in bello*, the reader would also do well to reflect upon the different ways that the relationship between just war and peace has been conceptualized over time. Cicero and Augustine, for instance, were explicit that a just war must only be fought for the sake of peace. While a few thinkers associated with the tradition are culpable of glorifying war, most obviously Lieber, the thrust of the tradition recognizes war as something inherently tragic and horrible, albeit sometimes necessary. Following from this view, the return to a just peace is posited as a most desirable outcome. Of course, there are concerns of what that peace should look like. Key to Augustine, and the classic just war doctrine as described by Johnson, is that justice and order define peace. Others recognize that peace with some "barbarians" might not be possible (Cicero, Vitoria, and Vattel). The idea of *jus post bellum* emerges with Suárez, and while Vattel also dedicates considerable ink to the challenge of peace, one of his staunchest critics, Kant, is perhaps the one who offers the most complete discussion.

The key point to note here, however, is that when one is charting the transmission of ideas across time, as this book seeks to do, one must be alert to the processes of both change and continuity that are present, and sensitive to how each informs or circumscribes the other. Following from this, and as we cautioned in the introduction and the reader will presumably have already discovered for him or herself, one will not find one single and correct version of just war theory emerging out of the pages of this volume. Rather, it showcases a myriad of different theories and notable disagreements across various eras. These are the very substance of the tradition, its marrow. For example, one can trace the influence of Cicero, as adapted by Augustine to the Christian era, then his general disappearance (perhaps replaced by the authority of Augustine and Gratian) until his clear revival in the works of Grotius and Vattel. Or one could look at how Augustine's ideas were taken out of context by Gratian, and then transmitted as authority to later Christian thinkers, before falling out of the tradition in the period of secularization, only to be revived in different and sometimes controversial ways by Ramsey, Elshtain and Johnson. And one could chart Vitoria's break with the Middle Ages, followed by the critical engagement with his ideas by Suárez, and later Grotius, Pufendorf and Vattel. And there are many more such intellectual threads to explore.

The authority of tradition

There is a clear sense that some ideas took on the status of authority (Augustine and Gratian during the Middle Ages, Vitoria at the dawn of the European imperialist age in the 16th century, Vattel during the period of great powers intrigue in the 18th century, but also that individual thinkers sought to offer counter argument or new insights. Las Casas, for example, departs from previous authorities when applying the just war tradition to the debates about the Spanish conquest of the New World. Vattel builds on Grotius, who built on Vitoria, to offer new insights in the Westphalian era, but while an authority for statesmen in his day, was heavily criticized by Kant and Lieber.

The importance of authority and debate takes on deeper significance because the majority of just war thinkers covered across the chapters were engaging with the concept of just war to respond to the international challenges of their time. The just war doctrines that emerged are thus the product of historical conditions, the weight each thinker placed on the authority of his or her intellectual forbearers, and the perceived need to innovate. They were not conceived in a political vacuum, isolated from the gravitas of war. The tradition is thus a living body of knowledge, whose contributors took war seriously. As a source of insight, delving deeper into the moments of disagreement and innovation enriches our understanding of the tradition. This holds true for the contemporary just war revival as well. The substantive differences between Johnson, Walzer and McMahan form the backbone of the modern day revival. Despite their methodological differences – it is worth noting that the just war tradition has never been a stranger to methodological plurality – their arguments represent three general strands of just war thinking: the historical (with a penchant for the classical just war paradigm), the legalist (with its deviations and caveats), and the revisionist (with its push towards reductive individualism). Like the thinkers of the past, each strand brings to the table its own assumptions and offers insights into present day dilemmas, with the disagreements between them, in keeping with the general characteristic our authors have noted across the volume, the source of considerable insight.

The approach presented here supposes that it is worthwhile and helpful to understand how just war thinking has developed. Acquiring a clearer sense of how just war thinking has evolved over time will better equip the reader to think about how it should be developed in the future. Yet this is not a straightforward task. The tradition can be a source of wisdom, insofar as understanding how others engaged the most pressing international relations problems can highlight moral dilemmas and tradeoffs, bring to the fore the assumptions that undergird our thinking about these issues, and, because of the plurality of theories within the tradition, point to alternative ways of thinking. We do, however urge caution, as there are pitfalls – what we called in the introduction the twin perils of anachronism and antiquarianism – to poaching the past for insight into today's problems. The reader should thus pay close attention to the specific language each thinker uses and the historical context and norms of the time. With this in mind, we identify several controversial themes that have been the subject of heated debate in contemporary times, which have historical precedent in the tradition.

Controversies

Preventive war is as controversial as it comes. Can one wage war against a distant but foreseeable threat? While contemporary international law says no, we do find arguments in favor within the tradition. Revisiting Gentili and Vattel, for example, opens insights into how one could justify preventive war both prior to and during the era of Westphalian sovereignty.

Humanitarian intervention drives at the core of the tensions within just war thinking. On the one hand, we find the sense of moral duty to aid the innocent other; but there is also the requirement to navigate norms of sovereignty and the fear that such interventions may not be successful, but rather, lead to more violence. The tradition offers a variety of arguments that defend the right to wage war to help those suffering the violence of their rulers. Vitoria, for example, proposes that "barbarians" have sovereignty, but proffers that one could wage a just war to impose a new regime to rescue the innocent who suffer under the tyranny of their mores. Suárez, Gentili, Grotius, and Pufendorf, despite some difference in how they viewed just war, also make arguments in favor. Las Casas stands out in opposition. Despite defending the Indians at every turn, he rejects war for the sake of humanitarian intervention because war, he observed, breeds hatred and unpredictable violence. Vattel's silence on the subject is also significant.

Punishment was a defining feature of the just war tradition across many of the phases we outlined above. It was a linchpin of just cause in Middle Ages, and then was central to the *jus ad bellum* in the period of secularization. One could hardly speak of just war without the notion of punishment being part of the discussion. And yet, it falls out over time. Rarely are our normative discussions about war today framed through the lens of punishment. The exception is, of course, the revisionist just war strand. McMahan challenges the backbone of modern just war thinking – the separation between *jus ad bellum* and *jus in bello*. His rejection of the moral equality of combatants and his argument that civilians might be morally liable to harm have spearheaded a new wave of thinking about just war. And yet McMahan draws attention to the notion of punishment that permeated the tradition, specifically in the thought of Vitoria, Suárez, Grotius, and Vattel. The divides separating Johnson, Walzer and McMahan are certainly clear, but paying deeper attention to the importance of punishment across the tradition offers a common language that may help bridge some of them.

Restraint in war is also a contentious topic. Two common, and somewhat contradictory, narratives of the just war tradition one hears are the following: it is a language that allows statesmen to justify just about any war, or, it is a moral framework designed to limit recourse to war and moderate the destruction of even just wars. In a sense, both are accurate descriptions if one were to pick and choose isolated elements, or focus on certain veins of the tradition, but neither is a true statement about the tradition *in toto*. One can, indeed, find arguments for many kinds of war, but there is a common thread across the tradition of right intention that does set some limits. And there is much debate about the dirty details of the justice of going to war. In terms of what one can do in war, there are clearly limits to the limits. The common caveat is the notion of necessity – and it is interesting to see how each thinker defines the contours of this caveat. While certainly more was permissible back in the day – few would find Vitoria's and Vattel's discussions of when one could put prisoners to death morally palatable today – there is a sense that the limits on war became progressively more restraining. And yet, there is another caveat that essentially allows just war to become limitless. Cicero, Vitoria, Gentili, and Vattel when they contemplate just wars against so-called barbarians, and even Walzer when he talks about supreme emergency, are examples of this limit to the limits. And again, Las Casas rises to the top as a counter-example. For better or for worse, just war parlance today does not shy away from the civilized-barbaric dichotomy – the war against the Islamic State group is one pertinent example. As we apparently inevitably embark upon that road, there is thus, we surmise, something important to be learned from the insights and follies of the tradition.

Conclusion

By returning to the tradition for examples of how to incorporate conflict with "barbarians" into the realm of morality, we become acutely aware of the relationship between just war discourse and power dynamics, between just war and imperial machinations. This opens up a path of critical inquiry into who sets the rules, (and their caveats, qualifications, and permissions), who might benefit from them and who does not, and how the rules might serve to disaffect groups who view war through different cultural lenses. Going down this path, the reader could engage Islamic, Hindu, Jewish, Native American and other ethical traditions to find, no doubt, points of overlap and divergence.

This kind of reflexivity is essential as we engage in the very debates about statecraft that drive international relations today, and by consequence, nourish the tradition itself. But, looking critically upon the ground covered by this book, what about reflexivity in terms of how we understand the just war tradition itself? This text has steered clear of controversy by selecting a relatively orthodox list of thinkers to focus upon. The reader should not mistake this list as final or exhaustive. There is an abundance of other candidates who might have also been considered. We might, for instance, have sought to incorporate chapters on Plato, Aristotle, Erasmus, Luther, or Thomas More, all of whom had interesting things to say about the idea and practice of just war; or indeed a host of other thinkers mentioned within these chapters as sources of influence or intellectual foils. Looking ahead, at the same time as we encourage anyone with an interest in the ethics of war to familiarize themselves the key thinkers of the just war tradition, we would also entreaty them to approach that task in a pluralist fashion, one that takes the selection of thinkers presented here as a starting rather than a stopping point.

Note

1   We also point the reader to the indispensable anthology – *The Ethics of War: Classic and Contemporary Readings* – edited by Reichberg, Syse, Begby (2006). This text has skillfully selected excerpts from over fifty key thinkers, including all the figures we cover (with the exception of Las Casas, Elshtain and McMahan).

Works cited

Linklater, Andrew. 2016. *Violence and Civilization in the Western States-Systems*. Cambridge: Cambridge University Press.
Reichberg, Gregory M., Syse, Henrik, and Begby, Endre. eds. 2006. *The Ethics of War: Classic and Contemporary Readings*. Oxford: Blackwell.

INDEX